Prentice Hall Brief Review

Physics:
The Physical Setting

Bernadine Hladik Cook

Ordering Information

Send orders to:
  Pearson
  PO Box 6820
  Chandler, AZ 85246

or call toll free:
  1-800-848-9500
  (8:00 A.M.-6:00 P.M. EST)

School orders:
  k12.oasis.pearson.com

Individual orders:
  pearsonschool.com/nybriefreviews

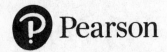

About the Author

Bernadine Hladik Cook received her B.S. in Physics from Clarkson and her M.S. in Science Education from the State University of New York at Oneonta. Prior to her retirement, she taught for 30 years in the Greater Johnstown School District and served as Science Department Chairperson for 16 of those years. For many years, she was a physics instructor in various enrichment programs for middle-level students at Rensselaer Polytechnic Institute. At Union College, she co-developed and co-directed a summer research program for secondary science teachers, which was funded by the National Science Foundation (NSF). For several years thereafter, Ms. Cook evaluated teacher enhancement proposals seeking funding from the NSF. During her teaching career, she was a workshop presenter at local, state, and national level science conferences. She has been a reviewer and contributing writer for Pearson Prentice Hall, providing laboratory activities, standardized test practice, and features. Ms. Cook was a member of both the NYS Physical Setting Physics Core Curriculum committee and the preceding NYS Regents Physics Syllabus committee. A lifetime member of the NYS section of the American Association of Physics Teachers (AAPT), she is a former secretary/treasurer and executive board member of that organization.

Acknowledgments begin on page I-6 and constitute an extension of this copyright page.

Regents Examinations and questions appear courtesy of the New York State Education Department/New York Regents Exam.

ISBN-13: 978-0-32-898854-9
ISBN-10: 0-32-898854-5

Brief Review in
Physics: The Physical Setting

New York Standards

Standard	Key Idea
KEY	**4.2.1**
	Major Understanding

PS Introduction	1.S1	4.5.1a
1.M1.1	1.S3.1	6.3.2
1.M2.1	1.S3.2	7.1
1.M3.1	2.1.2	

1.M1.1	4.5.1i	4.PS5.1iii
1.M2.1	4.5.1j	4.PS5.1iv
1.M3.1	4.5.1k	4.PS5.1v
1.S1	4.5.1l	4.PS5.1vi
1.S3.1	4.5.1n	4.PS5.1vii
1.S3.2	4.5.1o	4.PS5.1viii
2.1.2	4.5.1p	4.PS5.1ix
4.5.1a	4.5.1q	4.PS5.1x
4.5.1b	4.5.1r	4.PS5.1xi
4.5.1c	4.5.1s	4.PS5.1xii
4.5.1d	4.5.1t	6.3.2
4.5.1e	4.5.1u	6.4.2
4.5.1f	4.PS4.1iv	7.1
4.5.1g	4.PS5.1i	
4.5.1h	4.PS5.1ii	

1.M1.1	4.4.1d	4.PS4.1i
1.M2.1	4.4.1e	4.PS4.1ii
1.M3.1	4.4.1f	4.PS4.1iii
1.S1	4.4.1g	4.PS4.1v
1.S3.1	4.4.1h	4.PS4.1vi
1.S3.2	4.4.1i	4.PS4.1vii
4.4.1a	4.4.1j	4.PS5.1xiii
4.4.1b	4.5.1a	6.3.2
4.4.1c	4.5.1m	

New York Standards

1.M1.1	4.4.1n	4.PS4.1ix
1.M2.1	4.4.1o	4.PS4.1x
1.M3.1	4.4.1p	4.PS4.1xi
1.S1	4.5.1a	4.PS4.1xii
1.S3.1	4.5.1s	4.PS4.1xiii
1.S3.2	4.5.1t	4.PS4.1xiv
2.1.2	4.5.1u	4.PS4.1xv
4.4.1j	4.5.3b	6.3.2
4.4.1k	4.5.3f	7.1
4.4.1l	4.5.3h	
4.4.1m	4.PS4.1viii	

1.M1.1	4.4.3g	4.PS4.3iii
1.M2.1	4.4.3h	4.PS4.3iv
1.S1	4.4.3i	4.PS4.3v
1.S3.1	4.4.3j	4.PS4.3vi
4.4.3a	4.4.3k	4.PS4.3vii
4.4.3b	4.4.3l	4.PS4.3viii
4.4.3c	4.4.3m	4.PS4.3ix
4.4.3d	4.4.3n	6.3.2
4.4.3e	4.PS4.3i	
4.4.3f	4.PS4.3ii	

1.M1.1	4.5.3a	4.5.3h
1.M2.1	4.5.3b	4.5.3i
1.M3.1	4.5.3c	4.5.3j
1.S1	4.5.3d	4.PS5.3i
1.S3.1	4.5.3e	4.PS5.3ii
4.4.1a	4.5.3f	6.2.1
4.5.1r	4.5.3g	6.3.2

Separate Answer Key Contents:

Diagnostic Tests with Answers

Answers to Review Questions

Answers to Regents Exam Practice Questions

Answers to Regents Examinations

About This Book

This book is designed to enhance review of the concepts, skills, and applications of The Physical Setting/Physics Core Curriculum that may be tested on the Physical Setting/Physics Regents Examination. Students can review topics in any order as each topic is independent of the others except for the introduction of vocabulary words.

Features

Content Review

The presentation features aids for accessing the basic content that will be tested on the Regents Examination as well as practice for interpreting and answering Regents Examination questions.

Illustrations Graphics visualize the concepts and vocabulary of physics as well as the types of drawings and graphs students will be required to interpret on the exam.

Vocabulary Many exam questions require an understanding of the language of physics.

Bold Words This vocabulary is listed at the beginning of a topic and defined within that topic.

Underlined Words These terms appear as bold in other topics or describe basic physics concepts.

Sample Problems Step-by-step detailed solutions guide the problem-solving process, reinforce content knowledge, and provide examples of types of problems found on the exam.

Review Questions More than 650 questions similar to those on the exam, appear throughout each topic to clarify and reinforce understanding.

Practice Questions for the New York Regents Exam

More than 550 practice questions are written and organized for each topic in the format of the exam.

Part A Multiple-choice questions test knowledge of concepts.

Part B Both multiple-choice and constructed-response questions test understandings and skills.

Part C Questions assess the ability to explain, analyze, and interpret physics processes and phenomena. The number in brackets tells how many credits the question is worth on an actual exam.

Reference and Support

Strategies for Answering Test Questions Support to help you interpret and answer the range of exam questions.

Appendix The *Reference Tables for the Physical Setting/Physics* are integral to this content review and are annotated with an Ⓡ. Review Questions and Practice Questions also refer students to them. When a formula that appears on the *Reference Tables for the Physical Setting/Physics* is first introduced in a topic, the formula is annotated with an Ⓡ.

Glossary All bold vocabulary words and underlined words appearing in the topics are defined.

Index Concepts in the topics are cross-referenced.

Regents Examinations

The most recent released Regents Examinations are reproduced at the end of this book to provide practice in taking actual Regents Examinations.

Answer Key with Diagnostic Tests A separate Answer Key includes all answers to the Review and Practice Questions plus topic-by-topic Diagnostic Tests to help determine which concepts require more intense review.

Strategies for
Answering Test Questions

This section provides strategies to help you answer various types of questions on the Regents Examination for The Physical Setting/Physics. Strategies are provided for answering multiple-choice and constructed-response questions as well as for questions based on diagrams, data tables, and graphs.

Strategies for Multiple-Choice Questions

Multiple-choice questions account for more than 50% of the Regents Examination for The Physical Setting/Physics. Parts A and B-1 are comprised totally of multiple-choice questions. Therefore, it is important to be good at deciphering multiple-choice questions. Here are a few helpful strategies. For any one question, not all strategies will need to be used. The numbers are provided for reference, not to specify an order (except for Strategies 1 and 2).

1. Always read the entire question, but wait to read the choices. (See Strategy 4.)

2. Carefully examine any data tables, diagrams, or relevant part(s) of the *Reference Tables for Physical Setting/Physics* associated with the question.

3. Underline key words and phrases in the question that signal what you should be looking for in the answer. This will make you read the question more carefully. This strategy applies mostly to questions with a long introduction.

4. Try to think of an answer to the question before looking at the choices given. If you think you know the answer, write it on a separate piece of paper before reading the choices. Next, read all of the choices and compare them to your answer before making a decision. Do not select the first answer that seems correct. If your answer matches one of the choices, and you are quite sure of your response, you are probably correct. Even if your answer matches one of the choices, carefully consider all of the answers because the obvious choice is not always the correct one.

If there are no exact matches, re-read the question and look for the choice that is most similar to your answer.

5. Eliminate any choices that you know are incorrect. Lightly cross out the numbers for those choices on the exam paper. Each choice you can eliminate increases your chances of selecting the correct answer.

6. If the question makes no sense after reading through it several times, leave it for later. After completing the rest of the exam, return to the question. Something you read on the other parts of the exam may give you some ideas about how to answer this question. If you are still unsure, go with your best guess. There is no penalty for guessing, but answers left blank will be counted as wrong. If you employ your best test-taking strategies, you just may select the correct answer.

Strategies for Constructed-Response Questions

Questions in Part B-2 and all questions in Part C of the Regents Examination for Physical Setting/Physics require a constructed response. You may be required to read one or more paragraphs (the stimulus) and then graph data, complete a data table, label or draw diagrams, design experiments, make calculations, or write short or extended responses. In addition, questions may ask you to hypothesize, interpret, analyze, evaluate data, or apply your scientific knowledge and skills to real-world situations.

The following procedure may prove helpful in answering many constructed-response questions. Strategies 2 through 10 are also useful to follow for multiple-choice questions involving calculations.

1. Read the stimulus carefully.

2. Read the question carefully to make certain you understand what is being asked.

3. Make a sketch of the situation.

4. Include on the sketch all values of quantities given in the statement of the problem.

To save time and space, represent quantities with appropriate symbols and be sure to include correct units with the numbers.

5. Include on your sketch quantities that can be inferred from the statement of the problem. For example, if the problem states that "an object falls freely from rest near Earth's surface," it can be inferred that $a = 9.81$ m/s^2 and $v_i = 0$ m/s.

6. Use the proper symbol for the quantity being sought.

7. Refer to the *Reference Tables for Physical Setting/Physics* to help decide which equations are relevant to solving the problem.

8. Solve the appropriate equation(s) for the variable being sought before substituting in any values.

9. Substitute the known values with their correct units into the equation(s). Expressing derived units in terms of fundamental units may help you determine if the answer has the correct unit.

10. Perform the required calculations, paying particular attention to exponents and significant figures. Simplify the units in the answer.

Check the accuracy of your work and the reasonableness of your answer. Be on the lookout for answers that are not physically possible.

Strategies for Questions Based on Diagrams

Both multiple-choice and extended-response questions frequently include diagrams. Usually the diagrams provide information needed to answer the question. The diagrams may be realistic, or they may be schematic. Schematic drawings show the relationships among parts and sometimes the sequence in a system. Follow these steps:

1. First study the diagram and think about what the diagram shows you. Be sure to read any information, such as titles or labels, that go with the diagram.

2. Read the question. Follow the strategies for either multiple-choice or constructed-response questions listed previously.

Strategies for Questions Based on Data Tables

Most data tables contain information that summarizes a topic. A table uses rows and columns to condense information and to present it in an organized way. Rows are the horizontal divisions going from left to right across the table, while columns are vertical divisions going from top to bottom. Column headings name the type of information included in a table. Sometimes different categories of information are listed down the left-hand column of the table. When answering a question with a data table, use the following strategies.

1. Find the title of the table. It is usually located across the top.

2. Determine the number of columns in the table and their purpose.

3. Determine the number of rows and their purpose.

4. Read down the columns and across the rows to determine what the relationships are.

5. Now you are ready to read the question with the data table. Answer the question by using the suggested strategies for multiple-choice or constructed-response questions listed previously.

Strategies for Questions Based on Graphs

Graphs represent relationships in a visual form that is easy to read. Line graphs show the relationship between two changing quantities, or variables.

When answering a question that includes a graph, first ask yourself these questions:

- What information does the graph provide?
- What are the variables?
- What seems to happen to one variable as the other changes?

After a careful analysis of the graph, use the appropriate strategies for multiple-choice or constructed-response questions.

Use of Reference Tables for Physical Setting/Physics to Help Answer Questions

On recent Regents Examinations, more than 35% of the questions have involved the use of the *Reference Tables for Physical Setting/Physics*. You should become thoroughly familiar with all details of these tables. Sometimes the questions will specifically refer you to the reference tables, but most often you will be expected to know what information is included within the reference tables. Listed below are some of the ways these reference tables are used in Regents Examination questions.

- finding a specific fact, such as the value of an electronvolt expressed in joules
- using a formula on the reference tables to solve a problem, such as determining the kinetic energy of a moving object
- graphing or recognizing the correct graph of data on the reference tables, such as the absolute index of refraction of a substance
- decoding a graphic symbol in a question, such as quark or lepton
- performing a procedure using part of the reference tables, such as approximating the wavelength of red light from the frequency data given in the electromagnetic spectrum
- interpreting data in the reference tables, such as the ionization energies for mercury

Measurement and Mathematics

How Scientists Study Measurement and Mathematics

Are angles always measured in degrees?

A protractor is a device used to measure the size of an angle in degrees. A protractor that is a semicircle has a range from 0° to 180°, because a circle has 360°. The reason there are 360° in a circle may be related to some ancient calendars using 360 days for a year. Early astronomers noticed that the stars seemed to move 1/360th of a circular path each night. Long before there were calculators, it was known that 360 was divisible by every number from 1 to 10 except 7, and that it had a total of 24 factors.

In higher levels of physics and mathematics, angles are often measured in radians. The radian measure of an angle has no dimensions. A full circle is equal to 2π radians, making 1 radian equal to $360°/2\pi$ or approximately 57°.

When using your calculator for angle calculations in this text and on the Regents examination, be sure to confirm that your calculator is in the correct mode. For example, the sine of 20.0 degrees is 0.342 and the sine of 20.0 radians is 0.912.

Measurement and Mathematics

Vocabulary

absolute error	fundamental unit	scalar
accepted value	independent variable	scientific notation
accurate	indirect squared proportion	SI prefix
constant proportion	inversely proportional	SI system
dependent variable	line of best fit	significant figures
derived unit	mass	slope
direct squared proportion	mean	standard deviation
directly proportional	percent error	unit
experimental value	precise	variance
extrapolation	range	vector
force		

Topic Overview

Note to student: *This topic explains some of the process skills based on Standards 1, 2, 6, and 7 that you will use in the study of physics. These skills will be applied to specific content in later topics. Material in this topic will not be tested as definitions or on a purely mathematical basis. However, these concepts and process skills are testable when they are incorporated into specific physics content based on Standard 4.*

Physics is based on observations and measurements of the physical world. Consequently, scientists have developed tools for measurement and adopted standard conventions for describing natural phenomena. These conventions are reviewed below.

Units

A **unit** is a standard quantity with which other similar quantities can be compared. All measurements must be made with respect to some standard quantity. For example, it makes no sense to say the distance between two cities is 26. Distance must be stated in terms of a standard unit. The distance between the cities might be 26 miles or 26 kilometers.

The SI System

The **SI system** provides standardized units for scientific measurements. All quantities measured by physicists can be expressed in terms of the seven **fundamental units** listed in Table 1-1. **Derived units** are combinations of two or more of the fundamental units and are used to simplify notation. Other systems of units are sometimes used when they are more appropriate because of the size of the quantity being measured.

Table 1-1. Units of Measure

Kind of Unit	Quantity Being Measured	Name of Unit	Symbol
Fundamental SI	length	meter	m
	mass	kilogram	kg
	time	second	s
	electric current	ampere	A
	temperature	kelvin	K
	amount of substance*	mole	mol
	luminous intensity*	candela	cd
Derived SI	frequency	hertz	Hz
	force	newton	N
	energy, work	joule	J
	quantity of electric charge	coulomb	C
	electric potential, potential difference	volt	V
	power	watt	W
	electrical resistance	ohm	Ω
	resistivity	ohm · meter	$\Omega \cdot m$
Non-SI	length	centimeter	cm
	mass	gram	g
	mass	universal mass unit	u
	time	hour	h
	energy, work	electronvolt	eV
	angle size	degree	°

*These quantities are not treated in this review.

SI Prefixes

SI prefixes are prefixes combined with SI base units to form new units that are larger or smaller than the base units by a multiple or submultiple of 10. The symbol for the new unit consists of the symbol for the prefix followed by the symbol for the base unit. Table 1-2 lists some common SI prefixes. For example, 1000 meters can be expressed as 1 kilometer or 1 km, and 0.01 meter can be expressed as 1 centimeter or 1 cm.

Symbols for Units and Quantities Symbols for SI units are printed in normal type. For example, m is the symbol for meter, and A is the symbol for ampere. Letter symbols are also used for the names of quantities in formulas. These symbols are printed in *italic* type. For example, *m* is the symbol for mass, and *A* is the symbol for area. Be careful not to confuse these different meanings of the same letters.

Dimensional Analysis Analyzing units can help in solving problems. The units on the left side of an equation must always be equivalent to the units on the right side of the equation. Quantities can be added or subtracted only if they have the same units. These facts can be used to check whether an answer is reasonable.

Table 1-2. Prefixes for Powers of 10

Prefix	Symbol	Notation
tera-	T	10^{12}
giga-	G	10^{9}
mega-	M	10^{6}
kilo-	k	10^{3}
deci-	d	10^{-1}
centi-	c	10^{-2}
milli-	m	10^{-3}
micro-	μ	10^{-6}
nano-	n	10^{-9}
pico-	p	10^{-12}

For example, dimensional analysis for the period of a simple pendulum is shown in Figure 1-1. The time T required to complete one cycle of motion is the period of the pendulum, ℓ is the length, and g is the acceleration due to gravity. Because the period represents time, the expression on the right side of the equation must also have the dimension time. The units of the acceleration due to gravity, m/s^2, can be expressed as length ℓ in meters divided by T^2 in seconds squared, or $\frac{\ell}{T^2}$.

The units of length divide out and $T = \sqrt{T^2}$. The factor 2π has no units so it is not considered in the analysis.

Review Questions

1. Which term is not a fundamental unit?

   (1) kilogram   (3) second
   (2) meter   (4) watt

2. Which quantity and unit are correctly paired?

   (1) electric current — coulomb
   (2) frequency — hertz
   (3) power — joule
   (4) resistivity — ohm

3. Which amount of power is the *smallest*?

   (1) 1 gigawatt
   (2) 2 kilowatts
   (3) 3 megawatts
   (4) 4 watts

4. Which length is the *shortest*?

   (1) 1 μm   (2) 2 mm   (3) 3 nm   (4) 4 cm

5. Continental drift speed is 1×10^{-9} meter per second. This is equivalent to a speed of

   (1) 1 Tm/s   (2) 1 Gm/s   (3) 1 nm/s   (4) 1 pm/s

6. The diameter of 12-gauge wire is 2.053×10^{-3} meter. This is equivalent to 2.053

   (1) km   (2) mm   (3) μm   (4) nm

7. The energy in half a tank of gasoline is 1,000,000,000 joules. Express this value in gigajoules.

8. The mean radius of Earth is 6,000,000 meters. Express this value in kilometers.

9. Which length is 10^6 times greater than a nanometer?

   (1) μm   (2) mm   (3) cm   (4) km

10. The period of rotation of the Sun is 2.125×10^6 seconds. This is equivalent to 2.125

    (1) μs   (2) ms   (3) Ms   (4) Ts

11. Human hair grows at the rate of 3 nanometers per second. This rate is equivalent to

    (1) 3×10^{-3} m/s   (3) 3×10^{-9} m/s
    (2) 3×10^{-6} m/s   (4) 3×10^{-12} m/s

12. The wavelength of red light is 7×10^{-7} meter. Express this value in nanometers.

13. If m represents mass in kg, v represents speed in m/s, and r represents radius in m, show that the force F in the formula $F = \frac{mv^2}{r}$ can be expressed in the unit kg · m/s^2.

14. If PE_s represents the potential energy stored in a spring in kg · m^2/s^2, and x represents the change in spring length from its equilibrium position in m, what is the unit for the spring constant k in the formula $PE_s = \frac{1}{2}kx^2$?

15. If F_e represents the electrostatic force in N that point charge q_1 in C exerts on point charge q_2 in C, and r represents the distance between the point charges in m, what is the unit for the electrostatic constant k in the formula $F = \frac{kq_1q_2}{r^2}$?

    (1) N · m^2/C^2
    (2) N · m^2
    (3) N · C^2/m^2
    (4) N · m^2/C

16. Using dimensional analysis, show that the expression $\frac{v^2}{d}$ has the same units as acceleration.

Tools for Measurement

In most laboratory investigations, you will make observations and measurements of physical quantities. You will be expected to select the appropriate piece of equipment, determine its scale, and make measurements to the proper number of significant figures.

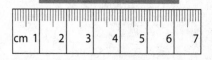

Figure 1-2. Metric ruler: The length of the wire is 5.20 cm.

Measuring Length

The length of an object or the total length of a path an object moves is measured with a metric ruler or meter stick. Path length is usually measured in meters, but occasionally centimeters are more appropriate. You can convert a measurement in centimeters to meters by dividing by 100. The piece of wire in Figure 1-2 has a length of 5.20 cm or 0.0520 m.

Measuring Mass

The **mass,** or amount of matter contained in an object, can be measured with an electronic balance or a triple-beam balance. It is important that the balance be zeroed before determining the mass of an object.

Figure 1-3. Electronic balance: The steel ball has a mass of 115.2 g.

The steel ball on the electronic balance in Figure 1-3 has a mass of 115.2 g or 0.1152 kg.

The block of wood on the triple-beam balance in Figure 1-4 has a mass of 208.50 g or 0.20850 kg. A mass that is determined in grams can be converted to kilograms by dividing by 1000.

Measuring Time

Elapsed time can be measured with a clock or stopwatch. As you know, one hour equals sixty minutes and one minute equals sixty seconds. Because many of the events you will be measuring in physics occur quickly, you may be asked to record elapsed time to the nearest hundredth of a second. The stopwatch in Figure 1-5 shows an elapsed time of 37.08 s.

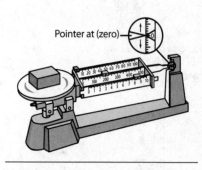

Figure 1-4. Triple-beam balance: The beam must be at zero when a reading of the mass is made.

Measuring Force

A push or pull on a mass is called a **force.** Forces are measured with a spring scale. Ranges on spring scales typically vary from 2.5 newtons to 20.0 newtons. Figure 1-6 shows a spring scale recording a force of 4.5 N as a block is lifted at constant speed.

Measuring an Angle

A common unit for measuring angles is the degree (°), which is one ninetieth of a right angle. The protractor is an instrument used for measuring angles in degrees. Figure 1-7 shows a protractor being used to measure angle *AOB*. The wedge point of the protractor is on *O*, and the diameter of the semicircle lies on *OA*, one side of the angle. The other side of the angle intersects the semicircle at 47°. This reading gives the number of degrees in the angle. If the sides of the angle to be measured are too short to intersect the semicircle, they can be extended.

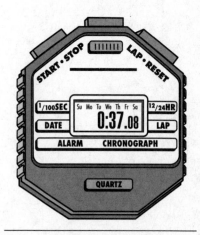

Figure 1-5. Stopwatch: Minutes are recorded to the left of the colon. Seconds (to the one-hundreth place) are recorded to the right of the colon. The elapsed time is 37.08 s.

Figure 1-6. **Spring scale:** Force or weight is measured with a spring scale. This scale reads 4.5 N.

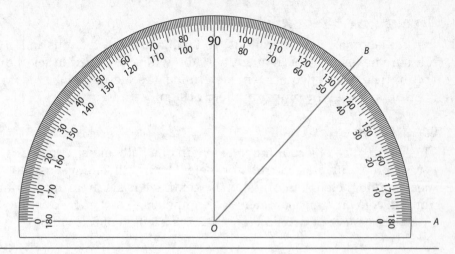

Figure 1-7. Protractor: Angle *AOB* has a measure of 47°.

Drawing an Angle To draw an angle of 25° with its vertex at point *P*, draw a line segment originating at *P*. Place the wedge point of the protractor on *P* and the diameter of the protractor semicircle along the line segment. Make a dot on the paper at the 25° mark on the inner set of degree readings. Draw a line from this point to *P*.

Trigonometry

The branch of mathematics that treats the relationships between the angles and sides of triangles is called trigonometry. Basic trigonometric relationships are used to solve some types of physics problems.
Figure 1-8 shows a right triangle. Notice that side *a* is opposite angle θ, side *b* is adjacent to angle θ, and side *c* is the hypotenuse opposite the right angle.

Important ratios of the sides of a right triangle in terms of angle θ include the following.

$$\sin \theta = \frac{a}{c}$$

$$\cos \theta = \frac{b}{c}$$

$$\tan \theta = \frac{a}{b}$$

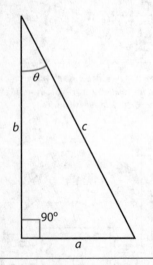

Figure 1-8. Right triangle

If the measure of angle θ is 30.°, the ratio of *a* to *c* is 0.50 because $\sin 30.° = 0.50$.

If you know the length of any two sides of a right triangle, you can find the length of the third side by using the Pythagorean theorem. The Pythagorean theorem is valid for right triangles only and has the following formula:

$$c^2 = a^2 + b^2$$

A block is displaced a vertical distance of 0.75 meter as it slides down a 1.25-meter long plane inclined to the horizontal, as shown in the following diagram.
(a) Calculate the horizontal displacement of the block.
(b) Calculate the angle the plane makes with the horizontal.

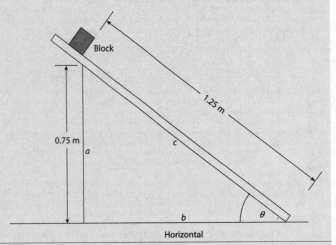

SOLUTION: Relate the Pythagorean theorem to the diagram. Identify the known and unknown values.

Known
$a = 0.75$ m
$c = 1.25$ m

Unknown
$b = ?$ m
$\angle \theta = ?$ °

1. Solve the formula for the Pythagorean theorem for the unknown, b.
$$c^2 = a^2 + b^2$$
$$b = \sqrt{c^2 - a^2}$$

2. Substitute the known values and solve.
$$b = \sqrt{(1.25 \text{m})^2 - (0.75 \text{ m})^2} = 1.0 \text{ m}$$

3. Write the formula for $\sin \theta$.
$$\sin \theta = \frac{a}{c}$$

4. Substitute the known values and solve for θ.
$$\sin \theta = \frac{0.75 \text{ m}}{1.25 \text{ m}}$$
$$\theta = 37°$$

Review Questions

17. A student measures a strip of metal using a metric ruler, as shown in the diagram below.

What is the length of the strip?
(1) 6.50 cm
(2) 56.5 mm
(3) 56.5 cm
(4) 5065 mm

18. The diagram below shows the cross-sectional area of a dowel.

Use a metric ruler to measure the diameter of the dowel to the nearest tenth of a centimeter.

19. Express a length of 52.5 centimeters in meters.

20. The diagram below shows an enlarged view of the beams on a triple-beam balance.

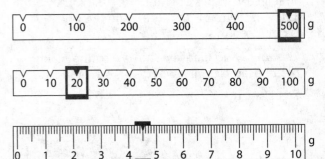

What is the reading for the mass that is being measured?
(1) 251.0 g
(2) 524.5 g
(3) 5245 g
(4) 5,002,045 g

21. The diagram below shows an enlarged view of the beams of a triple-beam balance.

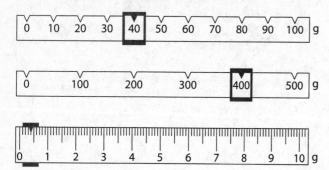

What is the reading, in kilograms, for the mass being measured?

22. The stopwatch below was used to time an event.

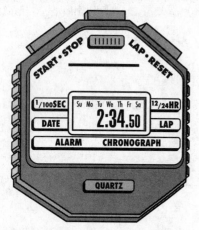

What is the elapsed time in seconds?

(1) 24.450 s   (3) 234.50 s
(2) 154.50 s   (4) 23,450 s

23. An electric lightbulb operates for 1 hour 15 minutes. What is the total time the light bulb operates in seconds?

24. An electric iron is operated for 18 minutes at 120 volts. What is the total time the iron is operated in seconds?

25. The following diagram shows a spring scale being used to pull a wooden block up a wooden incline.

What is the magnitude of the force recorded on the spring scale?

26. The diagram below shows a spring scale attached to a wooden block as it is being pulled across a horizontal surface.

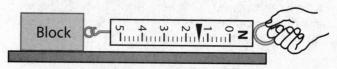

What is the magnitude of the force exerted on the spring scale?

27. The diagram below represents a ramp inclined to the horizontal at angle θ. The upper end of the ramp is 37 centimeters above the horizontal.

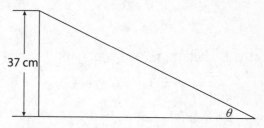

a) Using a protractor measure angle θ.
b) Calculate the length of the ramp.

28. The diagram below represents a ramp inclined at angle θ to the horizontal.

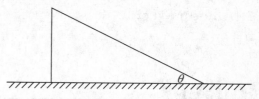

a) Using a protractor measure angle θ to the nearest degree.
b) What is sin θ?
c) What is cos θ?

29. On the diagram below, use a protractor and a straightedge to construct an angle of 40.° with the normal to the surface at point *P*.

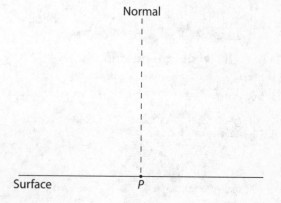

30. The diagram below shows one end of a ladder resting against the side of a building 6.1 meters above the level ground. The other end of the ladder makes an angle of 60.° with the ground.

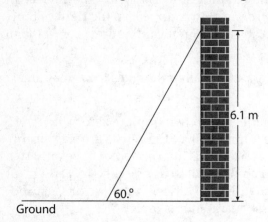

Using the scale in the drawing *or* a trigonometric function:

a) Calculate the length of the ladder.
b) Calculate how far the base of the ladder is from the building.

31. A child flying a kite lets out 50. meters of string. The string makes an angle of 30.° with the ground, as shown in the diagram below.

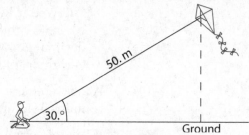

Calculate the height of the kite above the ground.

32. A forest ranger, 35 meters above the ground in a tower, observes a blazing fire. The angle of depression to the base of the fire is 20.°, as shown in the diagram below.

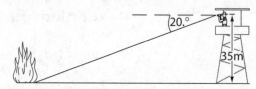

Calculate the distance from the tower to the fire.

Uncertainty in Measurement

When a quantity is measured, the measurement always consists of some digits that are certain plus one digit whose value has been estimated. Thus, every measurement has an experimental uncertainty. The uncertainty can result from the quality and limitations of the measuring instrument, the skill of the person using the instrument, and the number of measurements made.

If several measurements taken of the same event are nearly identical, the measurements are said to be **precise.** If a measurement is very close to the accepted value found in a handbook, the measurement is said to be **accurate.** For example, the accepted value for the acceleration due to gravity near Earth's surface is 9.81 m/s². If a student measures this quantity as 9.98 m/s², 9.98 m/s², and 9.99 m/s², the measurements are precise, but not accurate.

Significant Figures (Significant Digits)

In a measured value, the digits that are known with certainty plus the one digit whose value has been estimated are called **significant figures** or significant digits. The greater the number of significant digits in a measurement, the greater the accuracy of the measurement.

Nonzero digits in a measurement are always significant. Zeroes appearing in a measurement may or may not be significant. The following rules should be applied *in order* to the zeroes in a measured value:

1. Zeroes that appear *before* a nonzero digit are *not* significant.
   Examples: 0.002 m (1 significant figure) and 0.13 g (2 significant figures)

2. Zeroes that appear *between* nonzero digits are significant. Examples: 0. 705 kg (3 significant figures) and 2006 km (4 significant figures)
3. Zeroes that appear *after* a nonzero digit are significant *only* if (a) followed by a decimal point. Examples: 40 s (1 significant figure) and 20. m (2 significant figures); *or* if (b) they appear to the right of the decimal point. Examples: 37.0 cm (3 significant figures) and 4.100 m (4 significant figures)

A measurement of 0.040 900 kg utilizes all of the rules for zeroes and contains 5 significant digits.

If a whole-number measurement ends in two or more zeroes, it is not possible to indicate that some, but not all, of the zeroes are significant. For example, a measurement of 5200 m is interpreted to have only two significant figures, although it could actually represent a measurement to the nearest 10 meters. This situation is avoided by the use of scientific notation, which will be discussed later in this topic.

Addition and Subtraction with Measured Values

Measured values must have the same units before they are added or subtracted. For example, if the dimensions of a rectangle are recorded as 4.3 cm and 0.085 m, both measurements must be expressed either in centimeters or in meters before they can be combined by addition to find the perimeter of the rectangle. After adding or subtracting measured values expressed in the same units, the sum or difference is rounded to the same decimal place value as the least sensitive measurement.

Example A below shows that subtracting a measurement known to the nearest thousandth of a meter from a measurement known to the nearest tenth of a meter produces a difference known to the nearest tenth of a meter.

Similarly, in Example B below, adding measurements to the nearest hundredth of a centimeter, tenth of a centimeter, and centimeter produces a sum to the nearest centimeter.

Example A	Example B
	24.82 cm
31.1 m	4.7 cm
− 2.461 m	+ 2 cm
28.639 m = 28.6 m	31.52 cm = 32 cm

Multiplication and Division with Measured Values

When multiplying or dividing measured values, the operation is performed and the answer is rounded to the same number of significant figures as appears in the value having the lowest number of significant figures. In the example that follows, 2.6 cm has two significant figures, whereas 200.0 cm has four. Thus, the product of the two values can have only two significant figures.

$$(200.0 \text{ cm})(2.6 \text{ cm}) = 520 \text{ cm}^2$$

Notice that although both measurements are accurate to the nearest tenth of a centimeter, the last significant figure in the product is in the tens place. Thus, the product of a measurement with four significant figures and a measurement with two significant figures has only two significant figures.

33. A student measures the speed of yellow light in water to be 2.00×10^8 meters per second, 1.87×10^8 meters per second, and 2.39×10^8 meters per second. If the accepted value for the speed is 2.25×10^8 meters per second, the student's measurements are

(1) precise, only
(2) accurate, only
(3) both precise and accurate
(4) neither precise nor accurate

34. A student measures the length of a quarter-mile lap around the school's track to be 402.3 meters, 402.3 meters, and 402.5 meters. If the accepted value for the path length is 402.3 meters, the student's measurements are

(1) precise, only
(2) accurate, only
(3) both precise and accurate
(4) neither precise nor accurate

35. Which length measurement contains three significant figures?

(1) 0.203 m   (3) 34.70 km
(2) 0.54 m   (4) 570 cm

36. To what number of significant figures is a measurement of 14,020 grams expressed?

(1) 5   (2) 2   (3) 3   (4) 4

37. What is the area of a rectangle having dimensions of 9.8 meters and 12.7 meters?

(1) 100 m²   (3) 124 m²
(2) 120 m²   (4) 124.46 m²

38. Which mass measurement is expressed to two significant figures?

(1) 0.040 kg   (3) 40 kg
(2) 0.4 kg   (4) 405 kg

39. To what number of significant figures is a measurement of 7002 meters expressed?

(1) 1   (3) 3
(2) 2   (4) 4

40. A car travels 685 meters in 27 seconds. What is the average speed of the car?

(1) 25.370 m/s   (3) 25.4 m/s
(2) 25.37 m/s   (4) 25 m/s

41. A radar signal traveling at 3.00×10^8 meters per second is sent from Earth to the Moon and is received back at Earth in 2.56 seconds. What is the distance from Earth to the Moon?

(1) 7.68×10^8 m   (3) 8×10^8 m
(2) 3.84×10^8 m   (4) 4×10^8 m

42. What is the sum of 3.04 meters, 4.134 meters, and 6.1 meters?

43. What is the sum of 0.027 kilogram and 0.0023 kilogram?

44. To what number of significant figures is the measurement 0.705 meter expressed?

45. To what number of significant figures is the measurement 470 meters expressed?

46. Express forty meters with four significant figures.

47. Calculate the area of a rectangle having a length of 41.6 centimeters and a width of 2.3 centimeters.

48. Safety guidelines recommend an area of 5.6 meters² per student in a laboratory setting. Would a room having dimensions of 13.2 meters and 10.6 meters accommodate 24 students and comply with these guidelines? Justify your answer.

Scientific Notation

Measurements that have very large or very small values are usually expressed in **scientific notation.** Scientific notation consists of a number equal to or greater than one and less than ten followed by a multiplication sign and the base ten raised to some integral power. The general form of a number expressed in scientific notion is $A \times 10^n$. All of the digits in A are significant. For numbers having an absolute value greater than one, n is positive. For numbers having an absolute value less than one, n is negative. For a number having an absolute value of one, n is zero. For example, the mean radius of Earth is 6,370,000 m or 6.37×10^6 m (3 significant figures). The universal gravitational constant is

0.000 000 000 066 7 N·m²/kg² or 6.67×10^{-11} N·m²/kg² (3 significant figures). The height of a physics student might be 1.75 meters or 1.75×10^0 meters (3 significant figures).

Addition and Subtraction Measurements written in scientific notation can be added or subtracted only if they are expressed in the same units and to the same power of ten. Sometimes, as in the example below, the power of ten must be changed first before adding or subtracting.

$$3.2 \times 10^2 \text{ m} + 4.73 \times 10^3 \text{ m} = 0.32 \times 10^3 \text{ m} + 4.73 \times 10^3 \text{ m} = 5.05 \times 10^3 \text{ m}$$

Multiplication and Division The commutative and associative laws for multiplication are used to find products and quotients of physical quantities written in scientific notation. Recall that the exponents are added when like bases are multiplied and the exponents are subtracted when like bases are divided. The general rule is as follows.

$$(A \times 10^n)(B \times 10^m) = (A \times B)(10^{n+m})$$
$$\text{and}$$
$$\frac{(A \times 10^n)}{(B \times 10^m)} = \frac{A}{B} \times 10^{n-m}$$

When multiplying and dividing measured values, the rules for significant figures apply to values expressed in scientific notation. Some examples follow.

$$(1.3 \times 10^5 \text{ m})(3.47 \times 10^2 \text{ m}) = 4.5 \times 10^7 \text{ m}^2$$
$$(1.3 \times 10^{-5} \text{ m})(3.47 \times 10^2 \text{ m}) = 4.5 \times 10^{-3} \text{ m}^2$$
$$(4.73 \times 10^5 \text{ m})(5.2 \times 10^2 \text{ m}) = 25 \times 10^7 \text{ m}^2 = 2.5 \times 10^8 \text{ m}^2$$
$$(8.4 \times 10^5 \text{ m}) \div (2.10 \times 10^2 \text{ m}) = 4.0 \times 10^3$$
$$(8.4 \times 10^5 \text{ m}) \div (2.10 \times 10^{-2} \text{ m}) = 4.0 \times 10^7$$
$$(2.10 \times 10^2 \text{ m}) \div (8.4 \times 10^5 \text{ m}) = 0.25 \times 10^{-3} = 2.5 \times 10^{-4}$$

SAMPLE PROBLEM A

Estimate the magnitude of the gravitational force that Earth exerts on the Moon and compare it with the actual value.

SOLUTION: Use the formula for the force due to gravity and the known values of the masses, the distance between centers, and the universal gravitational constant.

Known

$$F_g = \frac{Gm_1m_2}{r^2}$$

$G = 6.67 \times 10^{-11}$ N·m²/kg²
$m_1 = 7.35 \times 10^{22}$ kg
$m_2 = 5.98 \times 10^{24}$ kg
$r = 3.84 \times 10^8$ m

Unknown

estimated $F_g = ?$ N

1. Substitute the known values in the formula for the force due to gravity.

$$F_g = \frac{(6.67 \times 10^{-11} \text{ N} \cdot \text{m}^2/\text{kg}^2)(7.35 \times 10^{22} \text{ kg})(5.98 \times 10^{24} \text{ kg})}{(3.84 \times 10^8 \text{ m})^2}$$

2. Estimate the answer by rounding off each value to the nearest whole number and combining them.

$$F_g = \frac{(7 \times 10^{-11})(7 \times 10^{22})(6 \times 10^{24}) \text{ N}}{16 \times 10^{16}}$$

$$F_g \text{ (estimated)} = 20 \times 10^{19} \text{ N} = 2 \times 10^{20} \text{ N}$$

3. Use a calculator to determine the actual magnitude of the force.

$$F_g \text{ (calculated)} = 1.99 \times 10^{20} \text{ N}$$

The estimated value is close to the calculated value.

As the Voyager spacecraft passed the planet Uranus, it sent signals back to Earth. Determine the order of magnitude of the time in seconds for a signal to reach Earth. The distance from Earth to Uranus is 2.71×10^{12} meters. The speed of light in a vacuum is 3.00×10^8 meters per second.

SOLUTION: Identify the known and unknown values.

Known
$d = 2.71 \times 10^{12}$ m
$v = 3.00 \times 10^8$ m/s

Unknown
$t = ?$ s

1. Round the known values to the nearest whole numbers and find the formula relating distance, time, and average speed.

$$\bar{v} = \frac{d}{t}$$

2. Solve for t. Substitute the rounded values and solve.

$$t = \frac{d}{\bar{v}} = \frac{3 \times 10^{12}\text{ m}}{3 \times 10^8\text{ m/s}} = 10^4\text{ s}$$

The order of magnitude is 10^4.

Estimation and Orders of Magnitude

The technique of estimating the answer to a problem before performing the calculations makes it possible to quickly verify the procedures to be used and determine the reasonableness of the answer as in Sample Problem A. Estimating answers using orders of magnitude also helps in evaluating the reasonableness of an answer, as illustrated in Sample Problem B.

Review Questions

49. Express the diameter of a nickel, 0.021 meter, in scientific notation.

50. Express the mass of a car, 1500 kilograms, in scientific notation.

51. The jet engines of a 747 exert a force of 770,000 newtons. Express this value in scientific notation.

52. Divide $1.494\,57 \times 10^{11}$ meters, the average distance from the Sun to Earth, by 3.00×10^8 meters per second, the speed of light in a vacuum. Write your answer in scientific notation with the correct units and the appropriate number of significant figures.

53. What is the approximate width of a person's little finger?
    (1) 1 m   (2) 0.1 m   (3) 0.01 m   (4) 0.001 m

54. The length of a high school classroom is probably closest to
    (1) 10^{-2} m   (2) 10^{-1} m   (3) 10^1 m   (4) 10^4 m

55. The thickness of a dollar bill is closest to
    (1) 1×10^{-4} m   (3) 1×10^{-1} m
    (2) 1×10^{-2} m   (4) 1×10^1 m

56. Which measurement of an average classroom door is closest to 10^0 meter?
    (1) thickness   (3) height
    (2) width   (4) surface area

57. A flowerpot falls from a third-story window ledge to the ground. The total distance the flowerpot falls is closest to
    (1) 10^0 m   (2) 10^1 m   (3) 10^2 m   (4) 10^3 m

58. The approximate diameter of a 12-ounce can of root beer is
    (1) 6.7×10^{-3} m   (3) 6.7×10^{-1} m
    (2) 6.7×10^{-2} m   (4) 6.7×10^0 m

59. What is the approximate mass of a chicken egg?
    (1) 1×10^1 kg   (3) 1×10^{-1} kg
    (2) 1×10^2 kg   (4) 1×10^{-4} kg

60. A mass of one kilogram of nickels has a monetary value in United States dollars of approximately
    (1) $1.00   (3) $10.00
    (2) $0.10   (4) $1000.00

61. The mass of a physics textbook is closest to
(1) 10^3 kg (2) 10^1 kg (3) 10^0 kg (4) 10^{-2} kg

62. The mass of a high-school football player is approximately
(1) 10^0 kg (2) 10^1 kg (3) 10^2 kg (4) 10^3 kg

63. What is the approximate mass of an automobile?
(1) 10^1 kg (2) 10^2 kg (3) 10^3 kg (4) 10^6 kg

64. Approximately how many seconds are in three hours?
(1) 10^2 s (2) 10^3 s (3) 10^4 s (4) 10^5 s

65. The weight of an apple is closest to
(1) 10^{-2} N (2) 10^0 N (3) 10^2 N (4) 10^4 N

66. Which object weighs approximately 1 newton?
(1) dime (3) physics student
(2) paper clip (4) golf ball

67. The weight of a chicken egg is approximately
(1) 10^{-3} N (2) 10^{-2} N (3) 10^0 N (4) 10^2 N

68. The speed of a rifle bullet is 7×10^2 meters per second and the speed of a snail is 1×10^{-3} meter per second. How many times faster than the snail does the bullet travel?

69. The power of sunlight striking Earth is 1.7×10^{17} watts. How many 100-watt incandescent light bulbs would produce this amount of power?

Note: Use information found on the first page of the *Reference Tables for Physical Setting/Physics* in answering questions 70 through 73.

70. The acceleration due to gravity is approximately
(1) 10^{-1} m/s^2 (3) 10^1 m/s^2
(2) 10^0 m/s^2 (4) 10^3 m/s^2

71. What is the order of magnitude of the ratio of the charge on an electron to the mass of an electron?

72. What is the order of magnitude of the ratio of the speed of light in a vacuum to the speed of sound in air at STP?

73. What is the order of magnitude of the ratio of the mass of the Moon to the mass of Earth?

Evaluating Experimental Results

Experimental measurements made in any laboratory must be evaluated before they can be published in a scientific journal. An evaluation procedure has been developed for this purpose.

Data Analysis

In an experiment, for example to determine the relationship between the period of a simple pendulum and its length, multiple measurements are made of a given or identical event. Although there is a **range** of measurements or difference between the highest and lowest value in the data set, most of the measurements are close to the mean.

The notation $\sum\limits_{i=1}^{n}$ is used to represent the sum of related terms. The index i is replaced by consecutive integers starting with the lower limit of summation written below the summation symbol Σ and ending with the upper limit of summation written above. Therefore, the **mean** or average $\bar{x}$ of a set of n measurements, where x_i is the individual measurement and f_i is the frequency of occurrence of that measurement, can be represented by Expression A below. The **variance** ν is the sum of the squares of the differences of the measurements from the mean, divided by the number of measurements, as shown in Expression B below. The **standard deviation** σ is the square root of the variance, shown by Expression C below.

Expression A

$$\bar{x} = \frac{\sum\limits_{i=1}^{n} x_i f_i}{\sum f_i}$$

Expression B

$$\nu = \frac{\sum\limits_{i=1}^{n} f_i (x_i - \bar{x})^2}{\sum f_i}$$

Expression C

$$\sigma = \sqrt{\nu} = \sqrt{\frac{\sum\limits_{i=1}^{n} f_i (x_i - \bar{x})^2}{\sum f_i}}$$

In a normal distribution, 68% of the data values lie between $\bar{x} - \sigma$ and $\bar{x} + \sigma$; 95% lie between $\bar{x} - 2\sigma$ and $\bar{x} + 2\sigma$; and 99.5% lie between $\bar{x} - 3\sigma$ and $\bar{x} + 3\sigma$.

SAMPLE PROBLEM

A student made seven measurements of the period of a simple pendulum of constant length released from the same point: 1.34 s, 1.28 s, 1.26 s, 1.28 s, 1.33 s, 1.33 s, and 1.28 s. Determine the range, mean, variance, and standard deviation for the data.

SOLUTION: Identify the known and unknown values.

Known
$T_1 = 1.34$ s
$T_2 = 1.28$ s
$T_3 = 1.26$ s
$T_4 = 1.28$ s
$T_5 = 1.33$ s
$T_6 = 1.33$ s
$T_7 = 1.28$ s

Unknown
range = ? s
mean $\bar{x}$ = ? s
variance v = ? s^2
standard deviation σ = ? s

1. Determine the range by subtracting the smallest measurement from the largest.
   1.34 s − 1.26 s = 0.08 s

2. Set up a chart to simplify finding the mean, variance, and standard deviation.

3. Write in column 1 the four values of T (x_i) that are different.

4. Write the frequency of each value of T in column 2.

5. Find the sum of the frequencies, Σf_i, and record it in column 2.
   $\Sigma f_i = 1 + 3 + 2 + 1 = 7$

6. Multiply the values in column 1 (x_i) by the values in column 2 (f_i). Record the results in column 3.
   $x_i f_i = (1.26 \text{ s})(1) = 1.26$ s
   $x_i f_i = (1.28 \text{ s})(3) = 3.84$ s
   $x_i f_i = (1.33 \text{ s})(2) = 2.66$ s
   $x_i f_i = (1.34 \text{ s})(1) = 1.34$ s

7. Calculate the sum of all the $x_i f_i$ values, $\Sigma x_i f_i$, by adding the values in column 3.
   $\Sigma x_i f_i = 1.26 \text{ s} + 3.84 \text{ s} + 2.66 \text{ s} + 1.34 \text{ s} = 9.10$ s

8. Determine the mean, $\bar{x}$, by dividing $\Sigma x_i f_i$ by Σf_i.
   $$\bar{x} = \frac{\sum_{i=1}^{n} x_i f_i}{\Sigma f_i} = \frac{9.10 \text{ s}}{7} = 1.30 \text{ s}$$

9. Subtract the mean from each value in column 1 and record the values in column 4.
   1.26 s − 1.30 s = −0.04 s
   1.28 s − 1.30 s = −0.02 s
   1.33 s − 1.30 s = + 0.03 s
   1.34 s − 1.30 s = + 0.04 s

10. Square the values in column 4 and record the results in column 5.
    $(-0.04 \text{ s})^2 = 0.0016 \text{ s}^2$
    $(-0.02 \text{ s})^2 = 0.0004 \text{ s}^2$
    $(+0.03 \text{ s})^2 = 0.0009 \text{ s}^2$
    $(-0.04 \text{ s})^2 = 0.0016 \text{ s}^2$

11. Multiply the values in column 5 by the frequencies in column 2. Record these products in column 6.
    $(0.0016 \text{ s}^2)(1) = 0.0016 \text{ s}^2$
    $(0.0004 \text{ s}^2)(3) = 0.0012 \text{ s}^2$
    $(0.0009 \text{ s}^2)(2) = 0.0018 \text{ s}^2$
    $(0.0016 \text{ s}^2)(1) = 0.0016 \text{ s}^2$

12. Add the values in column 6.
    $\Sigma(x_i - \bar{x})^2 f_i = 0.0016 \text{ s}^2 + 0.0012 \text{ s}^2 + 0.0018 \text{ s}^2 + 0.0016 \text{ s}^2 = 0.0062 \text{ s}^2$

13. Determine the variance using the following formula.
    $$v = \frac{\sum_{i=1}^{4} f_i(x_i - \bar{x})^2}{\Sigma f_i} = \frac{0.0062 \text{ s}^2}{7} = 8.9 \times 10^{-4} \text{ s}^2$$

14. Determine the standard deviation using the following formula.
    $$\sigma = \sqrt{v} = \sqrt{\frac{\sum_{i=1}^{4} f_i(x_i - \bar{x})^2}{\Sigma f_i}}$$
    $$= \sqrt{8.9 \times 10^{-4} \text{ s}^2} = 0.030 \text{ s}$$

x_i (s)	f_i	$x_i f_i$ (s)	$x_i - \bar{x}$ (s)	$(x_i - \bar{x})^2$ (s^2)	$(x_i - \bar{x})^2 f_i$ (s^2)
1.26	1	1.26	−0.04	0.0016	0.0016
1.28	3	3.84	−0.02	0.0004	0.0012
1.33	2	2.66	+0.03	0.0009	0.0018
1.34	1	1.34	+0.04	0.0016	0.0016
	$\Sigma f_i = 7$	$\Sigma x_i f_i = 9.10$ s			$\Sigma(x_i - \bar{x})^2 f_i = 0.0062$ s^2

Percent Error

Measurements made during laboratory work may stand alone or be incorporated into one or more formulas to yield an **experimental value** for a physical quantity. In some instances, scientists have determined the most probable value or **accepted value** for quantities and published them in reference books. The difference between an experimental value and the published accepted value is called the **absolute error.** The **percent error** of a measurement can be calculated by dividing the absolute error by the accepted value and multiplying the quotient by 100.

$$\text{Percent error} = \frac{\text{absolute error}}{\text{accepted value}} \times 100$$

SAMPLE PROBLEM

In an experiment, a student determines that the acceleration due to gravity in the laboratory is 9.98 meters per second². Calculate the percent error. (According to the *Reference Tables for Physical Setting/Physics*, the accepted value for the acceleration due to gravity is 9.81 meters per second².)

SOLUTION: Identify the known and unknown values.

Known
Experimental value of
  $g = 9.98$ m/s²
Accepted value of
  $g = 9.81$ m/s²

Unknown
Percent error = ? %

1. Determine the absolute error by finding the difference between the experimental measurement and the accepted value.

  Absolute error = 9.98 m/s² − 9.81 m/s²
          = 0.17 m/s²

2. Use the following formula to determine percent error.

  $$\text{Percent error} = \frac{\text{absolute error}}{\text{accepted value}} \times 100$$

3. Substitute the known and calculated values and solve.

  $$\text{Percent error} = \frac{0.17 \text{ m/s}^2}{9.81 \text{ m/s}^2} \times 100 = 1.7\%$$

Review Questions

74. In an experiment, a student measures the speed of sound in air to be 318 meters per second at STP. If the accepted value for the speed of sound under those conditions is 331 meters per second, what is the student's percent error?

    (1) 3.9%   (2) 3.93%   (3) 4.09%   (4) 4.1%

75. In an experiment, a student measures the speed of yellow light in water to be 2.00×10^8 meters per second. The accepted value for the speed is 2.25×10^8 meters per second. Calculate the student's percent error.

76. In an experiment a student obtained a value of 9.6 meters per second² for the acceleration due to gravity. The accepted value is 9.81 meters per second². Calculate the student's percent error.

Base your answers to questions 77 through 79 on the table below, which lists winning times to the nearest hundredth of a minute for the women's 400.-meter freestyle race at the Olympics.

Year	Time (min)
1960	4.66
1964	4.73
1968	4.51
1972	4.32
1976	4.17
1980	4.15
1984	4.12
1988	4.07

77. Find the range.

78. Determine the mean to the nearest hundredth of a minute.

79. Determine the standard deviation of these times to the nearest hundredth of a minute.

Base your answers to questions 80 through 82 on the data table below, which shows the frequency of the average daily temperatures during the month of June.

Temperature (°F)	Frequency
63	5
70.	3
78	4
79	3
80.	6
84	4
96	5

80. Find the range.

81. Determine the mean to the nearest tenth of a degree.

82. Determine the standard deviation to the nearest tenth of a degree.

Base your answers to questions 83 through 85 on the data table below, which shows the average snowfall in centimeters recorded one winter at a ski resort over a period of days.

Snowfall (cm)	Frequency
18	6
19	4
20.	4
21	3
24	5
26	3

83. Find the range.

84. Determine the mean to the nearest tenth of a centimeter.

85. Determine the standard deviation to the nearest tenth of a centimeter.

Graphing Data

The data collected in a physics experiment are often represented in graphical form. A graph makes it easier to determine whether there is a trend or pattern in the data.

Making a Graph

By convention, the **independent variable,** the one the experimenter changes, is graphed on the x- or horizontal axis. The **dependent variable,** the one that changes as a result of the changes made by the experimenter, is graphed on the y- or vertical axis. The axes are labeled with the quantities and their units are given in parenthesis. An appropriate, linear scale that accommodates the range of data is determined for each axis. It is not necessary to label every grid line. The graph should be titled as the dependent variable versus the independent variable. After the data points are plotted, a smooth line of best fit is drawn. The **line of best fit** is a straight or curved line which approximates the relationship among a set of data points. This line usually does not pass through all measured points. Sometimes the line of best fit is extrapolated. **Extrapolation** means extending the line beyond the region in which data was taken. This is important because the point where the extended line intersects the horizontal or vertical axis has physical significance.

The **slope,** or inclination of a graphed line, often has a physical meaning. On an x-y coordinate system, the slope of a line is defined as the ratio $\frac{\Delta y}{\Delta x}$ for any two points on the line. See Figure 1-9.

$$\text{slope} = \frac{\Delta y}{\Delta x} = \frac{\text{vertical change}}{\text{horizontal change}}$$

$$\text{slope} = \frac{\text{change in dependent variable}}{\text{change in independent variable}}$$

Figure 1-9. Slope defined

SAMPLE PROBLEM

The position of a moving car was measured at one-second intervals and recorded in the table.

Plot the data on the grid provided and draw the line of best fit. Calculate the slope of the line of best fit.

Time (s)	Position (m)
0.0	0
1.0	18
2.0	40.
3.0	62
4.0	80.
5.0	100.

SOLUTION: Using the information in the table, plot the data and draw the line of best fit.

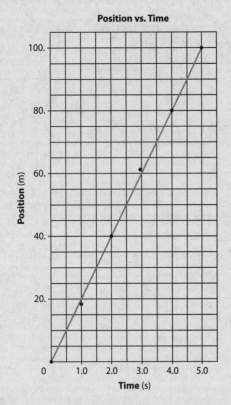

Position vs. Time

Calculate the slope of the line.

$$slope = \frac{change\ in\ position}{change\ in\ time}$$

$$slope = \frac{100.\ m - 40.\ m}{5.0\ s - 2.0\ s}$$

$$slope = 20.\ m/s$$

In determining the slope of a graphed line, points directly from the data table can only be used if those points lie on the line of best fit. (**Note to student:** Although the formula for slope does not appear on the *Reference Tables for Physical Setting/Physics*, calculating slope is testable.)

A horizontal line has a slope of zero. If a line is nearly horizontal, its slope has a small absolute value. If a line slants steeply, its slope has a large absolute value. A line that slopes downward to the right has a negative slope. Figure 1-10 illustrates some slopes of straight and curved lines.

Mathematical Relationships

Some of the common relationships that exist between quantities measured in physics are revealed by the shapes of graphs.

- Two quantities are **directly proportional** if an increase in one causes an increase in the other. The quotient of the quantities is a non-zero constant. The direct proportion $y = 2x$ or $\frac{y}{x} = 2$ is illustrated in Figure 1-11A.
- Two quantities are **inversely proportional** if an increase in one causes a decrease in the other. The product of the quantities is a non-zero constant. The equation $y = \frac{12}{x}$ or $xy = 12$ expresses the inverse proportion shown in Figure 1-11B.
- Two quantities have a **constant proportion** if an increase in one causes no change in the other. The equation $y = 6$, illustrated in Figure 1-11C, is a constant proportion.
- Two quantities have a **direct squared proportion** if an increase in one causes a squared increase in the other. The direct squared proportion $y = x^2$ is shown in Figure 1-11D.
- Two quantities have an **indirect squared proportion** if an increase in one causes a squared decrease in the other. The equation $y = \frac{12}{x^2}$ expresses the indirect squared proportion illustrated in Figure 1-11E.
- Figure 1-11F represents the equation $y = \sqrt{x}$.

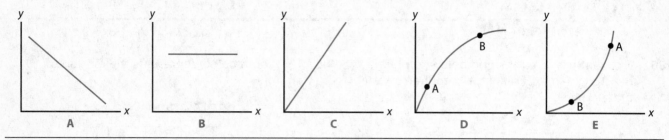

Figure 1-10. Slopes of common curves: The line in graph A has a negative slope. The line in graph B has a slope of zero. The line in graph C has a positive slope. In graphs D and E, the slope at point A is greater than at point B.

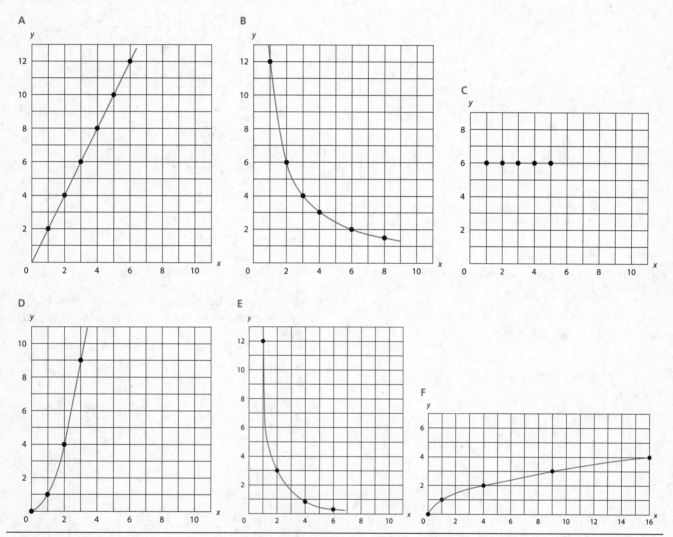

Figure 1-11. Graphs showing shapes of different proportions: (A) The graph of the direct proportion $y = 2x$ (B) The graph of the inverse proportion $y = \dfrac{12}{x}$ (C) The graph of the constant proportion $y = 6$ (D) The graph of the direct squared proportion $y = x^2$ (E) The graph of the indirect squared proportion $y = \dfrac{12}{x^2}$ (F) The graph of $y = \sqrt{x}$.

86. A student prepared the grid below to plot data collected in an experiment. List *four* errors the student made.

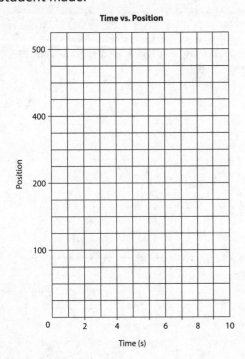

Time vs. Position

87. Which graph shows a properly drawn line of best fit?

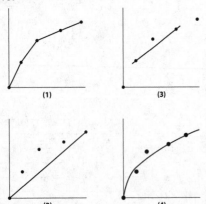

88. A student varied the length of a simple pendulum and measured its period, which is the time required to complete one cycle of motion. In this experiment, time represents the variable that is

(1) dependent and graphed on the horizontal axis

(2) independent and graphed on the horizontal axis

(3) dependent and graphed on the vertical axis

(4) independent and graphed on the vertical axis

89. The graph below represents the motion of an object.

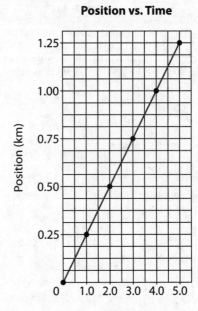

Position vs. Time

The slope of the line is

(1) 0.25 m/s   (3) 0.25 km/s

(2) 1.5 m/s   (4) 1.5 km/s

90. Which graph best represents the relationship between the cross-sectional area of a wire and its radius?

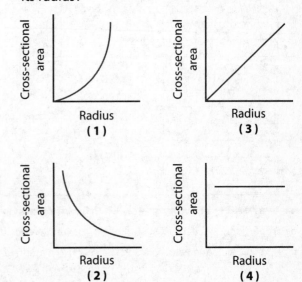

91. The graph that follows represents the relationship between light intensity and distance from a light source.

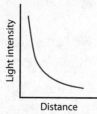

Distance

What kind of proportion exists between light intensity and distance?

(1) constant   (3) direct squared
(2) direct   (4) indirect squared

92. Sketch a graph that represents the relationship between the radius of a circle and its circumference.

93. According to Kepler's laws of planetary motion the ratio of the mean radius of the orbit of a planet cubed to the period of revolution of the planet squared is constant for all planets orbiting the Sun. Sketch a graph representing this relationship.

Scalar and Vector Quantities

Physical quantities can be categorized as either scalar or vector quantities. As physical quantities are introduced in this text, their scalar or vector nature will be indicated.

A **scalar** quantity has magnitude only, with no direction specified. Time and mass are scalar quantities. For example, 30 seconds and 45 kilograms are scalar quantities. The measurement of a scalar quantity is indicated by a number with an appropriate unit. Scalar quantities are added and subtracted according to the rules of arithmetic.

A **vector** quantity has both magnitude and direction. Velocity is a vector quantity because it must be described not only by a number with an appropriate unit, but also by a specified direction. For example, the velocity of a car might be described as 25 meters per second, due north. Vector quantities are added and subtracted using geometric or algebraic methods. These methods will be illustrated later in the text.

Solving Equations Using Algebra

Several axioms or statements are used in solving an equation for an unknown quantity. These axioms, which can be assumed to be true, include the following.

- If equals are added to equals, the sums are equal.
- If equals are subtracted from equals, the remainders are equal.
- If equals are multiplied by equals, the products are equal.
- If equals are divided by equals, the quotients are equal.
- A quantity may be substituted for its equal.
- Like powers or like roots of equals are equal.

You should make use of these axioms to isolate the unknown on the left side of an equation before substituting known values. Always include the units with the values in an equation. Although it is not necessary to align equal signs in the solution of an equation, it may help you keep your work orderly.

Mathematicians have agreed on the following order to be used in performing a series of operations:

1. Simplify the expression within each set of parentheses.
2. Perform exponents.
3. Perform the multiplications and divisions in order from left to right.
4. Do the additions and subtractions from left to right.

"*Please excuse my dear Aunt Sue*" is a useful memory device for this order: *p*arentheses, *e*xponents, *m*ultiplication and *d*ivision in order, and finally *a*ddition and *s*ubtraction in order.

Review Questions

94. Solve the following formulas for *r*.

(a) $F = \dfrac{mv^2}{r}$

(b) $A = \pi r^2$

(c) $C = 2\pi r$

(d) $F = G\dfrac{m_1 m_2}{r^2}$

95. Solve the following formulas for *d*.

(a) $\bar{v} = \dfrac{d}{t}$

(b) $P = \dfrac{Fd}{t}$

(c) $v_f^2 = v_i^2 + 2ad$

96. Solve the following formulas for *v*.

(a) $KE = \dfrac{1}{2}mv^2$

(b) $p = mv$

(c) $n = \dfrac{c}{v}$

97. Solve the following formulas for *I*.

(a) $R = \dfrac{V}{I}$

(b) $W = VIt$

(c) $P = I^2 R$

98. Express 1/299 792 458 second, the time it takes light to travel one meter in a vacuum, in scientific notation.

99. What is the approximate length of a baseball bat?

(1) 10^{-1} m   (3) 10^1 m
(2) 10^0 m   (4) 10^2 m

Base your answers to questions 100 and 101 on the diagram below, which represents a toy car traveling at constant speed *v* up an incline from point *A* to point *B*, a distance of 1.4 meters.

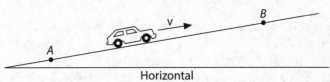

Horizontal

100. Determine the measure of the angle that the incline makes with the horizontal.

101. Calculate the vertical change in the car's position.

Base your answers to questions 102 and 103 on the graph below, which represents the velocity of an object traveling in a straight line as a function of time.

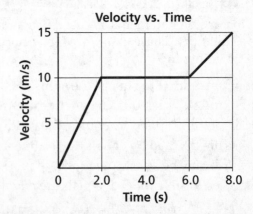

102. Calculate the total area under the curve.

103. Calculate the slope of the line in the time interval 6.0 seconds to 8.0 seconds.

Mechanics

How Scientists Study Mechanics

? *If a moving car is accelerating, is the speed of the car increasing?* **?**

Acceleration and velocity are vector quantities, having both magnitude (size) and direction. The acceleration of a car can be produced by a change in the magnitude of the car's velocity (speed) or by a change in the direction of the car's velocity.

Suppose a car is initially traveling at 12.0 meters/second to the east. If the car accelerates at 2.0 meters/second^2 to the east for 4.0 seconds, the final velocity of the car is 20.0 meters/second to the east. The speed of the car increases 8.0 meters/second in this 4.0-second interval. On the other hand, if a car initially traveling at 12.0 meters/second to the east accelerates at 2.0 meters/second^2 to the west for 4.0 seconds, the final velocity of the car is 4.0 meters/second to the east. The speed of the car decreases 8.0 meters/second in this 4.0-second interval even though the car is accelerating.

If a car travels along a horizontal circular path, the car experiences acceleration directed toward the center of the circular path. This acceleration is called centripetal acceleration. Although the car may be traveling at a constant speed, the car's direction of travel continuously changes and thus the car is accelerating.

Vocabulary

acceleration	gravitational field strength	linear motion	speed
centripetal acceleration	gravitational force	mechanics	static friction
centripetal force	gravity	meter	tangent
closed system	horizontal component	momentum	unbalanced force
coefficient of friction	impulse	net force	uniform circular motion
displacement	inertia	newton	uniform motion
distance	instantaneous velocity	normal force	vacuum
equilibrium	kinetic friction	pendulum	vector component
free fall	kilogram	period (of a pendulum)	velocity
free-body diagram	law of conservation of momentum	resolution of forces	vertical component
friction		resultant	weight
gravitational field		second	

Kinematics

The branch of physics that deals with forces and the way they produce and change motion is called **mechanics.** Kinematics is the mathematical treatment of the motions of bodies without regard to the forces that produce the motion.

Distance and Displacement

When an object moves from one point to another, it experiences a change in position relative to some arbitrary reference point. **Distance** is the total length of a path that an object travels. Distance is a scalar quantity, which means it has magnitude but not direction. **Displacement** is the change in the position of an object described by a vector that begins at the initial position of the object and ends at its final position. Because displacement is a vector quantity, it has both magnitude and direction. Distance and displacement are usually measured in meters, centimeters, or kilometers. The **meter,** m, is the fundamental SI unit of length.

The following example illustrates the difference between distance and displacement. A car is driven on the NYS Thruway from Buffalo to Albany to New York City. The distance traveled by the car is approximately 418 miles or 673 kilometers. The magnitude of the total displacement of the car, however, is only the length of the vector connecting Buffalo and New York City—approximately 313 miles or 504 kilometers. Two or more displacement vectors can be combined to obtain the vector sum, or resultant, as the following sample problem shows.

A student walks 5.0 meters due east and then 12.0 meters due north. Calculate the magnitude and direction of the student's resultant displacement, R.

SOLUTION: Identify the known and unknown values.

Known

$d_1 = 5.0$ m east

$d_2 = 12.0$ m north

Unknown

$R = ?$ m at ?°

1. Make a sketch of the situation.

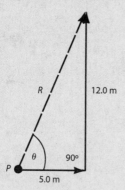

Because east and north are perpendicular to each other, the two displacements form the legs of a right triangle. The resultant displacement is the hypotenuse of the triangle.

2. Write the Pythagorean Theorem.
$$c^2 = a^2 + b^2$$

3. Solve the equation for c.
$$c = \sqrt{a^2 + b^2}$$

4. Substitute R for c, then substitute the known values and solve.
$$R = \sqrt{(5.0\text{ m})^2 + (12.0\text{ m})^2} = 13\text{ m}$$

5. Write a trigonometric function to determine θ.
$$\tan \theta = \frac{\text{side opposite } \angle \theta}{\text{side adjacent to } \angle \theta}$$

6. Substitute the known values and solve.
$$\tan \theta = \frac{12.0\text{ m}}{5.0\text{ m}}$$
$$\theta = 67°$$
The resultant is 13 meters at 67° north of east.

Displacements along the same straight line can be combined by simple addition or subtraction to find the resultant. If the successive displacements in the previous problem had been 5.0 meters east and 12.0 meters east, the resultant would have been 17.0 meters east. Also, if the student had walked 5.0 meters east, and then 12.0 meters west, the resultant would have been 7.0 meters west.

When successive displacements are not along the same straight line, the resultant can be found either graphically, by making a scaled vector diagram using a metric ruler and a protractor, or algebraically using the law of cosines and the law of sines. Because the laws of cosines and sines are not provided in the *Reference Tables for Physical Setting/Physics*, this type of algebraic solution is not testable.

Speed and Velocity

The position of an object in motion changes with time. The **speed,** v, of an object is the distance that the object moves in a unit of time. Speed is a scalar quantity. The average speed, $\bar{v}$, of an object is given by this formula

$$\bar{v} = \frac{d}{t}$$ Ⓡ

Distance d is in meters and the time interval t is in seconds. The **second,** s, is the fundamental SI unit of time. Thus, the average speed $\bar{v}$ is in meters per second, or m/s, a derived SI unit. If the object's speed is constant

SAMPLE PROBLEM

A person walks 5.0 meters due east and 12.0 meters at 60.° north of east. Find the magnitude and direction of the person's resultant displacement.

SOLUTION: Identify the known and unknown values.

Known

d_1 = 5.0 m east

d_2 = 12.0 m at 60.° north of east

Unknown

R = ? m at ?°

1. Construct a scale drawing. A scale of 1.0 cm = 4.0 m is used, but a scale of 1.0 cm = 2.0 m would provide more accurate results.

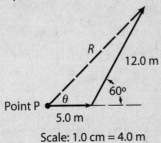

12.0 m

60°

R

θ

Point P

5.0 m

Scale: 1.0 cm = 4.0 m

2. Use a ruler to measure the length of the resultant vector.

   Resultant vector R measures 3.75 cm.

3. Use the scale of the drawing to convert R in centimeters to meters.

   R = (3.75 cm)(4.0 m/cm) = 15 m

4. Use a protractor to measure θ.

   θ = 43°. Thus, the resultant R is 15 m at 43° north of east.

---

during the entire time interval, $\bar{v}$ is its constant speed, and the object is said to be in **uniform motion.** If the speed of the object varies, the motion is nonuniform.

The **velocity** of an object is the time rate of change of its displacement. Velocity is a vector quantity having direction as well as magnitude. The magnitude of an object's velocity is its speed. For example, if one car travels at 88 kilometers per hour due east and a second car travels at 88 kilometers per hour due north, both cars have the same speed. However, the velocities of the cars differ because the direction of travel is not the same. In physics, the terms speed and velocity are not interchangeable.

Linear motion refers to an object's change of position along a straight line. On a straight path, there are only two possible directions for the velocity. One of these is called the positive direction. The opposite direction, then, is the negative direction. Depending upon the direction of the motion, changes in displacement are also positive or negative. When referring to linear motion in this text, the symbol v is used for both velocity and speed, and the symbol d is used for both displacement and distance.

Graphs of Linear Motion Graphs of position versus time are commonly used to represent the linear motion of an object. The independent variable, time, is recorded on the horizontal axis, and the dependent variable, position, is recorded on the vertical axis. Because $\bar{v} = \frac{d}{t}$, the magnitude of the slope of a position versus time graph at any point equals the object's speed at that instant, and the algebraic sign of the slope indicates whether the velocity is in the positive or negative direction. A straight line indicates constant velocity. A straight horizontal line represents zero velocity, that is, an object at rest. If a position-time graph is a curved line, the velocity is not constant. The slope of the tangent to the curve at any point is called the instantaneous velocity of the object. The **tangent** to a curve at any point on the curve is defined as the line passing through the point and having a slope equal to the slope of the curve at that point. **Instantaneous velocity** is the velocity of an object at any particular instant in time. The term is applied to the motion of an object that is not traveling at constant velocity. The steeper the slope of a position versus time graph, the greater the instantaneous speed. Figure 2-1 shows examples of graphs of linear motion.

Acceleration

The time rate of change of velocity is **acceleration,** a, a vector quantity represented by this formula.

$$a = \frac{\Delta v}{t}$$ Ⓡ

The change in velocity Δv is in meters per second and t is the time interval in seconds. Thus, acceleration can be expressed with the unit meters per second per second, or meters per second^2, m/s^2.

Note that the formula, as written without a bar over the a to indicate average, implies constant, or uniform, acceleration. This text does not address nonuniform acceleration.

The average speed $\bar{v}$ of an object accelerating uniformly from an initial speed v_i to a final speed v_f is given by this formula.

$$\bar{v} = \frac{v_i + v_f}{2}$$

This formula is valid only when the acceleration is constant. This formula does not appear on the *Reference Tables for Physical Setting/Physics*, but it is acceptable to use where appropriate.

Velocity versus time graphs can be used to represent accelerated linear motion, as shown in Figure 2-2. The independent variable, time, is measured on the horizontal axis, and the dependent variable, velocity, is recorded on the vertical axis. Because $a = \frac{\Delta v}{t}$, the magnitude of the slope of a velocity versus time graph at any point equals the object's acceleration at that instant, and the algebraic sign of the slope indicates whether the acceleration is in the positive or negative direction. For example, a horizontal line with zero slope indicates constant speed or no acceleration. A straight line with a positive slope shows increasing speed or constant acceleration. A straight line with negative slope shows decreasing speed or constant negative acceleration (deceleration).

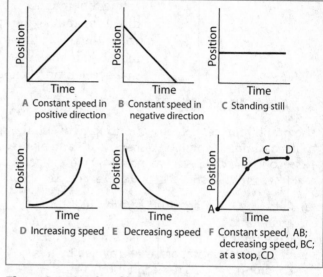

Figure 2-1. Graphs of linear motion, drawn on position-time axes

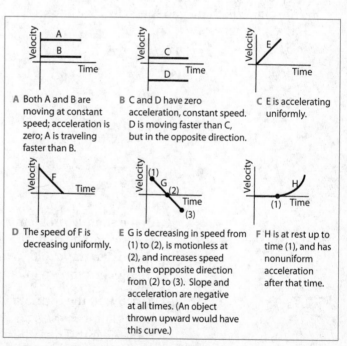

Figure 2-2. Graphs of various types of motion in a straight line path, drawn on velocity-time axes

A line that intersects the horizontal time axis indicates a change in direction, that is, the speed in one direction decreases to zero at the time when the graph line intersects the horizontal axis, and then the speed increases in the opposite direction. A curved velocity-time line indicates that acceleration is not constant.

SAMPLE PROBLEM

The graph represents the relationship between the speed of a child coasting downhill on a skateboard and elapsed time. At 1.0 second the child is traveling at 4.0 meters per second, and at 4.0 seconds her speed is 10.0 meters per second.

(a) Calculate the magnitude of the child's acceleration.
(b) Determine the average speed of the child.
(c) Calculate the total distance traveled by the child during this 3.0-second interval.

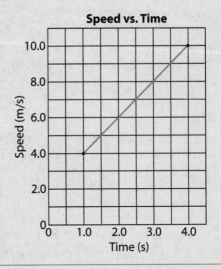

SOLUTION: Identify the known and unknown values.

Known
$t_i = 1.0$ s
$t_f = 4.0$ s
$v_i = 4.0$ m/s
$v_f = 10.0$ m/s

Unknown
$a = ?$ m/s^2
$\bar{v} = ?$ m/s
$d = ?$ m

1. The slope of the graph is the magnitude of the child's acceleration. Determine the slope by dividing the change in speed by the change in time.

$$a = \frac{\Delta v}{t} = \frac{10.0 \text{ m/s} - 4.0 \text{ m/s}}{4.0 \text{ s} - 1.0 \text{ s}} = 2.0 \text{ m/s}^2$$

2. Write the formula for average speed.

$$\bar{v} = \frac{v_i + v_f}{2}$$

Substitute the known values and solve.

$$\bar{v} = \frac{4.0 \text{ m/s} + 10.0 \text{ m/s}}{2} = 7.00 \text{ m/s}$$

The average speed is the vertical coordinate of the midpoint of the graphed line segment.

3. Write the formula that relates distance, average speed, and time.

$$\bar{v} = \frac{d}{t}$$

Solve the equation for d.

$$d = \bar{v}t$$

Substitute the known values and solve.

$$d = (7.00 \text{ m/s})(3.0 \text{ s}) = 21 \text{ m}$$

In the sample problem above, the distance traveled by the child could have been found by determining the area under the graph line. That area has the shape of a trapezoid, which can be separated into a rectangle and a triangle, as shown in Figure 2-3.

Recall that the formula for the area of a rectangle is $A = bh$ and that the formula for the area of a triangle is $A = \frac{1}{2}bh$ where b is the base and h is the height. Thus, the area under the line is the sum of the area of the rectangle and the area of the triangle. For the purpose of this calculation, these quantities may be represented as meters.

That is,

$$A_{\text{rectangle}} = bh = (3.0 \text{ s})(4.0 \text{ m/s}) = 12 \text{ m}$$

$$A_{\text{triangle}} = \frac{1}{2}bh = \frac{1}{2}(3.0\text{s})(6.0 \text{ m/s}) = 9.0 \text{ m}$$

$$A_{\text{total}} = 12 \text{ m} + 9.0 \text{ m} = 21 \text{ m}$$

The total distance is 21 meters, as calculated in the sample problem. Thus, the physical significance of the area under the line of a speed versus time graph is the distance traveled.

Final Velocity and Distance Traveled During Constant Acceleration

Acceleration is defined by the formula $a = \frac{\Delta v}{t}$. Because Δ always represents a change in a variable, that is, final conditions minus initial conditions, it follows that $a = \frac{v_f - v_i}{t}$. Solving for the final speed v_f yields this formula.

$$v_f = v_i + at \qquad \text{®}$$

This expression can be combined with $d = \bar{v}t$ and $\bar{v} = \frac{v_i + v_f}{2}$ to obtain a useful expression for displacement d that involves initial velocity v_i, the acceleration a, and time t.

$$d = \bar{v}t = \left(\frac{v_i + v_f}{2}\right)t = \frac{1}{2}(v_i + v_f)t = \frac{1}{2}(v_i + v_i + at)t$$

Thus, the equation becomes the following.

$$d = v_i t + \frac{1}{2}at^2 \qquad \text{®}$$

This formula is valid only when acceleration is constant.

The velocity of an object as a function of its displacement can be determined without knowing the elapsed time. From the previous derivation, the following equation can be written.

$$d = \frac{1}{2}(v_i + v_f)t$$

Solving the equation $v_f = v_i + at$ for t yields

$$t = \frac{v_f - v_i}{a}$$

Combining these expressions yields

$$d = \frac{1}{2}(v_f + v_i)\left(\frac{v_f - v_i}{a}\right) = \frac{v_f^2 - v_i^2}{2a}$$

Solving for the final velocity yields

$$v_f^2 = v_i^2 + 2ad \qquad \text{®}$$

This formula is valid only for constant acceleration.

In many problems involving motion, the object is initially at rest and v_i is zero. In such cases, terms containing v_i drop out of the motion formulas

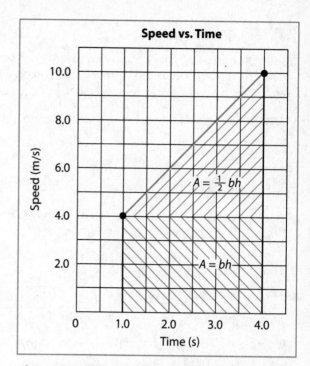

Figure 2-3. The area under a speed vs. time graph: The magnitude of the area of the rectangle is 12 m and the magnitude of the area of the triangle is 9 m. The magnitude of the total area is 21 m, which is the total distance in meters traveled by the child.

A car is originally traveling at 15.0 meters per second (approximately 34 miles per hour) on a straight, horizontal road. The driver applies the brakes, causing the car to decelerate uniformly at 4.00 meters per second^2 until it comes to rest. Calculate the car's stopping distance.

SOLUTION: Identify the known and unknown values.

Known	Unknown
v_i = 15.0 m/s	d = ? m
v_f = 0.0 m/s	
a = −4.00 m/s^2	

The acceleration is negative because its direction is opposite the direction of the moving car.

1. Write the formula that relates initial and final velocities, acceleration, and distance.

$$v_f^2 = v_i^2 + 2ad$$

2. Solve the equation for distance, d.

$$d = \frac{v_f^2 - v_i^2}{2a}$$

3. Substitute the known values and solve.

$$d = \frac{(0.0 \text{ m/s})^2 - (15.0 \text{ m/s})^2}{2(-4.00 \text{ m/s}^2)}$$

$$d = \frac{-225 \text{ m}^2/\text{s}^2}{-8.00 \text{ m/s}^2} = 28.1 \text{ m}$$

ALTERNATE SOLUTION:

1. Write the formula that defines acceleration.

$$a = \frac{\Delta v}{t}$$

2. Solve the equation for t.

$$t = \frac{\Delta v}{a}$$

3. Substitute the known values and solve.

$$t = \frac{0.0 \text{ m/s} - 15.0 \text{ m/s}}{-4.00 \text{ m/s}^2} = 3.75 \text{ s}$$

4. Write the formula that relates distance, initial velocity, acceleration, and time.

$$d = v_it + \frac{1}{2}at^2$$

5. Substitute the known values and solve for d.

$$d = (15.0 \text{ m/s})(3.75 \text{ s}) + \tfrac{1}{2}(-4.00 \text{ m/s}^2)(3.75 \text{ s})^2$$

$$d = 56.3 \text{ m} + (-28.1 \text{ m}) = 28.2 \text{ m}$$

If the initial speed was doubled to 30.0 meters per second (or 67 miles per hour), the stopping distance would quadruple!

and the equations are simplified. In addition, the symbol for v_f can be written as v. Thus, for objects starting from rest and accelerating uniformly,

$$a = \frac{v}{t} \qquad d = \frac{1}{2}at^2 \qquad \bar{v} = \frac{v}{2} \qquad v^2 = 2ad$$

Freely Falling Objects

In a **vacuum,** which is a space in which there is no matter, a coin and a feather fall with the same acceleration due to gravity, g. **Gravity** is the force between the mass of Earth and the mass of any object in the vicinity of Earth. According to the *Reference Tables for Physical Setting/Physics,* near the surface of Earth g is a constant 9.81 meters per second^2. The ideal falling motion of an object acted upon only by the force of gravity is called **free fall.**

Although the acceleration due to gravity is the same for all objects in a vacuum, in air the acceleration of the feather is less than that of the coin because the shape and exposed area of the feather result in greater air resistance.

If an object falls freely from rest (air resistance is neglected), its speed and position at any instant in time are given by $v = gt$ and $d = \frac{1}{2}gt^2$. Table 2-1 shows the speed and distance traveled by an object falling freely from rest near Earth's surface in the absence of air resistance.

Table 2-1. Free Fall of an Object Starting from Rest

Time of fall (s)	Speed (m/s)	Distance traveled (m)
0.00	0.00	0.00
1.00	9.81	4.91
2.00	19.6	19.6
3.00	29.4	44.1
4.00	39.2	78.5
5.00	49.1	123

1. If a boy runs 125 meters north, and then 75 meters south, his total displacement is

(1) 50. m north   (3) 200. m north
(2) 50. m south   (4) 200. m south

2. A student walks 3 blocks south, 4 blocks west, and 3 blocks north. What is the resultant displacement of the student?

(1) 10. blocks east   (3) 4 blocks east
(2) 10. blocks west   (4) 4 blocks west

3. A girl attempts to swim directly across a stream 15 meters wide. When she reaches the other side, she is 15 meters downstream. Calculate the magnitude of her displacement.

4. What is the average speed of an object that travels 6.00 meters north in 2.00 seconds and then travels 3.00 meters east in 1.00 second?

(1) 9.00 m/s   (3) 3.00 m/s
(2) 0.333 m/s   (4) 4.24 m/s

5. In a 4.0-kilometer race, a runner completes the first kilometer in 5.9 minutes, the second kilometer in 6.2 minutes, the third kilometer in 6.3 minutes, and the final kilometer in 6.0 minutes. The average speed of the runner for the race is approximately

(1) 0.16 km/min   (3) 12 km/min
(2) 0.33 km/min   (4) 24 km/min

6. The graph below shows the relationship between the position of an object moving in a straight line and elapsed time.

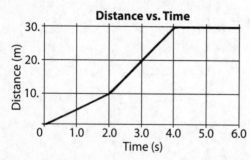

Distance vs. Time

What is the speed of the object during the time interval $t = 2.0$ seconds to $t = 4.0$ seconds?

(1) 0.0 m/s   (2) 5.0 m/s   (3) 7.5 m/s   (4) 10. m/s

7. A particle is accelerated uniformly from rest to a speed of 50. meters per second in 5.0 seconds. The average speed of the particle during this 5.0-second time interval is

(1) 5.0 m/s   (2) 10. m/s   (3) 25 m/s   (4) 50. m/s

8. Which statement best describes the movement of an object with zero acceleration?

(1) The object must be at rest.
(2) The object must be slowing down.
(3) The object may be speeding up.
(4) The object may be in motion.

9. A particle has a constant acceleration of 2.0 meters per second^2. Calculate the time required for the particle to accelerate from 8.0 meters per second to 28 meters per second.

10. If an object is traveling east with a decreasing speed, the direction of the object's acceleration is

(1) north   (2) south   (3) east   (4) west

Base your answers to questions 11 and 12 on the following graph, which represents the relationship between velocity and time of travel for four cars, A, B, C, and D, in straight-line motion.

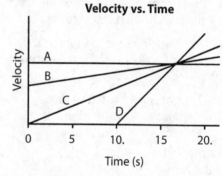

Velocity vs. Time

11. Which car has the greatest acceleration during the time interval 10. seconds to 15 seconds?

12. Which car travels the greatest distance during the time interval 0 second to 10. seconds?

(1) A only
(2) B only
(3) C only
(4) The distance traveled is the same for cars A, B, and C.

13. Starting from rest, an object rolls freely down a 10.-meter long incline in 2.0 seconds. The acceleration of the object is

(1) 5.0 m/s   (3) 10. m/s
(2) 5.0 m/s^2 (4) 10. m/s^2

14. A car accelerates uniformly from rest at 3.2 meters per second^2. Calculate the speed of the car when it has traveled a distance of 40. meters.

Base your answers to questions 15 through 19 on the graph below, which represents the relationship between speed and time for an object in straight-line motion.

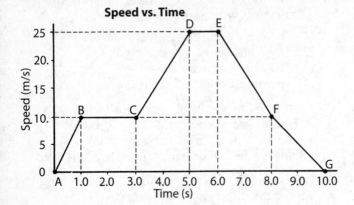

Speed vs. Time

15. Calculate the acceleration of the object during the time interval $t = 3.0$ seconds to $t = 5.0$ seconds.

16. Determine the average speed of the object during the time interval $t = 6.0$ seconds to $t = 8.0$ seconds.

17. Calculate the total distance traveled by the object during the first 3.0 seconds.

18. Identify the interval during which the magnitude of the object's acceleration is greatest.

19. During the interval $t = 8.0$ seconds to $t = 10.0$ seconds, the speed of the object is
    (1) zero
    (2) increasing
    (3) decreasing
    (4) constant, but not zero

_____

20. The graph below represents the relationship between distance and time of travel for an object moving in a straight line.

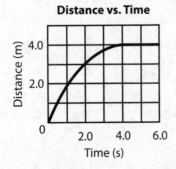

Distance vs. Time

Determine the instantaneous speed of the object at 1.5 seconds.

21. A boat heads directly eastward across a river at 12 meters per second. If the current in the river is flowing at 5.0 meters per second due south, what is the magnitude of the boat's resultant velocity?
    (1) 7.0 m/s (2) 8.5 m/s (3) 13 m/s (4) 17 m/s

22. Which pair of graphs represents the same motion?

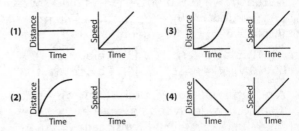

23. The graph below represents the motion of a body moving along a straight line.

Which quantity related to the motion of the body is constant?
    (1) speed   (3) acceleration
    (2) velocity   (4) displacement

Base your answers to questions 24 through 28 on the following four graphs, which represent the relationship between speed and time for four different objects, A, B, C, and D moving, in a straight line.

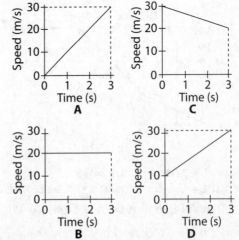

24. Which object had a retarding force acting on it?

25. Which object was *not* accelerating?

26. Which object traveled the greatest distance in the 3.0-second time interval?

27. Which object had the greatest acceleration?

28. Compared to the average speed of object A, the average speed of object D is

(1) less   (3) the same
(2) greater

---

29. An object initially traveling at 20. meters per second west accelerates uniformly at 4.0 meters per second² east for 2.0 seconds. The displacement of the object during these 2.0 seconds is

(1) 32 m east   (3) 48 m east
(2) 32 m west   (4) 48 m west

30. An object initially traveling at 20. meters per second south accelerates uniformly at 6.0 meters per second² north and is displaced 25 meters. The final velocity of the object is

(1) 26 m/s north   (3) 10. m/s north
(2) 26 m/s south   (4) 10. m/s south

31. The time-rate of change of displacement is

(1) acceleration   (3) speed
(2) distance   (4) velocity

Base your answers to questions 32 through 35 on the following graph, which represents the relationship between the displacement of an object and time.

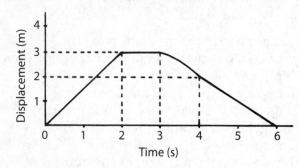

Displacement vs. Time

32. How far is the object from the starting point at the end of 3 seconds?

33. During which time interval is the object at rest?

34. What is the average velocity of the object from $t = 0$ to $t = 3$ seconds?

(1) 1 m/s   (2) 2 m/s   (3) 3 m/s   (4) 0 m/s

35. During which time interval is the object accelerating?

---

36. Which quantity is constant for a freely falling object near Earth's surface?

(1) displacement   (3) velocity
(2) speed   (4) acceleration

37. Which graph best represents the motion of an object falling from rest near Earth's surface? [Neglect friction.]

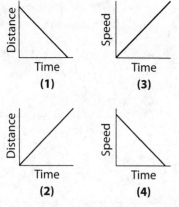

38. What is the total distance that an object near the surface of Earth falling freely from rest travels in 3.0 seconds?

(1) 88 m   (2) 44 m   (3) 29 m   (4) 9.8 m

39. An object starts from rest and falls freely near Earth's surface for 3.00 seconds. Calculate the final speed of the object.

40. An object is thrown vertically upward from the surface of Earth. Which graph best represents the relationship between velocity and time for the object as it rises and then returns to Earth?

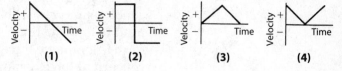

Statics

The branch of mechanics that treats forces which act on objects at rest is called <u>statics</u>. A force is a push or pull measured in newtons, N, a derived unit in the SI system. Force is a vector quantity.

Concurrent Forces

Two or more forces that act on the same object at the same time are called concurrent forces. The single force that is equivalent to the combined effect

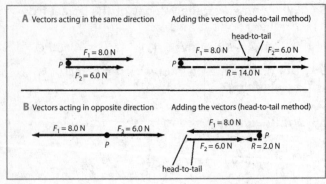

A Vectors acting in the same direction   Adding the vectors (head-to-tail method)

$F_1 = 8.0$ N
P
$F_2 = 6.0$ N

head-to-tail
$F_1 = 8.0$ N $F_2 = 6.0$ N
P
$R = 14.0$ N

B Vectors acting in opposite direction   Adding the vectors (head-to-tail method)

$F_1 = 8.0$ N $F_2 = 6.0$ N
P

$F_1 = 8.0$ N
P
$F_2 = 6.0$ N $R = 2.0$ N
head-to-tail

Figure 2-4. The resultants R of concurrent forces acting along the same straight line: (A) acting in the same direction, and (B) acting in opposite directions

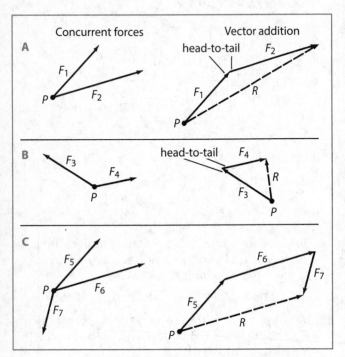

Concurrent forces   Vector addition

A
F_1
P
F_2

head-to-tail F_2
F_1 R
P

B
F_3
F_4
P

head-to-tail F_4
R
F_3
P

C
F_5
P
F_6
F_7

F_6
F_7
F_5
R
P

Figure 2-5. Adding force vectors by the triangle method

of these concurrent forces is called the **resultant.** The process of combining the magnitude and direction of concurrent forces to determine their resultant is called the composition of forces. If two concurrent forces F_1 and F_2 act in the same direction, the angle between the forces is 0° and the resultant force is the sum, $F_1 + F_2$, of their magnitudes acting in the same direction as the individual forces. This is the largest resultant the two forces can have. If the two forces act in opposite directions, the angle between the forces is 180.° and the resultant force is the difference, $F_1 - F_2$, between their magnitudes, acting in the direction of the larger force. This is the smallest resultant the two forces can have. Figure 2-4 illustrates these concepts for an 8.0-newton force and a 6.0-newton force acting concurrently on point P.

Triangle Method of Adding Concurrent Forces The resultant of two concurrent forces F_1 and F_2 acting at an angle between 0° and 180.° can be found by the triangle method of vector addition. In this method, each force is represented by a vector drawn to scale, with its length corresponding to the magnitude of the force and its direction corresponding to the direction of the force. To add the two vectors, place the tail of the second vector F_2 at the head of the first vector F_1. The resultant is the vector drawn from the tail of F_1 to the head of F_2, as shown in Figure 2-5.

The magnitude of the resultant is found by measuring the vector length with a ruler and then multiplying by the scale. The direction of the vector is determined by using a protractor to measure the angle of the resultant with respect to a compass point. In Figure 2-5A, the resultant has a greater magnitude than either force. In Figure 2-5B, the magnitude of the resultant is smaller than either force. Figure 2-5C correctly implies that the resultant of any number of concurrent forces acting on an object can be found by adding their vectors head to tail. The final resultant is the net force acting on the object. The net force is the single force that is equivalent to the combined effect of concurrent forces acting on an object.

If two concurrent forces act at right angles to each other, the head to tail method of vector addition produces a right triangle in which the hypotenuse is the resultant. In this case, the resultant vector is often found algebraically using the Pythagorean theorem, $c^2 = a^2 + b^2$. Figure 2-6 illustrates this method for an 8.0-newton force to the east and a 6.0-newton force to the north acting concurrently on point P.

Parallelogram Method of Adding Concurrent Forces An alternate graphical method for determining the vector sum of two concurrent forces acting

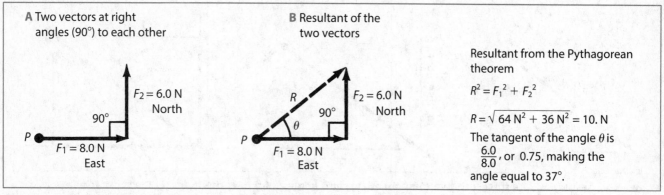

A Two vectors at right angles (90°) to each other

$F_2 = 6.0\ N$ North

90°

P

$F_1 = 8.0\ N$ East

B Resultant of the two vectors

R

90°

θ

$F_2 = 6.0\ N$ North

P

$F_1 = 8.0\ N$ East

Resultant from the Pythagorean theorem

$$R^2 = F_1^2 + F_2^2$$

$$R = \sqrt{64\ N^2 + 36\ N^2} = 10.\ N$$

The tangent of the angle θ is $\frac{6.0}{8.0}$, or 0.75, making the angle equal to 37°.

Figure 2-6. **Finding the resultant of two concurrent forces acting at right angles (90°) to each other**

at any angle is the parallelogram method shown in Figure 2-7. The two vectors are drawn to scale with both tails originating at the same point. A parallelogram is then constructed with the force vectors as adjacent sides. Recall that a parallelogram is a quadrilateral having opposite sides parallel and equal in length. The diagonal of the parallelogram drawn from the vertex of the original two vector tails is the resultant.

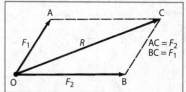

Figure 2-7. Finding the resultant of two concurrent forces at any angle to each other using the parallelogram method

The parallelogram method makes it obvious that as the angle between two vectors increases from 0° to 180.° the magnitude of the resultant decreases from a maximum, $F_1 + F_2$ at 0°, to a minimum, $F_1 - F_2$ at 180°.

Resolution of Forces

Just as force vectors can be added to provide the magnitude and direction of the resultant force, force vectors can be resolved or broken up into component vectors. The process of determining the magnitude and direction of the components of a force is called **resolution of forces.** Although a force vector could be resolved into any number of components, it is usually resolved into two components that are perpendicular to each other. The **vector components** of a force vector F are the concurrent forces whose vector sum is F. If the force is resolved into two components at right angles to each other, vector F is a diagonal of the rectangle formed in the parallelogram method. Perpendicular component forces are usually given directions such as east-west and north-south, perpendicular and parallel to the ground, or perpendicular and parallel to an incline.

Graphical Method of Resolving a Force into Components Figure 2-8 shows a 50.-newton force at 37° north of east being resolved into two perpendicular component forces by the graphical method. Force F_1 is along the north-south axis and force F_2 is along the east-west axis. The magnitude of each force is found by drawing a perpendicular to each axis from the head end of the given vector. The line drawn from the origin, O, to each intersection with the axes determines the magnitude of each component vector. The components are measured to be $F_1 = 30.\ N$ north and $F_2 = 40.\ N$ east. Note that the vector sum of the components is equal to the original force F.

Algebraic Method of Resolving a Force into Components It is also possible to determine algebraically the perpendicular components of a force or any other vector. Figure 2-9 shows how vector A, which is at an angle θ with the horizontal, can be resolved into components at right angles to each other. Recall that in a right triangle, the sine of one of the acute angles is the ratio of the side opposite the angle to the hypotenuse and that the

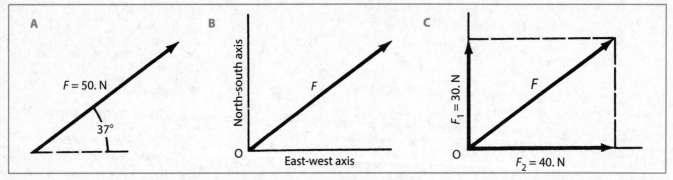

Figure 2-8. Resolution of a force into two components at right angles (90°) to each other: (A) The vector to be resolved is a force vector F of 50. N directed at 37° north of east. (B) Horizontal (east-west) and vertical (north-south) axes are constructed at the tail of the vector. (C) Dashed lines that start at the head of vector F and extend perpendicularly to the axes define two new vectors F_1 and F_2 that are the vertical and horizontal components of the original force vector F. To the scale of the drawing, F_1 measures 30. N north and F_2 measures 40. N east.

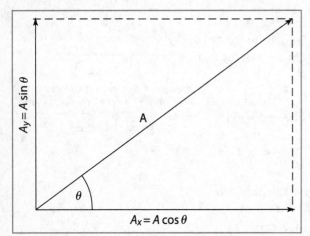

Figure 2-9. A force vector A resolved into horizontal and vertical components

cosine of the angle is the ratio of the adjacent side of the angle to the hypotenuse. Thus, for any vector A, making angle θ with the horizontal, the following apply.

$$A_x = A \cos \theta$$
$$A_y = A \sin \theta$$

Ⓡ

Thus, the components of a vector can be readily determined without making a scale drawing.

Component forces have practical applications, such as pushing a lawnmower or pulling a suitcase by an extended handle at constant speed along the ground. In pulling a suitcase, the magnitude of the force that needs to be exerted depends upon the angle of the extended handle with the ground. The suitcase is moved only by the component of the applied force parallel to the ground. This component is a smaller fraction of the applied force when the angle the extended handle makes with the ground is larger. Thus, a greater force must be applied as the angle between the extended handle and the ground becomes larger.

Equilibrium

The vector sum of the concurrent forces acting on an object is called the **net force,** F_{net}. If the net force acting on an object is zero, the object is in **equilibrium.** An object at rest is said to be in <u>static equilibrium</u>.

In the example illustrated in Figure 2-6, the resultant of an 8.0-newton force to the east and a 6.0-newton force to the north is a 10.-newton force at 37° north of east. If a third force of 10. newtons acting at 37° south of west was applied, the net force would be zero. A force that is equal in magnitude and opposite in direction to the resultant of concurrent forces produces equilibrium.

Figure 2-10A shows a sign hanging from the side of a building. Because the sign is at rest, it is in static equilibrium and the net force on the sign is zero. But three forces are acting on the sign. They are its weight F_g acting perpendicular to the ground, the force exerted by the cable F_1 pulling in the direction of the cable toward the building, and the outward push F_2 of the horizontal rod.

Figure 2-10B is a free-body diagram for the sign. A **free-body diagram** is a sketch, or scale drawing, that shows all the forces acting concurrently on an object. In this example, the weight of the sign must be equal in magnitude and opposite in direction to the vector sum or resultant of the forces exerted by the rod and the cable. This diagram, drawn to scale, indicates that the weight of the sign is smaller than the magnitude of either of the forces used to support it from the building.

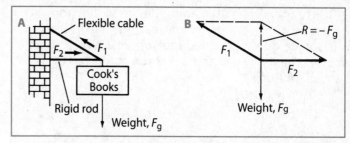

Figure 2-10. (A) **The sign is supported by a flexible cable and a rigid rod.** (B) **A free-body diagram showing the relationships among the forces on the sign while it is in static equilibrium**

Review Questions

41. The vector diagram below shows two concurrent forces, *A* and *B*.

Which vector diagram best represents the resultant force?

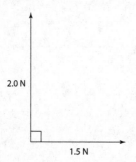

(1)   **(3)**

(2)   **(4)**

42. The vector diagram below represents two concurrent forces.

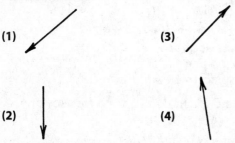

2.0 N

1.5 N

What is the magnitude of the resultant force?

(1) 2.5 N   (2) 3.5 N   (3) 3.0 N   (4) 4.0 N

43. The magnitude of the resultant of two concurrent forces is a minimum when the angle between them is

(1) 0°   (2) 45°   (3) 90.°   (4) 180.°

44. The vector diagram below represents two forces acting concurrently on an object at point *P*.

Which vector diagram best represents the resultant force?

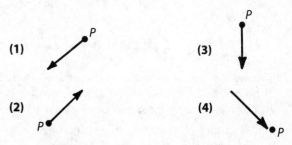

(1)   **(3)**

(2)   **(4)**

45. As the angle between two concurrent forces of 5.0 newtons and 7.0 newtons increases from 0° to 180.°, the magnitude of their resultant changes from

(1) 0.0 N to 35 N   (3) 12.0 N to 2.0 N
(2) 2.0 N to 12.0 N   (4) 12.0 N to 0.0 N

46. A resultant force with a magnitude of 20. newtons can be produced by two concurrent forces having magnitudes of

(1) 5.0 N and 10. N   (3) 20. N and 50. N
(2) 20. N and 20. N   (4) 30. N and 5.0 N

47. The diagram below represents two force vectors, *A* and *B*.

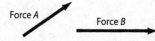

Force A   Force B

Which vector best represents the force that could act concurrently with force *A* to produce force *B*?

(1)   **(2)**   **(3)**   **(4)**

48. Three forces with magnitudes of 10. newtons, 8 newtons, and 6 newtons acting concurrently on an object produce equilibrium. The resultant of the 6-newton and 8-newton forces has a magnitude of

(1) 0.0 N
(2) between 0.0 N and 10. N
(3) 10. N
(4) more than 10. N

49. What is the total number of components into which a single force can be resolved?

(1) an unlimited number
(2) two components
(3) three components
(4) four components at right angles to each other

50. A lawnmower is pushed with a constant force *F*, as shown in the following diagram.

As angle *θ* between the lawnmower handle and the horizontal increases, what happens to the horizontal and vertical components of *F*?

(1) The horizontal component decreases and the vertical component decreases.
(2) The horizontal component decreases and the vertical component increases.
(3) The horizontal component increases and the vertical component decreases.
(4) The horizontal component increases and the vertical component increases.

51. The following diagram shows a person exerting a 300.-newton force on the handle of a shovel that makes an angle of 60.° with the horizontal ground.

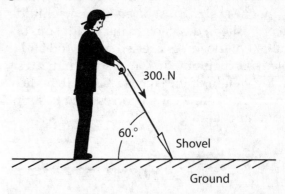

Calculate the magnitude of the component of the force perpendicular to the ground.

52. A vector makes an angle *θ* with the horizontal. The horizontal and vertical components of the vector will be equal in magnitude if angle *θ* is

(1) 30.°   (2) 45°   (3) 60.°   (4) 90.°

53. Which terms represent a vector quantity and the scalar quantity of the vector's magnitude, respectively?

(1) acceleration and velocity
(2) mass and force
(3) speed and time
(4) displacement and distance

54. The fundamental units for a force of one newton are

(1) meters / second^2
(2) kilograms
(3) meters / second^2 / kilogram
(4) kilogram • meters / second^2

Dynamics

The branch of mechanics that deals with how the forces acting on an object affect its motion is called <u>dynamics</u>. The physical laws that govern dynamics were formulated by Isaac Newton.

Newton's Three Laws of Motion

Recall that when the net force acting on an object is zero, it is said to be in equilibrium. An object in static equilibrium is at rest. An object in dynamic equilibrium moves with a constant velocity, that is, at constant speed in a straight line.

Newton's First Law According to Newton's first law, an object maintains a state of equilibrium, remaining at rest or moving with constant velocity, unless acted upon by an unbalanced force. An **unbalanced force** is a nonzero net force acting on an object. According to the first law, an unbalanced force always produces a change in an object's velocity, a vector quantity. This change in velocity produces an acceleration because the object's speed, or direction of motion, or both speed and direction are changing. The inertia of an object is independent of its speed or velocity.

The law of inertia is another name for the first law. **Inertia** is the resistance of an object to a change in its motion. The inertia of an object is directly proportional to its mass. The fundamental SI unit of mass is the **kilogram,** kg. Mass is a scalar quantity.

Inertia can have a devastating effect on a person not wearing a seat belt in a car traveling at high speed. If the car runs off the road and collides with a tree, the force of the collision causes the car to rapidly decelerate. However, the force does not act on the passengers in the car. They continue to move with the same velocity as before the collision, until they are decelerated by colliding with the dashboard or front window. When seat belts are used, the passengers are fastened to the car and decelerate upon impact at the same rate as the car.

Newton's Second Law According to Newton's second law, when an unbalanced force acts on an object, the object is accelerated in the same direction as the force. The acceleration is directly proportional to the magnitude of the unbalanced force and inversely proportional to the mass of the object, as shown in this formula.

$$a = \frac{F_{net}}{m}$$ ®

Mass m is in kilograms, acceleration a is in meters per second^2, and the net force F_{net} is in newtons. One **newton** is equal to the force that imparts an acceleration of one meter per second^2 to a one-kilogram mass. The newton, N, is the derived SI unit of force. One newton equals one kilogram • meter per second^2, kg • m/s^2.

Simple laboratory experiments can be performed to verify Newton's second law. In one experiment, the net force on a cart originally at rest on a horizontal surface is varied and the resulting acceleration calculated by timing the motion of the cart for some distance. The data is plotted with force as the independent variable on the horizontal axis and acceleration as the dependent variable on the vertical axis. Figure 2-11 shows such a graph.

The slope of the line of best fit is $\frac{\Delta a}{\Delta F}$ and is equal to $\frac{1}{m}$. Therefore, the reciprocal of the slope of the line of best fit is the mass of the object being accelerated. Sometimes the axes are reversed so that the mass of the object can be determined directly from the slope.

Newton's Third Law According to Newton's third law, when one object exerts a force on a second object, the second object exerts a force on the first that is equal in magnitude and

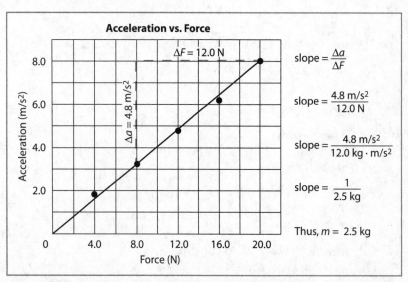

Figure 2-11. The slope of the line on an acceleration-force graph gives the reciprocal of the mass of the object being accelerated. Note in the calculation that the newton, N, is equivalent to a kilogram · meter per second^2.

opposite in direction. The two equal and opposing forces constitute an action/reaction pair. The third law indicates that for every action force there is an equal and opposite reaction force. This means that a single force cannot be generated in nature. When one force is generated, another force of equal magnitude and opposite direction must also be generated.

SAMPLE PROBLEM

A 10.-newton force gives a mass m_1 an acceleration a. A 20.-newton force gives another mass m_2 the same acceleration a. What is the ratio of m_1 to m_2?

SOLUTION: Identify the known and unknown values.

Known

$F_1 = 10.\ N$

$F_2 = 20.\ N$

Unknown

$\dfrac{m_1}{m_2} = ?$

1. Write the formula that defines acceleration.

$$a = \frac{F_{net}}{m}$$

2. Solve the equation for m.

$$m = \frac{F_{net}}{a}$$

3. Substitute the known values for each mass.

$$m_1 = \frac{10.\ N}{a} \text{ and } m_2 = \frac{20.\ N}{a}$$

4. Divide the first equation by the second.

$$\frac{m_1}{m_2} = \frac{10.\ N/a}{20.\ N/a} = \frac{1}{2}$$

SAMPLE PROBLEM

The diagram at the right shows two forces F_1 and F_2 applied to a 2.0-kilogram box originally at rest on a horizontal frictionless surface. Calculate the magnitude and direction of the acceleration of the box.

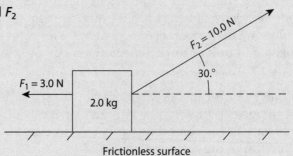

$F_2 = 10.0\ N$

30.°

$F_1 = 3.0\ N$

2.0 kg

Frictionless surface

SOLUTION: Identify the known and unknown values.

Known
$m = 2.0\ kg$

Unknown
$a = ?\ m/s^2$ to the?

From the diagram:

$F_1 = 3.0\ N$ to the left
$F_2 = 10.0\ N$ to the right at 30.° above the horizontal

1. Write the formula for the horizontal component of a vector.

$A_x = A \cos \theta$

2. Substitute F_{2_x} for A_x, then substitute the known values and solve.

$F_{2_x} = F_2 \cos \theta = (10.0\ N)(\cos 30.°) = 8.7\ N$

3. Determine the net force in the horizontal direction acting on the box.

$F_{net_x} = F_{1_x} + F_{2_x} = -3.0\ N + 8.7\ N = 5.7\ N$

4. Write the formula that defines Newton's second law.

$$a = \frac{F_{net}}{m}$$

5. Substitute the known values and solve.

$$a = \frac{5.7\ N}{2.0\ kg} = 2.9\ m/s^2 \text{ to the right}$$

A baseball bat striking a ball is an example of an action-reaction pair. If the bat exerts a 50.-newton force on the baseball, the ball exerts a 50.-newton force on the bat in the opposite direction. Each member of the action/reaction pair of forces acts on a different object; one force acts on the ball and the other on the bat. If no other forces are present, the objects are accelerated in opposite directions as long as the forces are applied.

Review Questions

55. As the mass of an object on Earth's surface decreases, what happens to the inertia and weight of the object?

(1) Inertia decreases, and weight decreases.
(2) Inertia decreases, and weight remains the same.
(3) Inertia increases, and weight decreases.
(4) Inertia remains the same, and weight remains the same.

56. Compared to the inertia of a 0.10-kilogram steel ball, the inertia of a 0.20-kilogram Styrofoam ball is

(1) one-half as great   (3) the same
(2) twice as great   (4) four times as great

57. A ball rolls through a hollow semicircular tube lying flat on a horizontal tabletop. On the following diagram, draw a line with an arrowhead to represent the path of the ball after emerging from the tube, as viewed from above.

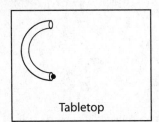

Tabletop

58. The following graph shows the relationship between the acceleration of an object and the net force on the object.

Acceleration vs. Force

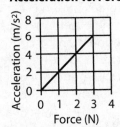

What is the mass of the object?

(1) 1 kg   (2) 2 kg   (3) 0.5 kg   (4) 0.2 kg

59. A cart is uniformly accelerating from rest. The net force acting on the cart is

(1) decreasing   (3) constant but not zero
(2) zero   (4) increasing

60. An 8.0-kilogram block and a 2.0-kilogram block rest on a horizontal frictionless surface. When horizontal force F is applied to the 8.0-kilogram block, it accelerates at 5.0 meters per second^2 east. If the same force was applied to the 2.0-kilogram block, the magnitude of the block's acceleration would be

(1) 1.3 m/s^2 (3) 10. m/s^2
(2) 2.5 m/s^2 (4) 20. m/s^2

61. A 6-newton force and an 8-newton force act concurrently on a box located on a frictionless horizontal surface. Which top-view diagram shows the forces producing the smallest magnitude of acceleration of the box?

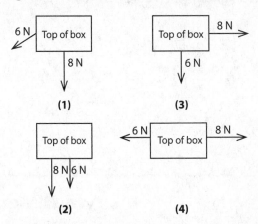

62. As the vector sum of all the forces acting on a moving object increases, the magnitude of the acceleration of the object

(1) decreases   (3) remains the same
(2) increases

63. An unbalanced force of 10.0 newtons north acts on a 20.0-kilogram mass for 5.0 seconds. Calculate the acceleration of the mass.

64 Two horizontal forces are applied to a 2.0-kilogram block on a frictionless, horizontal surface, as shown in the following diagram.

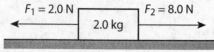

$F_1 = 2.0\,N$ 2.0 kg $F_2 = 8.0\,N$

Frictionless horizontal surface

The acceleration of the block is

(1) 5.0 m/s² to the right
(2) 5.0 m/s² to the left
(3) 3.0 m/s² to the right
(4) 3.0 m/s² to the left

65. Which graph best represents the motion of an object on which the net force is zero?

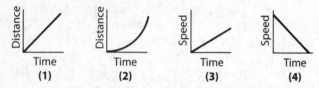

Distance	Distance	Speed	Speed
Time	Time	Time	Time
(1)	(2)	(3)	(4)

66. The vector diagram below represents force *F* acting on point *P*.

P   Force

Which vector diagram represents the pair of concurrent forces that would produce equilibrium when added to force *F*?

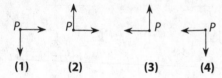

(1)   (2)   (3)   (4)

67. Which graph best represents the motion of an object that has no unbalanced force acting on it?

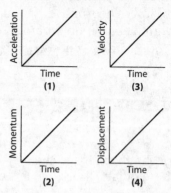

(1)   (3)
(2)   (4)

68. Four forces act on an object, as shown in the following diagram.

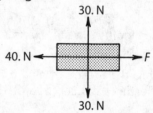

30. N
40. N   F
30. N

If the object is moving with a constant velocity, what is the magnitude of force *F*?

69. A 1.0-kilogram book rests on a horizontal tabletop. The magnitude of the force of the tabletop on the book is

(1) 1.0 kg   (2) 9.8 kg   (3) 1.0 N   (4) 9.8 N

70. In the following diagram, an inflated balloon released from rest moves horizontally with velocity *v*.

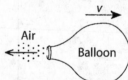

v
Air
Balloon

What is the most likely cause of this velocity?

Two-Dimensional Motion and Trajectories

The motion of an object traveling in a two-dimensional plane can be described by separating its motion into the horizontal (x) and vertical (y) components of its displacement, velocity, and acceleration. A component parallel to the horizon is a **horizontal component** and a component at right angles to the horizon is a **vertical component**. If air resistance is neglected, an example of two-dimensional motion is the motion of a cannonball projected near the surface of Earth at an angle above the horizontal. If gravity is the only unbalanced force acting on the cannonball, the vertical component of the ball's motion is identical to that of a freely falling body, and the horizontal component is uniform motion. Although the two motions occur simultaneously, the two components of the motion are independent. Thus, if the object's initial velocity is known, the motion of the object in Earth's gravitational field can be described by the superposition of the two motions.

A Projectile Fired Horizontally

An object projected horizontally from some height above Earth's surface obeys Newton's laws of motion. If air resistance is neglected, the horizontal component of the velocity of the object remains constant. The initial vertical velocity of the object is zero but the vertical velocity increases as the object accelerates downward due to gravity. Figure 2-12A shows a ball falling freely straight downward from rest. Figure 2-12B shows a ball that has a horizontal component of velocity as it falls downward.

Whether an object is dropped from rest or projected horizontally, the vertical distance fallen by the object is the same at any particular instant of time, as can be seen by comparing the vertical position of the ball at 1.00-second intervals in Figure 2-12A and B. This example illustrates that a ball thrown horizontally at 10.0 meters per second from a height of 44.1 meters above level ground, will hit the ground at the same time as another ball dropped from the same height at the same time.

In addition to showing the positions of the ball after an elapsed time of 1.00, 2.00, and 3.00 seconds, Figure 2-12B shows (by means of velocity vectors) the vertical and horizontal components of the velocity. At any particular time after the ball is released, the vertical component of velocity of an object projected horizontally is the same as the vertical component of velocity of an object dropped from rest. However, the vertical component of the ball's velocity increases, as the ball is accelerated by gravity. Thus, the vertical distance the ball falls in the third second is greater than the vertical distance the ball falls in the second second.

When air resistance is neglected, there is no acceleration or change in velocity in the horizontal direction. In Figure 2-12B, the horizontal displacement of the ball is a constant 10.0 meters in each 1.00-second interval. If the horizontal velocity of the ball had been greater, the object would have traveled a greater horizontal distance in the first 3.00 seconds of travel.

A Projectile Fired at an Angle

A golf ball is an example of an object that is projected with an initial velocity at an angle above the horizontal. Such a projectile rises to some height above Earth and then falls back to the ground. The projectile's motion can be studied by resolving the initial velocity into its horizontal and vertical components and then calculating the motions resulting from the two components. If air resistance is ignored, the horizontal component

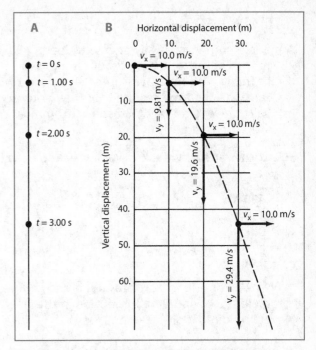

Figure 2-12. **(A)** The position of a ball at 1.00-second intervals as it falls from rest in a vacuum near Earth's surface. The vertical scale in drawing B also applies to drawing A. **(B)** The position of the same ball at 1.00-second intervals after it has been rolled off the edge of a building with an initial horizontal velocity of 10.0 m/s. The arrows are velocity vectors giving the horizontal and vertical components of the velocity when the ball is at each position. Note that the horizontal component of the ball's velocity is the same after each second but the vertical component increases with time as the ball is accelerated by gravity. Note also that in both A and B, the vertical distance the ball has fallen at the end of each second is the same.

SAMPLE PROBLEM

A plane flying horizontally at an altitude of 490 meters and having a velocity of 250 meters per second east, drops a supply packet to a work crew on the ground. It falls freely without a parachute. [Assume no wind and negligible air resistance.]
(a) Calculate the time required for the packet to hit the ground.
(b) Calculate the horizontal distance from the target area that the plane must drop the packet.

SOLUTION: Identify the known and unknown values.

Known
$d_y = 490$ m
$v_x = 250$ m/s
$v_{i_y} = 0.0$ m/s
$a_y = g = 9.81$ m/s^2
$a_x = 0.00$ m/s^2

Unknown
$t = ?$ s
$d_x = ?$ m

1. Write a formula that relates the distance, acceleration, and time for motion in the vertical direction.

$$d_y = v_{i_y}t + \tfrac{1}{2}a_yt^2$$

Because v_{i_y} is zero, the equation becomes

$$d_y = \frac{1}{2}a_yt^2$$

2. Solve the equation for t and substitute g for acceleration.

$$t = \sqrt{\frac{2d_y}{g}}$$

3. Substitute the known values and solve.

$$t = \sqrt{\frac{2(490 \text{ m})}{9.81 \text{ m/s}^2}} = 10. \text{ s}$$

4. Write a formula that relates the distance, acceleration, and time for motion in the horizontal direction.

$$d_x = v_{i_x}t + \tfrac{1}{2}a_xt^2$$

Because $a_x = 0.0$ m/s^2 the equation becomes $d_x = v_{i_x}t$.

5. Substitute the known values and solve.

$$d_x = (250 \text{ m/s})(10. \text{ s}) = 2.5 \times 10^3 \text{ m}$$

The plane must drop the packet 2.5×10^3 meters west of the target.

---

of the velocity remains constant. The object's vertical motion is accelerated by the force of gravity.

If a golf ball is projected with initial velocity v_i at an angle θ above the horizontal, v_i can be separated into perpendicular components, as shown in Figure 2-13.

Recall from page 36 that any vector, A, making an angle θ with the horizontal can be resolved into horizontal and vertical components. The two components of velocity can be determined using these formulas.

Horizontal component: $v_{i_x} = v_i \cos \theta$
Vertical component: $v_{i_y} = v_i \sin \theta$

The vertical component of the velocity gradually decreases to zero as the golf ball reaches the highest point in its trajectory. When the vertical component of the velocity is zero, all of the velocity is in the horizontal. Then the vertical component gradually increases along the ball's downward path due to the constant acceleration of gravity. See Figure 2-14.

To find the time t for the projectile to reach its maximum height, solve the equation $v_f = v_i + at$ for t.

$$t = \frac{v_f - v_i}{a}$$

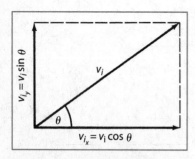

Figure 2-13. An initial velocity vector resolved into horizontal and vertical components

Then, substitute the appropriate values for the vertical velocity and acceleration. If upward in the vertical direction is considered positive, then g, a downward acceleration, is negative. At the highest point, the vertical velocity of the projectile is zero. Thus $t = \frac{v_i \sin \theta}{g}$. It can be shown that the time for the projectile to reach its maximum height is the same as the time to fall back to the ground from that height. Therefore the total time of travel to return to ground level is $\frac{2v_i \sin \theta}{g}$.

The horizontal distance traveled by a projectile is called its <u>range</u>. For any given initial velocity, the range is a maximum when $\theta = 45°$. For any given initial speed of a projectile, the range of the projectile is the same for complementary angles above the horizontal, neglecting friction. For example, a projectile launched with an initial velocity of 15 meters per second at 20.° above the horizontal has the same range as a projectile launched with an initial velocity of 15 meters per second at 70.° above the horizontal. However, the time of flight and maximum height above the horizontal are greater for the launch at 70.°. The actual range of a projectile (when air resistance is present) is shorter than the calculated ideal range.

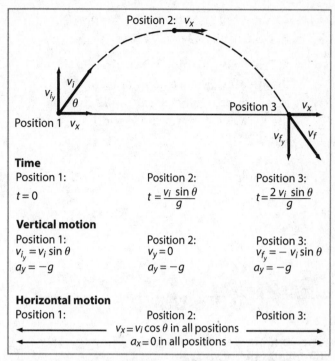

Figure 2-14. The motion of a projectile that is fired at angle θ above the horizontal and returns to the horizontal. [Neglect friction.]

SAMPLE PROBLEM

A small missile is fired with a velocity of 300. meters per second at an angle of 30.0° above the ground. After a total flight time of 30.6 seconds, the missile returns to the level ground. [Neglect air resistance.]
(a) Calculate the initial horizontal and vertical components of the velocity.
(b) Calculate the maximum height of the missile above the ground.
(c) Calculate the total horizontal range of the missile.

SOLUTION: Identify the known and unknown values.

Known
$v_i = 300.$ m/s
$\theta = 30.0°$
$t = 30.6$ s
$a_y = g = -9.81$ m/s^2
$a_x = 0.00$ m/s^2

Unknown
$v_{i_x} = ?$ m/s
$v_{i_y} = ?$ m/s
$d_y = ?$ m
$d_x = ?$ m

1. Write the formulas that resolve the initial velocity vector into horizontal and vertical components.

   $v_{i_x} = v_i \cos \theta$
   $v_{i_y} = v_i \sin \theta$

2. Substitute the known values and solve.

   $v_{i_x} = (300.$ m/s$)(\cos 30.0°) = 260.$ m/s
   $v_{i_y} = (300.$ m/s$)(\sin 30.0°) = 150.$ m/s

3. Find the time for the missile to reach its highest point.

   Because the total time of flight is 30.6 s, the time to reach the maximum height is $\frac{1}{2}(30.6$ s$) = 15.3$ s.

4. Write the formula that relates distance, average velocity, and time in the vertical direction.

   $d_y = \bar{v}_y t_{rise}$

   At the highest point, velocity in the vertical direction is zero. Average velocity = $\frac{1}{2}(v_i + v_f) = \frac{1}{2}(150.$ m/s $+ 0$ m/s$) = 75.0$ m/s.

5. Substitute the known values and solve.

$d_y = (75.0 \text{ m/s})(15.3 \text{ s}) = 1150 \text{ m}$

- An alternate solution is to write the formula that relates displacement, time, and acceleration, $d = v_i t + \frac{1}{2}at^2$ and substitute the known values for the vertical direction. That is

$d_y = (150. \text{ m/s})(15.3 \text{ s}) + \frac{1}{2}(-9.81 \text{ m/s}^2)(15.3 \text{ s})^2$

$d_y = 1150 \text{ m}$

- Another alternate solution is to write the formula that relates final velocity, initial velocity, acceleration, and displacement, $v_f^2 = v_i^2 + 2ad$. Solve the equation for d to yield $d = \frac{v_f^2 - v_i^2}{2a}$. Then substitute the known values for the vertical direction. That is

$d = \frac{(0 \text{ m/s})^2 - (150. \text{ m/s})^2}{2(-9.81 \text{ m/s}^2)} = 1150 \text{ m}$

6. Write the equation that relates distance, velocity, and time in the horizontal direction.

$d_x = \bar{v}_x t_{total}$

7. Substitute the known values and solve.

$d_x = (260. \text{ m/s})(30.6 \text{ s}) = 7960 \text{ m}$

Review Questions

Base your answers to questions 71 through 75 on the following information.

A ball of mass m is thrown horizontally with speed v from a height h above level ground. [Neglect friction.]

71. If the height above the ground from which the ball is thrown was increased, the time of flight of the ball would

(1) decrease   (2) increase   (3) remain the same

72. If the initial speed of the ball was increased, the time of flight of the ball would

(1) decrease   (2) increase   (3) remain the same

73. If the initial speed of the ball was increased, the horizontal distance traveled by the ball would

(1) decrease   (2) increase   (3) remain the same

74. As time elapses before the ball strikes the ground, the horizontal velocity of the ball

(1) decreases   (3) remains the same
(2) increases

75. Compared to the total horizontal distance traveled by the ball in the absence of air resistance, the total horizontal distance traveled by the ball with air resistance is

(1) shorter   (2) longer   (3) the same

76. A student throws a baseball horizontally at 25 meters per second from a cliff 45 meters above the level ground. Approximately how far from the base of the cliff does the ball hit the ground? [Neglect air resistance.]

(1) 45 m   (2) 75 m   (3) 140 m   (4) 230 m

77. A ball rolls down a curved ramp, as shown in the following diagram.

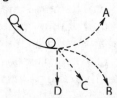

Which dotted line best represents the path of the ball after leaving the ramp?

78. Above a flat horizontal plane, arrow A is shot horizontally from a bow at a speed of 20 meters per second, as shown in the following diagram. A second arrow B is dropped from the same height and at the same instant as A is fired.

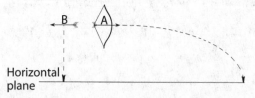

Compare the amount of time A takes to strike the plane to the amount of time B takes to strike the plane. [Neglect friction.]

79. A rock is thrown horizontally from the top of a cliff at 12 meters per second. Calculate the time required for the rock to fall 45 meters vertically.

80. A ball is thrown horizontally at a speed of 24 meters per second from the top of a cliff. If the ball hits the ground 4.0 seconds later, approximately how high is the cliff?

(1) 6.0 m   (2) 39 m   (3) 78 m   (4) 96 m

81. The following diagram shows the muzzle of a cannon located 50. meters above the ground. When the cannon is fired, a ball leaves the muzzle with an initial speed of 250 meters per second. [Neglect air resistance].

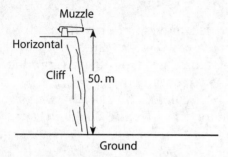

Which action would most likely increase the time of flight of a ball fired by the cannon?

(1) pointing the muzzle of the cannon toward the ground
(2) moving the cannon closer to the edge of the cliff
(3) positioning the cannon higher above the ground
(4) giving the ball a greater initial horizontal velocity

82. A football player kicks a ball with an initial velocity of 25 meters per second at an angle of 53° above the horizontal. The vertical component of the initial velocity of the ball is

(1) 25 m/s (2) 20. m/s (3) 15 m/s (4) 10. m/s

83. The path of a projectile fired at an angle of 30.° above the horizontal is best described as

(1) parabolic   (3) circular
(2) linear   (4) hyperbolic

84. A projectile is fired with velocity of 150. meters per second at an angle of 30.° above the horizontal. Calculate the magnitude of the horizontal component of the velocity at the time the projectile is fired.

85. Projectile A is fired with velocity v at an angle of 30.° above the horizontal. Projectile B is fired with velocity v at an angle of 40.° above the horizontal. Compared to the magnitude of the horizontal component of v at the time projectile A is fired, the magnitude of the horizontal component of v at the time projectile B is fired is

(1) smaller   (2) larger   (3) the same

86. A projectile is launched at an angle of 60.° above the horizontal. Compared to the vertical component of the initial velocity of the projectile, the vertical component of the projectile's velocity when it has reached its maximum height is

(1) smaller   (2) larger   (3) the same

87. A projectile is launched at an angle of 30.° above the horizontal. Neglecting air resistance, what are the projectile's horizontal and vertical accelerations when it reaches its maximum height?

Uniform Circular Motion

According to Newton's first law of motion, an unbalanced force acting on an object always produces a change in the object's velocity. If the force has a component in the direction of the object's motion, the magnitude of the velocity changes. However, if the force is applied perpendicular to the direction of motion, only the direction of the velocity changes; its magnitude remains the same. In both instances, the object accelerates because velocity changes with time. If the applied force has a constant magnitude and always acts perpendicular to the direction of the object's velocity, the object moves in a circular path at constant speed, experiencing **uniform circular motion.**

Centripetal Acceleration

An object moving uniformly in a circular path always has **centripetal acceleration,** which is an acceleration directed toward the center of the circle. "Center-seeking" centripetal acceleration is a vector quantity whose magnitude is directly proportional to the square of the speed of the object and inversely proportional to the radius of the circular path in which it travels. Centripetal acceleration is represented by this formula.

$$a_c = \frac{v^2}{r}$$

Ⓡ

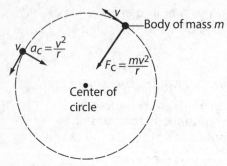

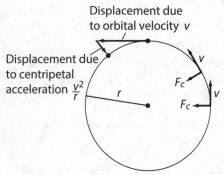

Figure 2-15. The relationship between velocity *v*, mass *m*, radius of curvature *r*, centripetal force F_c, and centripetal acceleration a_c for a body in uniform circular motion: The velocity vector is tangent to the circle. Both the centripetal force and the centripetal acceleration are directed toward the center of the circle. The radius of curvature is the radius of the circle.

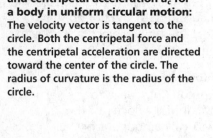

The speed *v* of the object is in meters per second, the radius of curvature *r* is in meters, and the centripetal acceleration a_c is in meters per second². The centripetal acceleration of an object is independent of the mass of the object.

Centripetal Force

The force needed to keep an object moving in a circular path is called **centripetal force,** F_c. Centripetal force is a force directed toward the center of curvature. Centripetal force, a vector quantity, produces centripetal acceleration. Newton's second law, $F = ma$, can be rewritten for the special case of circular motion as $F_c = ma_c$. Substituting in the expression for centripetal acceleration, $a_c = \frac{v^2}{r}$, yields this formula.

$$F_c = \frac{mv^2}{r}$$

Mass *m* is in kilograms, speed *v* is in meters per second, radius *r* is in meters, and centripetal force F_c is in kilogram · meters per second², or newtons. Figure 2-15 shows the relationship between these quantities for an object in uniform circular motion.

An object in uniform circular motion travels at constant speed in its circular path because there is no net force acting on the object in its direction of motion. That is, the object's tangential velocity is constant. However, the object is not in equilibrium because centripetal force acts perpendicular to the tangential velocity and produces a constant acceleration towards the center of curvature. Thus, although the magnitude of the object's velocity (speed) remains constant, the direction of the object's velocity is always changing, as shown in Figure 2-16.

Figure 2-16. The velocity, acceleration, and displacement of a body in uniform circular motion: The velocity vector is always tangent to the circle and perpendicular to the centripetal acceleration. The acceleration causes a continuous change in the direction of the velocity and a continuous displacement to the circular path.

SAMPLE PROBLEM

A 1.5-kilogram cart moves in a horizontal circular path of 1.3-meter radius at a constant speed of 2.0 meters per second.
(a) Calculate the magnitude of the centripetal acceleration of the cart.
(b) Calculate the magnitude of the centripetal force on the cart.

SOLUTION: Identify the known and unknown values.

Known
$m = 1.5$ kg
$r = 1.3$ m
$v = 2.0$ m/s

Unknown
$a_c = ?$ m/s²
$F_c = ?$ N

1. Write the formula for centripetal acceleration.

$$a_c = \frac{v^2}{r}$$

2. Substitute the known values and solve.

$$a_c = \frac{(2.0 \text{ m/s})^2}{1.3 \text{ m}} = \frac{4.0 \text{ m}^2/\text{s}^2}{1.3 \text{ m}} = 3.1 \text{ m/s}^2$$

3. Write the formula for centripetal force.

$$F_c = \frac{mv^2}{r}$$

4. Substitute the known values and solve.

$$F_c = \frac{(1.5 \text{ kg})(2.0 \text{ m/s})^2}{1.3 \text{ m}} = \frac{(1.5 \text{ kg})(4.0 \text{ m}^2/\text{s}^2)}{1.3 \text{ m}}$$

$$F_c = 4.6 \text{ N}$$

Another way to solve (b) is to substitute the calculated value of a_c from part (a) for v^2/r.

$$F_c = ma_c = (1.5 \text{ kg})(3.1 \text{ m/s}^2) = 4.7 \text{ N}$$

Base your answers to questions 88 through 96 on the following information and diagram.

A 2.0-kilogram cart travels counter-clockwise at a constant speed of 6.0 meters per second in a horizontal circle of radius 3.0 meters.

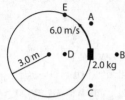

88. Calculate the magnitude and direction of the centripetal acceleration of the cart at the position shown.

89. Calculate the magnitude of the centripetal force acting on the cart.

90. If the mass of the cart was doubled, the magnitude of the centripetal force acting on the cart would be

    (1) halved   (3) quartered
    (2) doubled   (4) quadrupled

91. If the radius of curvature of the path was doubled, the magnitude of the centripetal acceleration of the cart would be

    (1) halved   (3) quartered
    (2) doubled   (4) quadrupled

92. If the speed of the cart was doubled, the magnitude of the centripetal force on the cart would be

    (1) halved   (3) quartered
    (2) doubled   (4) quadrupled

93. If the mass of the cart was halved, the magnitude of the centripetal acceleration of the cart would

    (1) decrease   (2) increase   (3) remain the same

94. In the position shown in the diagram, towards which point is the centripetal force acting on the cart directed?

95. In the position shown in the diagram, towards which point is the velocity of the cart directed?

96. Which factor, when doubled, would produce the greatest change in the magnitude of the centripetal force acting on the cart?

    (1) mass of the cart
    (2) radius of curvature of the path
    (3) speed of the cart
    (4) weight of the cart

97. As the time taken for a car to make one lap around a circular track decreases, the centripetal acceleration of the car

    (1) decreases (2) increases (3) remains the same

98. The tangential acceleration of a cart moving at a constant speed in a horizontal circle is

    (1) 0.0 m/s^2
    (2) 9.8 m/s^2 in the direction of the velocity
    (3) constant in magnitude and directed radially toward the center of curvature
    (4) constant in magnitude and directed radially away from the center of curvature

99. The centripetal acceleration of a ball of mass m moving at constant speed v in a horizontal circular path of radius r is

    (1) zero
    (2) constant in direction, but changing in magnitude
    (3) constant in magnitude, but changing in direction
    (4) changing in both magnitude and direction

Base your answers to questions 100 through 103 on the following information and diagram.

A 5.0-kilogram cart travels clockwise in a horizontal circle of radius 2.0 meters at a constant speed of 4.0 meters per second

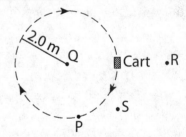

100. Towards which point is the velocity of the cart directed at the position shown?

101. Towards which point is the centripetal acceleration of the cart directed at the position shown?

102. If the mass of the cart was doubled, the magnitude of the cart's centripetal acceleration would be

    (1) unchanged   (3) halved
    (2) doubled   (4) quadrupled

103. The magnitude of the centripetal force acting on the cart is

    (1) 8.0 N   (2) 20. N   (3) 40. N   (4) 50. N

Newton's Universal Law of Gravitation

Every body in the universe exerts a force of attraction on every other body. According to Newton's universal law of gravitation, any two bodies attract each other with a force that is directly proportional to the product of their masses and inversely proportional to the square of the distance between their centers. The attractive force that one object exerts on another object due to their masses is called **gravitational force,** which is given by this formula.

$$F_g = \frac{Gm_1m_2}{r^2}$$

(R)

In the formula F_g is the gravitational force in newtons, m_1 and m_2 are the masses of the objects in kilograms, r is the distance between the centers of the objects in meters, and G is the universal gravitational constant 6.67×10^{-11} N·m^2 / kg^2. The universal law of gravitation is valid only for spherical masses of uniform density and masses that are small compared to the distance between their centers.

According to the law, the gravitational force that mass m_1 exerts on mass m_2 is equal in magnitude and opposite in direction to the gravitational force that mass m_2 exerts on mass m_1. If the distance between the centers of the two masses is doubled, the magnitude of the gravitational force is quartered. If one of the two masses is doubled and the distance between their centers remains constant, the magnitude of the gravitational force is doubled.

SAMPLE PROBLEM

Calculate the magnitude of the gravitational force of attraction that Earth exerts on the Moon.

SOLUTION: Identify the known and unknown values. Obtain needed values from the *Reference Tables for Physical Setting/Physics.*

Known
$m_{Earth} = 5.98 \times 10^{24}$ kg
$m_{Moon} = 7.35 \times 10^{22}$ kg
$r_{Earth\ to\ Moon} = 3.84 \times 10^8$ m
$G = 6.67 \times 10^{-11}$ N • m^2 / kg^2

1. Write the formula for the gravitational force.
$$F_g = \frac{Gm_1m_2}{r^2}$$

Unknown
$F_g = ?$ N

2. Substitute the known values and solve.
$$F_g = \frac{(6.67 \times 10^{-11}\ \text{N·m}^2/\text{kg}^2)(5.98 \times 10^{24}\ \text{kg})(7.35 \times 10^{22}\ \text{kg})}{(3.84 \times 10^8\ \text{m})^2}$$

$$F_g = 1.99 \times 10^{20}\ \text{N}$$

Gravitational Field Strength A region in space where a test particle would experience a gravitational force is called a **gravitational field.** Every mass is surrounded by a gravitational field. A unit test mass is used to map a gravitational field, such as the one that surrounds Earth.

Figure 2-17A shows gravitational force vectors associated with a test mass at various locations above Earth's surface. The direction of the vectors indicates that the test mass is always attracted to Earth, and the magnitude of the vectors indicates that the force on the test mass increases as it gets closer to Earth. In Figure 2-17B, the force vectors have been joined to form lines of gravitational force. The imaginary line along which a test mass would move in a gravitational field is called a line of gravitational force.

In Figure 2-17 the gravitational field lines are directed radially toward the center of Earth, that is, normal to Earth's surface. The concentration of the field lines increases as Earth's surface is approached. This indicates that gravitational field strength, a vector quantity, increases as the distance from Earth decreases. At any point in a gravitational field, **gravitational field strength,** g, equals the force per unit mass at that point. The relationship is expressed by this formula.

$$g = \frac{F_g}{m} \quad \text{®}$$

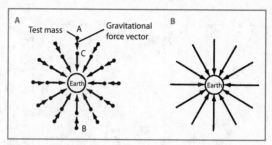

Figure 2-17. The gravitational field around Earth: (A) When the test mass is at points *A* or *B*, the magnitude of the gravitational force is the same because both points are the same distance from the center of Earth. At point *C* the gravitational force is greater than at points *A* and *B* because *C* is closer to the center of Earth. (B) The force vectors have been joined to form lines of gravitational force.

On a mass m in kilograms the gravitational force F_g is in newtons, and the gravitational field strength g is in newtons per kilogram, N/kg. Gravitational field strength has the same direction as the gravitational force acting on the mass.

The unit for gravitational field strength is the same as the unit for acceleration. Because 1 newton = 1 kilogram · meter/second², then

$$1 \frac{\text{newton}}{\text{kilogram}} = 1 \frac{\cancel{\text{kilogram}} \cdot \text{meter/second}^2}{\cancel{\text{kilogram}}}$$

$$= 1 \text{ meter/second}^2$$

Recall that the acceleration of an object equals the ratio $\frac{F_{net}}{m}$ from the equation $a = \frac{F_{net}}{m}$. Consequently g is the acceleration produced on a mass m by the gravitational force F_g. Therefore, the gravitational field strength g is the same as the acceleration due to gravity. For short distances near the surface of Earth, the gravitational field is considered to be uniform and g is the same for all masses:

$$g \text{ (gravitational field strength)} = 9.81 \text{ N/kg}$$

$$g \text{ (acceleration due to gravity)} = 9.81 \text{ m/s}^2$$

Do not confuse g the acceleration due to gravity (9.81 m/s²) with G the universal gravitational constant (6.67 × 10⁻¹¹ N · m²/kg²).

Weight

The gravitational force with which a planet attracts a mass is called **weight.** If M is the mass of Earth, m is the mass of an object on Earth's surface, and r is the distance from the center of Earth, it can be seen from Newton's universal law of gravitation that the weight F_g of an object on Earth's surface is directly proportional to its mass m because all the other quantities in the equation are constant. Weight is a vector quantity (force) directed toward the center of a planet that is measured in newtons, whereas mass is a scalar quantity measured in kilograms. The weight of an object decreases with increasing distance from the center of a planet because the gravitational field strength decreases. But the mass of an object is constant because it is independent of its location in any gravitational field.

The weight of an object can be determined by solving the gravitational field strength equation for F_g ($F_g = mg$) and substituting values for the mass and the acceleration due to gravity. The result shows that the weight F_g of a 1.00-kilogram object on Earth's surface is 9.81 newtons. The weight

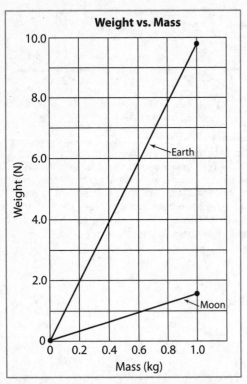

Weight vs. Mass

[Graph: Weight (N) on y-axis from 0 to 10.0, Mass (kg) on x-axis from 0 to 1.0. Two lines labeled "Earth" (steep) and "Moon" (shallow).]

Figure 2-18. On a weight-mass graph the slope of the line equals the acceleration due to gravity or gravitational field strength.

of a 1.00-kilogram object on the Moon is less than 9.81 newtons because the gravitational field strength on the surface of the Moon is less than on Earth. The difference results from the smaller mass of the Moon.

A graph of weight versus mass for a series of objects located at the same point in a gravitational field is a straight line whose slope is g, the acceleration due to gravity or gravitational field strength. Figure 2-18 shows the lines produced from data collected on the surface of Earth and the surface of the Moon. The slope of the line for Earth is six times as great as the slope of the line for the Moon.

If a person stands on a scale in an elevator at rest, the scale registers the downward force of the person's weight. The elevator floor exerts an upward force to balance this weight. However, when the elevator starts to rise, it must exert an additional upward force to accelerate the person's mass. By the law of action-reaction, the person's body must exert an equal force downward in addition to its weight. Thus, the scale on an elevator accelerating upward registers an increased total force or weight for a person. When the elevator stops accelerating and rises at constant speed, there is no additional force and the scale reading returns to the person's weight alone. If the elevator were to accelerate downward, the scale would register a force less than the weight of the person at rest.

Review Questions

104. Which diagram best represents the gravitational forces, F_g, between a satellite, S, and Earth?

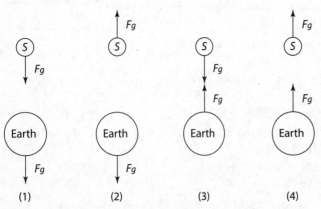

(1)   (2)   (3)   (4)

105. When a satellite is a distance d from the center of Earth, the magnitude of the gravitational force that the satellite exerts on Earth is F. What is the magnitude of the gravitational force that the satellite exerts on Earth when the satellite's distance from the center of Earth is $3d$?

106. The magnitude of the gravitational force that object A exerts on object B is 20. newtons. If the mass of each object is doubled, the magnitude of the gravitational force that A exerts on B is

(1) 5.0 N   (2) 10. N   (3) 20. N   (4) 80. N

107. Which graph best represents the relationship between the magnitude of the gravitational force that one point mass exerts on another point mass and the distance between them?

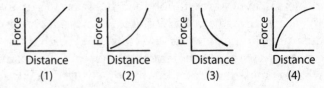

(1)   (2)   (3)   (4)

108. The following diagram represents a car stopped on a hill.

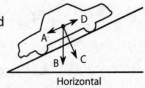

Which vector best represents the weight of the car?

109. Calculate the weight of a 5.00-kilogram object at the surface of Earth.

110. Which graph best represents the relationship between the mass of an object and its distance from the center of Earth?

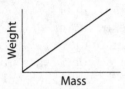

Distance Distance Distance Distance
(1)   **(2)**   **(3)**   **(4)**

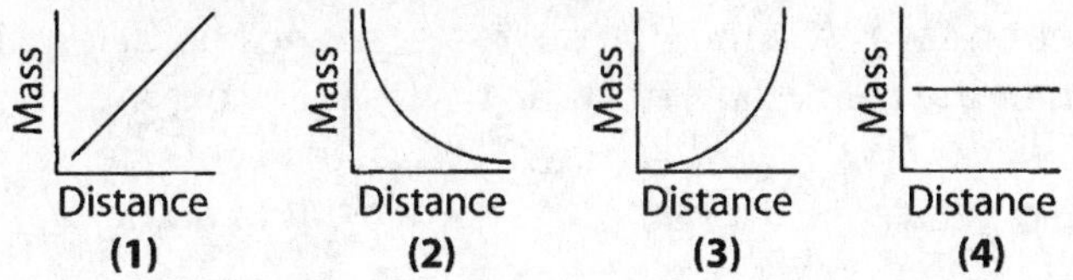

111. The following graph shows the relationship between weight and mass for a series of objects.

What is represented by the slope of the graph?

112. A 60.-kilogram astronaut weighs 96 newtons on the surface of the Moon. Calculate the acceleration due to gravity on the Moon.

113. Which graph best represents the relationship between acceleration due to gravity for objects near the surface of Earth and the mass of the objects? [Neglect friction.]

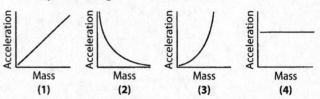

Mass Mass Mass Mass
(1) **(2)** **(3)** **(4)**

114. As an astronaut travels from the surface of Earth to a position that is four times as far away from the center of Earth, the astronaut's

(1) mass decreases
(2) mass remains the same
(3) weight increases
(4) weight remains the same

115. An 800-newton person is standing in an elevator. If the upward force of the elevator on the person is 600 newtons, the person is

(1) at rest
(2) accelerating upward
(3) accelerating downward
(4) moving downward at constant speed

Friction

The force that opposes the relative motion of two objects in contact is called **friction.** A vector quantity, friction is always parallel to the two surfaces in contact and acts in the direction that opposes the slipping motion. The force of friction, F_f, is directly proportional to the magnitude of the normal force, F_N. The **normal force** is the force pressing the two contacting surfaces together. On a horizontal surface, the normal force is equal in magnitude and opposite in direction to the weight, F_g or mg, of the object resting on the surface. For an object on a surface inclined at an angle θ to the horizontal, the normal force is equal in magnitude and opposite in direction to the component of the object's weight perpendicular to the inclined surface. That is, on an incline, the magnitude of the normal force F_N is equal to $F_g \cos \theta$ or $mg \cos \theta$. The force of friction, which depends upon the nature of the two surfaces in contact, is given by this formula.

$$F_f = \mu F_N$$ Ⓡ

The constant, μ, is the **coefficient of friction,** which is the ratio of the frictional force to the normal force, and thus has no unit.

The formula implies that the frictional force is independent of the area in contact and the speed of motion. For example, a rectangular block of wood, smooth on all sides, has dimensions 4.0 cm × 6.0 cm × 10. cm, and thus, has three different surfaces with areas 24 cm², 40. cm², and 60. cm². If the block slides along a horizontal surface, it makes no difference which face of the block is in contact with the surface because the normal force (the weight of the block) is the same in each case. The magnitude of the frictional force depends only on the weight of the block.

Static and Kinetic Friction

There are several kinds of friction. **Static friction** is the force that opposes the start of motion, whereas **kinetic friction** is the friction between objects in contact when they are in motion. Once motion starts, kinetic friction decreases. The force of kinetic friction for two surfaces in contact is less than the force of static friction for the same two surfaces, so the coefficient of kinetic friction is less than the coefficient of static friction. For example, according to the *Reference Tables for Physical Setting/Physics*, the coefficient of kinetic friction for copper on steel is 0.36 and the coefficient of static friction for copper on steel is 0.53.

Figure 2-19 shows forces acting concurrently on a 10.0-newton wooden block in equilibrium on a wooden horizontal surface. In each case, the normal force is equal in magnitude and opposite in direction to the weight of the block. In Figure 2-19A, the applied horizontal force is equal in magnitude but opposite in direction to the maximum static friction force. In Figure 2-19B, the horizontal force applied to move the block at constant speed to the right is equal in magnitude but opposite in direction to the force of kinetic friction. When the block is moved to the right at constant speed, the net force acting on the block in the horizontal direction is zero, and the block is in equilibrium.

Using the information in Figure 2-19, the coefficients of static and kinetic friction are

$$\mu_s = \frac{F_{f_s}}{F_N} = \frac{4.2 \text{ N}}{10.0 \text{ N}} = 0.42$$

and

$$\mu_k = \frac{F_{f_k}}{F_N} = \frac{3.0 \text{ N}}{10.0 \text{ N}} = 0.30$$

The values agree with those found in the *Reference* Ⓡ *Tables for Physical Setting/Physics*.

Determining the Coefficient of Friction A graph of frictional force versus normal force (weight) for a wooden block in contact with a wooden horizontal surface is a straight line for both static friction and kinetic friction. (Experimentally, the weight of the block can be varied by resting masses on top of it, thus keeping the nature of the two surfaces in contact the same at all times.) The slopes of the lines are the coefficient of static friction and the coefficient of kinetic friction, respectively. Figure 2-20 shows the lines that would result for data collected for a wooden block on a wooden table. The slope of the static friction line is 0.42 and the slope of the kinetic friction line is 0.30.

Friction on an Inclined Surface If an object is on a surface inclined at angle θ to the horizontal, the object's weight can be resolved into two

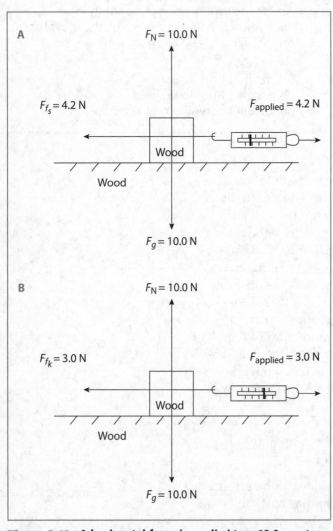

Figure 2-19. A horizontal force is applied to a 10.0-newton wooden block on a horizontal wooden surface: (A) A maximum static friction force keeps the box from moving. (B) The box moves at constant speed to the right when the applied force equals the force of kinetic friction. Note: The vectors are *not* drawn to scale.

components, one perpendicular to the inclined surface and the other parallel to the surface. The perpendicular component of the object's weight, $F_g \cos \theta$ or $mg \cos \theta$, is equal in magnitude and opposite in direction to the normal force and has no effect on the motion of the object. The object cannot move in the direction of either force. Only the component of the object's weight parallel to the inclined surface $F_g \sin \theta$ or $mg \sin \theta$ tends to accelerate the object down the incline. As the angle that the incline makes with the horizontal increases, the component of the object's weight parallel to the incline increases, and the acceleration of the object down the incline increases. This acceleration is opposed by the friction between the object and the incline. The magnitude of the force of friction is directly proportional the normal force, which is equal in magnitude but opposite in direction to the perpendicular component of the object's weight. Thus, as the angle of inclination increases, the component of the objects's weight perpendicular to the incline decreases, and the magnitude of the frictional force decreases. The steeper the slope of the incline, the greater the acceleration of the object down the incline.

Fluid Friction Fluid friction, which results from an object moving through a fluid such as air depends upon the surface area and the speed of the object moving through the fluid.

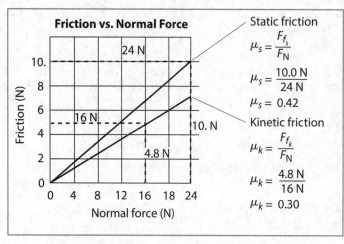

Figure 2-20. **Finding the coefficients of static and kinetic friction by determining the slopes of the lines on a friction-normal force graph**

Review Questions

116. An empty wooden crate slides across a warehouse floor. If the crate was filled, the coefficient of kinetic friction between the crate and the floor would

(1) decrease (2) increase (3) remain the same

117. An empty wooden crate slides across a warehouse floor. If the crate was filled, the magnitude of the force of kinetic friction between the crate and the floor would

(1) decrease (2) increase (3) remain the same

118. As an object initially at rest on a horizontal surface is set in motion, the magnitude of the force of friction between the object and the surface

(1) decreases (2) increases (3) remains the same

119. As a thrown baseball is acted on by air friction, the thermal energy of the ball

(1) decreases (2) increases (3) remains the same

120. Each of the following diagrams shows a different block being pushed to the right by a horizontal force across a horizontal surface at constant velocity.

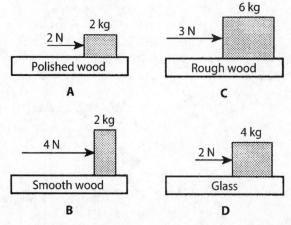

In which two diagrams is the force of friction the same?

Base your answers to questions 121 to 123 on the information below.

A force of 10. newtons toward the right is exerted on a wooden crate initially moving to the right on a horizontal wooden floor. The crate weighs 25 newtons.

121. Calculate the magnitude of the force of friction between the crate and the floor.

122. What is the magnitude of the net force acting on the crate?

123. Is the crate accelerating? Explain your answer.

---

124. The diagram below represents a 10.-newton block sliding at constant speed down a plane that makes an angle of 30.° with the horizontal.

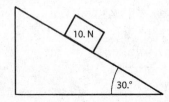

The magnitude of the frictional force acting on the block is

(1) 5.0 N   (2) 10. N   (3) 49 N   (4) 98 N

125. Sand is often placed on an icy road because the sand

(1) decreases the coefficient of friction between the tires of a car and the road
(2) increases the coefficient of friction between the tires of a car and the road
(3) decreases the gravitational force on a car
(4) increases the normal force of a car on the road

126. A 10.-kilogram rubber block is pulled horizontally at constant velocity across a sheet of ice. Calculate the magnitude of the force of friction acting on the block.

Base your answers to questions 127 through 130 on the following information and diagram.

A horizontal force is used to pull a 5.0-kilogram cart at a constant speed of 5.0 meters per second across the floor. The force of friction between the cart and the floor is 10. newtons.

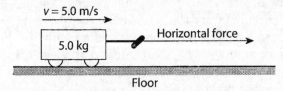

Floor

127. What is the magnitude of the horizontal force along the handle of the cart?

128. Calculate the weight of the cart.

129. Compare the weight of the cart to the normal force.

130. Calculate the coefficient of kinetic friction between the cart and the floor.

---

131. A constant horizontal force of 5.2 newtons is applied to a wooden block to slide it at constant speed across a wooden table. Calculate the weight of the block.

132. A wooden block is at rest on a wooden inclined plane. As the angle the plane makes with the horizontal is increased, the coefficient of static friction between the block and the plane

(1) decreases
(2) increases
(3) remains the same

133. A wooden block is at rest on a wooden inclined plane. As the angle the plane makes with the horizontal is increased, the magnitude of the force of static friction between the block and the plane

(1) decreases
(2) increases
(3) remains the same

Momentum

The product of an object's mass and velocity is a vector quantity called **momentum.** It is given by this formula.

$$p = mv$$ Ⓡ

Mass m is in kilograms, velocity v is in meters per second, and momentum p is in kilogram · meters per second. The direction of an object's momentum is the same as the direction of its velocity. The SI unit for momentum is kilogram · meters per second, kg · m/s.

Impulse and Change in Momentum

The product of the net force acting on an object and the time during which the force acts is called **impulse.** Impulse, a vector quantity having the same direction as the net force, is given by this formula.

$$J = F_{net}t$$ Ⓡ

The average force F is in newtons, t is the time during which the force acts in seconds, and J is the impulse in newton · seconds. The SI unit for impulse is the newton · second, N · s.

The impulse imparted to an object can also be determined graphically. A horizontal force of varying magnitude is applied over time to an object on a horizontal surface and a graph of force versus time is plotted. The area under the line equals the impulse imparted to the object.

According to Newton's second law an unbalanced force acting on an object causes it to accelerate. This acceleration produces a change in the object's velocity and consequently its momentum, as shown by the following equations.

$$F_{net} = ma = m\frac{\Delta v}{t} \text{ or } F_{net}t = m\Delta v$$

Because $F_{net}t$ equals the impulse and $m\Delta v$ equals the change in momentum, it follows that

$$J = F_{net}t = \Delta p$$ Ⓡ

The direction of the impulse imparted to an object is the same as the direction of the object's change in momentum. If an object is in equilibrium, there is no change in its momentum and, thus, no impulse imparted to it.

SAMPLE PROBLEM

A 5.0-kilogram object has an initial velocity of 8.0 meters per second due east. An unbalanced force acts on the object for 3.0 seconds, causing its velocity to decrease to 2.0 meters per second east. Calculate the magnitude and direction of the unbalanced force.

SOLUTION: Identify the known and unknown values.

Known
$m = 5.0$ kg
$v_i = 8.0$ m/s east
$v_f = 2.0$ m/s east
$t = 3.0$ s

Unknown
$F_{net} = ?$ N to the ?

1. Write the formula relating impulse and change in momentum and the formula for momentum.
$J = F_{net}t = \Delta p$ and $p = mv$

2. Combine the formulas.
$F_{net}t = m\Delta v$

3. Solve the equation for F.
$$F_{net} = \frac{m\Delta v}{t} = \frac{m(v_f - v_i)}{t}$$

4. Substitute the known values and solve.
$$F_{net} = \frac{(5.0 \text{ kg})(2.0 \text{ m/s} - 8.0 \text{ m/s})}{3.0 \text{ s}} = \frac{-30. \text{ kg} \cdot \text{m/s}}{3.0 \text{ s}}$$

$F_{net} = -10. \text{ kg} \cdot \text{m/s}^2 = -10. \text{ N}$
The force is 10. N directed to the west.

In baseball, both the batter hitting the ball and the outfielder catching the ball are aware of the relationship between impulse and momentum. The batter "follows through" to keep the bat in contact with the ball as long as possible. The greater the time during which the force of impact acts on the ball, the larger the impulse imparted to it, the greater its final momentum, and the longer the distance of travel. The outfielder catching the ball tries to prolong the time of slowing the ball by moving the gloved hand back in the direction of the ball's motion. By increasing the time during which the gloved hand acts on the ball to reduce its momentum to zero, the force needed to produce the necessary impulse and the "sting" are reduced.

Conservation of Momentum

A group of objects, not acted upon by any external force, is called a **closed system.** According to Newton's third law, within such a system the force F exerted by one mass m_1 in the system on a second mass m_2 must be equal in magnitude and opposite in direction to the force that m_2 exerts on m_1. Because the force F acts on both masses for exactly the same amount of time, the magnitude of the impulse on each mass is the same. Consequently, the change in momentum for each mass has the same magnitude, but they are in opposite directions. The relationship is expressed in this way.

$$m_1 \Delta v_1 = -m_2 \Delta v_2, \text{ or } m_1 \Delta v_1 + m_2 \Delta v_2 = 0$$

The total change in momentum due to the interaction of masses m_1 and m_2 is zero. This relationship is summed up in the **law of conservation of momentum** which states that the total momentum of the objects in a closed system is constant. The law is given by this formula.

$$p_{before} = p_{after}$$

Momentum p is in kilogram • meters per second, kg • m/s.

Ⓡ

SAMPLE PROBLEM

A 1.0-kilogram cart A is initially at rest on a horizontal frictionless air track. A 0.20-kilogram cart B is moving to the right at 10.0 meters per second on the same track. Cart B collides with cart A causing cart A to move to the right at 3.0 meters per second. Calculate the velocity of cart B after the collision.

SOLUTION: Identify the known and unknown values. Let velocity to the right be positive.

Known
$m_A = 1.0$ kg
$m_B = 0.20$ kg
$v_{A_i} = 0.0$ m/s
$v_{B_i} = 10.0$ m/s
$v_{A_f} = 3.0$ m/s

Unknown
$v_{B_f} = ?$ m/s to the ?

1. Write the formula that equates the momentum of the system before and after the collision.

$p_{after} = p_{before}$

$m_A v_{A_f} + m_B v_{B_f} = m_A v_{A_i} + m_B v_{B_i}$

2. Solve the equation for v_{B_f}.

$$v_{B_f} = \frac{m_A v_{A_i} + m_B v_{B_i} - m_A v_{A_f}}{m_B}$$

3. Substitute the known values and solve.

$$v_{B_f} = \frac{(1.0 \text{ kg})(0.0 \text{ m/s}) + (0.20 \text{ kg})(10.0 \text{ m/s}) - (1.0 \text{ kg})(3.0 \text{ m/s})}{0.20 \text{ kg}}$$

$v_{B_f} = -5.0$ m/s

The velocity of cart B after the collision is 5.0 m/s to the left.

134. As an object falls freely toward Earth, the object's momentum

(1) decreases (2) increases (3) remains the same

135. Which term identifies a scalar quantity?

(1) acceleration   (3) speed
(2) momentum   (4) displacement

136. What is the magnitude of the velocity of a 25-kilogram object that has a momentum of 100. kilogram · meters per second?

(1) 0.25 m/s   (3) 40. m/s
(2) 2500 m/s   (4) 4.0 m/s

137. What is the momentum of a 1,200-kilogram car traveling at 15 meters per second due east?

(1) 80. kg · m/s due east
(2) 80. kg · m/s due west
(3) 1.8×10^4 kg · m/s due east
(4) 1.8×10^4 kg · m/s due west

138. A constant unbalanced force acts on an object for 3.0 seconds, producing an impulse of 6.0 newton • seconds east. Determine the magnitude and direction of the force.

139. A 10.-newton force to the east acts on an object for 0.010 second. What force to the east, acting on the object for 0.050 second, would produce the same impulse?

(1) 1.0 N   (2) 2.0 N   (3) 5.0 N   (4) 10. N

Base your answers to questions 140 and 141 on the graph below, which represents the relationship between the net force acting on an object and the time during which the force acts.

Force vs. Time

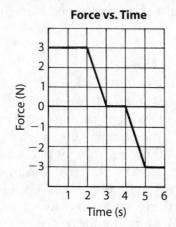

140. During which time interval is the velocity of the object constant?

141. Determine the net impulse imparted to the object during the 6-second time interval.

142. What is the magnitude of the net force acting on a 2.0×10^3-kilogram car as it accelerates from rest to a speed of 15 meters per second in 5.0 seconds?

(1) 6.0×10^3 N   (3) 3.0×10^4 N
(2) 2.0×10^4 N   (4) 6.0×10^4 N

143. A 5.00-kilogram mass is traveling at 100. meters per second. Determine the speed of the mass after an impulse with a magnitude of 30.0 newton • seconds is applied.

144. A 2,400-kilogram car is traveling at a speed of 20. meters per second. Compared to the magnitude of the force required to stop the car in 12 seconds, the magnitude of the force required to stop the car in 6.0 seconds is

(1) half as great   (3) the same
(2) twice as great   (4) four times as great

145. A 2.0-kilogram cart moving due east at 6.0 meters per second collides with a 3.0-kilogram cart moving due west. The carts stick together and come to rest after the collision. Calculate the initial speed of the 3.0-kilogram cart.

146. A 0.180-kilogram cart traveling at 0.80 meter per second to the right collides with a 0.100-kilogram cart initially at rest. The carts lock together upon collision. Calculate the final velocity of the carts.

147. A 2.0-kilogram cart traveling north at 4.0 meters per second collides head on with a 1.0-kilogram cart traveling south at 8.0 meters per second. What is the magnitude of the total momentum of the two carts immediately after the collision?

(1) 0.0 kg · m/s   (3) 16 kg · m/s
(2) 8.0 kg · m/s   (4) 32 kg · m/s

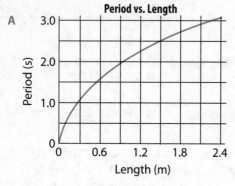

Period vs. Length

(graph A: Period (s) vs. Length (m))

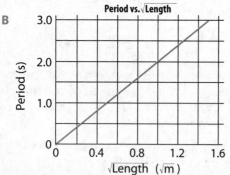

Period vs. √Length

(graph B: Period (s) vs. √Length (√m))

Figure 2-21. Graphs of experimental data of the period versus the length and square root of length of a simple pendulum: (A) shows that the period is not directly proportional to the length. **(B)** confirms the equation that defines the period of a pendulum. The period is directly proportional to the square root of the length.

The Simple Pendulum

A simple **pendulum** consists of a bob or mass m attached to a string of negligible mass. The length of the pendulum ℓ is measured from the pivot point at one end of the string to the center of the bob, where all the mass is assumed to be concentrated. In the equilibrium position, the string is perpendicular to the ground. To set the pendulum in motion, the bob is displaced from the equilibrium position by lifting it in the gravitational field. The angle the string makes with the equilibrium position is called the amplitude, θ.

Period of a Simple Pendulum

If friction is negligible, the variables associated with a simple pendulum are mass, length, amplitude, and gravitational field strength. The time required for the displaced pendulum to complete one cycle of motion is called the **period,** T. The number of cycles the pendulum completes per unit time is called the frequency, f. The period of the pendulum is related to the frequency by the equation $T = \frac{1}{f}$ where period is in seconds and frequency is in hertz (Hz), or $1/s$.

It can be found experimentally that for amplitudes less than 15°, the period of a simple pendulum is independent of the mass of the bob, and independent of the amplitude. However, the period is affected by the length of the pendulum ℓ and the acceleration due to gravity g. The period is given by this formula.

$$T = 2\pi\sqrt{\frac{\ell}{g}}$$

The length l is in meters, the acceleration due to gravity g is in meters per second^2, and the period T is in seconds. **Note to student:** This formula does not appear on the *Reference Tables for Physical Setting/Physics*, and is not testable. However, plotting given data for the period of a simple pendulum versus length or the period versus the square root of length and interpreting the resulting graphs is testable. Figure 2-21 shows two graphs produced as a result of varying the length of a simple pendulum and measuring its period.

Equilibrium and Nonequilibrium Forces

When a pendulum is in the equilibrium position, two forces act on the bob, the weight F_g and the tension in the string F_T. The tension is equal in magnitude and opposite in direction to the weight, so there is no net force on the bob. If the bob is displaced from equilibrium and the pendulum has an amplitude θ, the pendulum is no longer in equilibrium. The tension in the string is still directed along the string, but it is not opposite in direction to the weight. If the weight of the bob is resolved into perpendicular components F_{g_x} and F_{g_y}, the tension in the string is found to be less than the weight of the bob. The net force on the bob, equal to the component of its weight, F_{g_x}, acts along the tangent to its path. This net force causes the bob to accelerate towards its equilibrium position.

Directions

Review the Test-Taking Strategies section of this book. Then answer the following questions. Read each question carefully and answer with a correct choice or response.

Part A

1 A student walks 1.0 kilometer due east and 1.0 kilometer due south. Then she runs 2.0 kilometers due west. The magnitude of the student's resultant displacement is
(1) 0 km   (2) 1.4 km   (3) 3.4 km   (4) 4.0 km

2 A car travels 20. meters east in 1.0 second. The displacement of the car at the end of this 1.0-second interval is
(1) 20. m
(2) 20. m/s
(3) 20. m east
(4) 20. m/s east

3 Two cars, A and B, are 400. meters apart. Car A travels due east at 30. meters per second on a collision course with car B, which travels due west at 20. meters per second. What is the total time that elapses before the two cars collide?
(1) 8.0 s   (2) 13 s   (3) 20. s   (4) 40. s

4 A baseball pitcher throws a fastball at 42 meters per second. If the batter is 18 meters from the pitcher, approximately how much time does it take for the ball to reach the batter?
(1) 2.3 s   (2) 1.9 s   (3) 0.86 s   (4) 0.43 s

5 The velocity of an object in linear motion changes from +25 meters per second to +15 meters per second in 2.0 seconds. What is the object's acceleration during this 2.0-second interval?
(1) $-20.$ m/s^2
(2) $+20.$ m/s^2
(3) -5.0 m/s^2
(4) $+5.0$ m/s^2

6 An object initially traveling in a straight line with a velocity of 5.0 meters per second north is accelerated uniformly at 2.0 meters per second^2 north for 4.0 seconds. What is the total distance traveled by the object in this 4.0-second interval?
(1) 36 m   (2) 24 m   (3) 16 m   (4) 4.0 m

7 An object initially at rest accelerates uniformly in a straight line at 5.0 meters per second^2, until it attains a speed of 30. meters per second. What is the total distance the object moves while accelerating?
(1) 180 m   (2) 150 m   (3) 3.0 m   (4) 90. m

8 A stone is dropped from a bridge 45 meters above the surface of a river. What is the time required for the stone to reach the water's surface? [Neglect friction.]
(1) 9.2 s   (2) 4.6 s   (3) 3.0 s   (4) 0.22 s

9 A ball is thrown straight up with a speed of 12 meters per second near the surface of Earth. What is the maximum height reached by the ball? [Neglect friction.]
(1) 15 m   (2) 7.3 m   (3) 1.2 m   (4) 0.37 m

10 An object falls freely from rest near the surface of Earth. What is the speed of the object when it has fallen 4.9 meters from its rest position?
(1) 4.9 m/s   (2) 9.8 m/s   (3) 24 m/s   (4) 96 m/s

11 Starting from rest, object A falls freely for 2.0 seconds and object B falls freely for 4.0 seconds. Compared with the distance fallen by object A, the distance fallen by object B is
(1) half as far
(2) twice as far
(3) three times as far
(4) four times as far

12 Two concurrent forces have a maximum resultant of 45 newtons and a minimum resultant of 5.0 newtons. What is the magnitude of each of these forces?
(1) 0.0 N and 45 N
(2) 5.0 N and 9.0 N
(3) 20. N and 25 N
(4) 0.0 N and 50. N

13 Two forces act concurrently on an object. The magnitude of the resultant will be greatest when the angle between the forces is
(1) 0°   (2) 60.°   (3) 90.°   (4) 180.°

14 Two concurrent forces act at right angles to each other on an object. If the magnitude of one of the forces is 40. newtons and the magnitude of the resultant of the two forces is 50. newtons, the magnitude of the other force must be
(1) 10. N   (2) 20. N   (3) 30. N   (4) 40. N

15 In the diagram below, a block is at rest on a plane inclined at an angle θ to the horizontal.

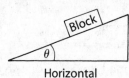

Horizontal

As angle θ is increased, what happens to the magnitude of the component of the block's weight parallel to the plane and the magnitude of the component of the block's weight perpendicular to the plane?
(1) Both components decrease.
(2) The parallel component decreases and the perpendicular component increases.
(3) The parallel component increases and the perpendicular component decreases.
(4) Both components increase.

16 Compared to 8 kilograms of feathers, 6 kilograms of lead has
(1) less mass and less inertia
(2) less mass and more inertia
(3) more mass and less inertia
(4) more mass and more inertia

17 A box, initially at rest on a level floor, is being acted upon by a horizontal force. Compared to the force required to start the box moving, the force required to keep the box moving at constant speed is
(1) smaller   (2) greater   (3) the same

18 A copper coin rests on a piece of cardboard placed on a beaker as shown in the following diagram.

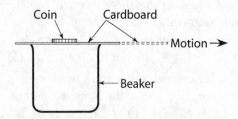

Which two properties of the coin best explain why the coin falls into the beaker when the cardboard is rapidly removed?
(1) weight and volume
(2) weight and inertia
(3) electrical resistance and volume
(4) electrical resistance and inertia

19 What is the magnitude of the force required to give an electron an acceleration of 1.00×10^2 meters per second^2?
(1) 9.11×10^{-33} N   (3) 9.11×10^{-29} N
(2) 9.11×10^{-31} N   (4) 1.10×10^{32} N

20 The diagram below shows a 4.0-kilogram object accelerating at 10. meters per second^2 on a rough horizontal surface.

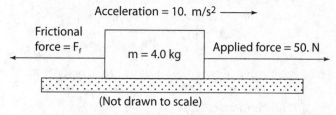

(Not drawn to scale)

What is the magnitude of the frictional force F_f acting on the object?
(1) 5.0 N   (2) 10. N   (3) 20. N   (4) 40. N

21 An object is moving on a horizontal frictionless surface. If the net force applied to the object in the direction of motion is doubled, the magnitude of the acceleration of the object is
(1) halved   (3) unchanged
(2) doubled   (4) quadrupled

22 In which situation is the net force on the object equal to zero?
(1) a satellite moving at constant speed around Earth in a circular orbit
(2) an automobile braking to a stop
(3) a bicycle moving at constant speed on a straight, level road
(4) a pitched baseball being hit by a bat

23 Equilibrium exists in a system where three forces are acting concurrently on an object. If the system includes a 5.0-newton force due north and a 2.0-newton force due south, the third force must be
(1) 7.0 N south   (3) 3.0 N south
(2) 7.0 N north   (4) 3.0 N north

24 A baseball bat moving at high speed strikes a feather. If air resistance is neglected, compared to the magnitude of the force exerted by the bat on the feather, the magnitude of the force exerted by the feather on the bat is
(1) smaller   (2) larger   (3) the same

25 A baseball player throws a ball horizontally. Which statement best describes the ball's motion after it is thrown? [Neglect friction.]
  (1) Its vertical speed remains the same and its horizontal speed increases.
  (2) Its vertical speed remains the same and its horizontal speed remains the same.
  (3) Its vertical speed increases and its horizontal speed increases.
  (4) Its vertical speed increases and its horizontal speed remains the same.

26 A red ball and a green ball are simultaneously thrown horizontally from the same height. The red ball has an initial speed of 40. meters per second and the green ball has an initial speed of 20. meters per second. Compared to the time it takes the red ball to reach the ground, the time it takes the green ball to reach the ground is
  (1) the same   (3) half as much
  (2) twice as much   (4) four times as much

27 A student throws a stone upward at an angle of 45° above the horizontal. Which statement best describes the stone at the highest point that it reaches?
  (1) Its acceleration is zero.
  (2) Its acceleration is a minimum, but not zero.
  (3) Its gravitational potential energy is a minimum.
  (4) Its kinetic energy is a minimum.

28 A projectile is launched with an initial velocity of 200 meters per second at an angle of 30° above the horizontal. What is the magnitude of the vertical component of the projectile's initial velocity?
  (1) $200 \text{ m/s} \times \cos 30°$ (3) $\dfrac{200 \text{ m/s}}{\cos 30°}$
  (2) $200 \text{ m/s} \times \sin 30°$ (4) $\dfrac{200 \text{ m/s}}{\sin 30°}$

29 An amusement park ride moves a rider at a constant speed of 14 meters per second in a horizontal circular path of radius 10. meters. What is the magnitude of the rider's centripetal acceleration in terms of g, the acceleration due to gravity?
  (1) $1\,g$ (2) $2\,g$ (3) $3\,g$ (4) $0\,g$

30 As a cart travels around a horizontal circular track, the cart must undergo a change in
  (1) velocity   (3) speed
  (2) inertia   (4) weight

31 A ball is projected horizontally to the right from a height of 50. meters, as shown in the following diagram.

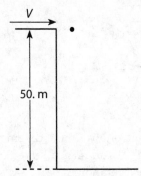

Which diagram best represents the position of the ball at 1.0-second intervals?

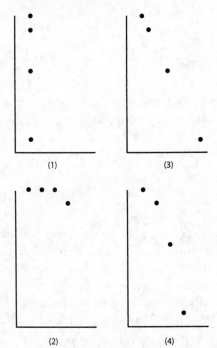

32 A convertible car with its top down is traveling at constant speed around a horizontal circular track, as shown in the following diagram.

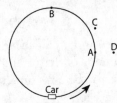

When the car is at point A, if a passenger in the car throws a ball straight up, the ball could land at point
  (1) A   (2) B   (3) C   (4) D

33 The diagram below represents a ball attached to one end of a string undergoing uniform circular motion as it travels clockwise.

At the moment shown in the diagram, what are the directions of both the ball's velocity and centripetal acceleration?

(1)   (3)

(2)   (4)

34 A satellite of mass m orbits Earth in a circular path of radius R. If centripetal force F_c is acting on the satellite, its speed is equal to

(1) $\sqrt{\dfrac{F_c R}{m}}$ (3) $\sqrt{\dfrac{F_c m}{R}}$

(2) $\dfrac{F_c R}{m}$ (4) $F_c m R$

35 If the mass of one of two particles is doubled and the distance between their centers is doubled, the magnitude of the force of attraction of one particle for the other particle is
(1) halved   (3) quartered
(2) doubled   (4) unchanged

36 What is the magnitude of the gravitational force that one 5.0-kilogram mass exerts on another 5.0-kilogram mass when the distance between their centers is 5.0 meters?
(1) 5.0×10^0 N   (3) 6.7×10^{-11} N
(2) 3.3×10^{-10} N   (4) 1.3×10^{-11} N

37 Two point masses m_1 and m_2 are located distance D apart. The magnitude of the gravitational force that m_1 exerts on m_2 can be quadrupled by changing the distance to
(1) $\frac{1}{2}D$ (2) $2D$ (3) $\frac{1}{4}D$ (4) $4D$

38 A 50-kilogram student, standing on Earth, attracts Earth with a force having a magnitude of
(1) 0 N   (3) 5×10^1 N
(2) 5 N   (4) 5×10^2 N

39 A 2.00-kilogram object weighs 19.6 newtons on Earth. If the acceleration due to gravity on Mars is 3.71 meters per second^2, what is the object's mass on Mars?
(1) 2.64 kg   (3) 19.6 N
(2) 2.00 kg   (4) 7.42 N

40 Which combination of units can be used to express the weight of an object?
(1) kilogram / second
(2) kilogram • meter
(3) kilogram • meter / second
(4) kilogram • meter / second^2

41 A 15-kilogram mass weighs 60. newtons on planet X. The mass is allowed to fall freely from rest near the surface of the planet. After falling for 6.0 seconds, the acceleration of the mass is
(1) 0.25 m/s^2 (3) 24 m/s^2
(2) 10. m/s^2 (4) 4.0 m/s^2

42 An object is allowed to fall freely from rest near the surface of a planet. If the object falls 54 meters in the first 3.0 seconds after it is released, what is the acceleration due to gravity on the planet?
(1) 6.0 m/s^2 (3) 12 m/s^2
(2) 9.8 m/s^2 (4) 18 m/s^2

43 The diagram below shows a sled and rider sliding down a snow-covered hill that makes an angle of 30.° with the horizontal.

Which vector best represents the direction of the normal force, F_N, exerted by the hill on the sled?

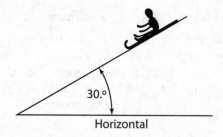

44 A different horizontal force is applied to each of four 1-kilogram blocks to slide them across a uniform horizontal steel surface at constant speed as shown. In which diagram is the coefficient of friction between the block and steel smallest?

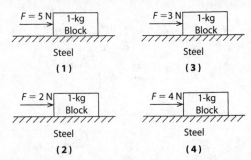

45 The magnitude of the momentum of an object is 64.0 kilogram • meters per second. If the magnitude of the velocity of the object is doubled, the magnitude of the object's momentum could be
(1) 32.0 kg • m/s
(2) 64.0 kg • m/s
(3) 128 kg • m/s
(4) 256 kg • m/s

46 A force of 20. newtons to the left is exerted on a cart for 10. seconds. For what period of time must a 50.-newton force to the right act to produce an impulse of equal magnitude on the cart?
(1) 10. s
(2) 2.0 s
(3) 5.0 s
(4) 4.0 s

47 A bullet traveling at 5.0×10^2 meters per second is brought to rest by a 50. newton • second impulse. What is the mass of the bullet?
(1) 2.5×10^4 kg
(2) 1.0×10^1 kg
(3) 1.0×10^{-1} kg
(4) 1.0×10^{-2} kg

48 A 5.0-kilogram cart traveling at 4.0 meters per second is brought to rest in 2.0 seconds. The magnitude of the average force used to stop the cart is
(1) 2.5 N
(2) 10. N
(3) 20. N
(4) 40. N

49 Two cars having different weights are traveling on a level surface at different constant velocities. Within the same time interval, greater force will always be required to stop the car that has the greater
(1) weight
(2) kinetic energy
(3) velocity
(4) momentum

50 A 0.050-kilogram bullet is fired from a 4.0-kilogram rifle which is initially at rest. If the bullet leaves the rifle with momentum having a magnitude of 20. kilogram • meters per second, the rifle will recoil with a momentum having a magnitude of
(1) 1600 kg • m/s
(2) 80. kg • m/s
(3) 20. kg • m/s
(4) 0.25 kg • m/s

51 A 2.0-kilogram toy cannon is at rest on a frictionless horizontal surface. A remote triggering device causes a 0.005-kilogram projectile to be fired from the cannon. Which equation describes the system after the cannon is fired?
(1) mass of cannon + mass of projectile = 0
(2) speed of cannon + speed of projectile = 0
(3) momentum of cannon + momentum of projectile = 0
(4) velocity of cannon + velocity of projectile = 0

52 Which pair of terms are vector quantities?
(1) force and mass
(2) distance and displacement
(3) acceleration and momentum
(4) velocity and speed

Part B

Base your answers to questions 53 through 58 on the following diagram and information. The diagram is drawn to a scale of 1.0 centimeter = 30. meters.

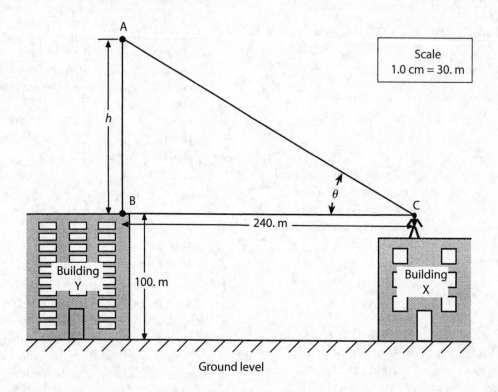

Ground level

A student on building X is located 240. meters from launch site B of a rocket on building Y. The rocket reaches its maximum altitude at point A. The student's eyes are level with the launch site on building Y. [Neglect friction.]

53 Using a protractor, measure the angle of elevation θ of the rocket. [1]

54 Determine the height h of the rocket above the student's eye level. [1]

55 Determine the total distance the rocket must fall from its maximum altitude to reach the ground. [1]

56 Calculate the total time required for the rocket to fall freely from point A back to ground level. [2]

57 Calculate the speed of the rocket as it reaches the ground after falling freely from point A. [2]

58 Sketch a graph to represent the relationship between velocity v and time t for the rocket from the time it is launched until it hits the ground. [1]

Base your answers to questions 59 through 62 on the information that follows.

A newspaper carrier on her delivery route travels 200. meters due north and then turns and walks 300. meters due east.

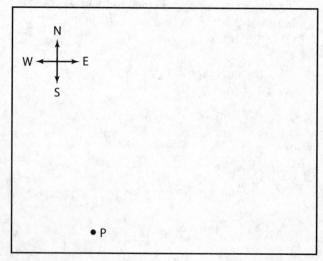

59 Using a ruler and a protractor and starting at point P, construct the sequence of two displacement vectors for the newspaper carrier's route. Use a scale of 1.0 centimeter = 50. meters. Label the vectors. [3]

60 Construct and label the vector that represents the carrier's resultant displacement from point P. [1]

61 Determine the magnitude of the carrier's resultant displacement. [1]

62 Using a protractor, measure the angle between north and the carrier's resultant displacement. [1]

Base your answers to questions 63 through 70 on the information that follows.

A stone is thrown with an initial velocity of 20. meters per second straight upward from the edge of a cliff 100. meters above a canyon floor. The stone just misses the cliff's edge on its way down. [Neglect friction.]

63 Calculate the time required for the stone to reach its maximum height. [2]

64 Calculate the maximum height of the stone above the edge of the cliff. [2]

65 Calculate the total time that elapses as the stone falls from its maximum height to the level from which it was thrown. [1]

66 What is the velocity of the stone upon returning to the level from which it was thrown? [1]

67 Calculate the velocity of the stone 6.0 seconds after it is thrown. [2]

68 Calculate the position of the stone 6.0 seconds after it is thrown. [2]

69 Sketch a graph to show the relationship between the stone's velocity and elapsed time from 0.0 second to 6.0 seconds. [1]

70 Sketch a graph to show the relationship between the stone's speed and elapsed time from 0.0 second to 6.0 seconds. [1]

Base your answers to questions 71 through 75 on the following speed-time graph, which represents the linear motion of a cart.

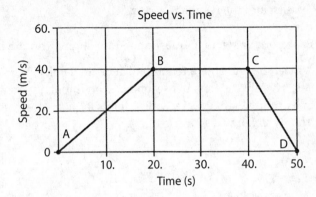

71 Calculate the magnitude of the acceleration of the cart during interval AB. [2]

72 Calculate the total distance traveled by the cart during interval ABC. [2]

73 Determine the average speed of the cart during interval CD. [1]

74 Describe the motion of the cart during interval CD. [1]

75 Identify the interval during which the net force acting on the cart is zero. [1]

Base your answers to questions 76 through 80 on the following information and vector diagram.

A 20.-newton force due north and a 40.-newton force due east act concurrently on a 10.-kilogram object located at point P.

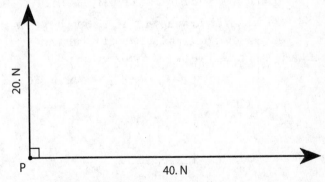

76 Use a ruler to determine the scale used in the vector diagram by finding the number of newtons represented by each centimeter. [1]

77 On the vector diagram, use a ruler and a protractor to construct the vector that represents the resultant force. [1]

78 Determine the magnitude of the resultant force. [1]

79 Using a protractor measure the angle between east and the resultant vector. [1]

80 Calculate the magnitude of the acceleration of the object. [2]

Base your answers to questions 81 through 87 on the information and diagram below.

A machine launches a tennis ball at an angle of 45° with the horizontal, as shown. The ball has an initial vertical velocity of 9.0 meters per second and an initial horizontal velocity of 9.0 meters per second. The ball reaches its maximum height 0.92 seconds after its launch. [Neglect friction and assume the ball lands at the same height from which it was launched.]

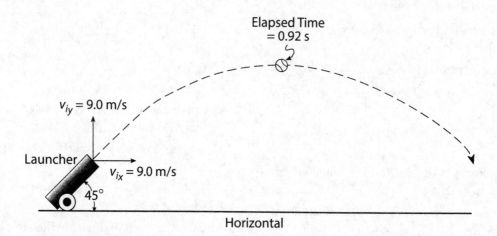

81 Calculate the speed of the ball as it leaves the launcher. [2]

82 Calculate the total horizontal distance traveled by the ball during the entire time it is in the air. [2]

83 Compare the vertical acceleration of the ball at the time of launch to the vertical acceleration of the ball at elapsed time 0.92 second. [1]

84 Sketch a graph to represent the relationship between the horizontal speed of the ball and elapsed time. [Neglect friction.]

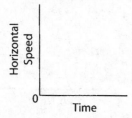

85 State the change, if any, in both the vertical component and horizontal component of the ball's velocity as it rises. [1]

86 On the diagram draw an arrow to show the direction of the ball's velocity at its maximum height. Label the arrow *v*. [1]

87 On the diagram draw an arrow to show the direction of the ball's acceleration at its maximum height. Label the arrow *a*. [1]

Base your answers to questions 88 through 93 on the following information and diagram.

A flat racetrack viewed from above has curves with radii of 50.0 meters and 100. meters. A car having a mass of 1.00×10^3 kilograms moves counterclockwise around the track at a constant speed of 20.0 meters per second. It takes the car 20.0 seconds to travel from C to D.

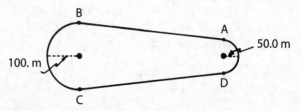

88 What is the magnitude of the net force acting on the car while it is moving from A to B? [1]

89 Calculate the net force acting on the car while it is moving from B to C. [2]

90 Calculate the distance from C to D. [2]

91 Compare the magnitude of the centripetal acceleration of the car while moving from D to A, to the magnitude of the centripetal acceleration of the car while moving from B to C. [1]

92 Compare the magnitude of the car's momentum at D to the magnitude of the car's momentum at B. [1]

93 Compare the magnitude of the centripetal acceleration of the car at A to the magnitude of the car's centripetal acceleration at A if additional passengers were riding in the car. [1]

Base your answers to questions 94 through 98 on the following information and data table.

An astronaut on a distant planet conducted an experiment to determine the gravitational acceleration on that planet. The data table shows the results of the experiment.

94 On the grid provided mark an appropriate scale on the axis labeled "Weight (N)." [1]

95 Plot the data points. [1]

96 Draw the best-fit line. [1]

97 Using the graph, calculate the acceleration due to gravity on the planet. [1]

98 On the same grid, draw a line to represent acceleration due to gravity on Earth. [2]

Base your answers to questions 99 through 104 on the following information.

A child pulls a cart with rubber wheels at constant speed across a dry, horizontal concrete surface by exerting a force of 50. newtons at an angle of 35° above the horizontal.

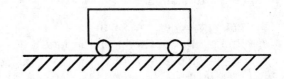

Data Table

Mass (kilograms)	Weight (newtons)
15	106
20.	141
25	179
30.	216
35	249

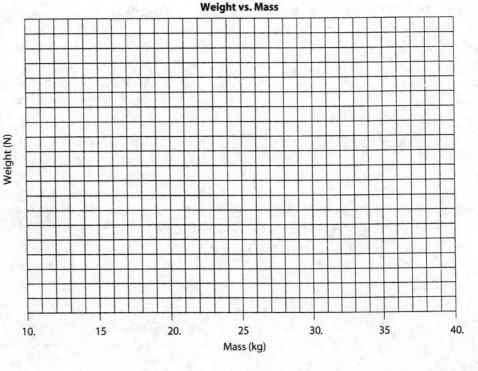

Weight vs. Mass

99 On the diagram, use a protractor and a ruler to construct a vector to represent the 50.-newton force acting on the cart. Use a scale of 1.0 centimeter = 10. newtons. Label the vector 50.-newton force and the angle 35°. [2]

100 Construct the horizontal component of the force vector to scale on the diagram and label it *H*. [1]

101 Determine the magnitude of the horizontal component of the force. [1]

102 What is the magnitude of the frictional force between the cart's rubber wheels and the concrete? [1]

103 Determine the magnitude of the normal force on the cart. [2]

104 Compare the magnitude of the normal force acting on the cart to the weight of the cart. [1]

Base your answers to questions 105 through 107 on the following information.

A block weighing 4.2 newtons, sliding from left to right in a straight line on a horizontal surface, is acted upon by a 2.4-newton friction force. The block will be brought to rest by the friction force in a distance of 4.0 meters.

105 On the diagram below, draw an arrow to identify the direction of each force on the block while it is still moving but being slowed by the friction force. Identify each force by appropriately labeling the arrow that represents its line of direction. [3]

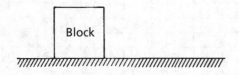

106 Calculate the magnitude of the acceleration of the block as it is brought to rest. [2]

107 Calculate the coefficient of friction between the two surfaces in contact. [2]

Base your answers to questions 108 through 110 on the following information and diagram.

Two railroad cars, A and B, are on a frictionless, level track. Car A has a mass of 2.0×10^3 kilograms and a velocity of 4.0 meters per second toward the right. Car B has a velocity of 1.5 meters per second toward the left. The magnitude of the momentum of cart B is 6.0×10^3 kilogram · meters per second. When the two cars collide, they lock together.

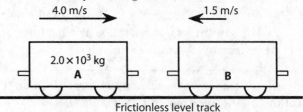

108 Calculate the magnitude of the momentum of car A before the collision. [2]

109 On the diagram below, construct a vector to represent the momentum of car A before the collision. Use a scale of 1.0 centimeter = 1.0×10^3 kilogram • meters per second [1]

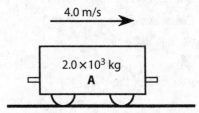

110 Describe the momentum of the two cars after the collision and justify your answer based on the initial momentum of both cars. [2]

Base your answers to questions 111 through 117 on the following information and data table.

A 1500-kilogram car is traveling due north at 24.0 meters per second when the driver sees an obstruction on the highway. The data table shows the velocity of the car at 1.0-second intervals as it is brought to rest on the straight, level highway.

Data Table	
Time (s)	Velocity (m/s)
0.0	24.0
1.0	19.0
2.0	14.0
3.0	10.0
4.0	4.0

111 Plot the data points for velocity versus time on the grid. [1]

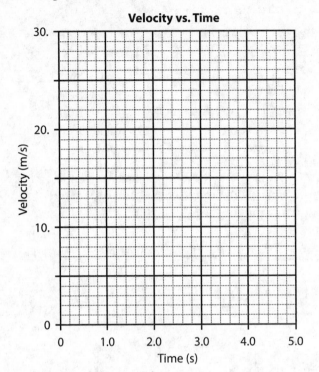

112 Draw the best-fit line. [1]

113 Using your graph, calculate the acceleration of the car. [2]

114 Using your graph, calculate the total distance traveled by the car as it is brought to rest. [2]

115 Calculate the magnitude of the car's total change in momentum as it is brought to rest. [2]

116 Calculate the magnitude and direction of the average force required to bring the car to rest. [2]

117 Compare the magnitude of the impulse imparted to the car to the magnitude of the car's change in momentum as it is brought to rest. [1]

Base your answers to questions 118 through 120 on the information and diagram below.

An object was projected horizontally from a tall cliff. The diagram below represents the path of the object, neglecting friction.

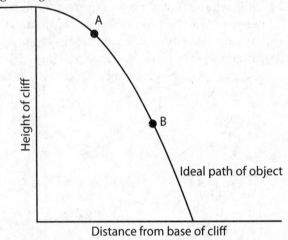

118 Compare the magnitude of the horizontal component of the object's velocity at point *A* to the magnitude of the horizontal component of the object's velocity at point *B*. [1]

119 Compare the magnitude of the vertical component of the object's velocity at point *A* to the magnitude of the vertical component of the object's velocity at point *B*. [1]

120 On the diagram sketch a likely path of the horizontally projected object, assuming it was subject to air resistance. [1]

121 The graph below represents the motion of an object traveling in a straight line as a function of time.

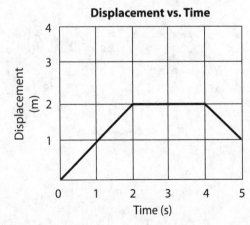

Determine the average speed of the object during the first 4.0 seconds. [1]

122 A group of bike riders took a 4.0-hour trip. During the first 3.0 hours they traveled a total of 50. kilometers, but during the last hour they traveled only 10. kilometers. Calculate the group's average speed for the entire trip. [2]

123 Which graph best represents the relationship between velocity and time for an object that has a uniform positive acceleration for 2 seconds, then moves at constant velocity for 1 second, and finally has a uniform negative acceleration for 3 seconds?

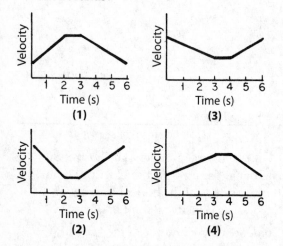

124 Which pair of graphs represents the same motion?

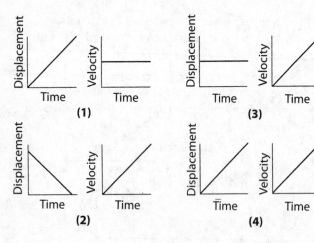

125 Which combination of graphs best describes the motion of a freely falling body? [Neglect friction.]

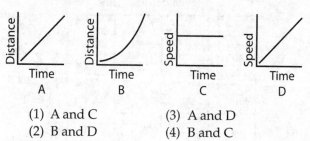

(1) A and C   (3) A and D
(2) B and D   (4) B and C

126 Which pair of forces acting concurrently on an object will produce the resultant of greatest magnitude?

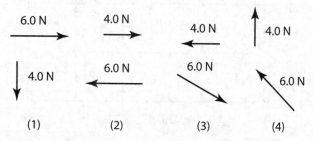

127 Two concurrent forces act on a point, as shown in the following vector diagram.

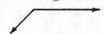

Which vector best represents their resultant?

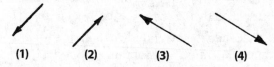

128 Two 30.-newton forces act concurrently on an object. In which diagram would the forces produce a resultant with a magnitude of 30. newtons?

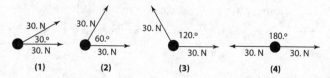

129 The vector that follows represents the resultant of two forces acting concurrently on an object at point *P*.

Which pair of vectors best represents two concurrent forces that combine to produce this resultant force vector?

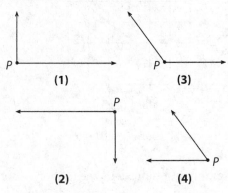

(1)   **(3)**

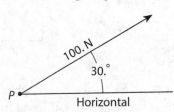

(2)   **(4)**

130 A 100.-newton force acts on point *P* as shown in the following diagram.

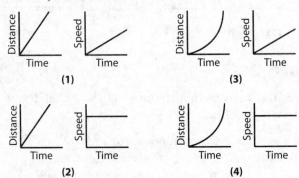

Determine the magnitude of the vertical component of this force. [1]

131 Which two graphs represent the motion of an object on which the net force is zero?

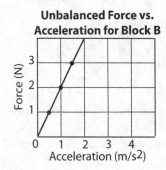

132 The following diagram represents a constant force acting on a box located on a frictionless horizontal surface.

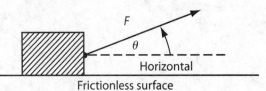

Frictionless surface

As the angle θ between the force and the horizontal is increased, the magnitude of the acceleration of the box
(1) decreases
(2) increases
(3) remains the same

133 A series of unbalanced forces was applied to each of two blocks A and B. The following graphs show the relationship between the magnitude of the unbalanced force and the magnitude of the acceleration for each block.

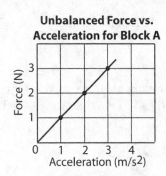

Compare the mass of block A to the mass of block B. [1]

134 The following diagram shows a block on a horizontal frictionless surface. A 100.-newton force acts on the block at an angle of 30.° above the horizontal.

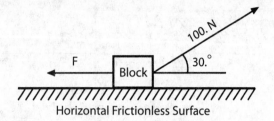

Horizontal Frictionless Surface

Calculate the magnitude of horizontal force *F* if it establishes equilibrium. [2]

135 Which graph best represents the motion of an object that is *not* in equilibrium as it travels along a straight line?

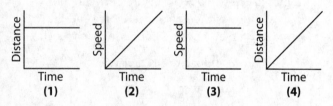

136 In the following diagram, a cyclist traveling at constant speed to the right drops a ball from her hand.

Which pair of graphs best represents the horizontal motion of the ball relative to the ground? [Neglect Friction.]

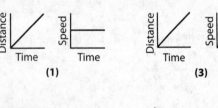

137 A projectile has an initial horizontal velocity of 15 meters per second and an initial vertical velocity of 25 meters per second. Determine the projectile's horizontal displacement if the total time of flight is 5.0 seconds. [Neglect friction.] [1]

138 The following graph shows the weight of three objects on planet X as a function of their masses.

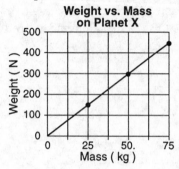

Determine the acceleration due to gravity on planet X. [1]

139 Which graph best represents the motion of an object with no unbalanced force acting on it?

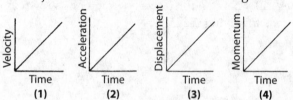

140 Which graph best represents the relationship between the mass *m* of a satellite launched from Earth and the distance *r* between the centers of the satellite and Earth?

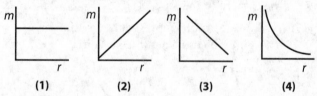

Part C

Base your answers to questions 141 and 142 on the following information.

A student walks from her house towards the bus stop, located 50. meters to the east. After walking 20. meters, she remembers that she left her lunch at the door. She runs home, picks up her lunch, walks again, and arrives at the bus stop.

141 On the grid, sketch a displacement versus time graph for the student's motion. [4]

142 Label the axes with appropriate values for time and displacement. [1]

Displacement vs. Time

Displacement

Time

Base your answers to questions 143 through 149 on the following information and data table.

Students decided to verify the value for acceleration due to gravity found in the *Reference Tables for Physical Setting/Physics* by performing a simple experiment. A ball bearing was dropped from the ceiling of the classroom and the time of fall measured. The twenty students took three measurements of the vertical distance and recorded an average value of 2.848 meters. Each student dropped the ball twice. The times of fall were recorded in the following tables, one showing the times as originally recorded and the other with the data sorted.

Unsorted		Sorted	
Time (s)		**Time (s)**	
0.97	0.87	0.50	0.76
0.86	0.75	0.56	0.77
1.00	0.68	0.57	0.77
0.81	0.72	0.61	0.77
0.98	0.78	0.66	0.78
0.77	0.77	0.67	0.78
0.87	0.80	0.68	0.78
0.87	0.75	0.68	0.80
0.88	0.77	0.69	0.80
0.71	0.78	0.69	0.81
0.73	0.69	0.69	0.83
0.72	0.69	0.71	0.86
0.78	0.68	0.72	0.87
0.76	0.87	0.72	0.87
0.75	0.75	0.73	0.87
0.76	0.50	0.75	0.87
0.69	0.57	0.75	0.88
0.83	0.67	0.75	0.97
0.56	0.66	0.75	0.98
0.80	0.61	0.76	1.00

143 What is the range of the data? [1]

144 Determine the mean of the data, to the nearest ten thousandth of a second and to the nearest hundredth of a second. [1]

145 Determine the standard deviation of the recorded values to the nearest hundredth of a second. [1]

146 What is the total number of values within one standard deviation from the mean? [1]

147 What percent of the data is within one standard deviation from the mean? [1]

148 Calculate the acceleration due to gravity on Earth based on the students' data. [2]

149 Determine the percent error. [1]

Base your answers to questions 150 through 153 on the following information and diagram.

A block weighing 100. newtons is positioned on an incline that makes an angle of 30.° with the horizontal. The magnitude of the friction force between the block and the incline is 10. newtons. A force of 120. newtons is applied by pulling on a rope that makes an angle of 30.° with the incline, as shown.

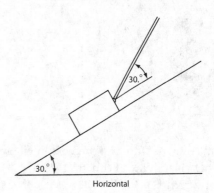

150 Draw a free-body diagram, and provide appropriate labels for each of the forces. [4]

151 Calculate the component of the block's weight parallel to the incline. [2]

152 Calculate the magnitude and direction of the component of the tension that is useful in moving the block up the incline. [2]

153 Calculate the magnitude and direction of the block's acceleration. [3]

Base your answers to questions 154 through 157 on the following information and diagrams.

A person standing on a scale in a stationary elevator weighs 735 newtons. The net force F_{net} on the person is zero because the normal force F_N is equal in magnitude but opposite in direction to the gravitational force F_g as shown.

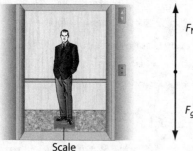

F_N

$F_{net} = 0$

F_g

Scale

154 On the following diagram, sketch an arrow to indicate the relative magnitude of the normal force on the person if the elevator is moving downward at a constant speed of 2.5 meters per second. [1]

F_g

Scale

155 What is the net force on the person when the elevator is moving at constant speed downward? [1]

156 On the following diagram, sketch an arrow to indicate the relative magnitude of the normal force on the person if the elevator is accelerating upward at 2.5 meters per second². [1]

F_g

Scale

157 Compare the reading on the scale when the elevator is accelerating upward to the reading on the scale when the elevator is stationary. [1]

Base your answers to questions 158 through 162 on the following information and diagram.

Students performed an experiment to study horizontal projectile motion. A 2.00-meter-long flexible plastic track was positioned so that one end was at the edge of a lab table and the other end was elevated, as shown.

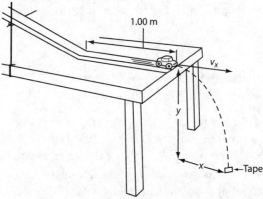

1.00 m

v_x

y

x Tape

A toy car was started from rest from the elevated end of the track and the time for the car to travel the 1.00-meter horizontal distance to the edge of the table was measured. The times for three trials were 0.453 second, 0.347 second, and 0.390 second. The car was caught as it left the tabletop. Students measured the vertical distance from the bottom of the car on the horizontal track to the floor and recorded an average distance of 0.926 meter.

158 Calculate the average horizontal speed of the car. [2]

159 Calculate the time required for the car, initially at rest, to fall freely from the tabletop to the floor. [2]

160 Calculate the horizontal distance the car would travel under these conditions if it wasn't caught. [2]

161 After having performed the calculations in questions 158 and 159, students measured the distance calculated in question 160 in a straight line from the horizontal track and directly beneath it on the floor. The spot was marked with a piece of masking tape. The car was then placed at the elevated end of the track and released from rest. State two reasons why the car landed about one centimeter short of the marked target. [2]

162 The experiment was repeated with the same car, but the elevated end of the track was positioned higher. Explain what effect releasing the car from rest at a greater height above the tabletop should have on (a) the average horizontal speed of the car [1], (b) the time required for the projected car to hit the floor after leaving the edge of the table [1], (c) the horizontal distance traveled by the car after it was projected from the tabletop [1].

Base your answers to questions 163 through 167 on the following information.

A child is moving at constant speed in a vertical circle on a ferris wheel. [Assume up is positive and down is negative.]

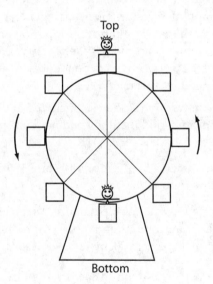

163 On the diagram, sketch and label arrows to represent the centripetal force, gravitational force, and normal force acting on the child at the bottom of the ride. [3]

164 On the diagram, sketch and label arrows to represent the three forces acting on the child at the top of the ride. [3]

165 Write an equation to show the relationship between the three forces acting on the child at the bottom of the ride. [1]

166 Write an equation to show the relationship between the three forces acting on the child at the top of the ride. [1]

167 The centripetal acceleration of a satellite in a circular orbit around Earth is produced by the gravitational force of attraction that the satellite exerts on Earth. Express the tangential speed v of the satellite in terms of the mass of Earth m_E and the distance r between the centers of the satellite and Earth. [2]

Base your answers to questions 168 through 170 on the information and diagram below.

A block of mass m slides at constant speed down a uniform plane inclined at an angle θ to the horizontal, as shown.

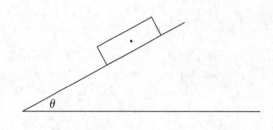

168 On the diagram, sketch and label arrows to represent the frictional force, the normal force, and the force of gravity acting on the block. [3]

169 Express the component of the block's weight parallel to the incline $F_{\parallel}$ and the component of the block's weight perpendicular to the incline $F_{\perp}$ in terms of F the weight of the block. [2]

170 Show that $\mu = \tan \theta$. [2]

Base your answers to questions 171 through 178 on the following information and diagram.

Two students, Julia and Tom, decided to perform an experiment to verify Newton's Second Law as applied to uniform circular motion; that is $F_c = \frac{mv^2}{r}$. In the lab, they collected the following materials: 15-centimeter long glass tube, fire-polished at each end and covered with rubber tubing, a piece of nylon line approximately one meter long, several two-holed rubber stoppers, a paper clip, masking tape, 36 identical iron washers, a stopwatch, and a triple-beam balance. An apparatus was assembled, with the intention of using it as shown below.

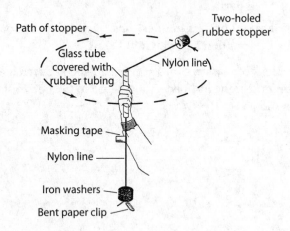

171 As the first objective Tom wrote: "To determine the relationship between the velocity of an object moving in a circular path and the magnitude of the centripetal force acting on the object." Julia objected stating they only could collect data that would enable them to determine the average speed of a rubber stopper in a circular path, but not its velocity. Identify which student was correct and explain why. [1]

172 Describe how the number of washers suspended at one end of the nylon cord could be converted into a measurement of the magnitude of the centripetal force acting on the stopper. [1]

173 To avoid having to use either the term velocity or speed, Tom changed their first objective to: "To determine the relationship between the period of revolution of an object moving in a circular path and the magnitude of the centripetal force acting on it." Using formulas found on the *Reference Tables for Physical Setting/Physics*, derive an expression for centripetal force in terms of r the radius of curvature of the path, m the object's mass, and T the period of revolution. [2]

174 List two *essential* pieces missing from their compilation of laboratory materials. [1]

175 The pair decided to time the motion of the stopper for thirty revolutions instead of making three separate trials of one revolution each and calculating an average to determine its period. Provide a rationale for this decision. [1]

176 *After securing all essential materials*, the pair proceeded with the collection of data. Julia practiced swinging the stopper overhead in a horizontal path, while keeping the radius of its path fixed. Once the technique was mastered the number of washers was varied for each trial from 36 to 4 washers in increments of 4 washers. Tom timed each event as noted in question 175. Identify four essential pieces of information that the students should have recorded in their data table. [2]

177 After the data was collected the students decided to graph their results. Sketch the general shape of the graph that should result for period of revolution versus magnitude of centripetal force. Label the axis with the dependent and independent variables. [2]

178 Explain why the students concluded at the end of the lab period that they had not had sufficient time to verify $F_c = \frac{mv^2}{r}$. [1]

Base your answers to questions 179 and 180 on the information below.

Friction provides the centripetal force that allows a 1,600-kilogram car to round a curve of radius 80. meters at a speed of 20. meters per second.

179 Calculate the minimum coefficient of friction needed between the tires and the road to round the curve. [4]

180 If the mass of the car were increased, how would that affect the maximum speed at which it could round the curve? [1]

Energy

How Scientists Study Energy

?

Does a power company sell power?

?

Both energy and work are equal to the product of power and time. Power is the time rate of doing work. A power company is always ready to supply electrical energy to its customers, but unless the energy is used, no work is done, and thus no energy is consumed. A 60-watt incandescent lamp operating for two seconds consumes twice as much energy as the same lamp operating for one second. The power company charges its customers for watt•seconds of energy or kilowatt•hours of energy rather than watts of power. One kilowatt•hour is equal to 1000 watts × 3600 seconds or 3.6×10^6 joules of energy. The kilowatt•hour meter found in a home or place of business records the total energy used by the consumer.

Vocabulary

battery	internal energy	potential energy
compression	joule	power
elastic potential energy	kinetic energy	simple pendulum
electromagnetic energy	law of conservation of energy	spring constant
elongation	mechanical energy	thermal energy
energy	motor	total energy
generator	nonideal mechanical system	watt
gravitational potential energy	nuclear energy	work
ideal mechanical system	photocell	

Work and Energy

Energy is the ability to do work. Energy is a scalar quantity. When work is done on or by a system, the total energy of the system is changed.

Work

Work is the transfer of energy to an object when the object moves due to the application of a force. The force can be entirely in the direction of the object's motion or have a component in the direction of the motion. Work is a scalar quantity. The amount of work done, W, is equal to the product of the force, F, along the direction of displacement, and the displacement d, of the object. The work done on the object produces a change in the object's total energy, ΔE_T:

$$W = Fd = \Delta E_T$$

The force F is in newtons and the displacement d is in meters. Thus, the work W or change in total energy ΔE_T can be expressed with the unit newton · meter. However, notice in the expressions below that 1 newton · meter equals 1 joule.

1 newton · meter = (1 kilogram · meter/second^2) (meter)
1 newton · meter = 1 kilogram · meter^2/second^2 = 1 joule

The **joule**, J, is a derived unit equal to the work done on an object when a force of one newton produces a displacement of one meter. Note that the amount of work done is independent of the time the force acts on the object.

When a force is applied to a mass, but the mass does not move, no work is done. If a student was to hold an object at a constant height above the ground, no work would be done no matter how heavy the object might be and how much effort the student expended.

A 2.3-kilogram block rests on a horizontal surface. A constant force with a magnitude of 5.0 newtons is applied to the block at an angle of 30.° to the horizontal, as shown in the diagram. The diagram is drawn to scale.

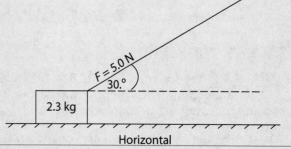

2.3 kg

Horizontal

SOLUTION: Calculate the work done in moving the block 2.0 meters to the right along the surface.

Known
$F = 5.0$ N
$m = 2.3$ kg
$d = 2.0$ m

Unknown
$F_x = ?$ N
$W = ?$ J

1. Find the component of the applied force that is in the x-direction, that is, in the direction of the displacement. There are two ways to do this.

   (a) Use the trigonometic relationship $F_x = F\cos\theta$. Substitute the known values and solve.

   $F_x = (5.0$ N$)(\cos 30.°) = 4.3$ N

   (b) Determine the scale in the diagram: 1.0 cm = 1.0 N. Project the 5.0-newton force onto the horizontal dashed line in the diagram and measure the line segment. This is the component of the applied force in the direction of motion, 4.3 N.

2. Use the formula that defines work to calculate the work done.

   $W = Fd$

3. Substitute the known values and solve.

   $W = (4.3$ N$)(2.0$ m$) = 8.6$ J

Power The rate at which work is done is a scalar quantity called **power.** By definition, power P is given by the formula $P = \frac{W}{t}$. However, $W = Fd$ and $\bar{v} = \frac{d}{t}$. Therefore, the formula can be rewritten as follows:

$$P = \frac{W}{t} = \frac{Fd}{t} = F\bar{v}$$

Ⓡ

F is the force applied to an object that causes it to move with an average speed $\bar{v}$. If work W is in joules and time t is in seconds, then power can be expressed in joules per second. One joule of work done per second equals one **watt,** W, the SI derived unit for power. If 1 watt = 1 joule/second and 1 joule = 1 kilogram · meter²/second², then 1 watt = 1 kilogram · meter²/second²/second = 1 kilogram · meter²/second³.

(Do not confuse the symbol W, which is used for the *quantity* of work, with the abbreviation W for the *unit* watt.)

Because power is inversely proportional to time, the less time required to do a given amount of work, the greater the power developed. For example, as the length of time it takes a student to swim 25 meters decreases, the power developed by the student increases.

From the definition of power, $P = \frac{W}{t}$, it follows that $W = Pt$. Thus, one watt of power used for one second transfers one joule of energy or does one joule of work. One joule is equivalent to one watt · second, and energy can be measured in watt · seconds. Electric utility companies charge their customers for kilowatt · hours of energy rather than for watts of power.

SAMPLE PROBLEM

A 7.80×10^2-newton man does 8.58×10^3 joules of work in 12.3 seconds by running up three flights of stairs to a landing vertically above his starting point. Calculate the power developed by the man during his run and his total vertical displacement.

SOLUTION: Identify the known and unknown values.

Known
$F_g = 7.80 \times 10^2$ N
$W = 8.58 \times 10^3$ J
$t = 12.3$ s

Unknown
$P = ?$ J/s or W
$d = ?$ m

1. Write the formula that defines power.

$$P = \frac{W}{t}$$

2. Substitute the known values and solve.

$$P = \frac{8.58 \times 10^3 \text{ J}}{12.3 \text{ s}} = 698 \text{ W}$$

3. To find the displacement, use the formula that defines work.

$$W = Fd$$

Solve the equation for d.

$$d = \frac{W}{F}$$

4. Substitute the known values and solve.

$$d = \frac{8.58 \times 10^3 \text{ J}}{7.80 \times 10^2 \text{ N}} = 11.0 \text{ m}$$

SAMPLE PROBLEM

A constant horizontal force of 6.0 newtons to the left is applied to a box on a counter to overcome friction. Calculate the power dissipated in moving the box 3.0 meters to the left along the counter in 1.5 seconds.

SOLUTION: Identify the known and unknown values.

Known
$F = 6.0$ N
$d = 3.0$ m
$t = 1.5$ s

Unknown
$P = ?$ W

1. Write the formula that defines power.

$$P = \frac{Fd}{t}$$

2. Substitute the known values and solve.

$$P = \frac{(6.0 \text{ N})(3.0 \text{ m})}{1.5 \text{ s}} = 12 \text{ W}$$

SAMPLE PROBLEM

In raising an object vertically at a constant speed of 2.0 meters per second, the power developed is 18 watts. Calculate the weight of the object.

SOLUTION: Identify the known and unknown values.

Known
$v = 2.0$ m/s
$P = 18$ W

Unknown
$F_g = ?$ N

1. Write the formula for power.

$$P = F\overline{v}$$

2. Solve the equation for F.

$$F = \frac{P}{v}$$

3. Substitute the known values and solve.

$$F = \frac{18 \text{ W}}{2.0 \text{ m/s}} = 9.0 \text{ N}$$

Because the object is raised at constant speed, it is in equilibrium. The force required to raise the object is equal in magnitude but opposite in direction to F_g, the weight of the object.

1. Which combination of units can be used to express work?

   (1) newton · second/meter
   (2) newton · meter/second
   (3) newton/meter
   (4) newton · meter

2. A jack exerts a vertical force of 4.5×10^3 newtons to raise a car 0.25 meter. How much work is done by the jack?

   (1) 5.6×10^{-5} J
   (2) 1.1×10^3 J
   (3) 4.5×10^3 J
   (4) 1.8×10^4 J

3. If a 2.0-kilogram mass is raised 0.050 meter vertically, the work done on the mass is approximately

   (1) 0.10 J
   (2) 0.98 J
   (3) 9.8 J
   (4) 40. J

4. A total of 640 joules of work is done on a 50.-kilogram object as it is moved 8.0 meters across a level floor by the application of a horizontal force. Determine the magnitude of the horizontal force applied to the object.

5. Work is being done when a force

   (1) acts vertically on a cart that can only move horizontally
   (2) is exerted by one team in a tug of war when there is no movement
   (3) is exerted while pulling a wagon up a hill
   (4) of gravitational attraction acts on a person standing on the surface of Earth

6. In the diagram below, a horizontal force with a magnitude of 20.0 newtons is used to push a 2.00-kilogram cart a distance of 5.00 meters along a level floor.

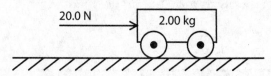

   Determine the amount of work done on the cart.

7. A constant force with a magnitude of 1.9×10^3 newtons is required to keep an automobile having a mass of 1.0×10^3 kilograms moving at a constant speed of 20. meters per second. The work done in moving the automobile a distance of 2.0×10^3 meters is

   (1) 2.0×10^4 J
   (2) 3.8×10^4 J
   (3) 2.0×10^6 J
   (4) 3.8×10^6 J

8. A student does 300. joules of work pushing a cart 3.0 meters due east and then does 400. joules of work pushing the cart 4.0 meters due north. The total amount of work done by the student is

   (1) 100. J   (3) 700. J
   (2) 500. J   (4) 2500 J

9. A constant horizontal force of 20.0 newtons east applied to a box causes it to move at a constant speed of 4.0 meters per second. Calculate how much work is done against friction on the box in 6.0 seconds.

10. A horizontal force with a magnitude of 3.0 newtons applied to a 7.0-kilogram mass moves the mass horizontally a distance of 2.0 meters. Determine the work done against gravity in moving the mass.

11. A student pulls a block along a horizontal surface at constant velocity. The diagram below shows the components of the force exerted on the block by the student.

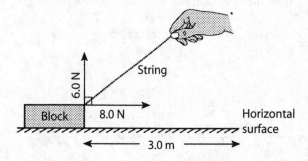

    Calculate the work done against friction.

12. A total of 8.0 joules of work is done when a constant horizontal force of 2.0 newtons to the left is used to push a 3.0-kilogram box across a counter top. Determine the total horizontal distance the box moves.

13. The diagram below shows a 9.8-newton cart being pulled 0.50 meter along a plane inclined at 15° to the horizontal. The amount of work required is 1.3 joules.

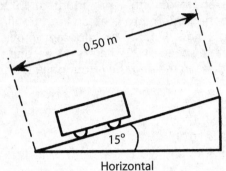

Horizontal

If the cart was raised 0.50 meter vertically instead of being pulled along the inclined plane, the amount of work done would be

(1) 0.0 J   (2) 1.3 J   (3) 4.9 J   (4) 9.8 J

14. A crane raises a 200-newton weight to a height of 50 meters in 5 seconds. The crane does work at the rate of

(1) 8×10^{-1} W   (3) 2×10^3 W
(2) 2×10^1 W   (4) 5×10^4 W

15. What is the maximum amount of work that a 5000.-watt motor can do in 10. seconds?

(1) 5.0×10^1 J   (3) 5.0×10^3 J
(2) 5.0×10^2 J   (4) 5.0×10^4 J

16. An engine rated at 5.0×10^4 watts exerts a constant force of 2.5×10^3 newtons on a vehicle. Determine the average speed of the vehicle.

17. The diagram below shows a 1.0×10^3-newton crate to be lifted at constant speed from the ground to a loading dock 1.5 meters high in 5.0 seconds.

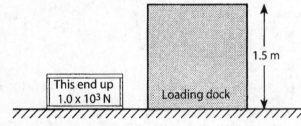

What power is required to lift the crate?

(1) 1.5×10^3 W   (3) 3.0×10^2 W
(2) 2.0×10^2 W   (4) 7.5×10^3 W

18. What is the average power developed by a motor as it lifts a 400.-kilogram mass at a constant speed through a vertical distance of 10.0 meters in 8.0 seconds?

(1) 320 W   (3) 4,900 W
(2) 500 W   (4) 32,000 W

19. Determine the power developed by a man weighing 6.0×10^2 newtons who climbs a rope at a constant speed of 2.0 meters per second.

20. Student A lifts a 40.-newton box from the floor to a height of 0.30 meter in 2.0 seconds. Student B lifts a 30.-newton box from the floor to a height of 0.40 meter in 4.0 seconds. Compared to student A, student B does

(1) less work but develops more power
(2) more work but develops less power
(3) the same work but develops less power
(4) the same work but develops more power

21. A 5.0×10^2-newton girl develops 250 watts of power as she runs up two flights of stairs to a landing a total of 5.0 meters vertically above her starting point. Calculate the time required for the girl to run up the stairs.

22. A motor having a maximum power rating of 8.1×10^4 watts is used to operate an elevator with a weight of 1.8×10^4 newtons. What is the maximum weight this motor can lift at an average speed of 3.0 meters per second?

(1) 6.0×10^3 N   (3) 2.4×10^4 N
(2) 1.8×10^4 N   (4) 2.7×10^4 N

23. A girl weighing 500. newtons takes 50.0 seconds to climb a flight of stairs 18 meters high. Calculate the girl's vertical power output.

24. If the time required for a student to swim 500. meters is doubled, the power developed by the student will be

(1) halved
(2) doubled
(3) quartered
(4) quadrupled

25. Calculate the average speed of a 4.0×10^2-newton weight being lifted vertically by a 2.00×10^3-watt motor.

Forms of Energy

As already noted, energy and work are related. The joule is the SI unit for both quantities, which are scalar. When one system does work on another system, the second system gains an amount of energy equal to the amount of work done on it. This process is called a transfer of energy.

Energy has many forms, including thermal, chemical, nuclear, electromagnetic, sound, and mechanical. Whatever its form, energy is measured by the amount of work it can do. **Thermal energy,** or heat, is the total kinetic energy possessed by the individual particles that comprise an object. (The term "thermal energy" is also used by nuclear physicists to describe the average kinetic energy, 0.025 electronvolt, possessed by neutrons at room temperature.)

Internal energy refers to the total potential energy and kinetic energy possessed by the particles that make up an object, but excludes the potential and kinetic energies of the system as a whole.

Nuclear energy is the energy released by nuclear fission, the division of a heavy atomic nucleus into parts of comparable mass, or nuclear fusion, the combining of two light nuclei to form a heavier nucleus.

Electromagnetic energy is the energy associated with electric or magnetic fields. Electromagnetic energy can take many forms, such as visible light, microwaves, and radio waves.

Devices for Converting Energy

A **photocell** (photovoltaic cell) is a device that converts light, a form of electromagnetic radiation, into electrical energy. A **generator** is a device that converts mechanical energy into electrical energy by rotating a large coil of wire in a magnetic field. On the other hand, a **motor** is a device that converts electrical energy into mechanical energy as a result of forces on a current-carrying conductor in a magnetic field. A **battery** is a direct-current voltage source that converts chemical, thermal, nuclear, or solar energy into electrical energy.

Potential Energy

The energy possessed by an object due to its position or condition is called **potential energy.** If there is no energy lost due to friction, the work done to bring the object to a different position or condition from its original condition or position is equal to the object's change in potential energy.

Gravitational Potential Energy If an object, originally at rest on Earth's surface, is lifted to some height, work is done *against* gravitational force. The work done in lifting the object to a height above Earth's surface is equal to the object's **gravitational potential energy** relative to Earth's surface. The work done is equal to the gravitational potential energy acquired by the object. If the object falls, work is done *by* gravity on the object, and the object loses gravitational potential energy. However, the work done by gravity on the object increases its energy of motion (kinetic energy) as the object's speed increases during its fall. This kinetic energy can, in turn, do an amount of work equal to the loss in gravitational potential energy.

Recall that work is described by the formula $W = Fd$. For a falling object, F equals F_g, the weight of the object given by the formula $F_g = mg$, and the displacement d corresponds to Δh, the change in height. Thus, the change in gravitational potential energy is given by the formula:

$$\Delta PE = mg\Delta h$$

The mass m is in kilograms, g is the acceleration due to gravity in meters per second^2 (or gravitational field strength in newtons per kilogram), and Δh is the change in height of the mass in meters. Thus ΔPE, the change in gravitational potential energy, can be expressed in kilogram · meter^2 per second^2 or joules. The change in gravitational potential energy of an object equals the product of its weight, mg, and its vertical change in height. This formula is valid only for displacements that are small compared to Earth's radius, so that g can be considered constant.

SAMPLE PROBLEM

Calculate the gravitational potential energy with respect to the floor gained by a 2.00-kilogram object as a result of being lifted from the floor to the top of a 0.92-meter high table.

SOLUTION: Identify the known and unknown values.

Known	Unknown
$m = 2.00$ kg	$\Delta PE = ?$ J
$h = 0.92$ m	
$g = 9.81$ m/s^2	

1. Write the formula for gravitational potential energy.

$\Delta PE = mg\Delta h$

2. Substitute the known values and solve.

$\Delta PE = (2.00 \text{ kg})(9.81 \text{ m/s}^2)(0.92 \text{ m}) = 18$ J

SAMPLE PROBLEM

A 15.3-newton book gains 18.4 joules of gravitational potential energy with respect to the floor as a result of being lifted from the floor to a shelf. Calculate the height of the shelf above the floor.

SOLUTION: Identify the known and unknown values.

Known	Unknown
$F_g = 15.3$ N	$\Delta h = ?$ m
$\Delta PE = 18.4$ J	

1. Write the formula for gravitational potential energy and solve for Δh.

$\Delta PE = mg\Delta h$

$\Delta h = \dfrac{\Delta PE}{mg}$

2. Substitute the known values and solve. The weight of the object, F_g, equals mg.

$\Delta h = \dfrac{18.4 \text{ J}}{15.3 \text{ N}} = 1.20$ m

26. Which term identifies a scalar quantity?

   (1) force   (3) displacement
   (2) energy   (4) velocity

27. Energy is measured in the same units as

   (1) force   (2) momentum   (3) power   (4) work

28. Which quantity and unit are correctly paired?

   (1) velocity; m/s^2 (3) energy; $kg \cdot m^2/s^2$
   (2) momentum;   (4) work; kg/m
       $kg \cdot m/s^2$

29. A unit for gravitational potential energy is the

   (1) watt   (3) newton
   (2) joule   (4) kilogram · meter/
                second

30. Which mass has the greatest gravitational potential energy with respect to the floor?

   (1) a 50.-kg mass resting on the floor
   (2) a 2.0-kg mass 10. m above the floor
   (3) a 10.-kg mass 2.0 m above the floor
   (4) a 6.0-kg mass 5.0 m above the floor

31. As an object slides across a rough horizontal surface, what happens to the object's gravitational potential energy with respect to the surface and speed?

   (1) Both gravitational potential energy and speed decrease.
   (2) Gravitational potential energy decreases and speed remains the same.
   (3) Gravitational potential energy remains the same and speed decreases.
   (4) Both gravitational potential energy and speed remain the same.

32. The diagram below represents a cart traveling with initial speed *v* from left to right along a frictionless surface.

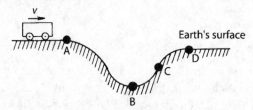

At which point is the gravitational potential energy of the cart least?

   (1) A   (2) B   (3) C   (4) D

33. Calculate the gravitational potential energy with respect to Earth's surface gained by a 5.00-kilogram mass as a result of being raised 2.00 meters from Earth's surface.

34. Which graph best represents the relationship between the gravitational potential energy *PE* with respect to the ground and height above the ground *h* for a freely falling object released from rest?

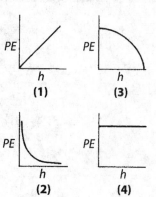

35. Three people of equal mass climb a mountain using paths A, B, and C shown in the diagram below.

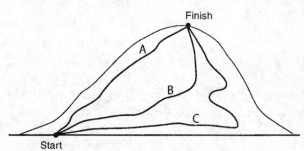

Along which path(s) does a person gain the greatest amount of gravitational potential energy from start to finish?

   (1) A only
   (2) B only
   (3) C only
   (4) The gain is the same along all paths.

36. A ball is thrown upward from Earth's surface. As the ball rises, what happens to its speed and gravitational potential energy with respect to Earth's surface?

   (1) Both speed and gravitational potential energy decrease.
   (2) Speed decreases and gravitational potential energy increases.
   (3) Speed increases and gravitational potential energy decreases.
   (4) Both speed and gravitational potential energy increase.

37. At the top of a frictionless inclined plane, a 0.50-kilogram block of ice possesses 6.0 joules of gravitational potential energy with respect to the bottom of the incline. After sliding halfway down the plane, the block's gravitational potential energy is

(1) 0.0 J   (2) 6.0 J   (3) 3.0 J   (4) 12 J

38. When a 5-kilogram mass is lifted from the ground to a height of 10 meters, the gravitational potential energy of the mass is increased by approximately

(1) 0.5 J   (3) 50 J
(2) 2 J   (4) 500 J

Elastic Potential Energy

The energy stored in a spring, when work is done in compressing or stretching it, is called **elastic potential energy.** The **compression** or **elongation** of a spring is the change in spring length from its equilibrium position when a force is applied to it. Provided the elastic limit of the spring is not exceeded, the compression or elongation of a spring is directly proportional to the applied force. This relationship, called Hooke's law, is given by the formula:

$$F_s = kx$$

In the equation, k is the **spring constant,** the constant of proportionality between the applied force F_s and the compression or elongation x of the spring. If F_s is in newtons and x is in meters, then k is in newtons per meter. The SI unit for the spring constant is the newton/meter, N/m.

A common laboratory activity is to vary the force applied to a spring and measure the resulting elongation or compression. Force is the independent variable and change in spring length is the dependent variable. However, force is often indicated on the vertical axis and change in spring length on the horizontal axis when the data from the experiment is graphed. If a graph of F_s versus x is plotted for the data collected for a given spring, the slope of the line of best fit is equal to the spring constant for that spring. For an ideal spring, the line is straight and passes through the origin. A stiff spring has a larger value of k than a weak spring.

If F_s versus x data for two different springs is plotted on the same grid and best-fit lines are drawn, the line for the stiffer spring has the greater slope. On the other hand, if change in spring length from its equilibrium position x is indicated on the vertical axis and the force applied to the spring F_s on the horizontal axis, the slope of the line of best fit is equal to $1/k$, the reciprocal of the spring constant. In this case the line for the stiffer spring has the lesser slope.

Potential Energy of a Spring

When no force is applied to a spring, there is no change in spring length from the equilibrium position. That is, when $F_s = 0$ N, $x = 0$ m. According to Hooke's law, as F_s increases, x increases. Because F_s increases uniformly from 0 to kx, the *average* applied force equals $\frac{1}{2}kx$. The work done in stretching the spring is equal to the product of the *average* force $\overline{F}_s$ and the elongation x.

SAMPLE PROBLEM

1. In an experiment, a student varied the force applied to a vertically-hung spring and measured the resulting elongation. The table shows the average elongation for three trials with each force.

Force (N)	Average Elongation (m)
0.00	0.000
1.00	0.040
2.00	0.075
3.00	0.120
4.00	0.165
5.00	0.200

2. Using the information in the data table and the grid provided:
(1) Mark an appropriate scale on the axis labeled "Average elongation (m)".
(2) Plot the data points.
(3) Draw the line of best fit.
(4) Use your graph to calculate the spring constant *k*.

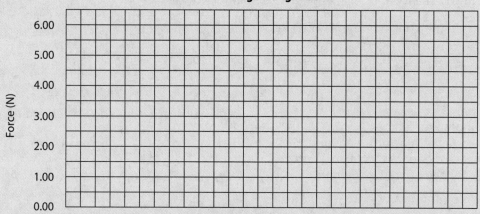

Force vs. Average Elongation

SOLUTION: The spring constant *k* is the slope of the line.

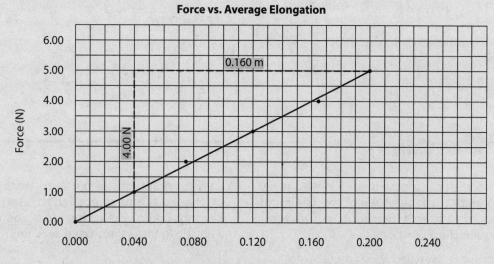

Force vs. Average Elongation

$$k = \frac{\Delta F}{\Delta x} = \frac{4.00 \text{ N}}{0.160 \text{ m}} = 25.0 \text{ N/m}$$

$$W = \overline{F}_s\, x = \frac{1}{2}\, kx \cdot x = \frac{1}{2}\, kx^2$$

Because the work done on the spring is equal to the spring's elastic potential energy PE_s, the equation can be rewritten in this way:

$$PE_s = \frac{1}{2}\, kx^2$$

®

The spring constant k is in newtons per meter, the change in spring length from the equilibrium position x is in meters, and the potential energy stored in the spring PE_s is in newton · meters, or joules. As the following Sample Problem shows, the area under an F_s versus x curve yields a number equal to the number of joules of work done in stretching the spring, and thus, the potential energy stored in the spring.

SAMPLE PROBLEM

Calculate the elastic potential energy stored in the spring in the previous Sample Problem when a force of 2.50 newtons is applied to it.

SOLUTION: Identify the known and unknown values.

Known
$F_s = 2.50$ N
$k = 25.0$ N/m

Unknown
$PE_s = ?$ J

1. Find A_Δ, the area under the curve in the previous Sample Problem. At $F = 2.50$ N the area is a triangle with height h equal to 2.50 N and base b equal to 0.100 m. Write the formula for the area of a triangle.

$$A_\Delta = \frac{1}{2}\, bh$$

2. Substitute the known values and solve.

$$A_\Delta = PE_s = \frac{1}{2}\,(0.100\text{ m})(2.50\text{ N})$$

$$PE_s = 0.125\text{ J}$$

An alternative solution is to use the relationship

$$F_s = kx$$

3. Solve the equation for x.

$$x = \frac{F_s}{k}$$

4. Substitute the known values and solve.

$$x = \frac{2.50\text{ N}}{25.0\text{ N/m}} = 0.100\text{ m}$$

5. Write the formula that relates PE_s and x.

$$PE_s = \frac{1}{2}\, kx^2$$

6. Substitute the known values and solve.

$$PE_s = \frac{1}{2}\,(25.0\text{ N})(0.100\text{ m})^2$$

$$PE_s = 0.125\text{ J}$$

Review Questions

39. A spring has a spring constant of 25 newtons per meter. Calculate the magnitude of the minimum force required to stretch the spring 0.25 meter from its equilibrium position.

40. When a spring is stretched 0.200 meter from its equilibrium position, it possesses a potential energy of 10.0 joules. What is the spring constant for this spring?

(1) 100. N/m   (3) 250. N/m
(2) 125 N/m   (4) 500. N/m

41. Which graph best represents the relationship between the force applied to a spring and the elongation of the spring? (Assume the spring's elastic limit has not been reached.)

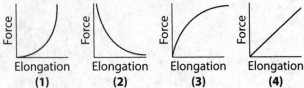

42. A 20.-newton weight is attached to a spring causing it to stretch, as shown in the diagram below.

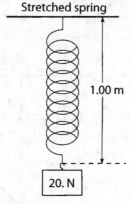

Unstretched spring   Stretched spring

0.50 m

1.00 m

20. N

What is the spring constant of this spring?

(1) 0.050 N/m   (3) 20. N/m
(2) 0.25 N/m   (4) 40. N/m

43. The graph below shows the relationship between the elongation of a spring and the force applied to the spring causing it to stretch.

Elongation vs. Applied Force

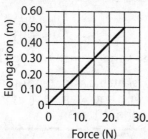

What is the spring constant for this spring?

(1) 0.020 N/m   (3) 25 N/m
(2) 2.0 N/m   (4) 50. N/m

44. A mass hanger is attached to a spring, as shown in the diagrams below.

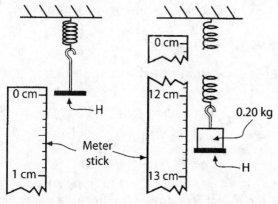

Unloaded   Loaded

What is the magnitude of the displacement of the mass hanger H after a 0.20-kilogram mass is loaded on it? [Assume the hanger is at rest in both positions.]

45. Graphs A and B represent the results of applying an increasing force to stretch a spring. The spring did not exceed its elastic limit.

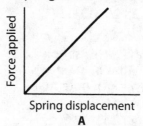 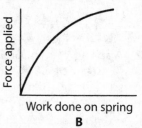

A   B

The spring constant can be represented by the

(1) slope of graph A
(2) slope of graph B
(3) reciprocal of the slope of graph A
(4) reciprocal of the slope of graph B

46. Force F is applied to a spring causing it to stretch a distance x. If force 2F is applied to the spring and the elasticity of the spring is not exceeded, the spring will stretch a distance

(1) x   (3) $\frac{x}{2}$
(2) 2x   (4) $\frac{x}{4}$

47. Which combination of fundamental units can be used to express the elastic potential energy stored in a compressed spring?

(1) $kg \cdot m/s^2$
(2) $kg \cdot m^2/s$
(3) $kg \cdot m^2/s^2$
(4) $kg \cdot m^2/s^3$

48. A force is applied to a spring causing it to stretch. If the applied force is halved, the potential energy stored in the spring will be

(1) halved
(2) doubled
(3) quartered
(4) quadrupled

49. A vertically hung 0.50-meter-long spring is stretched from its equilibrium position to a length of 1.00 meter by a weight attached to the spring. If 15 joules of elastic potential energy are stored in the spring, what is the value of the spring constant?

(1) 30. N/m
(2) 60. N/m
(3) 120 N/m
(4) 240 N/m

50. A spring has a spring constant of 120 newtons per meter. Calculate the elastic potential energy stored in the spring when it is stretched 2.0 centimeters.

51. A force of 0.2 newton is needed to compress a spring a distance of 0.02 meter. The potential energy stored in this compressed spring is

(1) 8×10^{-5} J   (3) 2×10^{-5} J
(2) 2×10^{-3} J   (4) 4×10^{-5} J

52. A spring of negligible mass with a spring constant of 2.0×10^2 newtons per meter is stretched 0.20 meter. How much potential energy is stored in the spring?

(1) 8 J   (3) 4 J
(2) 8.0 J   (4) 4.0 J

53. In the diagram below, a child compresses the spring in a pop-up toy 0.020 meter.

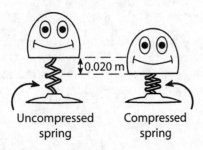

Uncompressed   Compressed
spring   spring

If the spring has a spring constant of 340 newtons per meter, how much elastic potential energy is being stored in the spring?

(1) 0.068 J   (3) 3.4 J
(2) 0.14 J   (4) 6.8 J

Base your answers to questions 54 through 56 on the graph below, which represents the relationship between the force applied to a spring and its elongation.

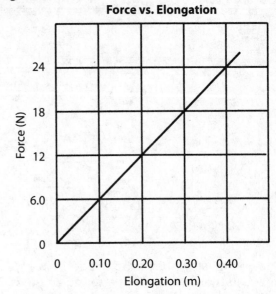

54. What is the total work done to stretch the spring 0.40 meter?

(1) 4.8 J   (3) 9.8 J
(2) 6.0 J   (4) 24 J

55. Calculate the spring constant k for the spring.

56. On the grid, sketch a line that represents the relationship between applied force and elongation for a stiffer spring.

Kinetic Energy

When a moving object strikes another object and displaces it, the moving object exerts a force on the second object and does work on it. The moving object possesses energy due to its motion. The energy an object possesses due to its motion is called **kinetic energy**. The formula for kinetic energy is $KE = \frac{1}{2}mv^2$ and can be derived from the definition of work and Newton's second law.

$$W = Fd \text{ and } F = ma$$

$$W = mad \text{ where } a = \frac{v}{t} \text{ from rest, } d = \bar{v}t \text{ and}$$

$$\bar{v} = \frac{v}{2} \text{ from rest.}$$

$$W = m \cdot \frac{v}{t} \cdot \bar{v}t = m \cdot \frac{v}{t} \cdot \frac{v}{2} \cdot t = \frac{1}{2}mv^2$$

The net work done in accelerating an object from rest to some speed is equal to the kinetic energy of the object. The following formula describes the relationship:

$$KE = \frac{1}{2}mv^2$$

Mass m is in kilograms, velocity or speed v is in meters per second, and kinetic energy KE is in kilogram $\cdot$ meter^2/second^2 or joules.

SAMPLE PROBLEM

Calculate the kinetic energy possessed by a 2.7-kilogram cart traveling at 1.5 meter per second.

SOLUTION: Identify the known and unknown values.

Known
$m = 2.7$ kg
$v = 1.5$ m/s

Unknown
$KE = ?$ J

1. Write the formula for kinetic energy.

$KE = \dfrac{1}{2}mv^2$

2. Substitute the known values and solve.

$KE = \dfrac{1}{2}(2.7 \text{ kg})(1.5 \text{ m/s})^2 = 3.0$ J

Note: If the weight of the cart had been given, it would have been necessary to use the formula

$g = \dfrac{F_g}{m}$ to determine the cart's mass.

Review Questions

57. If the speed of a car is doubled, its kinetic energy is

(1) halved
(2) doubled
(3) quartered
(4) quadrupled

58. A 1.0×10^3-kilogram car is moving at a constant speed of 4.0 meters per second. What is the kinetic energy of the car?

(1) 1.6×10^3 J
(2) 2.0×10^4 J
(3) 8.0×10^3 J
(4) 4.0×10^3 J

59. A 3.0-kilogram cart possesses 96 joules of kinetic energy. Calculate the speed of the car.

60. A cart of mass m traveling at speed v has kinetic energy KE. If the mass of the cart is doubled and the speed is halved, the kinetic energy of the cart will be

(1) half as great
(2) twice as great
(3) one-fourth as great
(4) four times as great

61. Which cart has the greatest kinetic energy?

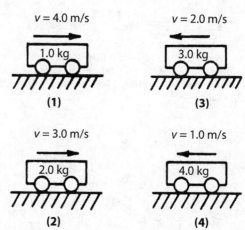

62. A 2.0-kilogram cart is initially at rest on a level floor. Determine the kinetic energy of the cart after a constant horizontal 8.0-newton force is applied to the cart over a distance of 1.5 meters.

63. A person does 100 joules of work in pulling back the string of a bow. What is the initial speed of a 0.5-kilogram arrow when it is fired from the bow?

(1) 20 m/s   (3) 200 m/s
(2) 50 m/s   (4) 400 m/s

64. An 8.0-kilogram object and a 4.0-kilogram object are released simultaneously from a height of 50. meters above the ground. After falling freely for 2.0 seconds, the objects have different

(1) accelerations   (3) kinetic energies
(2) speeds   (4) displacements

65. The work done in raising an object must result in an increase in the object's

(1) internal energy
(2) kinetic energy
(3) gravitational potential energy
(4) elastic potential energy

66. Two cars having different weights are traveling on a level surface at different constant velocities. Within the same time interval, greater force is always required to stop the car that has the greater

(1) weight   (3) velocity
(2) kinetic energy   (4) momentum

Work-Energy Relationship

If there is no friction, all the work done in lifting an object to a new height is equal to the object's increase in gravitational potential energy. The change in potential energy depends only on the change in height, not on the path taken. For example, the work done in lifting a 10.0-kilogram box from the floor to a 0.92-meter high tabletop is equal to the box's change in gravitational potential energy.

$$W = \Delta PE = mg\Delta h = (10.0 \text{ kg})(9.81 \text{ m/s}^2)(0.92 \text{ m}) = 90. \text{ J}$$

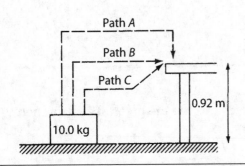

Figure 3-1. A conservative force: Because the force of gravity is a conservative force, the same amount of work is done when raising the box from the floor to the tabletop regardless of which path is followed.

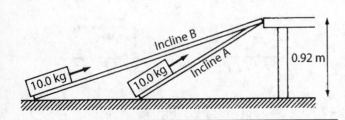

Figure 3-2. A nonconservative force: Because friction is a nonconservative force, moving the box from the floor to the tabletop requires more work on incline B than on incline A. In this case, the path makes a difference in the amount of work required. (Read the explanation in the text.)

Figure 3-1 shows that the work done in moving the box from the floor to the tabletop is the same regardless of the path taken. When work done against a force is independent of the path taken, the force is said to be a <u>conservative force</u>. The force of gravity is an example of a conservative force. The elastic force of a spring is also a conservative force. Potential energy has meaning only in relation to work done against conservative forces.

Air resistance and friction are examples of <u>nonconservative forces</u>. The work done against a nonconservative force is dependent upon the path taken. In Figure 3-2, the same box is moved from the floor to the tabletop by sliding it along an inclined plane A. Once again, 90. joules of work is done to change the gravitational potential energy of the box, but because additional work must be done against friction, the total work done is greater than 90. joules.

If inclined plane B is used instead of inclined plane A, the work done against friction, $W_f = F_f d$, is greater, even though the coefficient of friction is the same for both planes. The force of friction F_f is greater when a plane is inclined at a smaller angle because the normal force F_N for the same object on the incline is larger and $F_f = \mu F_N$. In addition, the frictional force acts over a greater distance on incline B. Because friction is a nonconservative force, the work required to raise the box from the floor to the top of the table on incline B is greater than the work required to raise it on incline A.

Conservation of Energy

A closed system is one in which there are no external forces doing work on the system, no external work being done by the system, and no transfer of energy into or out of the system. In a closed system, the sum of the potential energy (gravitational and/or elastic), kinetic energy, and internal energy remains constant. Although the energy within a closed system may be transformed from one type to another, the total energy of the system always remains the same. These ideas are expressed in the **law of conservation of energy,** which states that energy cannot be created or destroyed. In other words, the sum of the *changes* in energy (potential, kinetic, and internal) within a closed system is zero.

Ideal Mechanical Systems

The sum of the kinetic and potential energies in a system is called the total **mechanical energy.** An **ideal mechanical system** is a closed system in which no friction or other nonconservative force acts. In an ideal mechanical system, the sum of the kinetic and potential energies is constant, or the sum of the *changes* in kinetic and potential energy is zero.

The relationship between the gravitational potential energy and kinetic energy for an ideal simple pendulum is shown in Figure 3-3. A **simple pendulum** consists of a mass (bob) attached to one end of a string or wire that is attached at the other end to a pivot point.

An object falling freely from rest in a vacuum is another example of an ideal mechanical system. If a stationary object having mass m is located a vertical distance h above Earth's surface, the object has initial gravitational potential energy, $PE_i = mgh$ with respect to Earth and kinetic energy, $KE_i = 0$. As the object falls, its gravitational potential energy decreases, but because its speed increases, the object's kinetic

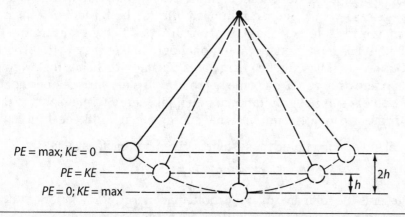

Figure 3-3. **The relationship between gravitational potential energy with respect to the lowest point and kinetic energy for an ideal simple pendulum**

energy increases. These energy changes can be expressed by the law of conservation of energy:

$$\Delta PE + \Delta KE = 0$$

or

$$\Delta KE = -\Delta PE$$

As the object falls from rest, its change in gravitational potential energy is given by $\Delta PE = -mgh$, and its change in kinetic energy is $\Delta KE = \frac{1}{2}mv^2$. These expressions can be substituted into the previous equations:

$$\frac{1}{2}mv^2 - mgh = 0$$

or

$$\frac{1}{2}mv^2 = mgh$$

The common factor, m, can be eliminated:

$$\frac{1}{2}v^2 = gh, \text{ so } v^2 = 2gh \text{ and } v = \sqrt{2gh}$$

The acceleration due to gravity, g, can be considered constant near Earth's surface, so the last equation can be used to determine the speed of an object falling from rest from a known height. Note that the speed of the object is independent of its mass.

Nonideal Mechanical Systems

When a system is acted upon by a nonconservative force, such as friction, it is called a **nonideal mechanical system.** In reality, friction opposes the motion of two objects in contact with each other and moving relative to each other. Frictional force converts some or all of the kinetic energy of a moving object into internal energy, that is, potential or kinetic energy of the individual particles that comprise the object. The "lost" kinetic energy usually appears as an increase in temperature of the objects in contact. For example, a simple pendulum set in motion in air does not swing back to its original release point. The pendulum experiences both friction at the pivot point and air resistance. A piece of paper dropped to the ground from some height has more initial gravitational potential energy with respect to the ground than it has kinetic energy at the instant it reaches the ground. A lead sphere dropped from some height onto a steel surface does not bounce; all of its initial gravitational potential energy with respect to the steel surface is converted into internal energy when it hits the steel.

The **total energy** of a nonideal system is given by this formula:

$$E_T = PE + KE + Q$$

Ⓡ

E_T represents the total energy, PE is potential energy, KE is kinetic energy, and Q is internal energy. All quantities are expressed in joules.

A 1.0-kilogram cart A and a 2.0-kilogram cart B are at rest on a frictionless table, as shown in the diagram. A cord and a spring of negligible mass join the two carts. The spring is compressed 0.060 meter between the two carts until the elastic's potential energy stored in the spring is 12 joules. When the cord is cut, the spring will force the carts apart.

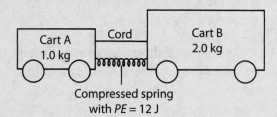

Cart A
1.0 kg

Cord

Cart B
2.0 kg

Compressed spring
with $PE = 12$ J

(1) Determine the total amount of work done in compressing the spring.
(2) Calculate the spring constant for the spring.
(3) Calculate the magnitude of the average force required to compress the spring 0.060 meter.
(4) Compare the following quantities while the spring is pushing the carts apart:
    (a) the forces acting on the two carts
    (b) the change in momentum of the two carts
    (c) the total initial and final momentum of the two carts
    (d) the acceleration of the two carts
(5) Calculate the final velocity of cart A.
(6) Determine the ratio of the maximum kinetic energy of cart A to the maximum kinetic energy of cart B.

SOLUTION: Identify the known and unknown values.

Known
$m_A = 1.0$ kg
$m_B = 2.0$ kg
$x = 0.060$ m
$PE_s = 12$ J

Unknown
$W = ?$ J
$k = ?$ N/m
$F_s = ?$ N
$v_{f_A} = ?$ m/s

1. The work done in compressing the spring is equal to the potential energy stored in the spring.

$W = PE_s = 12$ J

2. Write the formula for the potential energy of a spring.

$$PE_s = \frac{1}{2}kx^2$$

Solve the equation for k.

$$k = \frac{2PE_s}{x^2}$$

Substitute the known values and solve.

$$k = \frac{2(12\text{ J})}{(0.060\text{ m})^2}$$

$k = 6.7 \times 10^3$ N/m

3. Write the formula for the average force needed to compress the spring.

$F_s = kx$

Substitute the known values and solve.

$F_s = (6.7 \times 10^3$ N/m$)(0.060$ m$)$
$F_s = 4.0 \times 10^2$ N

4. The forces are equal in magnitude and opposite in direction.

Momentum must be conserved. Thus, the change in momentum is equal in magnitude and opposite in direction for the two carts at all times.

The total momentum is zero at all times, because the carts were initially at rest.

The forces on the two carts are equal in magnitude and the mass of A is one half the mass of B. Thus, the acceleration of cart A is twice that of cart B and opposite in direction.

5. Write an equation for the relationship between the initial and final momentum of the system. Because momentum must be conserved, the initial momentum of the system, which is zero, must equal the final momentum.

$$p_{before} = p_{after} = 0$$

Write this equality in terms of mass and velocity.

$$m_A v_A + m_B v_B = 0$$

Solve the equation for v_B.

$$m_B v_B = -m_A v_A$$

$$v_B = -\frac{m_A v_A}{m_B}$$

Substitute known values and solve.

$$v_B = -\frac{(1.0\ \text{kg})v_A}{2.0\ \text{kg}}$$

$$v_B = -\frac{1}{2}v_A$$

Recognizing that energy is conserved, write an equation that equates the total initial energy of the system and the total final energy of the system.

$$PE_i + KE_i + PE_{s_i} = PE_f + KE_f + PE_{s_f}$$

$$PE_i = PE_f,\ PE_{s_f} = 0,\ \text{and}\ KE_i = 0$$

Thus, because energy is conserved, the final kinetic energy of the two carts equals the initial potential energy of the spring.

$$PE_{s_i} = KE_f$$

Write an equation in terms of mass and velocity that states this relationship.

$$PE_{s_i} = \frac{1}{2}m_A(v_A)^2 + \frac{1}{2}m_B(v_B)^2$$

Substitute known values and solve for v_A.

$$12\ \text{J} = \frac{1}{2}(1.0\ \text{kg})(v_A)^2 + \frac{1}{2}(2.0\ \text{kg})\left(-\frac{v_A}{2}\right)^2$$

$$12\ \text{J} = (0.50\ \text{kg})(v_A)^2 + (1.0\ \text{kg})\left(\frac{v_A^2}{4}\right)$$

$$12\ \text{J} = (0.75\ \text{kg})v_A^2$$

$$v_A^2 = 16\ \text{J/kg} = 16\ \frac{\text{kg}\cdot\text{m}^2/\text{s}^2}{\text{kg}}$$

$$v_A = 4.0\ \text{m/s}$$

6. It has already been determined that the speed of cart B is one-half that of cart A, thus

$$\frac{KE_A}{KE_B} = \frac{\frac{1}{2}m_A v_A^2}{\frac{1}{2}m_B v_B^2} = \frac{\frac{1}{2}(1.0\ \text{kg})(4.0\ \text{m/s})^2}{\frac{1}{2}(2.0\ \text{kg})(2.0\ \text{m/s})^2} = \frac{2}{1}$$

Review Questions

67. As the speed of an object falling toward Earth increases, the gravitational potential energy of the object with respect to Earth

(1) decreases　　　(3) remains the same
(2) increases

68. At what point in its fall does the kinetic energy of a freely falling object equal its gravitational potential energy with respect to the ground?

(1) at the start of the fall
(2) halfway between the start and the end
(3) at the end of the fall
(4) at all points during the fall

69. A 2.0-kilogram mass falls freely for 10. meters near the surface of Earth. The total kinetic energy gained by the object during its free fall is approximately

(1) 400 J　(2) 200 J　(3) 100 J　(4) 50 J

70. A 20.0-kilogram object falls freely from rest and strikes the ground with 1,962 joules of kinetic energy. Calculate how far above the ground the object was when it was released.

71. A 1.0-kilogram mass gains kinetic energy as it falls freely from rest a vertical distance d. How far would a 2.0-kilogram mass have to fall freely from rest to gain the same amount of kinetic energy?

(1) d　　(2) $2d$　　(3) $\dfrac{d}{2}$　　(4) $\dfrac{d}{4}$

72. A basketball player, who weighs 600 newtons, jumps 0.5 meter vertically off the floor. Calculate her kinetic energy just before hitting the floor.

73. As an object falls freely in a vacuum, the total mechanical energy of the object

(1) decreases　　　　(3) remains the same
(2) increases

Base your answers to questions 74 through 76 on the information and diagram below.

A 10-kilogram block starts from rest at point A and slides along a frictionless track. [Neglect air resistance.]

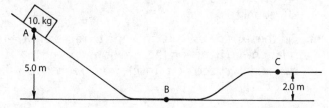

74. As the block moves from point A to point B, the total amount of gravitational potential energy that changes to kinetic energy is approximately
    (1) 5 J (2) 20 J (3) 50 J (4) 500 J

75. What is the approximate speed of the block at point B?
    (1) 1 m/s (2) 10 m/s (3) 50 m/s (4) 100 m/s

76. What is the approximate gravitational potential energy of the block at point C?
    (1) 20 J (2) 200 J (3) 300 J (4) 500 J

Base your answers to questions 77 and 78 on the information and diagram below.

An ideal simple pendulum is released from rest at position *A* and swings freely through position *B*. [Assume that the gravitational potential energy of the system is zero at *B*.]

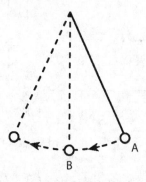

77. Compared to the pendulum's kinetic energy at position *B*, its gravitational potential energy at position *A* is
    (1) half as great   (3) the same
    (2) twice as great   (4) four times as great

78. As the pendulum swings from position *A* to position *B*, the total mechanical energy of the pendulum
    (1) decreases   (3) remains the same
    (2) increases

Base your answers to questions 79 through 81 on the information and diagram below.

A 1.00-kilogram block is held at rest on a frictionless plane inclined at 30.° to the horizontal.

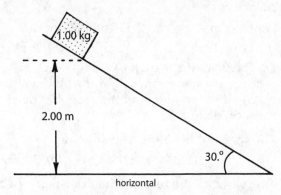

79. The block is released and slides down the length of the incline. Determine the block's kinetic energy at the bottom of the incline.

80. If the angle between the plane and the horizontal is increased, the magnitude of the force required to hold the block at rest on the incline will
    (1) decrease
    (2) increase
    (3) remain the same

81. As the block slides down the incline, the sum of its gravitational potential energy with respect to the horizontal and kinetic energy
    (1) decreases
    (2) increases
    (3) remains the same

Base your answers to questions 82 through 86 on the information and diagram below.

A 2.0-kilogram block is placed on a frictionless track at point A and released from rest. [Assume that the gravitational potential energy of the system is zero at point E.]

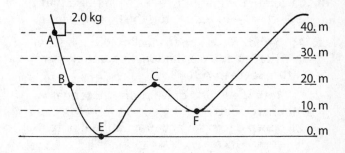

82. Calculate the gravitational potential energy of the system at point A.

83. Compared to the kinetic energy of the block at point *B*, the kinetic energy of the block at point *E* is

(1) the same   (3) half as great

(2) twice as great   (4) four times as great

84. On the diagram, mark an X on the track to indicate the maximum height the block will reach above point *E* after the block has passed through point *E*.

85. The speed of the block at point *C* is

(1) 0 m/s   (2) 10. m/s   (3) 14 m/s   (4) 20. m/s

86. Compared to the total mechanical energy of the system at point *A*, the total mechanical energy of the system at point *F* is

(1) less   (2) more   (3) the same

Base your answers to questions 87 through 93 on the information and diagram below.

A 10.0-kilogram box starts from rest at point A and is accelerated uniformly to point B in 4.0 seconds by the application of a constant horizontal force *F*. At point *B*, the speed of the box is 10.0 meters per second as it begins to move up a plane inclined at 30.° to the horizontal. [Neglect friction.]

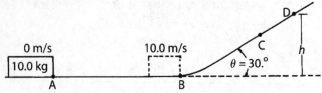

87. Calculate the kinetic energy of the box at point *B*.

88. Calculate the magnitude of force *F*.

89. Calculate the distance the box travels in moving from point *A* to point *B*.

90. Calculate the magnitude of the impulse that would be required to stop the box at point *B*.

91. As the box moves up the incline, what happens to its speed and gravitational potential energy with respect to $\overline{AB}$?

(1) Both speed and gravitational potential energy decrease.

(2) Speed decreases and gravitational potential energy increases.

(3) Speed remains the same and gravitational potential energy decreases.

(4) Speed remains the same and gravitational potential energy increases.

92. The box comes to rest at a vertical height of *h* (point D) when ∠θ = 30.°. If ∠θ was increased to 40.°, the box would come to rest at a vertical height

(1) less than *h*

(2) greater than *h*

(3) equal to *h*

93. On the axes below, sketch a line to represent the relationship between the kinetic energy of the box and its speed as it travels from point *A* to point *B*.

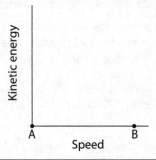

Base your answers to questions 94 through 97 on the information and diagram below.

A 1.00-kilogram sphere M, suspended by a string from point P, is lifted to a height *h*. The sphere is released and passes through the lowest point in its swing at a speed of 10.0 meters per second. [Neglect friction.]

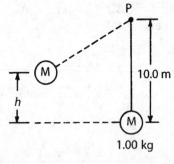

94. Calculate the height from which the sphere was released.

95. Calculate the magnitude of the centripetal force on the sphere as it passes through the lowest point in its swing.

96. The magnitude of the centripetal force on the sphere could be halved as it passes through the lowest point in its swing by doubling the

(1) weight of the sphere, only

(2) length of the string, only

(3) height *h* and the weight of the sphere

(4) the length of the string and height *h*

97. Compared to the sphere's speed through the lowest point of its swing when released from h, the sphere's speed through the lowest point when released from $2h$ would be

(1) lower   (2) greater   (3) the same

98. In the diagram below, a toy car having a mass of 4.00×10^{-2} kilogram starts from rest at point A and travels 3.60 meters along a uniform track until coming to rest at point B.

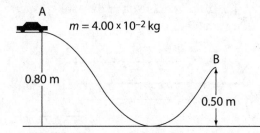

A
$m = 4.00 \times 10^{-2}$ kg
0.80 m
B
0.50 m

Calculate the magnitude of the frictional force acting on the car. [Assume the frictional force is constant.]

99. A car has a mass of 1.00×10^3 kilograms. Calculate the work done in moving the car at constant speed a distance of 250 meters along a horizontal asphalt-paved road.

Base your answers to questions 100 and 101 on the information and diagram below.

A 20.0-newton force is needed to pull a 5.00-kilogram object up a hill at a constant speed of 2.0 meters per second.

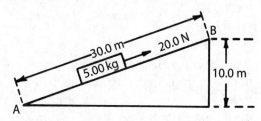

B
30.0 m
20.0 N
5.00 kg
10.0 m
A

100. Determine the work done against gravity in moving the object from point A to point B.

101. Determine the work done against friction in moving the object from point A to point B.

102. As a block slides across a table, its speed decreases while its temperature increases. Which two changes occur in the block's energy as it slides?

(1) a decrease in kinetic energy and an increase in internal energy
(2) an increase in kinetic energy and a decrease in internal energy
(3) a decrease in both kinetic energy and internal energy
(4) an increase in both kinetic energy and internal energy

103. The graph below represents the kinetic energy, gravitational potential energy, and total mechanical energy of a moving block.

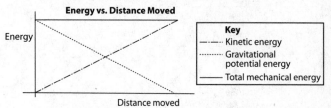

Energy vs. Distance Moved

Energy

Key
Kinetic energy
Gravitational potential energy
Total mechanical energy

Distance moved

Which best describes the motion of the block?

(1) accelerating on a flat horizontal surface
(2) sliding up a frictionless incline
(3) falling freely
(4) being lifted at constant velocity

104. An object is thrown vertically upward. Which pair of graphs best represents the object's kinetic energy and gravitational potential energy as functions of its displacement while it rises?

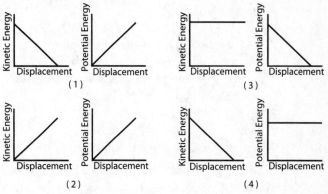

Kinetic Energy   Potential Energy
Displacement   Displacement
(1)

Kinetic Energy   Potential Energy
Displacement   Displacement
(3)

Kinetic Energy   Potential Energy
Displacement   Displacement
(2)

Kinetic Energy   Potential Energy
Displacement   Displacement
(4)

Directions

Review the Test-Taking Strategies section of this book. Then answer the following questions. Read each question carefully and answer with a correct choice or response.

Part A

1 Which variable expression is correctly paired with its corresponding unit?

(1) $\dfrac{\text{mass} \cdot \text{distance}}{\text{time}}$ and watt

(2) $\dfrac{\text{mass} \cdot \text{distance}^2}{\text{time}}$ and watt

(3) $\dfrac{\text{mass} \cdot \text{distance}^2}{\text{time}^2}$ and joule

(4) $\dfrac{\text{mass} \cdot \text{distance}}{\text{time}^3}$ and joule

2 What is an essential characteristic of an object in equilibrium?
(1) zero velocity
(2) zero acceleration
(3) zero potential energy
(4) zero kinetic energy

3 A net force with a magnitude of 5.0 newtons moves a 2.0-kilogram object a distance of 3.0 meters in 3.0 seconds. What is the total work done on the object?
(1) 1.0 J
(2) 10. J
(3) 15 J
(4) 30. J

4 A force is applied to a block causing it to accelerate along a horizontal, frictionless surface. The energy gained by the block is equal to the
(1) work done on the block
(2) power applied to the block
(3) impulse applied to the block
(4) momentum given to the block

5 A 2.2-kilogram mass is pulled by a horizontal 30.-newton force to the right through a distance of 5.0 meters as shown in the diagram below.

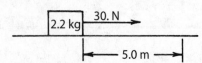

What is the total amount of work done on the mass?
(1) 11 J
(2) 66 J
(3) 150 J
(4) 330 J

6 In the diagram below, a 1.0-kilogram mass falls a vertical distance of 0.50 meter, causing a 2.0-kilogram mass to slide the same distance along a tabletop.

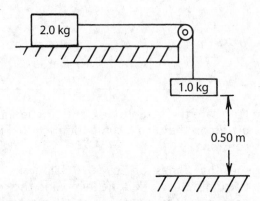

What is the total work done by the falling mass?
(1) 1.5 J
(2) 4.9 J
(3) 9.8 J
(4) 15 J

7 A horizontal force with a magnitude of 40. newtons is used to push a block along a level table at a constant speed of 2.0 meters per second. How much work is done on the block in 6.0 seconds?
(1) 80. J
(2) 120 J
(3) 240 J
(4) 480 J

8 A force with a magnitude of 100. newtons is used to push a trunk to the top of an incline 3.0 meters long. Then a force with a magnitude of 50. newtons is used to push the trunk for 10. meters along a horizontal platform. What is the total work done on the trunk?
(1) 8.0×10^2 J
(2) 5.0×10^2 J
(3) 3.0×10^2 J
(4) 9.0×10^2 J

9 The amount of work done against friction to slide a box in a straight line across a uniform, horizontal floor depends most on the
(1) time taken to move the box
(2) distance the box is moved
(3) speed of the box
(4) direction of the box's motion

10 The diagram below shows two identical wooden planks, A and B, at different incline angles. The planks are used to slide concrete blocks from the bed of a truck.

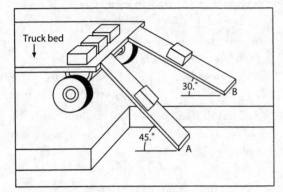

Compared to the amount of work done against friction by a block sliding down plank A, the work done against friction by a block sliding down plank B is

(1) less   (3) the same
(2) more

11 A 95-kilogram student climbs 4.0 meters up a rope in 3.0 seconds. What is the power output of the student?

(1) 1.3×10^2 W   (3) 1.2×10^3 W
(2) 3.8×10^2 W   (4) 3.7×10^3 W

12 What is the minimum power required for a conveyor to raise an 8.0-newton box 4.0 meters vertically in 8.0 seconds?

(1) 260 W   (3) 32 W
(2) 64 W   (4) 4.0 W

13 A weightlifter lifts a 200-kilogram mass a vertical distance of 0.5 meter in 0.1 second. What is the lifter's power output?

(1) 1×10^{-4} W   (3) 1×10^4 W
(2) 4×10^{-4} W   (4) 4×10^4 W

14 A 4.0×10^3-watt motor applies an 8.0×10^2-newton force to move a boat at constant speed. How far does the boat move in 16 seconds?

(1) 3.2 m   (2) 5.0 m   (3) 32 m   (4) 80. m

15 A boat weighing 9.0×10^2 newtons requires a horizontal force of 6.0×10^2 newtons to move it across the water at 1.5×10^1 meters per second. The boat's engine must provide energy at the rate of

(1) 2.5×10^{-2} J   (3) 7.5×10^3 J
(2) 4.0×10^1 W   (4) 9.0×10^3 W

16 As a ball falls freely toward the ground, what happens to the ball's speed and gravitational potential energy with respect to the ground?

(1) Both speed and gravitational potential energy decrease.
(2) Speed decreases and gravitational potential energy increases.
(3) Speed increases and gravitational potential energy decreases.
(4) Both speed and gravitational potential energy increase.

17 An object of mass m is lifted a vertical distance h above the surface of Earth at constant speed v in time t. The total gravitational potential energy with respect to Earth's surface gained by the object is equal to the

(1) average force applied to the object
(2) total weight of the object
(3) total work done on the object
(4) total momentum gained by the object

18 A box weighing 1.0×10^2 newtons is dragged to the top of an incline, as shown in the diagram below.

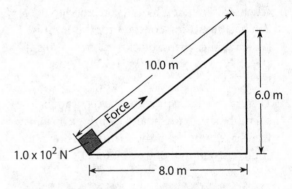

With respect to the bottom of the incline, the gravitational potential energy of the box at the top of the incline is

(1) 1.0×10^2 J   (3) 8.0×10^2 J
(2) 6.0×10^2 J   (4) 1.0×10^3 J

19 What is the spring constant of a spring of negligible mass that gains 6.0 joules of elastic potential energy as a result of being compressed 0.40 meter?

(1) 2.4 N/m   (3) 38 N/m
(2) 15 N/m   (4) 75 N/m

20 Spring *A* has a spring constant of 140 newtons per meter and spring *B* has a spring constant of 280 newtons per meter. Both springs are stretched the same distance. Compared to the elastic potential energy stored in spring *A*, the elastic potential energy stored in spring *B* is
(1) the same   (3) half as great
(2) twice as great   (4) four times as great

21 A vertical spring 0.100 meter long is elongated to a length of 0.119 meter when a 1.00-kilogram mass is attached to the bottom of the spring. The spring constant of this spring is
(1) 9.8 N/m   (3) 98 N/m
(2) 82 N/m   (4) 520 N/m

22 A force with a magnitude of 10. newtons is required to hold a stretched spring 0.20 meter from its rest position. What is the elastic potential energy stored in the stretched spring?
(1) 1.0 J   (2) 2.0 J   (3) 5.0 J   (4) 50. J

23 When a mass is placed on a spring with a spring constant of 15 newtons per meter, the spring is compressed 0.25 meter. How much elastic potential energy is stored in the spring?
(1) 0.47 J   (2) 0.94 J   (3) 1.9 J   (4) 3.8 J

24 A vertically hung spring stretches 0.075 meter when a 5.0-newton block is attached to the spring. What is the spring constant for this spring? [Assume the spring-block system is at rest.]
(1) 38 N/m   (3) 130 N/m
(2) 67 N/m   (4) 650 N/m

25 The unstretched spring in the diagram below has a length of 0.40 meter and a spring constant *k*. A weight is hung from the spring causing it to stretch to a length of 0.60 meter.

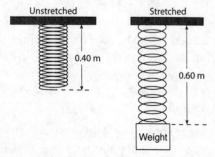

How many joules of elastic potential energy are stored in this stretched spring?
(1) 0.020 × *k*   (3) 0.18 × *k*
(2) 0.080 × *k*   (4) 2.0 × *k*

26 The diagram below shows block A having mass 2*m* and speed *v*, and block B having mass *m* and speed 2*v*.

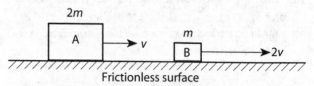

Compared to the kinetic energy of block A, the kinetic energy of block B is
(1) the same   (3) one-fourth as great
(2) twice as great   (4) four times as great

27 An object with a speed of 20. meters per second has a kinetic energy of 400. joules. The mass of the object is
(1) 1.0 kg   (2) 2.0 kg   (3) 0.50 kg   (4) 40. kg

28 A total of 10.0 joules of work is done in accelerating a 20.-newton object from rest across a horizontal frictionless table. What is the total kinetic energy gained by the object?
(1) 0.0 J   (2) 2.0 J   (3) 10. J   (4) 200 J

29 A baseball bat strikes a ball with a force with a magnitude of 2.0×10^4 newtons. If the bat stays in contact with the ball for a distance of 5.0×10^{-3} meter, what kinetic energy will the ball acquire from the bat?
(1) 1.0×10^2 J   (3) 2.5×10^1 J
(2) 2.0×10^2 J   (4) 4.0×10^2 J

30 An object 8 meters above the ground has *Z* joules of gravitational potential energy with respect to the ground. If the object falls freely, how many joules of kinetic energy will it have gained when it is 4 meters above the ground?
(1) Z   (2) 2Z   (3) $\frac{Z}{2}$ (4) 0

31 A girl rides an escalator that moves her upward at constant speed. As the girl rises, how do her kinetic energy and gravitational potential energy with respect to the bottom of the escalator change?
(1) Kinetic energy decreases and potential energy decreases.
(2) Kinetic energy decreases and potential energy increases.
(3) Kinetic energy remains the same and potential energy decreases.
(4) Kinetic energy remains the same and potential energy increases.

32 A 0.10-kilogram ball dropped vertically from a height of 1.00 meter above the floor bounces back to a height of 0.80 meter. The mechanical energy "lost" by the ball as it bounces is
(1) 0.020 J   (3) 0.78 J
(2) 0.20 J   (4) 0.98 J

33 A stone is dropped in air from a height of 50 meters above the ground. As the stone falls, what happens to the stone's kinetic energy and internal energy?
(1) Kinetic energy decreases and internal energy decreases.
(2) Kinetic energy decreases and internal energy increases.
(3) Kinetic energy increases and internal energy decreases.
(4) Kinetic energy increases and internal energy increases.

34 An aluminum pie pan is attached to a string and suspended from a hook, as shown in the diagram below. The pan is released from position A and swings through the air to position B.

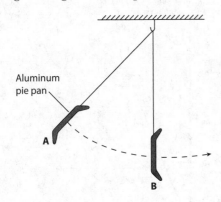

Aluminum pie pan

A

B

What is the relationship between the kinetic energy at position B, KE_B, and the gravitational potential energy at position A, PE_A with respect to B?
(1) KE_B is equal to PE_A minus work done against friction.
(2) KE_B is equal to the PE_A plus work done against friction.
(3) KE_B is equal to PE_A.
(4) KE_B is equal to $2PE_A$.

35 The bottom of a heavy block is covered with sandpaper. The block is repeatedly slid 1.0 meter at constant speed across a uniform, horizontal wooden plank by the application of a constant horizontal force. As the coefficient of friction between the sandpaper and the plank decreases, the amount of work done in sliding the block 1.0 meter along the plank at constant speed
(1) decreases   (3) remains the same
(2) increases

Part B

36 In the diagram below, a box is pulled at constant speed across the floor by the application of a constant force with a magnitude of 120 newtons acting at an angle of 37° to the horizontal.

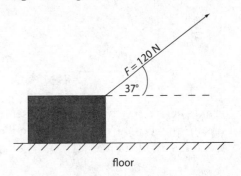

$F = 120$ N

37°

floor

Calculate the total work done in pulling the box 10. meters across the floor. [2]

37 A 20.-newton block is at rest at the bottom of a frictionless incline, as shown in the diagram below.

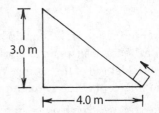

3.0 m

4.0 m

Calculate the work that must be done against gravity to move the block to the top of the incline. [2]

38 A student applies a constant horizontal force having a magnitude of 20. newtons to move a crate at a constant speed of 4.0 meters per second across a rough floor. Calculate the total work done by the student on the 80.-kilogram crate in 6.0 seconds. [3]

39 A student running up a flight of stairs increases her speed at a constant rate. Which graph best represents the relationship between work and time for the student's run up the stairs?

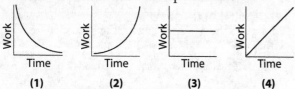

  (1)   (2)   (3)   (4)

40 On the axes below, sketch a line to represent the relationship between gravitational potential energy PE with respect to the ground and height h above the ground for an object near the surface of Earth. [1]

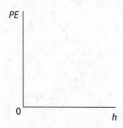

41 On the axes below, sketch a line to represent the relationship between the elongation of an ideal spring and the applied force. [1]

42 A graph represents the relationship between the weight attached to a suspended spring and the resulting total length of the spring. What does the horizontal intercept of the graph represent? [1]

43 On the axes below, sketch a line to represent the relationship between the elastic potential energy stored in a spring PE_s and the change in the length of the spring from its equilibrium position x. [1]

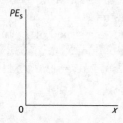

44 On the axes below, sketch a line to represent the relationship between the kinetic energy KE of a moving object and its speed v. [1]

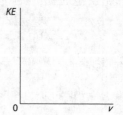

Base your answers to questions 45 through 47 on the graph below, which shows the relationship between the force applied to an ideal spring and the compression of the spring.

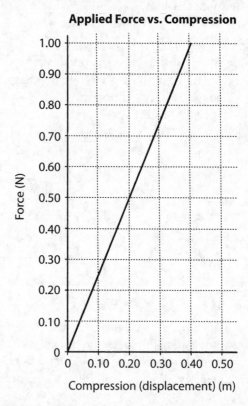

45 Calculate the spring constant for the spring. [2]

46 Calculate the elastic potential energy stored in the spring when it is compressed 0.20 meter. [2]

47 Determine the total work done in compressing the spring 0.20 meter. [1]

48 A cart of mass M on a frictionless track starts from rest at the top of a hill having height h_1, as shown in the diagram below.

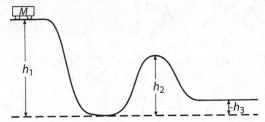

What is the kinetic energy of the cart when it reaches the top of the next hill h_2?

(1) Mgh_1 (3) $Mg(h_2 - h_3)$
(2) $Mg(h_1 - h_2)$ (4) 0

Base your answers to questions 49 through 53 on the information and graph below.

A 2.0-kilogram object moves along a horizontal frictionless surface. The graph shows the relationship between the object's velocity and elapsed time.

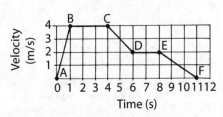

49 Calculate the distance the object moves during interval EF. [2]

50 What is the net force on the object during the interval DE? [1]

51 Calculate the magnitude of the momentum of the object during interval BC. [2]

52 Calculate the kinetic energy of the object during interval BC. [2]

53 Identify an interval during which work is *not* being done on the object. [1]

Base your answers to questions 54 through 58 on the information and diagram below.

A 3.0-kilogram mass is being moved at constant speed across a horizontal surface by a constant 6.0-newton horizontal force to the left.

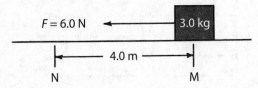

54 What is the change in kinetic energy of the mass as it is moved from point M to point N? [1]

55 Calculate the total work done in 2.0 seconds if energy is supplied at a rate of 10.0 watts. [2]

56 What is the magnitude of the force of friction acting on the mass? [1]

57 Calculate the magnitude of the acceleration that would be produced by the 6.0-newton force if the surface the mass slides on was frictionless. [2]

58 Calculate the gravitational potential energy of the 3.0-kilogram mass with respect to the horizontal surface if the mass was raised to a height of 4.0 meters. [2]

Base your answers to questions 59 through 63 on the information and diagram below.

A simple pendulum with a 2.00-kilogram bob and a length of 10.0 meters is released from rest at position 1 and swings without friction through position 4. At position 3, its lowest point, the speed of the bob is 6.00 meters per second.

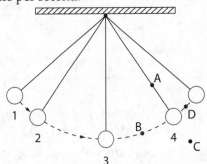

59 At which point does the bob have its maximum kinetic energy? [1]

60 Calculate the gravitational potential energy of the bob at position 1 with respect to position 3. [2]

61 At position 4, toward which point, A, B, C, or D, is the centripetal force directed? [1]

62 Calculate the magnitude of the centripetal acceleration of the bob at position 3. [2]

63 Compare the sum of the kinetic and potential energies of the bob at position 1 (with respect to position 3) to the sum of the kinetic and potential energies of the bob at position 2 (again, with respect to position 3). [1]

Base your answers to questions 64 through 66 on the information and diagram below, which is drawn to a scale of 1.0 centimeter = 3.0 meters.

A 650-kilogram roller coaster car starts from rest at the top of the first hill of its track and glides freely. [Neglect friction.]

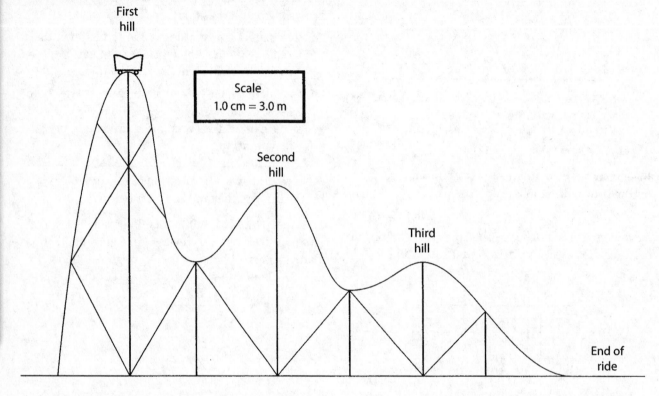

64 Using a metric ruler and the scale 1.0 cm = 3.0 m, determine the height of the first hill. [1]

65 Calculate the gravitational potential energy of the car at the top of the first hill with respect to the end of the ride. [2]

66 Compare the kinetic energy of the car at the top of the second hill to its kinetic energy at the top of the third hill. [1]

Base your answers to questions 67 through 70 on the information below.

A 6.00-kilogram concrete block is dropped from the top of a tall building. The block falls a distance of 55.0 meters and has a speed of 30.0 meters per second when it hits the ground.

67 Calculate the gravitational potential energy of the block with respect to the ground at the instant it is released. [2]

68 Calculate the kinetic energy of the block at the point of impact. [2]

69 Determine the total amount of mechanical energy "lost" by the block as it falls. [1]

70 Explain what happens to the mechanical energy that is "lost" by the block. [1]

Base your answers to questions 71 through 74 on the information and data table below.

A student performs a laboratory activity in which a constant 15-newton force acts on a 2.0-kilogram mass. The work done over time is summarized in the data table.

Time (s)	Work (J)
0	0
1.0	32
2.0	59
3.0	89
4.0	120.

71 Using information in the data table, construct a graph on the grid provided following the directions below:
- Mark an appropriate scale on the axis labeled "Work (J)." [1]
- Plot the data points. [1]
- Draw the best-fit line. [1]

Work vs. Time

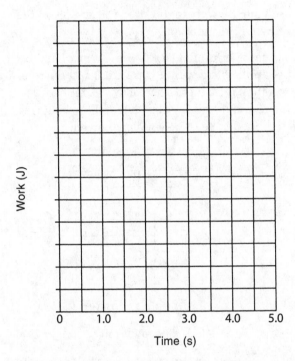

Time (s)

72 Calculate the slope of the line of best fit. [2]

73 What is the physical significance of the slope of the graph? [1]

74 Based on your graph, how much time did it take to do 75 joules of work? [1]

Base your answers to questions 75 through 77 on your knowledge of physics.

75 Explain why it requires more work to stop a ferry boat than a canoe if both are originally traveling with the same velocity. [1]

76 A 2.0-kilogram ball is used as the bob of a pendulum suspended from the ceiling of a classroom. The bob is drawn from its equilibrium position and released from the tip of a student's nose. Explain why, if the student does not move, there is no danger of the student being struck on the return swing. [1]

77 A 700.-newton physics teacher runs at constant speed up a flight of stairs rising 6.0 meters in 7.0 seconds. Explain why the teacher can claim he is more powerful than five 100-watt incandescent light bulbs. [1]

Part C

78 Determine the relationship between joules and 1.00 kilowatt · hour. [1]

79 The diagram below shows a small mass sliding along a frictionless track having a loop of radius r.

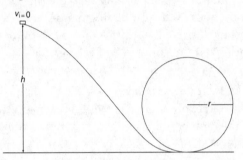

Using your knowledge of energy and circular motion, prove that if the object is to remain on the track at the top of the loop, the minimum height h from which the object must be released from rest is $\frac{5r}{2}$. [4]

80 A ballistic pendulum is a device consisting of a large block of wood having mass m_w suspended from two light-weight wires. The device is used to measure the initial speed v_{B_i} of a bullet having mass m_B. The bullet is shot into the wood and stopped. The block with embedded bullet has speed v_f immediately after the collision. As the diagram below shows, the bullet-block system swings through some vertical distance h, as mechanical energy is conserved.

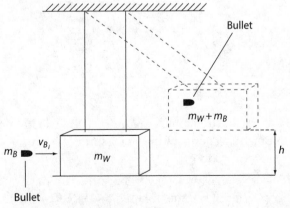

Derive an expression for the vertical distance h in terms of m_w, m_B, v_{B}, and g. [3]

81 When a mass m, hanging from a spring with spring constant k, is set into up-and-down simple harmonic motion, it has a period of vibration T, which is given by the equation $T = 2\pi\sqrt{\frac{m}{k}}$. The amount of elastic potential energy PE_s stored in this spring at any given instant is dependent on its spring constant k and its elongation x. Derive an expression for the potential energy stored in the spring, PE_s, in terms of m, T, and x. [2]

82 A spring in a toy car is compressed a distance, x. When released, the spring returns to its original length, transferring its energy to the car. Consequently, the car having mass m moves with speed v. Derive the spring constant, k, of the car's spring in terms of m, x, and v. [Assume an ideal mechanical system with no loss of energy.] [2]

83 A cart with mass m possesses kinetic energy KE. Write an expression to represent the magnitude of the momentum p of the cart in terms of m and KE. [1]

Base your answers to questions 84 through 87 on the information and diagrams below.

A block of mass m falls from rest a vertical distance h before striking a spring and compressing it a distance $-y$. The spring has spring constant k. At the point where the block first makes contact with the uncompressed spring, the block has speed v and distance is assumed to be zero. [Assume an ideal system.]

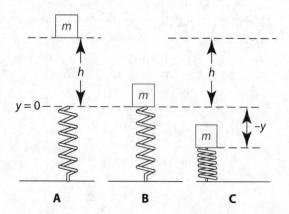

84 Write an equation that represents the gravitational potential energy of the block-spring system, as illustrated in A. [1]

85 Derive an expression for the speed v of the block in terms of h at the instant it makes contact with the uncompressed spring. [1]

86 When the block comes to rest, the spring is compressed a distance $-y$. Write an equation that represents the conservation of energy of the block-spring system in B and C in terms of the variables stated in the problem or other conventional terms. [2]

87 Derive an expression for the spring constant k in terms of g, v, m, and y. [1]

Base your answers to questions 88 and 89 on the following information.

A student performed an experiment in which the force applied to a spring was varied and the resulting elongation measured. The data was graphed, as shown, and the spring constant of the spring was determined to be 60. newtons per meter.

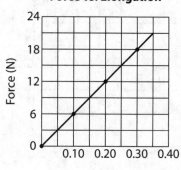

The equivalent spring constant for multiple springs connected in parallel is given by the following equation:

$$k_{eq\ parallel} = k_1 + k_2 + k_3 + \ldots$$

For multiple springs connected in series the equivalent spring constant is given by the equation:

$$\frac{1}{k_{eq\ series}} = \frac{1}{k_1} + \frac{1}{k_2} + \frac{1}{k_3} + \ldots$$

In these equations, k_1, k_2, and k_3 are the spring constants of the individual springs.

88 On a grid, draw a line to represent two identical springs with a spring constant of 60. newtons per meter connected in series. Label the line $k_{eq\ series}$. [1]

89 On the grid draw a line to represent the same two springs connected in parallel. Label the line $k_{eq\ parallel}$. [1]

Base your answers to questions 90 through 92 on the following information and diagram.

A simple pendulum of length ℓ has a bob of mass m. The bob is released from rest at point A and swings to point B directly below the pivot point. At B the cord comes in contact with a peg located a distance r above the center of the bob. This causes the bob to travel in a circular path to point C, as shown. [Neglect friction. Assume a gravitational potential energy of zero at point B.]

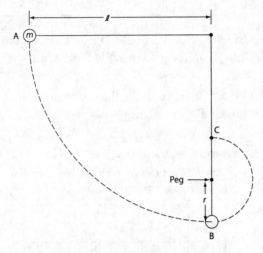

90 Derive an expression for the speed v_B of the bob at point B in terms of ℓ and g. [2]

91 Write an expression for the gravitational potential energy of the bob at point C. [1]

92 Derive an expression for the speed v_C of the bob at point C in terms of ℓ, r, and g. [2]

Base your answers to questions 93 through 96 on the information below.

The driver of a car made an emergency stop on a straight horizontal road. The wheels locked and the car skidded to a stop. The marks made by the rubber tires on the dry asphalt are 16 meters long, and the car's mass is 1200 kilograms.

93 Determine the weight of the car. [1]

94 Calculate the magnitude of the frictional force the road applied to the car in stopping it. [2]

95 Calculate the work done by the frictional force in stopping the car. [2]

96 Assuming that energy is conserved, calculate the speed of the car before the brakes were applied. [2]

Base your answers to questions 97 through 99 on the information below.

A 50.-kilogram child running at 6.0 meters per second jumps onto a stationary 10.-kilogram sled. The sled is on a level frictionless surface.

97 Calculate the speed of the sled with the child after she jumps onto the sled. [2]

98 Calculate the kinetic energy of the sled with the child after she jumps onto the sled. [2]

99 After a short time, the moving sled with the child aboard reaches a rough level surface that exerts a constant frictional force of 54 newtons on the sled. How much work must be done by friction to bring the sled with the child to a stop? [1]

Base your answers to questions 100 through 102 on the information and diagram below.

A 1000.-kilogram empty cart moving with a speed of 6.0 meters per second is about to collide with a stationary loaded cart having a total mass of 5000. kilograms, as shown. After the collision, the carts lock and move together. [Assume friction is negligible.]

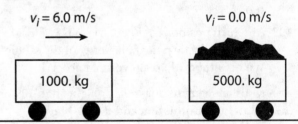

100 Calculate the speed of the combined carts after the collision. [2]

101 Calculate the kinetic energy of the combined carts after the collision. [2]

102 How does the kinetic energy of the combined carts after the collision compare to the kinetic energy of the carts before the collision? [1]

Base your answers to questions 103 through 105 on the information and diagram below.

A mass, *M*, is hung from a spring and reaches equilibrium at position *B*. The mass is then raised to position *A* and released. The mass oscillates between positions *A* and *C*. [Neglect friction.]

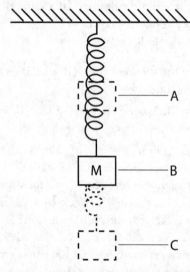

103 At which position, *A*, *B*, or *C*, is mass *M* located when the kinetic energy of the system is at a maximum? Explain your choice. [1]

104 At which position, *A*, *B*, or *C*, is mass *M* located when the gravitational potential energy of the system is at a maximum? Explain your choice. [1]

105 At which position, *A*, *B*, or *C*, is mass *M* located when the elastic potential energy of the system is at a maximum? Explain your choice. [1]

Base your answers to questions 106 through 109 on the following information and data table.

The spring in a dart launcher has a spring constant of 140 newtons per meter. The launcher has six power settings, 0 through 5, with each successive setting having a spring compression 0.020 meter beyond the previous setting. During testing, the launcher is aligned to the vertical, the spring is compressed, and a dart is fired upward. The maximum vertical displacement of the dart in each test trial is measured. The results of the testing are shown in the table.

Data Table		
Power Setting	Spring Compression (m)	Dart's Maximum Vertical Displacement (m)
0	0.000	0.00
1	0.020	0.29
2	0.040	1.14
3	0.060	2.57
4	0.080	4.57
5	0.100	7.10

Using the information in the data table, construct a graph on the grid provided following the directions below.

106 Plot the data points for the dart's maximum vertical displacement versus spring compression. [1]

107 Draw the line or curve of best fit. [1]

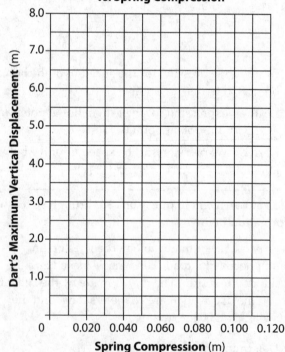

Dart's Maximum Vertical Displacement vs. Spring Compression

108 Using information from your graph, calculate the energy provided by the compressed spring that causes the dart to achieve a maximum vertical displacement of 3.50 meters. [2]

109 Determine the magnitude of the force, in newtons, needed to compress the spring 0.040 meter. [1]

Electricity and Magnetism

How Scientists Study Electricity and Magnetism

? *Is a 60-watt incandescent light bulb always more powerful than a 30-watt incandescent light bulb?* ?

At normal operating temperatures, a 60-watt lamp has half the resistance of a 30-watt lamp, which has a thinner filament. When operated in parallel, the potential difference across each lamp is the same, but the current through the 60-watt lamp is twice that through the 30-watt lamp. Because power is the product of potential difference and current, the 60-watt lamp is twice as powerful as the 30-watt lamp, when connected in parallel.

When the lamps are connected in series, the current is the same through each lamp, but the potential difference across the 60-watt lamp is less than that across the 30-watt lamp, because the 30-watt lamp has more resistance. Because power equals VI, and I is the same for both lamps, VI is greater for the 30-watt lamp, making it more powerful than the 60-watt lamp.

The lamps consume 60 watts and 30 watts, respectively, only when operated, as designated, in parallel at 120 volts in a household circuit.

Electricity and Magnetism

Vocabulary

ammeter	electromagnetic wave	north magnetic pole
ampere	electron	ohm
battery	electronvolt	ohm · meter
cell	electrostatic force	Ohm's law
conductivity	elementary charge	parallel circuit
conductor	equivalent resistance	potential difference
coulomb	induced potential difference	proton
Coulomb's law	joule	resistance
current	law of conservation of charge	resistivity
electric circuit	magnet	resistor
electric field	magnetic field	series circuit
electric field line	magnetic field strength	switch
electric field strength	magnetic field (flux) lines	variable resistor
electrical energy	magnetic force	volt
electrical power	magnetism	voltmeter
electromagnetic induction	neutron	watt

Electrostatics

The study of electric charges at rest, and their electric fields and potentials, is called electrostatics. Charges are said to be "at rest" if there is no net transfer of charge.

Microstructure of Matter   The smallest unit of an element is the atom. Atoms are composed of several different subatomic particles—electrons, protons, and neutrons. A typical atom consists of a cloud of electrons surrounding a central dense core known as the nucleus. The nucleus always contains protons and usually contains neutrons. The **electron** is the fundamental negatively charged (−) particle of matter. The **proton** is the fundamental positively charged (+) particle of matter. The **elementary charge,** e, is equal in magnitude to the charge on an electron ($-e$) or the charge on a proton ($+e$). Although the charge on the proton is equal in magnitude to the charge on the electron, the mass of the proton is much greater than the mass of the electron. **Neutrons,** which are found in the nucleus, are neutral (no charge) subatomic particles that have nearly the same mass as protons. Because they contain equal numbers of protons and electrons, all atoms are electrically neutral.

Charged Objects   Protons and neutrons cannot be removed from an atom by ordinary means. Because of this, electrically charged objects are usually formed when neutral objects lose or gain electrons. Electrons are often removed from an atom when energy is imparted to the atom by friction, heat, or light. When an atom gains or loses electrons, it becomes a charged particle known as an ion. An object with an excess of electrons is negatively charged, and an object with a deficiency of electrons is positively charged.

Two objects with the same sign of charge (both positive or both negative) that are located near each other are repelled by an electrical force. A negatively charged object and a positively charged object that are near each other are attracted by an electrical force. As explained in the next section, neutral objects and charged objects can also be attracted to each other.

Figure 4-1. Opposite charges attract: The tiny pieces of paper are attracted to the comb. The magnitude of the electrostatic force is greater than the magnitude of Earth's gravitational force acting on the piece of paper being lifted.

Transfer of Charge If a system consists only of neutral objects, it has a total net charge of zero. If objects in the system are rubbed together, electrons may be transferred between the objects. This, however, does not change the overall charge on the system—the system as a whole remains neutral. If one of the objects loses electrons and becomes positively charged, the object in contact with it acquires the electrons and becomes negatively charged.

If you run a plastic comb through your hair, electrons are transferred from your hair to the comb. Your hair becomes positively charged and the comb becomes negatively charged. If you then bring the comb near neutral pieces of paper on a tabletop, the charges within the paper are rearranged, as shown in Figure 4-1.

Law of Conservation of Charge The statement that in a closed, isolated system, the total charge of the system remains constant is known as the **law of conservation of charge.** Charges within the system may be transferred from one object to another, but charge is neither created nor destroyed.

SAMPLE PROBLEM

The diagram below shows the initial charges and positions of three metal spheres, R, S, and T, on insulating stands.

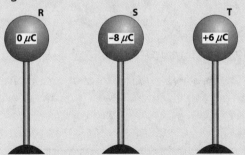

Sphere R is brought into contact with sphere S and then removed. Then sphere S is brought into contact with sphere T and removed. What is the charge on sphere T after this procedure is completed?

SOLUTION: When spheres R and S are brought into contact, they share the $-8~\mu C$ charge equally. Thus each sphere possesses $-4~\mu C$ when they are separated. When spheres S and T are brought into contact, they also share the charge evenly.

$$\frac{-4~\mu C + 6~\mu C}{2} = \frac{+2~\mu C}{2} = +1~\mu C$$

The final charge on sphere T is $+1~\mu C$. Note also that charge is conserved; the initial charge of the system equals the final charge of the system.

$$-8~\mu C + 6~\mu C = -4~\mu C + 1~\mu C + 1~\mu C = -2~\mu C$$

Quantity of Charge Electric charge, q, is a scalar quantity. The SI unit of charge is the **coulomb,** C. One coulomb is equal to 6.25×10^{18} elementary charges. The charge on an electron $(-e)$ is -1.6×10^{-19} coulomb, and the charge on a proton $(+e)$ is $+1.6 \times 10^{-19}$ coulomb. The net charge on a charged object is always an integral multiple of e, that is, charge is quantized. For example, an object may have a net charge of 8.0×10^{-19} C (equivalent to $+5e$) or -1.6×10^{-18} C (equivalent to $-10e$), but it cannot have a charge of 2.4×10^{-19} C (equivalent to $\frac{3}{2} e$).

Coulomb's Law The size or magnitude of the **electrostatic force** that one point charge exerts on another point charge is directly proportional to the product of the charges and inversely proportional to the square of the distance between them. This relationship, called **Coulomb's law,** is given by this formula

Ⓡ
$$F_e = \frac{kq_1q_2}{r^2}$$

The electrostatic force F_e is in newtons, q_1 and q_2 are the charges in coulombs, and r is the distance of separation in meters. The electrostatic constant, k, is equal to 8.99×10^9 N $\cdot$ m²/C². The electrostatic force is directed along the line joining the charges. The force that q_1 exerts on q_2 is equal in magnitude but opposite in direction to the force that q_2 exerts on q_1. The Coulomb's law formula is valid for charged objects whose dimensions are small compared to the distance separating the objects.

SAMPLE PROBLEM

Calculate the electrostatic force that a small sphere, A, possessing a net charge of $+2$ microcoulombs exerts on another small sphere, B, possessing a net charge of -3.0 microcoulombs when the distance between their centers is 10.0 meters.

SOLUTION: Identify the known and unknown values.

Known
$k = 8.99 \times 10^9$ N $\cdot$ m²/C²
$q_1 = +2.0 \times 10^{-6}$ C
$q_2 = -3.0 \times 10^{-6}$ C
$r = 10.0$ m

Unknown
$F_e = ?$ N

1. Write the formula for Coulomb's law.

$F_e = \frac{kq_1q_2}{r^2}$

2. Substitute the known values and solve.

$$F_e = \frac{\left(8.99 \times 10^9\ \frac{\text{N} \cdot \text{m}^2}{\text{C}^2}\right)(+2.0 \times 10^{-6}\,\text{C})(-3.0 \times 10^{-6}\,\text{C})}{(1.00 \times 10^1\,\text{m})^2}$$

$$F_e = \frac{\left(8.99 \times 10^9\ \frac{\text{N} \cdot \cancel{\text{m}^2}}{\cancel{\text{C}^2}}\right)(-6.0 \times 10^{-12}\,\cancel{\text{C}^2})}{1.00 \times 10^2\,\cancel{\text{m}^2}}$$

$F_e = -5.4 \times 10^{-4}$ N

The negative sign indicates a force of attraction.

Review Questions

1. What is the charge of a proton?

  (1) 9.11×10^{-31} C   (3) 1.60×10^{-19} C

  (2) 1.67×10^{-27} C   (4) 6.25×10^{18} C

2. A charge of 100 elementary charges is equivalent to

  (1) 1.60×10^{-21} C   (3) 6.25×10^{16} C

  (2) 1.60×10^{-17} C   (4) 6.25×10^{20} C

3. State *both* the sign and magnitude of the charge on a proton, an electron, and a neutron in terms of *e*, the elementary charge.

4. The diagram below represents two electrically charged identical-sized metal spheres, *A* and *B*.

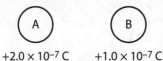

If the spheres are brought into contact, which sphere will have a net gain of electrons?

(1) *A*, only
(2) *B*, only
(3) both *A* and *B*
(4) neither *A* nor *B*

5. A small, uncharged metal sphere is placed near a large, negatively charged sphere. Which diagram best represents the charge distribution of the smaller sphere?

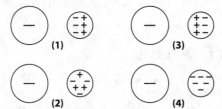

6. Which net charge could be found on an object?

(1) 8.00×10^{-20} C
(2) 2.40×10^{-19} C
(3) 3.20×10^{-19} C
(4) 6.25×10^{-18} C

7. A positively charged glass rod attracts object *X*. The net charge of object *X*

(1) may be zero or negative
(2) may be zero or positive
(3) must be negative
(4) must be positive

8. After two neutral solids, A and B, were rubbed together, Solid A acquired a net negative charge. Solid B, therefore, experienced a net

(1) loss of electrons
(2) increase of electrons
(3) loss of protons
(4) increase of protons

9. A rod and a piece of cloth are rubbed together. If the rod acquires a charge of $+1 \times 10^{-6}$ coulomb, the cloth acquires a charge of

(1) 0 C
(2) $+1 \times 10^{-6}$ C
(3) -1×10^{-6} C
(4) $+1 \times 10^{+6}$ C

10. Two identical spheres, A and B, carry charges of +6 microcoulombs and −2 microcoulombs, respectively. If these spheres touch, what will be the resulting charge on sphere A?

11. The diagram below shows the initial charges and positions of three identical metal spheres, X, Y, and Z, which have been placed on insulating stands. All three spheres are simultaneously brought into contact with each other and then returned to their original positions.

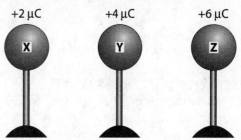

Which statement best describes the charge of the spheres after this procedure is completed?

(1) All the spheres are neutral.
(2) Each sphere has a net charge of $+4 \ \mu$C.
(3) Each sphere retains the same charge that it had originally.
(4) Sphere Y has a greater charge than sphere X or sphere Z.

12. Two oppositely charged metal spheres are brought toward each other. Which graph best represents the relationship between the magnitude of the electrostatic force one sphere exerts on the other sphere and the distance between their centers?

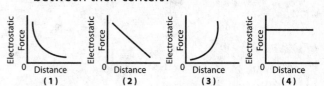

13. The electrostatic force of attraction between two small spheres that are 1.0 meter apart is *F*. If the distance between the spheres is decreased to 0.5 meter, the electrostatic force will be

(1) $\frac{F}{2}$
(2) $2F$
(3) $\frac{F}{4}$
(4) $4F$

14. Two identical small spheres possessing charges q_1 and q_2 are separated by distance *r*. Which change would produce the greatest increase in the magnitude of the electrostatic force that one sphere exerts on the other?

(1) doubling charge q_1
(2) doubling *r*
(3) doubling *r* and charge q_1
(4) doubling *r* and charges q_1 and q_2

15. The diagram below shows two metal spheres suspended by strings and separated by a distance of 3.0 meters. The charge on sphere A is $+5.0 \times 10^{-4}$ coulomb, and the charge on sphere B is $+3.0 \times 10^{-5}$ coulomb.

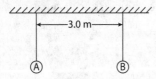

What forces does sphere A exert on sphere B?

(1) an attractive gravitational force and a repulsive electrostatic force of 15 N

(2) an attractive gravitational force and a repulsive electrostatic force of 45 N

(3) a repulsive gravitational force and an attractive electrostatic force of 15 N

(4) a repulsive gravitational force and an attractive electrostatic force of 45 N

16. If the charge is doubled on each of two small spheres having a fixed distance between their centers, the magnitude of the electrostatic force that one sphere exerts on the other will be

(1) halved
(2) doubled
(3) quartered
(4) quadrupled

17. A point charge A of $+3.0 \times 10^{-7}$ coulomb is placed 2.0×10^{-2} meter from a second point charge B of $+4.0 \times 10^{-7}$ coulomb. Calculate the magnitude of the electrostatic force that charge A exerts on charge B.

SAMPLE PROBLEM

Calculate the magnitude of the electric field strength at a point in a field where an electron experiences a force with a magnitude of 1.0×10^{-15} newton.

SOLUTION: Identify the known and unknown values.

Known	Unknown
$F_e = 1.0 \times 10^{-15}$ N	$E = ?$ N/C
$q = 1.60 \times 10^{-19}$ C	

1. Write the formula the defines electric field strength.

$$E = \frac{F_e}{q}$$

2. Substitute the known values and solve.

$$E = \frac{1.0 \times 10^{-15} \text{ N}}{1.60 \times 10^{-19} \text{ C}} = 6.3 \times 10^3 \text{ N/C}$$

Electric Fields

An **electric field** is the region around a charged particle through which a force is exerted on another charged particle. An **electric field line** is the imaginary line along which a positive test charge would move in an electric field. The direction of an electric field is the direction of the force on a stationary positive test charge located at any point on a field line. On a curved field line, the direction of the field at any point is the tangent drawn to the field line at that point. Electric field lines begin on positive charges (or at infinity) and end on negative charges (or infinity). Field lines never intersect.

Electric field strength, E, is the force on a stationary positive test charge per unit charge in an electric field. It is given by this formula

$$E = \frac{F_e}{q}$$ Ⓡ

The electrostatic force F_e is in newtons, the charge q is in coulombs, and the electric field strength E is in newtons per coulomb. Because it has both magnitude and direction, electric field strength is a vector quantity.

Field Around a Point Charge or Sphere Field lines extend radially outward from a positive point charge and radially inward toward a negative point charge. On a sphere, charge is distributed uniformly, and electric field lines are normal (perpendicular) to the surface. According to Coulomb's law, the electric field strength around a point charge or charged sphere varies inversely with the square of the distance from the point charge or sphere. The electric field strength within a hollow, charged conducting sphere is zero.

Field Between Two Oppositely Charged Parallel Plates If the distance separating two oppositely charged parallel plates is small compared to their area, the electric field between the plates is uniform. The electric field lines are parallel to each other, so the field strength is the same at every point between the plates. Figure 4-2 shows the electric fields surrounding charged objects.

The magnitude of the electric force on an electron or a proton located at any point between two given oppositely charged parallel plates is the same. The electric force acting on either of these charged particles causes it to accelerate toward the plate of opposite sign. That is, the particle's speed increases as it approaches the plate of opposite sign.

Potential Difference If the direction of an electric field is such that it opposes the motion of a charged particle, work must be done to move the particle in that direction. The **potential difference** between two points in an electric field is the work done (or change in potential energy) per unit charge as a charged particle is moved between the points. Potential difference is a scalar quantity given by this formula.

$$V = \frac{W}{q}$$

The work W is in joules, the charge q is in coulombs, and the potential difference V is in joules per coulomb. If one joule of work is done to move one coulomb of charge between two points in an electric field, a potential difference of one **volt** is said to exist between the two points. That is, 1 joule/coulomb = 1 volt. The volt, V, is the derived SI unit for potential difference.

If an elementary charge is moved against an electric field through a potential difference of one volt, the work done on the charge is calculated as shown below.

$$W = Vq = (1.00 \text{ V})(1.60 \times 10^{-19} \text{ C}) = 1.60 \times 10^{-19} \text{ J}$$

This amount of work (1.60×10^{-19} J), or gain in potential energy, is called the **electronvolt,** eV. That is, $1.00 \text{ eV} = 1.60 \times 10^{-19}$ J.

SAMPLE PROBLEM

Moving a point charge of 3.2×10^{-19} coulomb between points A and B in an electric field requires 4.8×10^{-18} joule of energy. Calculate the potential difference between these points.

SOLUTION: Identify the known and unknown values.

Known	*Unknown*
$q = 3.2 \times 10^{-19}$ C	$V = ?$ V
$W = 4.8 \times 10^{-18}$ J	

1. Write the formula that defines potential difference.

$$V = \frac{W}{q}$$

2. Substitute the known values and solve.

$$V = \frac{4.8 \times 10^{-18} \text{ J}}{3.2 \times 10^{-19} \text{ C}} = 15 \text{ V}$$

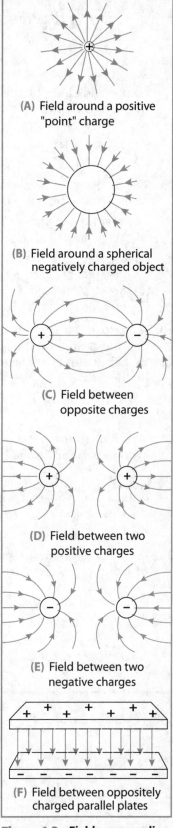

(A) Field around a positive "point" charge

(B) Field around a spherical negatively charged object

(C) Field between opposite charges

(D) Field between two positive charges

(E) Field between two negative charges

(F) Field between oppositely charged parallel plates

Figure 4-2. Fields surrounding charged objects

18. What is the magnitude of the electrostatic force experienced by one elementary charge at a point in an electric field where the magnitude of the electric field strength is 3.0×10^3 newtons per coulomb?

(1) 1.0×10^3 N   (3) 3.0×10^3 N
(2) 1.6×10^{-19} N   (4) 4.8×10^{-16} N

19. The diagram below shows some of the lines of electric force around a positive point charge.

The magnitude of the strength of the electric field is

(1) greatest at point A
(2) greatest at point B
(3) greatest at point C
(4) equal at points A, B, and C

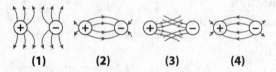

20. A charged particle is placed in an electric field *E*. If the charge on the particle is doubled, the magnitude of the force exerted on the particle by the field *E* is

(1) unchanged   (3) halved
(2) doubled   (4) quadrupled

21. Which diagram best illustrates the electric field around two unlike charges?

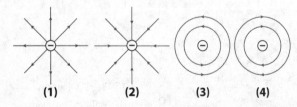

    (1)   **(2)**   **(3)**   **(4)**

22. Which diagram best represents the electric field of a point negative charge?

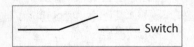

    (1)   **(2)**   **(3)**   **(4)**

23. How much energy is needed to move one electron through a potential difference of 1.0×10^2 volts?

(1) 1.0 J   (3) 1.6×10^{-17} J
(2) 1.0×10^2 J   (4) 1.6×10^{-19} J

24. In an electric field, 6.0 joules of work are done to move 2.0 coulombs of charge from point A to point B. Calculate the potential difference between points A and B.

25. A helium ion with a charge of +2e is accelerated by a potential difference of 5.0×10^3 volts. What is the kinetic energy acquired by the ion?

(1) 3.2×10^{-19} eV   (3) 5.0×10^3 eV
(2) 2.0 eV   (4) 1.0×10^4 eV

26. Calculate the potential difference across a 6-ohm resistor if 4 joules of work are required to move 2 coulombs of charge through the resistor.

27. An electron is accelerated from rest through a potential difference of 200. volts. What is the work done on the electron in electronvolts?

28. The uniform electric field between two oppositely charged parallel plates does work on a series of small positively charged spheres in moving them from one plate to the other. The graph below represents the relationship between the work done on the spheres and their respective charges.

What does the slope of the graph represent?

Electric Current

Electric **current** is the rate at which charge passes a given point in a circuit. Current is a scalar quantity. An **electric circuit** is a closed path along which charged particles move. A **switch** is a device for making, breaking, or changing the connections in an electric circuit. Figure 4-3 shows the symbol for a switch.

Unit of Current The SI unit of electric current, *I*, is the **ampere,** A. It is a fundamental unit. The coulomb, C, the unit of charge, is a derived unit defined to be the amount of charge that passes a point when a current of one ampere flows for one second. This relationship can be expressed as follows:

— Switch

Figure 4-3. The symbol for a switch Ⓡ

$$I = \frac{\Delta q}{t}$$

The current I is in amperes, charge q is in coulombs, and time t is in seconds. An **ammeter** is a device used to measure current. The symbol for an ammeter is shown in Figure 4-4.

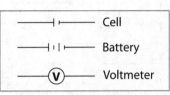

Figure 4-4. The symbol for an ammeter

Conditions Necessary for an Electric Current In addition to a complete circuit, a difference in potential between two points in the circuit must exist for there to be an electric current. The potential difference may be supplied by a **cell,** a device that converts chemical energy to electrical energy, or a **battery,** a combination of two or more electrochemical cells. The potential difference can be measured with a device called a **voltmeter.** These devices are represented in an electric circuit diagram by the symbols shown in Figure 4-5.

Figure 4-5. Symbols for sources of potential difference (voltage) and a voltmeter for measuring potential difference

Positive charges tend to move from points of higher potential to points of lower potential, or from positive potential to negative potential. Negative charges tend to move in the opposite direction. The direction of a current in an electric circuit can be defined as either of these directions. In some mathematical treatments it is convenient to treat the current as flowing from positive to negative, that is, as conventional current. However, it is more natural to choose the electron flow as the direction of current, because most currents consist of electrons in motion. This is the definition used in this book.

Conductivity in Solids For a current to exist in an electric circuit, the circuit must consist of materials through which charge can move. The ability of a material to conduct electricity depends on the number of free charges per unit volume and on their mobility. **Conductivity** is a property of a material that depends on the availability of charges that are relatively free to move under the influence of an electric field. Pure metals have many electrons, and these electrons are not bound, or are only loosely bound, to any particular atom. Consequently, metals are good **conductors,** because their electrons move readily. In nonmetallic elements or compounds, electrons are tightly bound and few are free to move. These types of materials are called <u>insulators,</u> because they are poor conductors.

Resistance and Ohm's Law Electrical **resistance,** R, is the opposition that a device or conductor offers to the flow of electric current. The resistance of a conductor is the ratio of the potential difference applied to its ends and the current that flows through it. This relationship, called **Ohm's law,** is expressed as follows.

$$R = \frac{V}{I}$$

The potential difference V is in volts, current I is in amperes, and resistance R is in volts per ampere. The **ohm,** Ω, is a derived SI unit equal to one volt per ampere. It should be noted that the equation is true for entire circuits or for any portion of a circuit, provided that the temperature does not change.

SAMPLE PROBLEM

A student measures a current of 0.10 ampere through a lamp connected by short wires to a 12.0-volt source. What is the resistance of the lamp?

SOLUTION: Identify the known and unknown values.

Known	*Unknown*
$V = 12.0$ V	$R = ? \ \Omega$
$I = 0.10$ A	

1. Write the formula for Ohm's law.

$$R = \frac{V}{I}$$

2. Substitute the known values and solve.

$$R = \frac{V}{I} = \frac{12.0 \text{ V}}{0.10 \text{ A}} = 120$$

A resistor was held at constant temperature in an operating electric circuit. A student measured the current through the resistor and the potential difference across it. The measurements are shown in the data table below.

Data Table	
Current (A)	Potential Difference (V)
0.010	2.3
0.020	5.2
0.030	7.4
0.040	9.9
0.050	12.7

(a) Using the information in the data table, construct a graph on the grid provided.

- Mark an appropriate scale on the axis labeled "Current (A)."
- Plot the data points.
- Draw the line or curve of best fit.

(b) Using your graph, find the slope of the best-fit line.

(c) Identify the physical quantity represented by the slope of the graph.

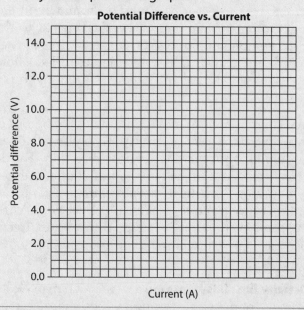

Potential Difference vs. Current

SOLUTION:

(a)

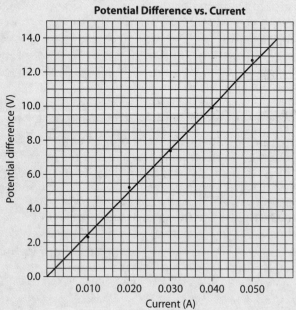

Potential Difference vs. Current

(b) Write the formula for slope.

$$\text{slope} = \frac{\text{rise}}{\text{run}} = \frac{\Delta V}{\Delta I}$$

Substitute values from places where the graphed line intersects the grid and solve. Points directly from the data table can be used only if those points lie on the line of best fit.

$$\text{slope} = \frac{10.0\ \text{V} - 2.5\ \text{V}}{0.040\ \text{A} - 0.010\ \text{A}} = 250\ \Omega$$

(c) The slope of the line represents the resistance of the resistor.

Factors that Affect the Resistance of a Conductor The resistance of a conducting wire increases with the increasing length of a wire because the current (electrons) encounter and collide with an increasing number of atoms. That is, the resistance R of a wire varies directly with its length L, or

$R \alpha L$. As the thickness of a wire decreases, there are fewer spaces between atoms in the cross-section through which electrons can travel in a given period of time. For example, if two wires have the same composition and length but one has half the diameter of the other, the thinner wire will have one-quarter the cross-sectional area, and therefore four times the resistance. That is, the resistance R of a wire varies inversely with its cross-sectional area A, or $R \alpha \frac{1}{A}$.

Resistivity, ρ, is a characteristic of a material that depends on its electronic structure and temperature. The resistance of a wire is directly proportional to its resistivity, that is, $R \alpha \rho$. Good conductors have low resistivities and good insulators have high resistivities. The SI unit for resistivity is the **ohm · meter,** or $\Omega \cdot$ m. As the temperature of a conductor increases, its resistivity increases. The *Reference Tables for Physical Setting/Physics* contain a chart listing resistivities of several metals at 20°C.

Combining the factors yields the following formula for the resistance of a wire.

$$R = \frac{\rho L}{A}$$

The resistivity ρ is in ohm · meters, length L is in meters, cross-sectional area A is in meters², and resistance R is in ohms.

SAMPLE PROBLEM

Calculate the resistance of a 4.00-meter length of copper wire having a diameter of 2.00 millimeters. Assume a temperature of 20°C.

SOLUTION: Identify the known and unknown values.

Known	*Unknown*
$\rho_{copper} = 1.72 \times 10^{-8} \Omega \cdot$ m	$R = ? \Omega$
$L = 4.00$ m	
$d = 2.00 \times 10^{-3}$ m	

1. Write the formula that defines resistance.

$$R = \frac{\rho L}{A}$$

2. Write the formula for the area of a circle given its radius. Recall that the radius equals one-half the diameter.

$$A = \pi r^2$$

3. Combine the equations.

$$R = \frac{\rho L}{\pi r^2}$$

4. Substitute the known values and solve.

$$R = \frac{\rho L}{A} = \frac{\rho L}{\pi (d/2)^2}$$

$$R = \frac{(1.72 \times 10^{-8} \Omega \cdot m)(4.00\ m)}{\pi (1.00 \times 10^{-3}\ m)^2}$$

$$R = 2.19 \times 10^{-2}\ \Omega$$

A **resistor** is a device designed to have a definite amount of resistance. It can be used in a circuit to limit current flow or provide a potential drop. A **variable resistor** is a coil of resistance wire whose effective resistance can be varied by sliding a contact point. As more of the coil is used in a circuit, the resistance of the circuit increases, and the current decreases. The symbols for a resistor and variable resistor are shown in Figure 4-6.

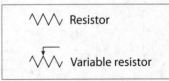

Figure 4-6. Symbols for a resistor and a variable resistor

29. A total of 20.0 coulombs of charge pass a given point in a conductor in 4.0 seconds. Calculate the current in the conductor.

30. A wire carries a current of 2.0 amperes. How many electrons pass a given point in this wire in 1.0 second?

(1) 1.3×10^{18} (3) 1.3×10^{19}
(2) 2.0×10^{18} (4) 2.0×10^{19}

31. Which condition must exist between two points in a conductor in order to maintain a flow of charge?

(1) a potential difference
(2) a magnetic field
(3) a low resistance
(4) a high resistance

32. A simple circuit consists of a variable resistor connected to a battery. An ammeter and a voltmeter are connected properly in the circuit to measure the current through and potential drop across the variable resistor. What is the effect of increasing the resistance of the variable resistor from 10^3 ohms to 10^4 ohms ? [Assume constant temperature.]

(1) The ammeter reading decreases.
(2) The ammeter reading increases.
(3) The voltmeter reading decreases.
(4) The voltmeter reading increases.

33. An electric circuit contains a variable resistor connected to a source of constant potential difference. Which graph best represents the relationship between current and resistance in this circuit?

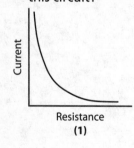
(1)

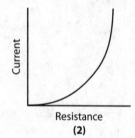
(2)

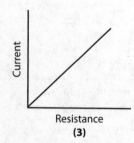
(3)

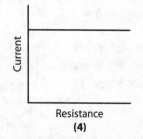
(4)

34. The graph below shows the relationship between potential difference and current in a simple circuit. [Assume constant temperature.]

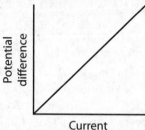

For any point on the line, what does the ratio of potential difference to current represent?

(1) resistivity in ohm·meters
(2) power in watts
(3) resistance in ohms
(4) charge in coulombs

35. A 20.-ohm resistor has 40. coulombs of charge passing through it in 5.0 seconds. Calculate the potential difference across the resistor.

36. The graph below represents the relationship between the potential difference across a metal conductor and the current through the conductor at constant temperature.

Potential Difference vs. Current

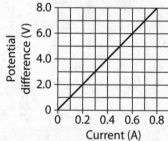

What is the resistance of the conductor?

37. A potential difference of 12 volts is applied across a circuit having a 4.0-ohm resistance. Calculate the current in the circuit.

38. In the diagrams below, ℓ represents a unit length of copper wire and A represents a unit cross-sectional area. Which copper wire has the smallest resistance at room temperature?

(1)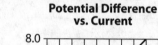

(2)

(3)

(4)

39. An incandescent lightbulb is supplied with a constant potential difference of 120 volts. As the filament of the bulb heats up, what happens to the resistance of the filament and the current through it?

(1) The resistance decreases, and the current decreases.
(2) The resistance decreases, and the current increases.
(3) The resistance increases, and the current decreases.
(4) The resistance increases, and the current increases.

40. The resistance of a wire at constant temperature depends on the wire's

(1) length, only
(2) type of metal, only
(3) length and cross-sectional area, only
(4) length, type of metal, and cross-sectional area

41. On the axes below, sketch the general shape of the graph that shows the relationship between the resistance of a copper wire of uniform cross-sectional area and the wire's length at constant temperature.

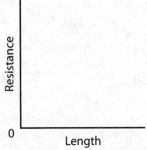

42. A piece of wire has a resistance of 8 ohms. What is the resistance of a second piece of wire of the same composition, same diameter, and at the same temperature, but with one half the length of the first wire?

43. An aluminum wire has a resistance of 48 ohms. A second aluminum wire of the same length and at the same temperature, but with twice the cross-sectional area, would have a resistance of

(1) 12 Ω   (2) 24 Ω   (3) 48 Ω   (4) 96 Ω

44. What is the resistance of a 10.0-meter-long copper wire having a cross-sectional area of 1.50×10^{-6} meter^2 at 20°C?

(1) 1.15×10^{-1} Ω   (3) 1.15×10^{-13} Ω
(2) 1.15×10^{-2} Ω   (4) 1.15×10^{-14} Ω

45. A 5.00-meter-long tin wire has a cross-sectional area of 2.00×10^{-6} meter^2 and a resistance of 0.35 ohm. Calculate the resistivity of this tin wire.

46. At 20°C carbon has a resistivity of 3.5×10^{-5} ohm·meter. What is the ratio of the resistivity of carbon to the resistivity of copper?

(1) 1:2
(2) 2:1
(3) 200:1
(4) 2000:1

47. Unlike most metals, the resistivity of carbon decreases with increasing temperature. As the temperature of carbon increases, its resistance

(1) decreases
(2) increases
(3) remains the same

48. An aluminum wire and a tungsten wire have the same cross-sectional area and the same resistance at 20°C. If the aluminum wire is 4.0×10^{-2} meter long, what is the length of the tungsten wire?

(1) 1.0×10^{-2} m
(2) 2.0×10^{-2} m
(3) 4.0×10^{-2} m
(4) 8.0×10^{-2} m

Electric Circuits

The simplest electric circuit consists of a source of electrical energy, such as a battery; connecting wires; and a circuit element, such as a lamp or a resistor, that converts electrical energy to light or heat. The current in the circuit is dependent on the potential difference V provided by the battery at the ends of the circuit element, and the resistance R of the circuit element. These quantities are related to each other by

Ohm's Law, $I = \dfrac{V}{R}$. Figure 4-7 shows a simple electric circuit.

When two or more resistors are present in a circuit, there are two basic methods of connecting them—in series or in parallel.

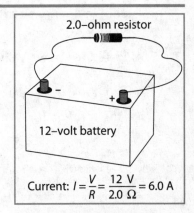

Current: $I = \dfrac{V}{R} = \dfrac{12 \text{ V}}{2.0 \text{ }\Omega} = 6.0 \text{ A}$

Figure 4-7. A simple circuit

Series Circuits A **series circuit** is a circuit in which all parts are connected end to end to provide a single path for the current. Figure 4-8 shows three resistors connected in series with a battery. The resistors are differentiated by the use of subscripts R_1, R_2, and R_3.

Since there is only one current path in a series circuit, the current is the same through each resistor. For resistors in series, the current is given by $I = I_1 = I_2 = I_3 = \ldots$. The applied potential difference at the terminals equals the sum of the potential differences across the individual resistors. That is, $V = V_1 + V_2 + V_3 + \ldots$. However, by Ohm's law $V = IR_{eq}$ where R_{eq} is the equivalent resistance of the entire circuit. **Equivalent resistance** is the single resistance that could replace the several resistors in a circuit. Substituting yields $IR_{eq} = I_1R_1 + I_2R_2 + I_3R_3 + \ldots$. However, because $I = I_1 = I_2 = I_3 = \ldots$, it follows that $IR_{eq} = IR_1 + IR_2 + IR_3 + \ldots$. Dividing each term in the equation by the common factor I yields $R_{eq} = R_1 + R_2 + R_3 + \ldots$.

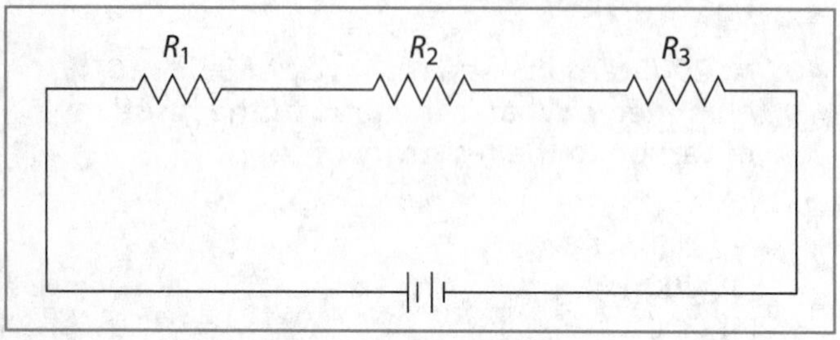

To summarize for series circuits:

$$I = I_1 = I_2 = I_3 = \ldots$$
$$V = V_1 + V_2 + V_3 + \ldots$$
$$R_{eq} = R_1 + R_2 + R_3 + \ldots$$

Figure 4-8. **Resistors in a series circuit**

SAMPLE PROBLEM

Three resistors, with resistances of 4.0 ohms, 6.0 ohms, and 8.0 ohms respectively, are connected in series to an applied potential difference of 36 volts. (a) Calculate the equivalent resistance. (b) Calculate the current through each resistor. (c) Calculate the potential drop across each resistor.

SOLUTION: Identify the known and unknown values.

Known	*Unknown*
Series circuit	$R_{eq} = ?\ \Omega$
$R_1 = 4.0\ \Omega$	$I_1, I_2, I_3 = ?\ A$
$R_2 = 6.0\ \Omega$	$V_1 = ?\ V$
$R_3 = 8.0\ \Omega$	$V_2 = ?\ V$
$V = 36\ V$	$V_3 = ?\ V$

1. Write the formula for the equivalent resistance in a series circuit.

$$R_{eq} = R_1 + R_2 + R_3$$

2. Substitute the known values into the equation and solve.

$$R_{eq} = 4.0\ \Omega + 6.0\ \Omega + 8.0\ \Omega = 18.0\ \Omega$$

3. Write the formula for Ohm's law.

$$R = \frac{V}{I}$$

4. Solve the equation for I and substitute R_{eq} for R.

$$I = \frac{V}{R_{eq}}$$

5. Substitute the known values and solve.

$$I = \frac{36\ V}{18.0\ \Omega} = 2.0\ A$$

The current is the same throughout a series circuit.

$$I = I_1 = I_2 = I_3 = 2.0\ A$$

6. Use Ohm's law to calculate the potential difference across each resistor.

$$V_1 = I_1R_1 = (2.0\ A)(4.0\ \Omega) = 8.0\ V$$
$$V_2 = I_2R_2 = (2.0\ A)(6.0\ \Omega) = 12\ V$$
$$V_3 = I_3R_3 = (2.0\ A)(8.0\ \Omega) = 16\ V$$

Note that when resistors in a circuit are connected in series, the sum of the potential differences across the individual resistors is equal to the applied potential difference.

$$V = V_1 + V_2 + V_3 = 8.0\ V + 12\ V + 16\ V = 36\ V$$

Parallel Circuits A **parallel circuit** is a circuit in which the elements are connected between two points, with one of the two ends of each component connected to each point. Consequently, there are two or more paths for current flow. As shown in Figure 4-9, current is divided among the branches of the circuit.

In a parallel circuit, the sum of the currents in the branches is equal to the total current from the source. That is, $I = I_1 + I_2 + I_3 + \ldots$. The potential difference across each branch of the parallel circuit is the same as that of the potential difference supplied by the source, so $V = V_1 = V_2 = V_3 = \ldots$.

However, according to Ohm's law $I = \dfrac{V}{R}$ for each branch of the circuit. Substituting yields

$I = \dfrac{V_1}{R_1} + \dfrac{V_2}{R_2} + \dfrac{V_3}{R_3} + \ldots$. By Ohm's law it is known that $I = \dfrac{V}{R_{eq}}$ for the circuit. Therefore,

$\dfrac{V}{R_{eq}} = \dfrac{V}{R_1} + \dfrac{V}{R_2} + \dfrac{V}{R_3} + \ldots$. Dividing each term by V yields

$\dfrac{1}{R_{eq}} = \dfrac{1}{R_1} + \dfrac{1}{R_2} + \dfrac{1}{R_3} + \ldots$.

To summarize for parallel circuits:

$$I = I_1 + I_2 + I_3 + \ldots$$
$$V = V_1 = V_2 = V_3 = \ldots$$
$$\dfrac{1}{R_{eq}} = \dfrac{1}{R_1} + \dfrac{1}{R_2} + \dfrac{1}{R_3} + \ldots$$

Note that in a parallel circuit the equivalent resistance R_{eq} is always less than the resistance of any branch. In addition, since V is the same for each branch, the current in each branch is inversely proportional to its resistance. As additional resistors or electrical devices are connected in parallel in a given circuit, the equivalent resistance of the circuit decreases. Consequently the total current in the circuit increases, perhaps to dangerous levels. A fuse or circuit breaker is inserted in the main line of each circuit in the home as a safety device. If the current becomes too large, the fuse or circuit breaker opens.

Meters in a Circuit As noted earlier, an ammeter is used to measure current and a voltmeter is used to measure potential difference. An ammeter is always connected in series with the circuit element being measured, whereas a voltmeter is always connected in parallel. The diagrams in Figure 4-10 show an ammeter and a voltmeter connected to determine the current through and potential difference across resistor R_1.

Conservation of Charge in Electric Circuits Charge in an electric circuit must be conserved. At any junction in a circuit, the sum of the currents entering the junction must equal the sum of the currents leaving it. Figure 4-11 illustrates the conservation of charge at a junction.

Electric Power Recall that power is the time rate of doing work or expending energy. That is $P = \frac{W}{t}$ where work W is in joules, time t is in seconds, and power P is in watts. The derived SI unit for power is the

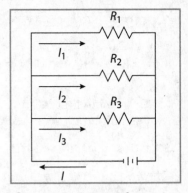

Figure 4-9. Currents in a parallel circuit: The total current I is divided among the three branches of the circuit.

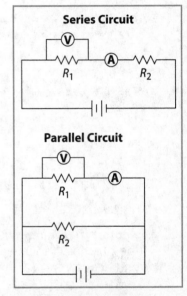

Figure 4-10. Connecting ammeters and voltmeters: The diagram shows how to use an ammeter and a voltmeter to measure the current through and the potential difference across the resistor R_1 in a series circuit and in a parallel circuit.

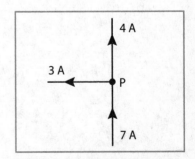

Figure 4-11. Current traveling near junction P in an electric circuit: Note that the sum of currents leaving the junction (3 A + 4 A) equals the current entering the junction (7 A).

SAMPLE PROBLEM

Three resistors of 4.0 ohms, 6.0 ohms, and 12 ohms are connected in parallel to an applied potential difference of 12 volts.

(a) Calculate the equivalent resistance.
(b) Determine the potential difference across each resistor.
(c) Calculate the current through each resistor.

SOLUTION: Identify the known and unknown values.

Known
Parallel circuit
$R_1 = 4.0\ \Omega$
$R_2 = 6.0\ \Omega$
$R_3 = 12.0\ \Omega$
$V = 12\ V$

Unknown
$R_{eq} = ?\ \Omega$
$V_1, V_2, V_3 = ?\ V$
$I_1 = ?\ A$
$I_2 = ?\ A$
$I_3 = ?\ A$

1. Write the formula for the equivalent resistance in a parallel circuit.
$$\frac{1}{R_{eq}} = \frac{1}{R_1} + \frac{1}{R_2} + \frac{1}{R_3}$$

2. Substitute the known resistance values and solve for R_{eq}.
$$\frac{1}{R_{eq}} = \frac{1}{4.0\ \Omega} + \frac{1}{6.0\ \Omega} + \frac{1}{12\ \Omega}$$
$$\frac{1}{R_{eq}} = \frac{3.0}{12\ \Omega} + \frac{2.0}{12\ \Omega} + \frac{1.0}{12\ \Omega}$$
$$R_{eq} = 2.0\ \Omega$$

3. The potential difference across each branch of the circuit is the same as the applied potential difference.
$$V = V_1 = V_2 = V_3 = 12\ V$$

4. Write the formula for Ohm's law.
$$R = \frac{V}{I}$$

5. Solve the equation for I.
$$I = \frac{V}{R}$$

6. Substitute the known values for each individual resistor and solve.
$$I_1 = \frac{V_1}{R_1} = \frac{12\ V}{4.0\ \Omega} = 3.0\ A$$
$$I_2 = \frac{V_2}{R_2} = \frac{12\ V}{6.0\ \Omega} = 2.0\ A$$
$$I_3 = \frac{V_3}{R_3} = \frac{12\ V}{12\ \Omega} = 1.0\ A$$

Note that when resistors are connected in parallel in a circuit, the sum of the currents in the resistors is equal to the total current (the current leaving the source).
$$I = I_1 + I_2 + I_3$$
$$I = 3.0\ A + 2.0\ A + 1.0\ A = 6.0\ A$$

Check: $I = \dfrac{V}{R_{eq}} = \dfrac{12\ V}{2.0\ \Omega} = 6.0\ A$

watt, W. In fundamental units, one watt equals one $\frac{\text{kilogram} \cdot \text{meter}^2}{\text{second}^3}$. Power is a scalar quantity.

Electrical power is the product of potential difference and current. That is, $P = VI$ where power P is in watts, potential difference V is in volts, and current I is in amperes. It can be seen that this equation is valid by analyzing the units.

$$(1\ \text{volt})(1\ \text{ampere}) = \left(1\frac{\text{joule}}{\text{coulomb}}\right)\left(1\frac{\text{coulomb}}{\text{second}}\right)$$
$$= 1\frac{\text{joule}}{\text{second}}$$
$$= 1\ \text{watt}$$

By Ohm's law $V = IR$, so IR can be substituted for V in the equation $P = VI$. This yields:

$$P = VI = (IR)I = I^2R$$

Because $I = \dfrac{V}{R}$, it follows by substitution that

$$P = VI = V\left(\dfrac{V}{R}\right) = \dfrac{V^2}{R}$$

These relationships are summarized below.

Ⓡ
$$P = VI = I^2R = \dfrac{V^2}{R}$$

Electrical Energy Recall from Topic 3 that energy is the capacity for doing work. In an electric circuit the total **electrical energy** W is equal to the product of the power consumed P and the time t of charge flow. That is,

Ⓡ
$$W = Pt = VIt = I^2Rt = \dfrac{V^2t}{R}$$

The SI derived unit for electrical energy is the **joule,** J. In fundamental units, one joule equals one $\frac{kilogram \cdot meter^2}{second^2}$. Electrical energy is a scalar quantity.

SAMPLE PROBLEM A

A potential difference of 60.0 volts is applied across a 15-ohm resistor. Calculate the power dissipated in the resistor.

SOLUTION: Identify the known and unknown values.

Known	Unknown
$V = 60.0$ V	$P = ?$ W
$R = 15\ \Omega$	

1. Write a formula for power in terms of potential difference and resistance.

$$P = \dfrac{V^2}{R}$$

2. Substitute the known values and solve.

$$P = \dfrac{(60.0\ V)^2}{15\ \Omega} = 240\ W$$

SAMPLE PROBLEM B

A current of 0.40 ampere is measured in a 150-ohm resistor. Calculate the total energy expended by the resistor in 30. seconds.

SOLUTION: Identify the known and unknown values.

Known	Unknown
$I = 0.40$ A	$W = ?$ J
$R = 150\ \Omega$	
$t = 30.$ s	

1. Write a formula for electrical energy or work in terms of current, resistance, and time.

$$W = I^2Rt$$

2. Substitute the known values and solve.

$$W = (0.40\ A)^2(150\ \Omega)(30.\ s) = 720\ J$$

Review Questions

49. A 4-ohm resistor and an 8-ohm resistor are connected in series. If the current through the 4-ohm resistor is 2 amperes, the current through the 8-ohm resistor is

(1) 1 A   (2) 2 A   (3) 0.5 A   (4) 4 A

50. If a 15-ohm resistor is connected in parallel with a 30.-ohm resistor, the equivalent resistance is

(1) 15 Ω (2) 2.0 Ω (3) 10. Ω (4) 45 Ω

51. Which two of the resistor arrangements below have the same equivalent resistance?

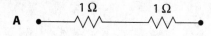
A

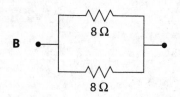
B

C

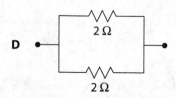
D

(1) A and B
(3) C and D
(2) B and C
(4) D and A

52. Which circuit would have the lowest voltmeter reading?

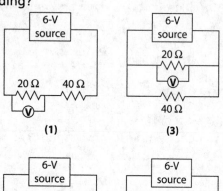

(1)   (3)

(2)   (4)

53. The circuit diagram below shows three voltmeters connected across resistors.

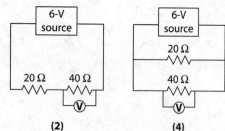

What is the reading of voltmeter V_2?

54. The diagram below shows two resistors connected to a 20.-volt battery.

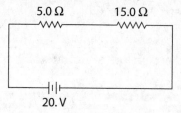

If the current through the 5.0-ohm resistor is 1.0 ampere, what is the current through the 15.0-ohm resistor?

55. The diagram below shows a circuit with three resistors.

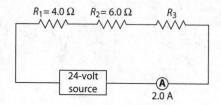

What is the resistance of resistor R_3?

(1) 6.0 Ω   (2) 2.0 Ω   (3) 12 Ω   (4) 4.0 Ω

56. An electric circuit contains an operating heating element and a lit lamp. Which statement best explains why the lamp remains lit when the heating element is removed from the circuit?

(1) The lamp has less resistance than the heating element.
(2) The lamp has more resistance than the heating element.
(3) The lamp and heating element are connected in series.
(4) The lamp and heating element are connected in parallel.

57. A 10.-ohm resistor and a 5.0-ohm resistor are connected as shown in the diagram below.

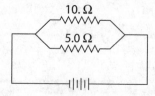

If the current through the 10.-ohm resistor is 1.0 ampere, then the current through the 5.0-ohm resistor is

(1) 15 A   (2) 2.0 A   (3) 0.50 A   (4) 0.30 A

58. In the circuit diagram below, ammeter A measures the current supplied by a 10.-volt battery.

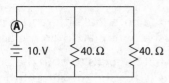

The current measured by ammeter A is

(1) 0.13 A   (2) 2.0 A   (3) 0.50 A   (4) 4.0 A

59. A physics student is given three 12-ohm resistors with instructions to create the circuit that would have the lowest possible resistance. The correct circuit would be a

(1) series circuit with an equivalent resistance of 36 Ω

(2) series circuit with an equivalent resistance of 4 Ω

(3) parallel circuit with an equivalent resistance of 36 Ω

(4) parallel circuit with an equivalent resistance of 4 Ω

60. Which circuit could be used to determine the total current and potential difference of a parallel circuit?

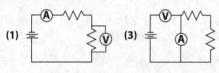

61. Which diagram below shows correct current direction in a circuit segment?

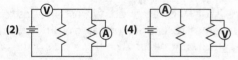

62. The diagram below shows currents in a segment of an electric circuit.

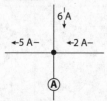

What is the reading of ammeter A?

63. The diagram below represents currents in branches of an electric circuit.

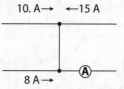

What is the reading on ammeter A?

64. An immersion heater has a resistance of 5.0 ohms while drawing a current of 3.0 amperes. What is the total electrical energy delivered to the heater during 4.0 minutes of operation?

(1) 1.8×10^2 J   (3) 1.1×10^4 J

(2) 3.6×10^3 J   (4) 5.4×10^4 J

65. In a simple circuit, two 3.0-ohm resistors are connected in series to a 12-volt battery. The rate at which electrical energy is expended in this circuit is

(1) 6.0 W   (2) 12 W   (3) 24 W   (4) 36 W

66. Which combination of current and potential difference would use energy at the greatest rate?

(1) 7 A at 110 V   (3) 3 A at 220 V

(2) 6 A at 110 V   (4) 4 A at 220 V

67. How much time is required for an operating 100-watt incandescent lightbulb to dissipate 10 joules of electrical energy?

(1) 1 s   (2) 0.1 s   (3) 10 s   (4) 1000 s

68. While operating at 120 volts, an electric toaster has a resistance of 15 ohms. The power used by the toaster is

(1) 8.0 W   (2) 120 W   (3) 960 W   (4) 1800 W

69. An electric dryer consumes 6.0×10^6 joules of energy when operating at 220 volts for 30. minutes. During operation, the dryer draws a current of

(1) 10. A   (2) 15 A   (3) 20. A   (4) 25 A

70. What is the total amount of electrical energy needed to operate a 1600-watt toaster for 60. seconds?

(1) 27 J   (2) 1500 J   (3) 1700 J   (4) 96,000 J

71. To increase the brightness of a desk lamp, a student replaces a 60-watt incandescent lightbulb with a 100-watt incandescent lightbulb. Compared to the 60-watt lightbulb, the 100-watt lightbulb has

(1) less resistance and draws more current
(2) less resistance and draws less current
(3) more resistance and draws more current
(4) more resistance and draws less current

Base your answers to questions 72 through 75 on the diagram below, which represents a circuit containing a 120-volt power supply with switches S_1 and S_2 and two 60.-ohm resistors.

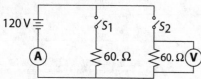

72. If switch S_1 is kept open and switch S_2 is closed, what is the circuit's resistance?

73. If switch S_2 is kept open and switch S_1 is closed, how much current will flow through the circuit?

74. When both switches are closed, what is the current in the ammeter?

75. When both switches are closed, what is the reading of the voltmeter?

Base your answers to questions 76 through 80 on the diagram below, which represents an electrical circuit.

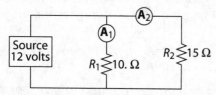

76. Calculate the equivalent resistance of the circuit.

77. Determine the potential difference across resistor R_2.

78. Calculate the magnitude of the current through ammeter A_1.

79. Compare the current in ammeter A_1 to the current in ammeter A_2.

80. Explain what happens to *both* the equivalent resistance of the circuit and the total current in the circuit, if another resistor is added to the circuit in parallel.

Base your answers to questions 81 through 85 on the following information and diagram.
Two resistors, R_1 and R_2, and an ammeter are connected to a constant 30.-volt source.
The equivalent resistance of the circuit is 6.0 ohms.

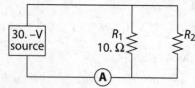

81. Determine the resistance of R_2.

82. Calculate the current through ammeter A.

83. Calculate the power developed in resistor R_1 alone.

84. Compare the potential difference across the source to the potential difference across R_2.

85. Explain what happens to *both* the potential difference across and the current through R_2, if the resistance of R_2 is increased.

Base your answers to questions 86 through 89 on the circuit diagram below.

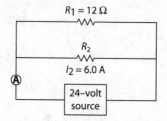

86. The current in ammeter A is
  (1) 1.0 A   (2) 2.0 A   (3) 6.0 A   (4) 8.0 A

87. What is the total energy used by the 12-ohm resistor in 30. minutes?
  (1) 48 J   (3) 1.1×10^4 J
  (2) 3.6×10^3 J   (4) 8.6×10^4 J

88. If resistance R_2 were removed, the potential difference across R_1 would
  (1) decrease   (3) remain the same
  (2) increase

89. If resistor R_2 is removed, what happens to the equivalent resistance of the circuit and the current in ammeter A?
  (1) The equivalent resistance decreases, and the current decreases.
  (2) The equivalent resistance decreases, and the current increases.
  (3) The equivalent resistance increases, and the current decreases.
  (4) The equivalent resistance increases, and the current increases.

Base your answers to questions 90 through 94 on the electric circuit below. Note that the switch is in the open position.

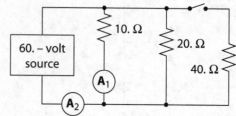

90. What is the reading of ammeter A_1?

    (1) 0.16 A   (2) 6.0 A   (3) 60. A   (4) 600 A

91. What is the reading of ammeter A_2?

    (1) 9.0 A   (2) 2.0 A   (3) 12 A   (4) 18 A

92. What is the power developed in the 10.-ohm resistor?

    (1) 6.0 W   (2) 36 W   (3) 360 W   (4) 600 W

93. Compared to the potential drop across the 10.-ohm resistor, the potential drop across the 20.-ohm resistor is

    (1) less   (2) greater   (3) the same

94. When the switch is closed, what happens to the current through ammeters A_1 and A_2?

    (1) The current through A_1 decreases, and the current through A_2 decreases.
    (2) The current through A_1 decreases, and the current through A_2 increases.
    (3) The current through A_1 remains the same, and the current through A_2 decreases.
    (4) The current through A_1 remains the same, and the current through A_2 increases.

Base your answers to questions 95 and 96 on the following information. An electric heater rated at 4800 watts is operated at 120 volts.

95. Calculate the resistance of the heater.

96. Calculate the amount of energy used by the heater in 10.0 seconds.

97. A resistor develops 15 watts of power when connected to a 12-volt battery. Calculate the amount of charge passing through the resistor in 1.0 minute.

98. An electric circuit consists of a 3.0-ohm resistor, R_1, and a variable resistor, R_2, connected in series to a 12-volt battery. At what value must the variable resistor be set to produce a current of 1.0 ampere through R_1?

    (1) 6.0 Ω   (2) 9.0 Ω   (3) 3.0 Ω   (4) 12 Ω

99. An operating electric circuit consists of a lamp and a length of nichrome wire connected in series to a 12-volt battery. As the temperature of the nichrome is decreased, what happens to the equivalent resistance of the circuit and the power developed by the lamp?

    (1) The equivalent resistance decreases, and the power developed by the lamp decreases.
    (2) The equivalent resistance decreases, and the power developed by the lamp increases.
    (3) The equivalent resistance increases, and the power developed by the lamp decreases.
    (4) The equivalent resistance increases, and the power developed by the lamp increases.

Magnetism

A **magnet** is a material in which the spinning electrons of its atoms are aligned with one another. This motion of charges relative to each other produces a **magnetic force.** Even if two magnets are at rest relative to each other, they exert magnetic force because the electrons within them are in motion. Many permanent magnets are made of an alloy of aluminum, nickel, and cobalt.

A magnet has two ends called poles, where the magnetic force is strongest. One end is called the north-seeking **magnetic pole** (N-pole), and the other end is the south-seeking magnetic pole (S-pole). No matter how many times a magnet is broken, each piece always has a north pole and a south pole. Like magnetic poles repel each other and unlike poles attract each other. **Magnetism** is the force of attraction or repulsion between magnetic poles. Unmagnetized pieces of iron and steel are readily magnetized by pulling them across a pole of a strong magnet or by having them interact with a direct current.

Earth is like a large magnet with a S-pole near the geographic North Pole (the northern end of its axis of rotation) and an N-pole near the geographic South Pole. The N-pole of a compass, a device having a magnetized needle that can spin freely, is attracted toward Earth's S-pole (geographic North

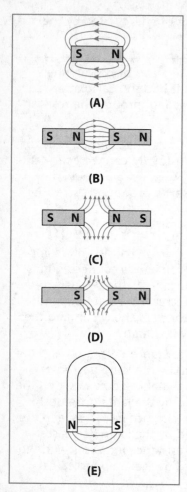

(A)

(B)

(C)

(D)

(E)

Figure 4-12. Magnetic field lines around some bar magnets and a horseshoe magnet

Pole). Earth's magnetic field results from the motion of its molten iron and nickel core.

Magnetic Fields The region where magnetic force exists around a magnet or any moving charged object is called its **magnetic field.** Just as a gravitational or electric field allows objects to interact without coming into direct contact with each other, a magnetic field allows magnets to interact without touching. A magnetic field exerts a force on any moving charge and can be measured and detected by this effect.

Magnetic Flux Lines Imaginary lines that map out the magnetic field around a magnet are known as **magnetic field lines** or **magnetic flux lines.** Iron filings sprinkled on a card and held above a magnet are often used to map a magnetic field. The filings show the effects of magnetic force in the region surrounding a magnet and produce a pattern similar to the magnetic field lines. Magnetic flux lines always form closed loops and never intersect. Concentrated lines of flux emerge from the N-pole of a magnet, curve around the magnet, and then enter the S-pole of the magnet. The direction of a magnetic field is defined as the direction in which the N-pole of a compass would point in the field. When the field lines are curved, the direction of the field is determined by the direction of the N-pole of a compass placed along the tangent to the field at that point. Figure 4-12 shows the locations of the lines of magnetic flux around some bar magnets and around a horseshoe magnet.

Magnetic Field Strength The number of magnetic lines of flux per unit area passing through a plane perpendicular to the direction of the lines is called the **magnetic field strength,** B, or flux density. Magnetic field strength is a vector quantity, as are gravitational field strength and electric field strength.

Review Questions

100. In order to produce a magnetic field, an electric charge must be

(1) stationary
(2) moving
(3) positive
(4) negative

101. The presence of a uniform magnetic field may be detected by using a

(1) stationary charge
(2) small mass
(3) beam of neutrons
(4) magnetic compass

102. Which term does *not* identify a vector quantity?

(1) electric charge
(2) magnetic field strength
(3) velocity
(4) acceleration

103. The diagram below shows a compass placed near the north pole, N, of a bar magnet.

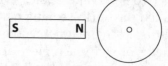

Which diagram best represents the position of the needle of a compass as it responds to the magnetic field of the bar magnet?

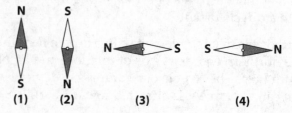

(1)   **(2)**   **(3)**   **(4)**

104. A student is given two pieces of iron and told to determine if one or both of the pieces are magnets. First, the student touches an end of one piece to one end of the other. The two pieces of iron attract. Next, the student reverses one of the pieces and again touches the ends together. The two pieces attract again. What does the student definitely know about the initial magnetic properties of the two pieces of iron? [1]

105. Which diagram correctly shows a magnetic field configuration?

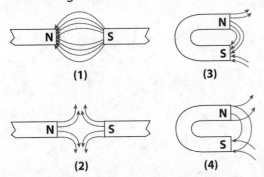

106. The diagram below shows two compasses located near the ends of a bar magnet. The north pole of compass X points toward end A of the magnet.

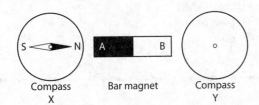

On the diagram draw the correct orientation of the needle of compass Y and label its polarity.

107. Which diagram best represents the lines of magnetic flux between the ends of two bar magnets?

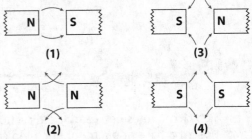

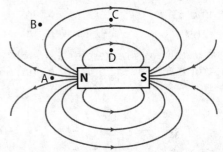

108. The diagram below represents the magnetic lines of force around a bar magnet.

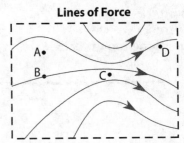

At which point is the magnitude of the magnetic field strength of the bar magnet greatest?

109. The diagram below represents magnetic lines of force within a region of space.

Lines of Force

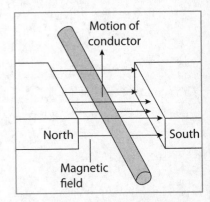

At which point is the magnetic field strongest?

Electromagnetic Induction

Electromagnetic induction is the process of generating a potential difference in a conductor due to relative motion between the conductor and a magnetic field. If the conductor "cuts" across the magnetic flux lines, a magnetic force acts on the electrons in the conductor, causing them to move from one end toward the other. This results in a difference in the amount of negative charge at each end of the conductor, in other words, a potential difference. The difference in potential created in a conductor due to its relative motion in a magnetic field is called an **induced potential difference**. Figure 4-13 shows a potential difference being induced in a conductor.

If the conductor is part of a complete circuit, an electric current is induced. If the conductor is moved parallel to the lines of flux (that is, it does not "cut" them) no potential difference is induced and there is no current, even if the conductor is part of a complete circuit.

Figure 4-13. Electromagnetic induction: The diagram shows the direction of motion of a straight conductor relative to a magnetic field that produces a maximum induced potential difference in the conductor.

Electromagnetic Radiation Oscillating or accelerating electric charges produce changing electric and magnetic fields that radiate outward into the surrounding space in the form of waves. Such a combined electric and magnetic wave is called an **electromagnetic wave.**

Review Questions

110. For which two angles between the direction of motion of a wire and a magnetic field can a potential difference be induced across the wire?

(1) 0° and 45°   (3) 45° and 90°
(2) 0° and 90°   (4) 45° and 180°

111. The diagram below represents a straight conductor between the poles of a permanent magnet.

In which direction should the wire be moved to induce a potential difference?

(1) toward N
(2) toward S
(3) toward the top of the page
(4) into the page

112. A conductor is moved perpendicularly through magnetic field B as represented in the diagram below.

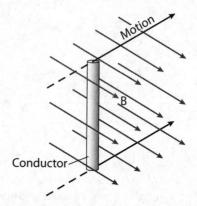

What is being induced in the conductor?

(1) potential difference
(2) resistance
(3) power
(4) current

Directions

Review the Test-Taking Strategies section of this book. Then answer the following questions. Read each question carefully and answer with a correct choice or response.

Part A

1 A sphere has a charge of -6.40×10^{-7} coulomb. Approximately how many electrons must be removed to make the sphere neutral?
(1) 2.50×10^{-13}
(3) 4.00×10^{12}
(2) 1.60×10^{12}
(4) 7.03×10^{24}

2 An inflated balloon that has been rubbed against a person's hair is touched to a neutral wall and remains attracted to it. Which diagram best represents the charge distribution on the balloon and wall?

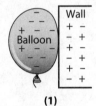
(1)

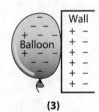
(3)

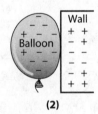
(2)

(4)

3 Which quantity of excess electric charge could be found on an object?
(1) 6.25×10^{-19} C
(2) 4.80×10^{-19} C
(3) 6.25 elementary charges
(4) 1.60 elementary charges

4 After a neutral object loses 2 electrons, it will have a net charge of
(1) $-2e$
(3) $-3.20 \times 10^{-19}\,e$
(2) $+2e$
(4) $+3.20 \times 10^{-19}\,e$

5 The electrostatic force between two positive point charges is F when the charges are 48 centimeters apart. When these point charges are placed 24 centimeters apart, the electrostatic force between them is
(1) $\dfrac{F}{4}$, and attracting
(3) $\dfrac{F}{4}$, and repelling
(2) $4F$, and attracting
(4) $4F$, and repelling

6 A repulsive electrostatic force of magnitude F exists between two metal spheres of identical charge q. The distance between the centers of the spheres is r. Which combination of changes would produce no change in the electrostatic force between the spheres?
(1) doubling q on one sphere while doubling r
(2) doubling q on both spheres while doubling r
(3) doubling q on one sphere while halving r
(4) doubling q on both spheres while halving r

7 The diagram below shows two identical metal spheres, A and B, separated by distance d. Each sphere has mass m and possesses charge $+q$.

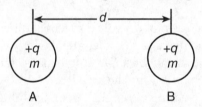

Which diagram best represents the electrostatic force F_e and the gravitational force F_g acting on sphere B due to sphere A?

8 An electrostatic force of 20.0 newtons is exerted on a charge of 8.00×10^{-2} coulomb at point P in an electric field. The magnitude of the electric field strength at P is
(1) 4.00×10^{-3} C/N
(3) 20.0 N/C
(2) $1.60\ \text{N} \cdot \text{C}$
(4) 2.50×10^2 N/C

9 If 6.40×10^{-19} joule of work is required to move a proton between two points A and B in an electric field, what is the potential difference between points A and B?
(1) 6.40×10^{-19} V
(3) 6.40 V
(2) 4.00×10^{-19} V
(4) 4.00 V

10 How much energy is required to move 3.20×10^{-19} coulomb of charge through a potential difference of 5.0 volts?
(1) 5.0 eV   (2) 2.0 eV   (3) 10. eV   (4) 16 eV

11 During a thunderstorm, a lightning strike transfers 12 coulombs of charge in 2.0×10^{-3} second. What is the average current produced in this strike?
(1) 1.7×10^{-4} A
(3) 6.0×10^3 A
(2) 2.4×10^{-2} A
(4) 9.6×10^3 A

12 A wire carries a current of 6.0 amperes. How much charge passes a point in the wire in 2.0 minutes?
(1) 720 C
(2) 360 C
(3) 3.0 C
(4) 12 C

13 A simple circuit has a total resistance of 1.00×10^2 ohms and an applied potential difference of 2.00×10^2 volts. The amount of charge passing any point in the circuit in 2.00 seconds is
(1) 1.26×10^{19} C
(3) 2.52×10^{19} C
(2) 2.00 C
(4) 4.00 C

14 Which changes would cause the greatest increase in the rate of flow of charge through a conducting wire?
(1) increasing the applied potential difference and decreasing the length of wire
(2) increasing the applied potential difference and increasing the length of wire
(3) decreasing the applied potential difference and decreasing the length of wire
(4) decreasing the applied potential difference and increasing the length of wire

15 A metal conductor is used in an electric circuit. The electrical resistance provided by the conductor could be increased by
(1) decreasing the length of the conductor
(2) decreasing the applied voltage in the circuit
(3) increasing the temperature of the conductor
(4) increasing the cross-sectional area of the conductor

16 A uniform aluminum wire has a resistance of 100 ohms. If the wire is cut into 10 equal lengths, the resistance of each piece will be
(1) $1\ \Omega$
(2) $10\ \Omega$
(3) $100\ \Omega$
(4) $1000\ \Omega$

17 A 6.50-meter-long copper wire at 20°C has a cross-sectional area of 3.0 millimeters². What is the resistance of the wire?
(1) $3.7 \times 10^{-8}\ \Omega$
(3) $3.7 \times 10^{-2}\ \Omega$
(2) $3.73 \times 10^{-8}\ \Omega$
(4) $3.73 \times 10^{-4}\ \Omega$

18 A 4.00-meter long aluminum wire at 20°C has a radius of 2.5×10^{-3} meter. What is the resistance of the wire?
(1) $1.4 \times 10^{-5}\ \Omega$
(3) $1.0 \times 10^{-2}\ \Omega$
(2) $5.7 \times 10^{-3}\ \Omega$
(4) $5.7 \times 10^{-1}\ \Omega$

19 In the circuit shown below, voltmeter V_2 reads 80. volts.

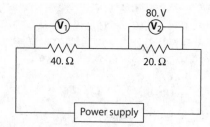

What is the reading of voltmeter V_1?
(1) 160 V
(2) 80. V
(3) 40. V
(4) 20. V

20 The diagram below shows three resistors connected to a 12-volt battery.

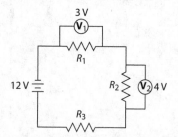

If voltmeter V_1 reads 3 volts and voltmeter V_2 reads 4 volts, what is the potential drop across resistor R_3?
(1) 12 V
(2) 5 V
(3) 0 V
(4) 4 V

21 A 3.0-om resistor and 4.0-ohm resistor are connected in series to a battery. If a 5.0-ohm resistor is added to this circuit in series, what happens to the potential difference across and the current through the 3.0-ohm resistor?
(1) The potential difference decreases, and the current decreases.
(2) The potential difference decreases, and the current increases.
(3) The potential difference remains the same, and the current increases.
(4) The potential difference remains the same, and the current remains the same.

22 The diagram below represents a series circuit containing three resistors.

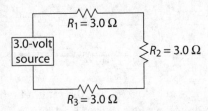

What is the current through resistor R_2?
(1) 1.0 A   (2) 0.33 A   (3) 3.0 A   (4) 9.0 A

23 Resistors R_1 and R_2 have an equivalent resistance of 6 ohms when connected in the circuit shown below.

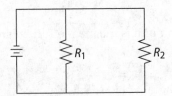

The resistance of R_1 could be
(1) 1 Ω   (2) 5 Ω   (3) 8 Ω   (4) 4 Ω

24 The diagram below shows three resistors connected to a 9-volt source.

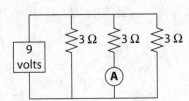

What is the current in ammeter A?
(1) 1 A   (2) 0.3 A   (3) 3 A   (4) 9 A

25 A 10-ohm and a 20-ohm resistor are connected in parallel to a constant voltage source. If the current through the 10-ohm resistor is 4 amperes, the current through the 20-ohm resistor is
(1) 1 A   (2) 2 A   (3) 8 A   (4) 4 A

26 Which circuit segment has an equivalent resistance of 6 ohms?

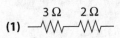
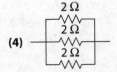

27 In which circuit shown below could the readings of voltmeters V_1 and V_2 and ammeter A be correct?

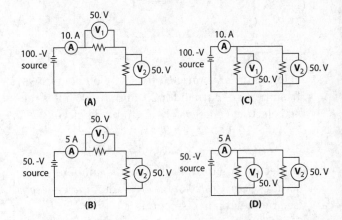

(1) A and B   (3) C and D
(2) B and C   (4) A and D

28 Ammeters A_1, A_2, and A_3 are placed in a circuit as shown below.

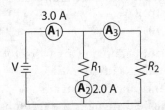

What is the reading of ammeter A_3?
(1) 1.0 A   (2) 2.0 A   (3) 3.0 A   (4) 5.0 A

29 The diagram below shows the current in a segment of a direct current circuit.

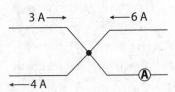

What is the reading of ammeter A?
(1) 1 A   (2) 5 A   (3) 7 A   (4) 8 A

30 An incandescent lightbulb operating at 120 volts draws a current of 0.50 ampere for 240 seconds. The power rating of the lightbulb is
(1) 30. W   (2) 60. W   (3) 75 W   (4) 120 W

31 The heating element on an electric heater dissipates 4.0×10^2 watts of power when connected to a 120-volt source. What is the electrical resistance of this heating element?
(1) 0.028 Ω   (2) 0.60 Ω   (3) 3.3 Ω   (4) 36 Ω

32 A 4.50-volt personal stereo uses 1950 joules of electrical energy in one hour. What is the electrical resistance of the personal stereo?
(1) 433 Ω
(2) 96.3 Ω
(3) 37.4 Ω
(4) 0.623 Ω

33 A clothes dryer connected to a 240-volt line draws 30. amperes of current for 20. minutes. What is the total electrical energy consumed by the dryer?
(1) 4.8×10^3 J
(3) 1.4×10^5 J
(2) 7.2×10^3 J
(4) 8.6×10^6 J

34 An electric iron draws a current of 5 amperes and has a resistance of 20 ohms. The amount of energy used by the iron in 40 seconds is
(1) 1×10^2 J
(3) 4×10^3 J
(2) 5×10^2 J
(4) 2×10^4 J

35 An operating 75-watt incandescent lamp is connected to a 120-volt outlet. How much electrical energy does the lamp use in 1.0 hour?
(1) 4.5×10^3 J
(3) 5.4×10^5 J
(2) 2.7×10^5 J
(4) 3.2×10^7 J

36 Which quantity and unit are correctly paired?
(1) power and watt•seconds
(2) resistance and ohm•meters
(3) electric field strength and newtons/ampere
(4) electric potential difference and joules/coulomb

37 The diagram below shows a point located between two magnetic poles.

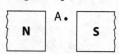

What is the direction of the magnetic field at point A?
(1) to the left
(2) to the right
(3) toward the top of the page
(4) toward the bottom of the page

38 Which diagram best represents the magnetic field near the poles of a horseshoe magnet?

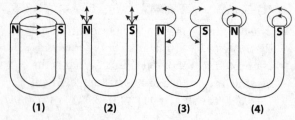

(1) (2) (3) (4)

39 Which diagram best represents the magnetic field between two magnetic north poles?

40 The diagram below shows the magnetic field that results when a piece of iron is placed between unlike magnetic poles.

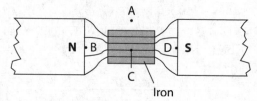

At which point is the magnetic field strength greatest?
(1) A
(2) B
(3) C
(4) D

41 In the diagram below, a steel paper clip is attached to a string, which is attached to a table. The clip remains suspended beneath a magnet.

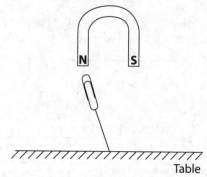

As the magnet is lifted, the paper clip begins to fall as a result of
(1) an increase in the potential energy of the clip
(2) an increase in the gravitational field strength near the magnet
(3) a decrease in the mass of the paper clip
(4) a decrease in the magnetic field strength near the clip

42 Which type of field is present near a moving electric charge?
(1) an electric field, only
(2) a magnetic field, only
(3) both an electric field and a magnetic field
(4) neither an electric field nor a magnetic field

43 In the diagram below a straight wire is at rest in a uniform magnetic field directed into the page.

Magnetic field

A potential difference will be induced in the wire if it is moved
(1) toward the top of the page
(2) toward the right of the page
(3) into the page
(4) out of the page

44 The diagram below shows the cross section of a wire that is perpendicular to the page in a uniform magnetic field directed to the right.

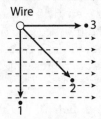

Toward which direction could the wire be moved to induce an electric potential?
(1) 1 only   (3) 3 only
(2) both 1 and 2   (4) both 1 and 3

Part B

45 In the diagram below, the open circle represents an uncharged metal sphere located midway between two charged spheres, A and B. On the diagram, using + for positive and − for negative, mark at least six charges to represent the arrangement of charges on the uncharged sphere. [1]

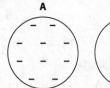

46 Charge A is +2.0 microcoulombs and charge B is +1.0 microcoulomb. If the magnitude of the electrostatic force that A exerts on B is 1.0×10^{-2} newton, what is the magnitude of the electrostatic force that B exerts on A? [1]

47 Calculate the charge to mass ratio $(\frac{e}{m})$ for an electron. [2]

48 Three identical metal spheres are mounted on insulating stands. Initially, sphere A has a net charge of q and spheres B and C are uncharged. Sphere A is touched to sphere B and removed. Then sphere A is touched to sphere C and removed. What is the final charge on sphere A in terms of q? [1]

49 In the diagram below, two identical spheres A and B have equal net positive charges.

On the diagram, sketch an arrow that best represents the direction of the resultant electric field at point P. [1]

Base your answers to questions 50 through 53 on the following information and diagram. Two small spheres A and B are separated by a distance of 0.50 meter. The charge on sphere A is +2.4 microcoulombs and the charge on sphere B is −2.4 microcoulombs.

A   B

$+2.4 \times 10^{-6}$ C -2.4×10^{-6} C

50 On the diagram sketch at least three electric field lines in the region between sphere A and sphere B. Draw an arrowhead on each field line to show the proper direction. [2]

51 Calculate the magnitude of the electrostatic force that sphere *A* exerts on sphere *B*. [2]

52 Using the axes below, draw the general shape of the graph representing the magnitude of the electrostatic force versus the distance separating the centers of the two oppositely charged spheres. [1]

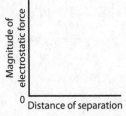

53 The two spheres are brought into contact and then separated. After separation, what is the charge on each sphere? [1]

Base your answers to questions 54 through 58 on the following information and diagram.

Two parallel plates are charged to a potential difference of 10.0 volts. Points A, B, and C are located in the region between the plates.

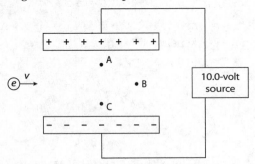

54 Sketch at least three electric field lines to represent the field in the region between the oppositely charged parallel plates. Draw lines with arrowheads in the proper direction. [2]

55 Describe the path an electron would travel if it were projected into the electric field with a velocity v, as shown. [1]

56 Compare the magnitude of the electric field strength at point B to the magnitude of the electric field strength at point A. [1]

57 Calculate the work done against the electric field in moving an electron from the positive plate to the negative plate. [2]

58 Determine the maximum speed of an electron that starts from rest at the negative plate and travels towards the positive plate. [1]

59 Which graph below best represents how the resistance R of a series of tungsten wires of uniform length and temperature varies with cross-sectional area A?

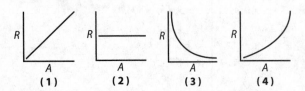

60 The table below shows the length and cross-sectional area of four pieces of copper wire at the same temperature.

Some Sizes of Copper Wire

Wire	Length (m)	Cross-sectional Area (m²)
A	10	2×10^{-6}
B	10	1×10^{-6}
C	1	2×10^{-6}
D	1	1×10^{-6}

Which wire has the highest resistance? [1]

Base your answers to questions 61 through 64 on the following information and graph.

Four different conductors of equal length and equal cross-sectional area were held at constant temperature while the potential difference across each was varied. The resulting current through each conductor was measured. The data are represented in the graph below.

Current vs. Potential Difference

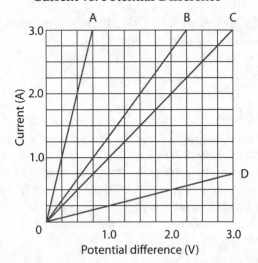

61 Which conductor has the greatest resistance? [1]

62 Which conductor has the smallest resistivity? [1]

63 Calculate the resistance of conductor B. [2]

64 Calculate the rate of energy use in conductor B at 1.5 volts. [2]

Base your answers to questions 65 through 67 on the circuit diagram below.

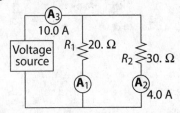

65 Determine the potential difference across the source. [1]

66 Calculate the current reading of ammeter A_1 [2].

67 Calculate the power dissipated by resistor R_2. [2]

Base your answers to questions 68 through 72 on the following information and diagram. A 5.0-ohm resistor, a 15.0-ohm resistor, and an unmarked resistor are connected as shown with a 15-volt source. The ammeter reads a current of 0.50 ampere.

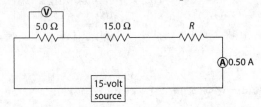

68 Calculate the reading of the voltmeter across the 5.0-ohm resistor. [2]

69 Calculate the total electrical energy used in the circuit in 10.0 minutes. [2]

70 Determine the value of the unmarked resistor. [1]

71 Compare the power dissipated by the 5.0-ohm resistor to the power dissipated by the 15.0-ohm resistor. [1]

72 The 5.0-ohm resistor is removed from the circuit and the remaining circuit elements reattached to the source in the same manner as in the original diagram. State the effect of this change on *both* the potential drop across resistor R and the current through the ammeter. [1]

Base your answers to questions 73 through 75 on the following information and diagram. Three resistors are connected in parallel across a 24-volt source. The ammeter reads 3.0 amperes.

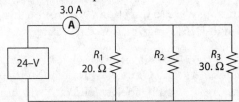

73 Determine the equivalent resistance of the circuit. [1]

74 Calculate the current in resistor R_1. [2]

75 The ratio of the current in R_3 to the current in R_2 is 4 : 5. What is the resistance of R_2? [1]

76 In the diagram below steel paper clips A and B are attached to a string, which is attached to the table. The clips remain suspended beneath a magnet.

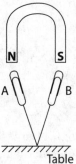

Label each of the paper clips in the diagram with its induced polarity. [1]

77 On the diagram of a bar magnet below, sketch at least four magnetic lines of flux with arrowheads to represent the magnetic field around the magnet. [2]

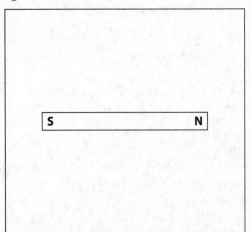

Base your answers to questions 78 through 80 on your knowledge of electricity.

78 Explain why it would be highly impractical to have household circuits wired in series. [1]

79 Explain why the tungsten filament of a 150-watt incandescent bulb is thicker and shorter than the filament of a 60-watt incandescent bulb. [1]

80 Explain why an electron appears to defy gravity as it accelerates upward between two oppositely charged parallel plates. [1]

81 The diagram below represents a particle of mass m and charge $+q$ located between two oppositely charged parallel plates. The electric field strength between the plates is E.

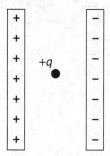

On the diagram draw and label all the force vectors acting on the particle. [2]

Part C

Base your answers to questions 82 and 83 on the following information and diagram.

Potential difference V exists between two oppositely charged parallel metal plates in a vacuum. An electron of mass m_e and charge e starts from rest at the negative plate and travels towards the positive plate. [Neglect the effect of gravity.]

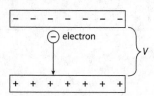

82 Derive an expression for the maximum speed v of the electron in terms of V, m_e, and e. [2]

83 The electron is replaced with a proton that starts from rest at the positive plate and travels toward the negative plate. Compare the maximum speed of the proton to the maximum speed of the electron in question 82 and give evidence to support your answer. [1]

84 According to Ohm's law an ohm is equivalent to a volt per ampere. The ohm can be expressed in terms of the fundamental units kilogram, meter, second, and ampere. Show $1\frac{V}{A} = 1\frac{kg \cdot m^3}{A^2 \cdot s^3}$ [3]

85 Derive an expression for the radius r of a conductor in terms of its length ℓ, resistance R, and resistivity ρ. [2]

Base your answers to questions 86 through 90 on the following information. An electric broiler is rated 1440 watts and 120 volts. The broiler is connected to a 120-volt line.

86 Draw a diagram of the circuit, showing a voltmeter and an ammeter properly connected to determine the actual power (wattage) of the broiler. [2]

87 Calculate the resistance of the heating coil, if the broiler is operating at the rated power. [2]

88 Calculate the energy the broiler produces in 10.0 minutes. [Assume all of the electrical energy used is converted to heat energy.] [2]

89 A 15-ampere fuse protects the electrical power supply line. Calculate how much additional current can be drawn from the line before the fuse blows and opens the circuit. [2]

90 A "short circuit" is a circuit containing a path of very low resistance in parallel with some other circuit element, such as a lamp. Explain the effect a short circuit would have on the power output of the broiler. [1]

Base your answers to questions 91 through 96 on the following information. A 3.0-ohm resistor and a 6.0-ohm resistor are connected in parallel to an applied potential difference of 12 volts.

91 Using appropriate symbols from the *Reference Tables for Physical Setting/Physics*, draw a labeled circuit diagram. [1]

92 Calculate the current in the 6.0-ohm resistor. [2]

93 Determine the potential drop across the 3.0-ohm resistor. [1]

94 Calculate the power developed in the circuit. [3]

95 An additional 2.0-ohm resistor is connected in parallel in the circuit. Explain what effect, if any, this action has on the amount of current drawn by the 6.0-ohm resistor. [1]

96 Compare the equivalent resistance of the 3.0-ohm resistor and the 6.0-ohm resistor when connected in parallel to their equivalent resistance when connected in series. [1]

Base your answers to questions 97 through 104 on the following information and data table.

A student performed an experiment with the intention of verifying Ohm's law for a household incandescent lightbulb labeled 150 W. In addition to the lightbulb, the student had available to him a socket appropriate for a lamp, a variable source of potential difference, an ammeter, a voltmeter, and connecting wires of negligible resistance. After correctly connecting the ammeter and voltmeter in a circuit with the bulb and source, the student increased the applied potential difference in increments of 1.0 volt and recorded the reading of the ammeter each time. The student took only one reading of the ammeter for each potential difference value. The student's data are shown in the table below.

Meter Readings	
Potential Difference (V)	Current (A)
0.0	0.00
1.0	0.08
2.0	0.16
3.0	0.20
4.0	0.22
5.0	0.24
6.0	0.26
7.0	0.27

97 Using appropriate symbols from the *Reference Tables for Physical Setting/Physics* and a box labeled "power source," draw and label a complete circuit showing:
- the lamp connected to the power source [1]
- the ammeter connected to measure the current through the lamp [1]
- the voltmeter connected to measure the potential difference across the lamp [1]

98 Using the information in the data table, construct a graph using the grid below by:
- plotting the data points [1]
- drawing the line or curve of best fit [1]
- writing an appropriate title above the grid [1]

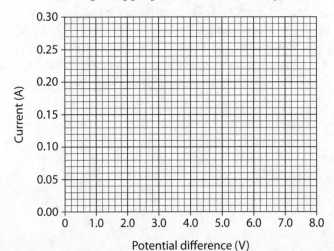

99 Calculate the slope of the graph at the 3.0-volt reading. [2]

100 What is the physical significance of the slope of the line at any point? [1]

101 The student concluded that the lamp does not obey Ohm's law. Based on your knowledge of physics and the graph, state the most likely reason why. [1]

102 On the same grid used in question 98, sketch a line representing a device that obeys Ohm's law. [1]

103 Calculate the maximum power developed by the lamp during the experiment. [2]

104 Explain why your answer to question 103 does *not* agree with the 150 W label on the bulb. [1]

Base your answers to questions 105 through 109 on the following information and data table.

In an experiment, a potential difference of 2.0 volts was applied to various lengths of wire of the same cross-sectional area and metallic composition at a temperature of 20°C. The resulting current was measured and the data recorded in the table below. The student calculated the resistance for each length of wire and recorded that in the table as well.

Results of Varying Wire Length			
Length (cm)	Potential Difference (V)	Current (mA)	Resistance
40.	2.0	500	4.0
80.	2.0	240	8.3
120.	2.0	170	12
160.	2.0	120	17
200.	2.0	100	20.

105 Using the information in the data table, construct a graph on the grid below by:
- plotting the data points [1]
- drawing the line or curve of best fit [1]
- writing an appropriate title above the grid [1]

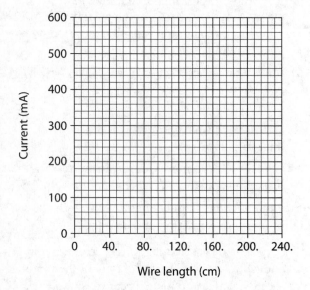

106 Based on your graph, state the relationship between current and wire length. [1]

107 What unit should be written on the data table for resistance? [1]

108 On the axes below sketch the general shape of the graph that shows the relationship between resistance and wire length based on information in the data table. [1]

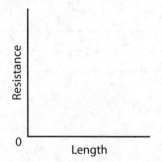

109 The diameter of the wire is 3.18×10^{-4} meter. Calculate the resistivity of the 200.-centimeter-long wire at 20°C. [3]

Base your answers to questions 110 through 114 on the following information and data table.

Three lamps were connected in a circuit with a battery of constant potential. The current, potential difference, and resistance for each lamp are listed in the data table below. [There is negligible resistance in the wires and the battery.]

	Current (A)	Potential Difference (V)	Resistance (Ω)
lamp 1	0.45	40.1	89
lamp 2	0.11	40.1	365
lamp 3	0.28	40.1	143

110 Using the circuit symbols found in the *Reference Tables for Physical Setting/Physics*, draw a circuit showing how the lamps and batter diagram are connected. [2]

111 What is the potential difference supplied by the battery? [1]

112 Calculate the equivalent resistance of the circuit. [2]

113 If lamp 3 is removed from the circuit, what would be the value of the potential difference across lamp 1 after lamp 3 is removed? [1]

114 If lamp 3 is removed from the circuit, what would be the value of the current in lamp 2 after lamp 3 is removed? [1]

Base your answers to questions 115 and 116 on the information below.

A lightweight sphere hangs by an insulating thread. A student wishes to determine if the sphere is neutral or electrostatically charged. She has a negatively charged hard rubber rod and a positively charged glass rod. She does not touch the sphere with the rods, but runs tests by bringing them near the sphere one at a time.

115 Describe the test result that would prove that the sphere is neutral. [1]

116 Describe the test result that would prove that the sphere is positively charged. [1]

How Scientists Study Waves

? **?**

Are radio waves sound waves?

Radio waves are electromagnetic waves that are produced by accelerating charged particles in an antenna. Radio waves do not require a medium for transmission. They travel through space at 3.00×10^8 meters per second.

On the other hand, sound waves are longitudinal waves that are usually produced by vibrating objects. Sound waves propagate through a medium as changes in pressure. Sound waves can be transmitted by solids, liquids, and gases, but they cannot travel through a vacuum. The speed of sound is 343 meters per second in air at 20° C.

Although radio waves travel in straight lines and the Earth's surface is curved, it is possible to transmit radio waves great distances from the source of production to point of reception. Radio waves with frequencies ranging from approximately 0.3 megahertz to 30 megahertz can reflect multiple times from the ionosphere surrounding Earth and from Earth's surface.

It takes less time for a radio wave to travel from California to New York than it does for the sound wave coming from a radio to travel across a room.

Vocabulary

absolute index of refraction	incident ray	reflected ray
amplitude	interference	refracted ray
angle of incidence	law of reflection	reflection
angle of reflection	longitudinal wave	refraction
angle of refraction	medium	resonance
antinode	natural frequency	Snell's law
constructive interference	node	speed
destructive interference	normal	standing wave
diffraction	period	superposition
Doppler effect	periodic wave	transverse wave
electromagnetic spectrum	phase	vacuum
electromagnetic wave	principle of superposition	wave
frequency	pulse	wave front
hertz	ray	wavelength

Introduction to Waves

A **wave** is a vibratory disturbance that propagates through a **medium** (body of matter) or field. Every wave has, as its source, a particle vibrating or oscillating about an average position. For example, a sound wave can be produced by a vibrating tuning fork and a radio wave can be generated by accelerating electrons in a transmitter.

Waves and Energy Transfer

Waves transfer energy from one place to another by repeated small vibrations of particles of a medium or by repeated small changes in the strength of a field. The source provides the initial vibrations, but there is no actual transfer of mass from the source. Only energy is transferred from the source. The propagation of mechanical waves, such as sound and water waves, requires a material medium. Electromagnetic waves, such as visible light and radio waves, can travel through a **vacuum,** which is a region of empty space.

Pulses and Periodic Waves

A wave may be classified as either a pulse or a periodic wave. A **pulse** is a single short disturbance that moves from one position to another in a field or medium. For example, a pulse produced on a stretched rope moves horizontally along the rope, as shown in Figure 5-1.

The speed of a pulse depends upon the type and properties of the medium. Pulse speed is constant if the medium is a uniform material with the same properties throughout. If the pulse reaches an interface or boundary of a new medium, part of the pulse is transmitted through the new medium, part is absorbed, and part is reflected back to the source. **Reflection** is the rebounding of a pulse or wave as it strikes a barrier.

Ceiling tiles, draperies, and carpeting help minimize noise levels in a room. These irregularly shaped surfaces absorb some of the energy of sound waves that strike them. The reflected sound waves have less energy than the original waves.

If the right end of the rope in Figure 5-1 was attached to a fixed unyielding body, such as a wall, the pulse would be completely reflected. None of the wave energy would be absorbed or transmitted. The reflected pulse, however, would be inverted, as shown in Figure 5-2.

This inversion can be explained by Newton's third law. When the pulse in Figure 5-2 arrives at the wall, the pulse exerts an upward force on the wall. Because the wall does not move, it exerts a force of equal magnitude on the rope in the opposite direction, which is downward. This reaction force inverts the pulse just before it is reflected back through the original medium.

If the initial disturbance that causes a pulse is repeated regularly, without interruption or change, a series of regular, evenly timed disturbances in the medium is produced. This series of regularly repeated disturbances of a field or medium is called a **periodic wave.**

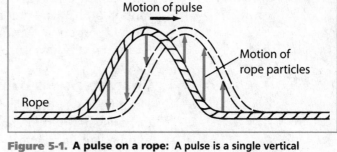

Figure 5-1. A pulse on a rope: A pulse is a single vertical disturbance transmitted horizontally at a definite speed.

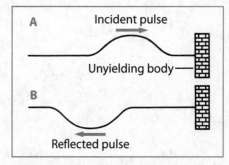

Figure 5-2. A pulse is reflected and inverted: (A) A wave pulse travels to the right along a rope attached to a brick wall. (B) When the pulse reaches the wall, it is reflected back toward the left in an inverted position.

Types of Wave Motion

A wave in which the motion of the vibratory disturbance is parallel to the direction of propagation or travel of the wave through the medium is called a **longitudinal wave.** Sound waves, compression waves in a spring, and earthquake P-waves are examples of longitudinal waves. A longitudinal wave is represented in Figure 5-3. Notice that the arrows indicating direction of motion of the wave and direction of particle motion are parallel to each other.

Another type of wave, a **transverse wave,** is one in which the motion of the vibratory disturbance is perpendicular, or at right angles to the direction of travel of the wave. An easy way to remember this is that the symbol for perpendicular lines, ⊥, is the first letter in the word transverse, T, inverted. The transverse wave shown in Figure 5-4 is produced in

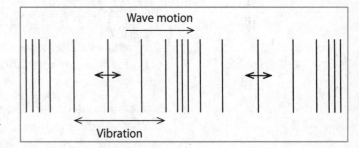

Figure 5-3. Longitudinal wave

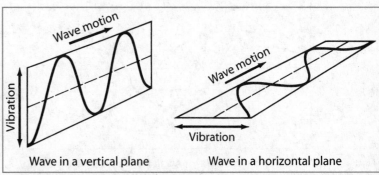

Figure 5-4. Transverse waves: These transverse waves have the same direction of travel but are in different planes.

a rope if the end is moved up and down or side to side. The direction of motion of the rope determines the plane of the wave's motion, which is always perpendicular to the rope's vibration. Electromagnetic waves and earthquake S-waves are examples of other transverse waves.

Characteristics of Periodic Waves

Periodic waves are not described solely by their type, such as longitudinal or transverse. Other characteristics distinguish an individual wave from another similar wave. Some of these characteristics are described below.

Frequency The complete series of changes at one point in a medium as a wave passes is called a cycle. The number of cycles, or complete vibrations, experienced at each point per unit time is called the **frequency,** f, of the wave. A frequency of 1 cycle per second is called 1 **hertz.** The hertz, Hz, is the derived SI unit of frequency. In fundamental units, 1 Hz equals 1/s, or s^{-1}, which can be read as *per second*.

The frequency of a sound wave determines its pitch, whereas the frequency of a light wave determines its color. The human ear can detect frequencies in the range of 20 to 20,000 hertz, and the human eye perceives frequencies of approximately 3.84×10^{14} to 7.69×10^{14} hertz.

Period The time required for one complete vibration to pass a given point in the medium is called the **period** of the wave and is denoted by T. Note that this is a capital letter. The period of a periodic wave is inversely proportional to frequency and is given by this formula.

$$T = \frac{1}{f}$$

The period T is in seconds and the frequency f is in hertz or per second. The second, s, is the SI unit for period.

Amplitude The graph of the displacement of a wave versus time is called the wave's waveform. The discussion that follows treats only the relatively simple sine wave, which has the shape of a sine curve. All complex waveforms may be analyzed in terms of the interactions of many different sine waves.

The **amplitude** of a mechanical wave is the maximum displacement of a particle of the medium from its rest or equilibrium position. The amplitude of a wave in a field is the maximum change in the field strength from its normal value.

In a transverse wave, the position of maximum displacement of a particle of the medium in the positive direction (for example, upward) is called a crest. The position of maximum displacement in the negative direction (downward) is called a trough. The greater the amplitude of the wave, the higher the crests and the lower the troughs. Transverse waves of various amplitudes are shown in Figure 5-5.

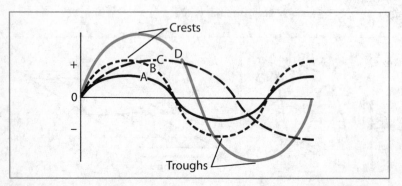

Figure 5-5. Wave amplitudes: Waves A and B have the same frequency but different amplitudes. Waves B and C have the same amplitudes but different frequencies. Wave D has the greatest amplitude of the four waves.

In a longitudinal wave, the periodic displacements of the particles of the medium produce regions of maximum compression called <u>condensations</u> that alternate with regions of maximum expansion called <u>rarefactions</u>. The greater the amplitude of the wave, the greater the compression of the particles in the condensations and the greater the separation of the particles in the rarefactions. Figure 5-6 shows condensations and rarefactions in a longitudinal wave.

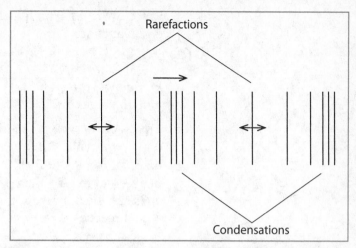

Figure 5-6. Condensations and rarefactions of a longitudinal wave

The amplitude of a wave is related to the amount of energy it transmits. The greater the amplitude of a light wave, the greater the light intensity or brightness. The greater the amplitude of a sound wave, the louder the sound. The amplitude of a sound wave is not related to its frequency or pitch.

Phase Points on successive wave cycles of a periodic wave that are displaced from their rest position by the same amount in the same direction and are moving in the same direction (away from or towards their rest positions) are said to have the same **phase,** or to be "in phase" with each other. For example, in a transverse wave, all the wave crests are in phase. In Figure 5-7 points A and E are in phase, B and F are in phase, and C and G are in phase.

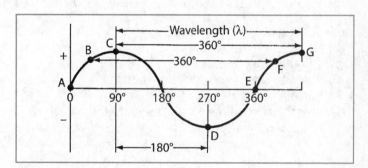

Figure 5-7. Phase relations in a wave

A simple way to determine if two points on a wave are in phase is to picture cutting out a template of the waveform between the points. If the template can be lifted, placed adjacent to one of the points, and traced without interruption to make the original sine waveform, the points are in phase.

Because there are 360° in a complete circle, one complete cycle of a periodic wave is often represented as equal to 360°. One half-cycle is then 180°. Points on a wave that are 180° apart are said to be "out of phase." In Figure 5-7, points C and D are out of phase.

Wavelength The distance between any two successive points in phase with one another in a periodic wave is called the **wavelength** of the wave. In Figure 5-7, the distance between points C and G, B and F, and A and E is one wavelength. Wavelength is represented by the symbol λ and is measured in units of length, such as meters and nanometers. If two points on a transverse wave are 180° out of phase, the distance between them is one-half wavelength or $\frac{1}{2}\lambda$.

The wavelength of a transverse wave is often measured between successive crests or troughs. The wavelength of a longitudinal wave is measured between successive condensations or rarefactions.

Speed of Waves The **speed** of a wave is equal to the product of its frequency and wavelength.

$$v = f\lambda$$

Frequency, f, is in hertz, wavelength, λ, is in meters, and speed, v, is in meters per second. This formula is valid for all waves in all media.

The speed of a wave depends upon its type and the medium through which it travels. Often at baseball games the bat is *seen* hitting the ball before the crack of the bat is *heard*. Why? Light travels at 3.00×10^8 meters per second in air, whereas sound travels only 346 meters per second in air at 25°C. The light from the bat hitting the ball reaches your eyes before the sound reaches your ears.

SAMPLE PROBLEM

The diagram shows a segment of a periodic wave in a spring traveling to the right to point I. The frequency of the wave is 2.0 hertz.

(a) What type of wave is represented in the diagram?
(b) What is the amplitude of the wave?
(c) What is the wavelength of the wave?
(d) Calculate the period of the wave.
(e) Calculate the speed of the wave.
(f) Identify two points on the wave that are in phase.
(g) Immediately after the wave moves through point I, in which direction will point H move?

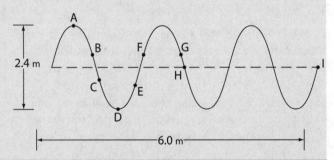

SOLUTION:

(a) The particles of the medium vibrate perpendicular to the direction of wave motion. Thus, the wave is transverse.

(b) The at-rest position is represented by the horizontal dashed line. Displacement is the vertical distance from the at-rest position to the curve. Therefore, the maximum displacement is $\frac{1}{2}$ the vertical height of the diagram or 1.2 m.

(c) Three complete wavelengths are shown. Divide the given length by 3.

$$\lambda = \frac{6.0 \text{ m}}{3} = 2.0 \text{ m}$$

(d) Use the formula for the period $T = \frac{1}{f}$. Substitute the known values and solve.

$$T = \frac{1}{f} = \frac{1}{2.0 \text{ Hz}} = 0.50 \text{ s}$$

(e) Write the formula for the speed of a wave $v = f\lambda$. Substitute the known values and solve.

$$v = f\lambda = (2.0 \text{ Hz})(2.0 \text{ m}) = 4.0 \text{ m/s}$$

(f) Notice that points B and C are moving in the same direction and are the same distance from the at-rest position of the medium, but they do not have the same displacement and thus are out of phase. Points B and F have the same displacement from the at-rest position, but are moving in opposite directions, up and down, respectively, and therefore are out of phase. Points B and G are in phase because they have the same displacement and are moving in the same direction. Points B and G are separated by a distance of one wavelength.

(g) The dashed line in the diagram below shows how the entire waveform would appear in the next instant of time. Point H moves up.

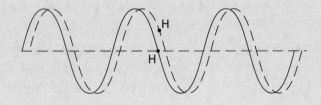

1. A single vibratory disturbance that moves from point to point in a medium is called
   - (1) a node
   - (2) a periodic wave
   - (3) an antinode
   - (4) a pulse

2. What generally occurs when a pulse reaches a boundary between two different media?
   - (1) All of the pulse is reflected.
   - (2) All of the pulse is absorbed.
   - (3) All of the pulse is transmitted.
   - (4) Part of the pulse is reflected, part is absorbed, and part is transmitted.

3. A tuning fork vibrating in air produces sound waves. These waves are best classified as
   - (1) transverse, because the air molecules are vibrating parallel to the direction of wave motion
   - (2) transverse, because the air molecules are vibrating perpendicular to the direction of wave motion
   - (3) longitudinal, because the air molecules are vibrating parallel to the direction of wave motion
   - (4) longitudinal, because the air molecules are vibrating perpendicular to the direction of wave motion

4. When a transverse wave moves through a medium, what is the action of the particles of the medium?
   - (1) They travel through the medium with the wave.
   - (2) They vibrate in a direction parallel to the direction in which the wave is moving.
   - (3) They vibrate in a direction perpendicular to the direction in which the wave is moving.
   - (4) They remain at rest.

5. Compression waves in a spring are an example of
   - (1) longitudinal waves
   - (2) transverse waves
   - (3) elliptical waves
   - (4) torsional waves

6. Wave motion in a medium transfers
   - (1) energy only
   - (2) mass only
   - (3) both energy and mass
   - (4) neither energy nor mass

7. Periodic waves are produced by a wave generator at the rate of one wave every 0.50 second. What is the period of the wave?

8. Which phrase best describes a periodic wave?
   - (1) a single pulse traveling at constant speed
   - (2) a single pulse traveling at varying speed in the same medium
   - (3) a series of pulses at irregular intervals
   - (4) a series of pulses at regular intervals

9. In the diagram below, the solid line represents a wave generated in a rope.

   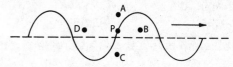

   As the wave moves to the right, point P on the rope is moving towards which position?
   - (1) A
   - (2) B
   - (3) C
   - (4) D

10. In the diagram below, a transverse wave is moving to the right on a rope.

    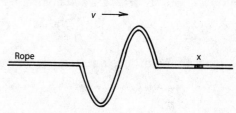

    In which direction will segment x move as the wave passes through it?
    - (1) down, only
    - (2) up, only
    - (3) down, then up, then down
    - (4) up, then down, then up

11. Which wave characteristic is defined as the number of cycles of a periodic wave occurring per unit time?

12. If the frequency of a sound wave is 440. cycles per second, the period of the wave is
    - (1) 2.27×10^{-3} s
    - (2) 0.752 s
    - (3) 1.33 s
    - (4) 3.31×10^2 s

13. If the frequency of a sound wave is doubled, the period of the sound wave is
    - (1) halved
    - (2) doubled
    - (3) unchanged
    - (4) quadrupled

14. The diagram below represents a transverse wave.

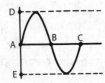

The amplitude of the wave is represented by the distance between points

(1) A and B   (3) A and D
(2) A and C   (4) D and E

15. If the frequency of a sound wave in air at STP remains constant, the wave's energy can be varied by changing its

(1) amplitude   (3) wavelength
(2) speed   (4) period

16. The diagram below shows a transverse wave.

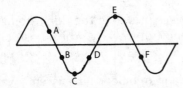

Which two points on the wave are in phase?

(1) A and E   (3) C and E
(2) B and F   (4) D and F

17. The diagram below shows a transverse wave.

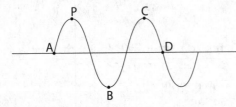

Which point on the wave is 180° out of phase with point P?

18. The diagram that follows shows a train of waves moving along a string.

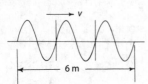

What is the wavelength?

19. The wavelength of the periodic wave shown in the diagram below is 4.0 meters.

What is the distance from point B to point C?

20. An 8.0-meter long ocean wave passes the end of a dock every 5.0 seconds. Calculate the speed of the wave.

21. A sound wave travels at 340 meters per second. Determine how far from the source the wave has traveled after 0.50 second.

22. The diagram below represents a wave traveling in a uniform medium.

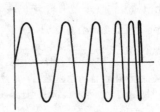

Which characteristic of the wave is constant?

(1) amplitude   (3) period
(2) frequency   (4) wavelength

Base your answers to questions 23 through 25 on the diagram below, which represents four transverse waves in the same medium.

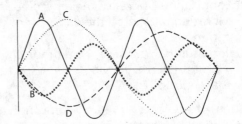

23. Which two waves have the same amplitude?

24. Which two waves have the same wavelength?

25. Which two waves have the same frequency?

26. A wave has a frequency of 2.0 hertz and a speed of 3.0 meters per second. The distance covered by the wave in 5.0 seconds is

(1) 30. m   (2) 15 m   (3) 7.5 m   (4) 6.0 m

27. A wave traveling at 5.00×10^4 meters per second has a wavelength of 2.50×10^1 meters. What is the frequency of the wave?

(1) 5.00×10^{-4} Hz   (3) 5.00×10^3 Hz
(2) 2.00×10^3 Hz   (4) 1.25×10^6 Hz

28. Sound waves with constant frequency of 250 hertz are traveling through air at STP. Calculate the wavelength of the sound waves.

29. Calculate the total distance a sound wave travels in air at STP in 3.00 seconds.

30. What type of wave is sound traveling in water?

Base your answers to questions 31 through 34 on the information and diagram below.

A periodic wave, having a frequency of 40. hertz, travels to the right in a uniform medium as shown.

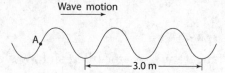
Wave motion

A

←——— 3.0 m ———→

31. On the diagram, draw one or more arrows to indicate the direction of motion of point A in the next instant of time.

32. On the diagram, label a point P that is in phase with point A.

33. Calculate the speed of the wave.

34. Calculate the period of the wave.

Base your answers to questions 35 and 36 on the information below.

The elapsed time between successive crests of a transverse wave passing a given point is 0.080 second.

35. Determine the period of the wave.

36. Calculate the frequency of the wave.

Base your answers to questions 37 through 39 on the information below.

The distance from one crest of a water wave to the next crest is 4.0 meters. One crest passes an observation point every 2.5 seconds.

37. Calculate the speed of the wave.

38. Calculate the time required for the wave to travel 50. meters.

39. Determine the total distance the wave travels in 4.0 seconds.

40. Write an equation that correctly relates the speed v, wavelength λ, and period T of a periodic wave.

41. A wave x meters long passes through a medium at y meters per second. The frequency of the wave could be expressed as

(1) $\dfrac{y}{x}$ Hz   (3) xy Hz

(2) $\dfrac{x}{y}$ Hz   (4) $(x + y)$ Hz

42. A unit for the amplitude of a transverse wave is

(1) m/s   (2) s   (3) Hz   (4) m

43. The diagram below shows a periodic wave W traveling to the right in a uniform medium.

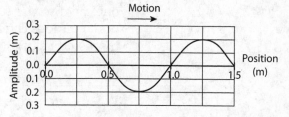
Motion

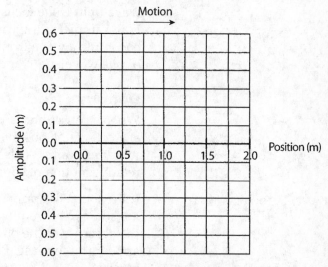

On the grid below sketch at least one cycle of a periodic wave having twice the amplitude and half the wavelength of wave W.

44. A sound wave is produced by a musical instrument for 0.40 second. If the frequency of the wave is 370 hertz, how many complete waves are produced in that time period?

45. If the frequency of a sound wave increases, the wavelength of the wave in air

(1) decreases (2) increases (3) remains the same

46. Which phrase best describes the wavelength of a sound wave in air at STP?

(1) inversely proportional to its amplitude and inversely proportional to its frequency
(2) inversely proportional to its amplitude and directly proportional to its frequency
(3) independent of its amplitude and inversely proportional to its frequency
(4) independent of its amplitude and directly proportional to its frequency

47. A water wave travels a distance of 10.0 meters in 5.0 seconds. What can be determined from this information?

(1) the speed of the wave only
(2) the period of the wave only
(3) the speed and frequency of the wave
(4) the period and frequency of the wave

Periodic Wave Phenomena

By observing two types of mechanical waves, transverse and longitudinal, one can discover some characteristics of waves and the behavior of waves under various conditions. Some of these characteristics and behaviors are discussed below.

Wave Fronts

When water drips from a leaky faucet into a water-filled sink, waves spread, or radiate, in concentric circles along the surface of the water from the point where the drips strike the surface. In a three-dimensional medium such as air, waves radiate in concentric spheres from a vibrating point. All points on a wave that are in phase comprise a wave front. A **wave front** is the locus of all adjacent points on a wave that are in phase. For example, in the waves in the sink, all of the points on one of the crests constitute a wave front. Two successive crests are separated by a distance of one wavelength and, therefore, are in phase.

Doppler Effect

When a source and an observer (receiver) of waves are moving relative to each other, the observed frequency is different from the frequency of the vibrating source. This change in observed or apparent frequency due to relative motion of source and observer is called the **Doppler effect.**

If the source is approaching the observer, or if the observer is approaching the source, the frequency appears to increase. If the source is receding from the observer or the observer is receding from the source, the frequency appears to decrease. Because the speed of the waves in the medium is not affected by the Doppler effect, it can be seen from the formula $v = f\lambda$ that the change in apparent wavelength is inversely proportional to the change in apparent frequency.

The wave front diagrams in Figure 5-8 illustrate the changes in apparent frequency and wavelength caused by the Doppler effect. In Figure 5-8A, the source is stationary, and the four successive wave fronts (1, 2, 3, and 4) are equally spaced circles in all directions. The observed wavelength and frequency are the same for all stationary observers. In Figure 5-8B, the source is moving from right to left. Each successive wave front has a different center. To a stationary observer at the left, the wavelengths appear shorter and the frequency higher; to a stationary observer at the right, the effect is the opposite.

The Doppler effect can cause changes in the apparent pitch of a sound wave because the ear perceives a sound wave of higher frequency as a sound of higher pitch. Thus the pitch of an approaching sound source is higher than its pitch when the source is stationary, and the pitch drops lower as the source passes the observer and begins to recede.

A Stationary source

Observer A perceives: normal λ, normal f

Observer B perceives: normal λ, normal f

B Source moving at constant velocity away from observer D and toward observer C

Observer C perceives: shorter λ, higher f

Observer D perceives: longer λ, lower f

Figure 5-8. The Doppler effect: (A) When the source is stationary, the wave fronts are equally spaced in all directions. (B) When the source is moving, the wave fronts are closer together in the direction in which the source is moving.

Visible light waves are subject to a similar effect. The human eye perceives light waves of different frequencies as differences in color. Light waves of the lowest frequency (longest wavelength) that the eye can detect are seen as red, while those of highest frequency (shortest wavelength) are seen as blue-violet. Other colors are distributed between these extremes in the visible spectrum. Because of the Doppler effect, the apparent color of an approaching light source is shifted toward the blue-violet end of the spectrum, while that of a receding source is shifted toward the red end. If the light source is a mixture of many frequencies, such as the light from a star, its light appears slightly bluer if it is approaching an observer, or slightly redder if it is receding, than it would appear if it were not moving relative to the observer.

Applications of the Doppler Effect The Doppler effect has practical applications in weather forecasting and police work. For example, the speed of a car can be determined by a computerized radar system. If a car is at rest and a beam of radio waves is directed at the car from a stationary source, the incident and reflected waves have the same frequency. If the car is moving toward the source of the radar, however, the reflected waves have a higher frequency than the waves emitted by the source. The greater the car's speed toward the radar source, the greater the Doppler shift in frequency. In a similar way, if the car is moving away from the source of radar, the frequency of the reflected waves decreases by an amount that depends upon the speed of the car. Thus, equipped with a "radar gun," a law-enforcement officer can detect speed-limit violators "coming or going."

Interference

Superposition occurs when two or more waves travel through the same medium simultaneously. The **principle of superposition** states that the resultant displacement at any point is the algebraic sum of the displacements of the individual waves. The effect of the superposition is called **interference**, which may be constructive or destructive. Although any number of waves may superpose, the discussion that follows is restricted to two waves.

Constructive interference occurs when the wave displacements of two in-phase waves in the same medium are in the same direction. The algebraic sum of the displacements is an amplitude greater than that of either of the original waves. Maximum constructive interference occurs when the waves are in phase and crest superposes on crest. Thus, maximum constructive interference occurs when the phase difference is equal to 0°, as shown in Figure 5-9A. The point of maximum displacement of a medium when two waves are interacting is called an **antinode**.

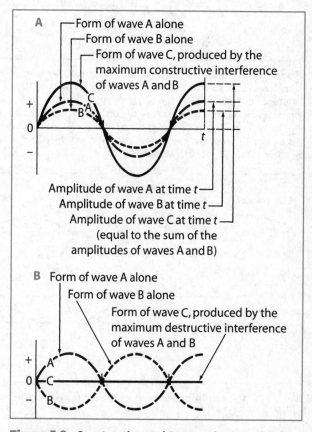

Figure 5-9. **Constructive and Destructive Interference:** (A) Waves A and B have the same frequency and a phase difference of 0°. As a result, they show maximum constructive interference, producing wave C. Note that the amplitudes of A and B always add up to the amplitude of C at every instant of time. This is demonstrated for the time t at the extreme right of the graph. (B) Waves A and B have the same frequency and the same amplitude, but a phase difference of 180°. As a result, they show maximum destructive interference. Notice that waves A and B cancel each other.

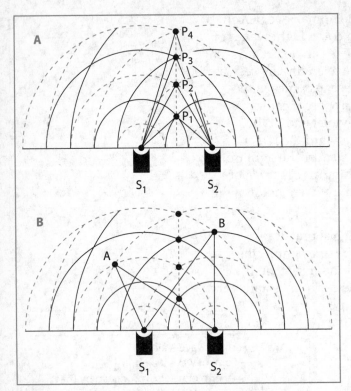

Figure 5-10. Interference of waves produced by two identical point sources: (A) Along antinodal line P_1P_4, the difference in path length from any point to S_1 and S_2 is 0λ. (B) Point A is an antinode because the distance AS_1 differs from the distance AS_2 by an even number of half-wavelengths. Point B is a node because the distance BS_1 differs from the distance BS_2 by an odd number of half-wavelengths.

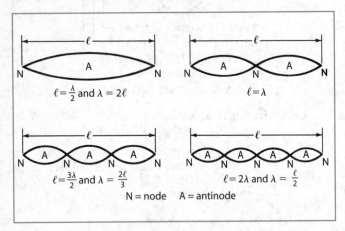

Figure 5-11. Standing waves of different wavelengths along a string

When two waves of equal frequency and amplitude whose phase difference is 180° or $\frac{1}{2}\lambda$ meet at a point (for example, crest to trough), there is maximum **destructive interference,** as shown in Figure 5-9B. Maximum destructive interference results in the formation of **nodes** (points or lines), which are regions of zero displacement of the medium. Intermediate degrees of interference occur between the regions of maximum constructive interference and maximum destructive interference.

Two Sources in Phase in the Same Medium When two in-phase point sources generate waves in the same medium, a symmetrical interference pattern results because of maximum constructive and destructive interference. Figure 5-10A shows two identical point sources, S_1 and S_2, producing wave crests (solid lines) and wave troughs (dashed lines) that interfere. The path difference from any point of constructive interference to the sources, S_1 and S_2, is an even number of half-wavelengths. For example, along antinodal line P_1P_4, the difference in path length from any point on the line to S_1 and S_2 is 0λ. In Figure 5-10B, point A is on an antinodal line because distance AS_1 differs from distance AS_2 by two half-wavelengths. On the other hand, point B is on a nodal line because distance BS_1 differs from distance BS_2 by an odd number of half-wavelengths. Nodal lines occur midway between antinodal lines.

Standing Waves

When two waves having the same amplitude and frequency travel in opposite directions through a uniform medium, a standing wave is formed. A **standing wave** is a pattern of wave crests and troughs that remains stationary in a medium. The nodes and antinodes are stationary and the wave appears to stand still. Standing waves are easily produced in a stretched string that is fixed at both ends. Wave trains traveling along the string are reflected at the ends and travel back with the same frequency and amplitude. Figure 5-11 illustrates several possible standing waves in a string. Note that a node appears at each end of the string. The distance between two successive nodes is equal to $\frac{1}{2}\lambda$.

Resonance

Every elastic body has a particular frequency called its **natural frequency** at which it will vibrate if disturbed. When a periodic force is applied to an elastic body, it absorbs energy and the amplitude of its vibration increases. The vibration of a body at its natural frequency because of the action of a vibrating source of the same frequency is called **resonance.** For example, a nonvibrating tuning fork, having a natural frequency of 512 hertz, will resonate when a vibrating tuning fork with a natural frequency of 512 hertz is brought near it. Furthermore, it is possible for an opera singer to shatter a glass by maintaining a note with a frequency equal to the natural frequency of the glass. The transfer of energy by resonance increases the amplitude of vibrations in the glass until its structural strength is exceeded. Probably the most dramatic example of resonance was the collapse of the Tacoma Narrows Bridge in the state of Washington in 1940. High winds set up standing waves in the bridge in addition to vibrations in a torsional (twisting) mode. Resonance increased the amplitude of vibrations until the bridge collapsed.

Diffraction

The spreading of waves into the region behind a barrier in the wave's path is called **diffraction.** Parallel water wave fronts incident on a small opening are diffracted to form concentric semicircular fronts. These semicircular fronts have the same wavelength as the incident wave if the medium is uniform throughout, as shown in Figure 5-12A. If the opening through which the wave is diffracted is much larger than one wavelength of the incident wave, diffraction effects are small, as shown in Figure 5-12B.

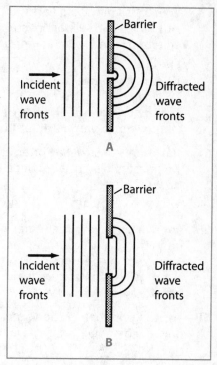

Figure 5-12. Diffraction of parallel wave fronts resulting from different sized openings in a barrier

Review Questions

48. What term describes the variations in the observed frequency of a sound wave when there is relative motion between the source and the receiver?

49. A source of waves and an observer are moving relative to each other. The observer will detect a steadily increasing frequency if

   (1) he moves toward the source at a constant speed

   (2) the source moves away from him at a constant speed

   (3) he accelerates toward the source

   (4) the source accelerates away from him

50. The driver of a car hears the siren of an ambulance that is moving away from her. If the actual frequency of the siren is 2000. hertz, the frequency heard by the driver may be

   (1) 1900. Hz

   (2) 2000. Hz

   (3) 2100. Hz

   (4) 4000. Hz

51. A police officer's stationary radar device indicates that the frequency of the radar wave reflected from an automobile is less than the frequency emitted by the radar device. This indicates that the automobile is

   (1) moving toward the police officer

   (2) moving away from the police officer

   (3) not moving

52. A stationary person makes observations of the periodic waves produced by a moving source. When the wave source recedes from the observer, he observes an apparent increase in the wave's

   (1) speed

   (2) frequency

   (3) wavelength

   (4) amplitude

53. When observed from Earth, the wavelengths of light emitted by a star are shifted toward the red end of the electromagnetic spectrum. This red shift occurs because the star is

(1) at rest relative to Earth
(2) moving away from Earth
(3) moving toward Earth at decreasing speed
(4) moving toward Earth at increasing speed

54. Maximum constructive interference occurs when the phase difference between the interfering waves is

(1) 0°   (2) 45°   (3) 90°   (4) 180°

55. Two waves having the same amplitude and frequency are traveling in the same medium. By how many degrees should the waves be out of phase to produce maximum destructive interference?

56. The diagram below shows a rope with two pulses moving along it in the directions shown.

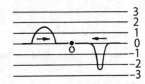

What is the resultant wave pattern at the instant when the maximum displacement of both pulses is at point O on the rope?

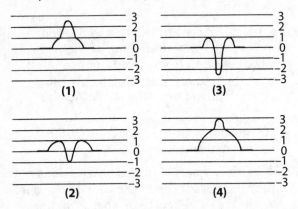

57. The diagram below shows four waves that pass simultaneously through a region.

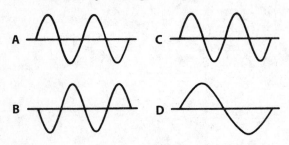

Which two waves will produce maximum constructive interference if they are combined?

58. Which pair of waves will produce a resultant wave with the smallest amplitude?

(1)    (3)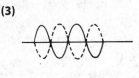

(2) 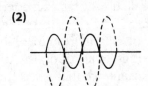   (4)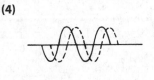

59. The diagram below represents two waves traveling simultaneously in the same medium.

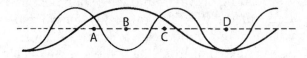

At which of the given points will maximum constructive interference occur?

60. Standing waves are produced by two waves traveling in opposite directions in the same medium. The two waves must have

(1) the same amplitude and the same frequency
(2) the same amplitude and different frequencies
(3) different amplitudes and the same frequency
(4) different amplitudes and different frequencies

61. The diagram below represents a wave moving toward the right side of this page.

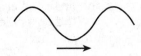

Which wave shown below could produce a standing wave with the original wave?

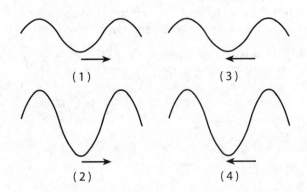

62. The diagram below shows a standing wave.

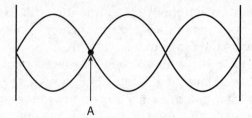

A

Point A on the standing wave is

(1) a node resulting from constructive interference
(2) a node resulting from destructive interference
(3) an antinode resulting from constructive interference
(4) an antinode resulting from destructive interference

Base your answers to questions 63 and 64 on the diagram below, which shows a standing wave in a rope.

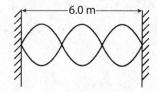

←—— 6.0 m ——→

63. How many nodes are represented?

64. If the rope is 6.0 meters long, what is the wavelength of the standing wave?

65. Two waves traveling in the same medium and having the same wavelength (λ) interfere to create a standing wave. What is the distance between two consecutive nodes on this standing wave?

(1) λ (2) $\frac{3\lambda}{4}$ (3) $\frac{\lambda}{2}$ (4) $\frac{\lambda}{4}$

66. The diagram below represents shallow water waves interacting with two slits in a barrier.

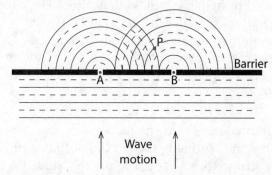

Wave motion

Identify *two* wave phenomena illustrated in the diagram.

67. An opera singer's voice is able to break a thin crystal glass if a note sung and the glass have the same natural

(1) speed   (3) amplitude
(2) frequency   (4) wavelength

68. When an opera singer hits a high-pitch note, a glass on the opposite side of the opera hall shatters. Which statement best explains this phenomenon?

(1) The amplitude of the note increases before it reaches the glass.
(2) The singer and the glass are separated by an integral number of wavelengths.
(3) The frequency of the note and the natural frequency of the glass are equal.
(4) The sound produced by the singer slows down as it travels from the air into the glass.

69. A wave is diffracted as it passes through an opening in a barrier. The amount of diffraction that the wave undergoes depends on both the

(1) amplitude and frequency of the incident wave
(2) wavelength and speed of the incident wave
(3) wavelength of the incident wave and the size of the opening
(4) amplitude of the incident wave and the size of the opening

70. Which diagram best illustrates diffraction of waves incident on a barrier?

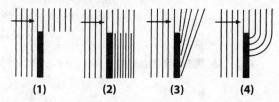

    (1)   **(2)**   **(3)**   **(4)**

71. The diagram below represents straight wave fronts approaching a narrow opening in a barrier.

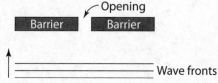

Opening

Barrier   Barrier

Wave fronts

Which diagram best represents the shape of the waves after passing through the opening?

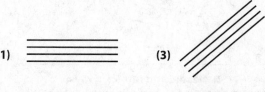

(1)   **(3)**

(2)   **(4)**

Light

The human eye can perceive only an extremely small fraction of the electromagnetic spectrum. That portion of the spectrum, which allows us to see, is called light and covers the range of wavelengths in air from approximately 4×10^{-7} to 7×10^{-7} meter. (The electromagnetic spectrum will be discussed in detail later in this topic.) Obviously, these wavelengths are too small to measure with a ruler as you might measure the wavelength of a transverse wave on a rope or a water wave in a shallow tank.

Speed of Light

Measurements of the speed of light to more than two or three significant figures could not be made until about 100 years ago. To three significant figures, the speed of light in a vacuum or air is 3.00×10^8 meters per second. Measurements of the speed of light are now recorded to nine significant figures. This more accurate data reveals that the speed of light in air is slightly less than it is in a vacuum. The speed of light in a vacuum is represented by the symbol c, an important physical constant.

The speed of light in a vacuum is the upper limit for the speed of any material body. No object can travel faster than c. The speed of light in a material medium is always less than c. The formula $v = f\lambda$ applies to light waves. Therefore, $c = f\lambda$, where f is the frequency of a light wave and λ is its wavelength in a vacuum.

Ray Diagrams

Because it is not possible to see individual wave fronts in a light wave, a ray is used to indicate the direction of wave travel. A **ray** is a straight line that is drawn at right angles to a wave front and points in the direction of wave travel. Ray diagrams show only the direction of wave travel, not the actual waves. An **incident ray** is a ray that originates in a medium and strikes a boundary or an interface of that medium with another medium. A **reflected ray** is a ray that has rebounded from a boundary or interface. A **refracted ray** is a ray that results from an incident ray entering a second medium of different optical density obliquely. Figure 5-13 shows these rays as well as the wave fronts whose motion they represent.

Incident, reflected, and refracted rays form corresponding angles measured from a line called the normal. The **normal** is a line drawn perpendicular to the barrier or to the interface between two media at the point where the incident ray strikes. In ray diagrams, all the rays and the normal lie in a single plane.

Reflection of Light

The **angle of incidence,** θ_i, is the angle between the incident ray and the normal to the surface at the point where the ray strikes the surface. The ray rebounds from the surface at the **angle of reflection,** θ_r, the angle between the reflected ray and the normal to the surface at the point

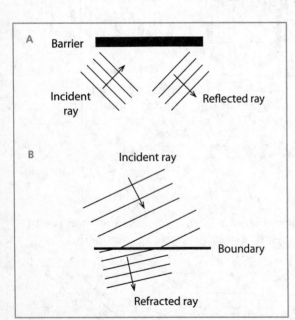

Figure 5-13. Reflected and refracted rays: (A) shows the direction of a reflected wave front at a barrier. (B) shows how a wave front changes at a boundary between air and a denser medium.

of reflection. The **law of reflection** states that the angle of incidence is equal to the angle of reflection.

$$\theta_i = \theta_r$$

Figure 5-14 illustrates the law of reflection. This law is valid for all types of waves including light, water, and sound waves. The reflection of sound waves is called an echo.

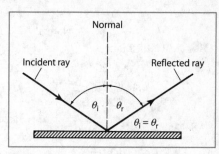

Figure 5-14. **The law of reflection: The angle of incidence equals the angle of reflection.**

Refraction of Light

Waves travel at different speeds in different media, so when a wave travels from one medium to another medium of different optical density, the speed of the wave changes. If the wave is incident on the interface between two media at an angle other than 90°, the direction of wave travel changes in the new medium. That means that both the speed and the direction of a wave usually change as the wave enters a new medium obliquely. The change in direction of a wave due to a change in speed at the boundary between two different media is called **refraction**. If the wave fronts of an incident wave are parallel to the interface, the angle of incidence is 0° and the wave may change speed upon entering the new medium, but the direction of the wave does not change.

The amount of refraction of a ray depends upon the properties of the two media at the interface and is measured by the angle of refraction. The **angle of refraction** is the angle between a ray emerging from the interface of two media and the normal to that interface at the point where the ray emerges.

Speed of Light and Refraction

When a light ray in air is incident on an interface with water at an angle of incidence of 0°, the ray of light slows down upon entering the more optically dense water, but does not change its direction of travel. Figure 5-15 shows an incident ray approaching the interface between air and water along the normal. The ray is not refracted as it travels from air into water. The ray travels more slowly in water than in air but its frequency remains the same. The speed of a wave is proportional to its wavelength when frequency is constant, so its wavelength in water is shorter than its wavelength in air.

The situation is different when a light ray passes obliquely from a less dense medium such as air into a more dense medium such as water. In this case, the ray is refracted towards the normal, as shown in Figure 5-16A. Upon entering the denser medium, the ray's frequency does not change, but its wavelength decreases as its speed decreases. If the path of the ray is from a more dense medium, such as water, into a less dense medium, such as air, the ray is refracted away from the normal, as shown in Figure 5-16B. Upon entering the less dense medium,

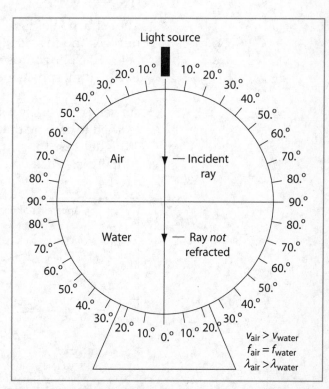

Figure 5-15. **Refraction of light: A light ray passes from a less optically dense medium, air, into a more optically dense medium, water, at an angle of incidence of 0°.**

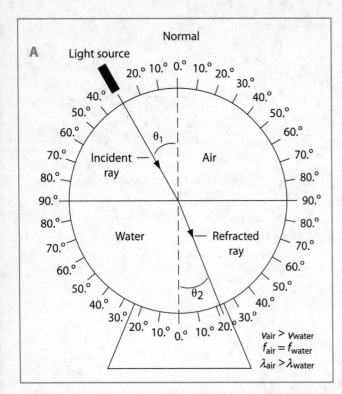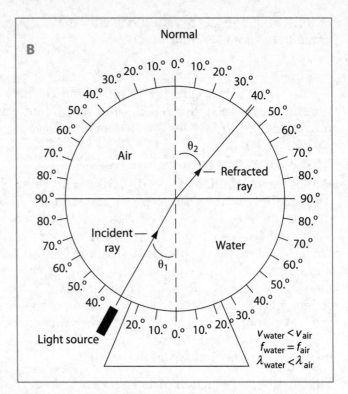

Figure 5-16. Additional examples of refraction of light: (A) A light ray passes obliquely from a less optically dense medium, air, into a more optically dense medium, water, at an angle of incidence of 30°. The ray is refracted toward the normal. (B) A light ray passes obliquely from a more optically dense medium, water, into a less optically dense medium, air, at an angle of incidence of 30°. The ray is refracted away from the normal.

the ray's frequency does not change, but its wavelength increases as its speed increases.

The refraction of light explains many everyday phenomena such as mirages and the visibility of the Sun after it has actually disappeared below the horizon, as illustrated in Figure 5-17. Because the density of Earth's atmosphere increases gradually as Earth's surface is approached from space, sunlight entering the atmosphere obliquely, as it does at sunset, is gradually refracted to produce a curved path. Your brain has learned to assume that light entering your eyes has been traveling in straight lines. Thus, at sunset you "see" the Sun higher in the sky than it actually is. When you "see" the Sun on the horizon, it has already set.

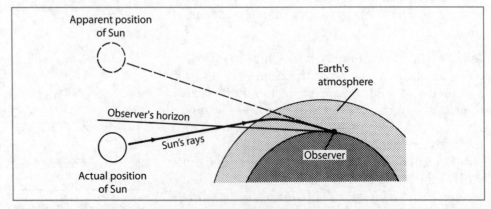

Figure 5-17. Curvature of the Sun's rays by refraction in Earth's atmosphere (not drawn to scale)

Another example of refraction is the apparent bending of a straw placed in a glass of water. The submerged portion of the straw appears to be closer to the surface than it actually is. Light from the submerged tip of the straw is bent away from the normal upon entering the less-dense air, as shown in Figure 5-18. To an observer, who interprets what is seen as light traveling in a straight line, the submerged tip of the straw seems closer to the surface than it actually is.

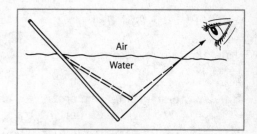

Figure 5-18. Refraction of light: Light rays from the tip of the straw are bent away from the normal as they emerge from the water. The effect is to make the straw appear to bend at the surface of the water.

Absolute Index of Refraction

The **absolute index of refraction,** n, is the ratio of the speed of light in a vacuum, c, to the speed of light in a material medium, v.

$$n = \frac{c}{v}$$

The absolute index of refraction has no units because both c and v are measured in the same units. The greater the value of n, the more optically dense the medium and the slower light travels in the medium. The absolute indices of refraction for a variety of materials are listed in the *Reference Tables for Physical Setting/Physics*.

Solving the equation for c yields $c = nv$. Thus, the following equations apply for two different media.

$$n_1 v_1 = n_2 v_2 \quad \text{or} \quad \frac{n_2}{n_1} = \frac{v_1}{v_2}$$

Also, the following equations apply for any two media.

$$v_1 = f\lambda_1 \quad \text{and} \quad v_2 = f\lambda_2$$

Note that the frequency of the wave does not change as the wave enters a new medium. Thus, the relationship between the speeds and wavelengths of the wave in the two media is this.

$$\frac{v_1}{v_2} = \frac{\lambda_1}{\lambda_2}$$

These relationships can be combined as follows.

$$\frac{n_2}{n_1} = \frac{v_1}{v_2} = \frac{\lambda_1}{\lambda_2}$$

Snell's Law

The mathematical relationship that governs the refraction of light as it passes obliquely from one medium to another of different optical density is called **Snell's law.**

$$n_1 \sin \theta_1 = n_2 \sin \theta_2$$

Angles θ_1 and θ_2 are the angles of incidence and refraction respectively, and n_1 and n_2 are the absolute indices of refraction of the incident and refractive media, respectively.

Snell's law can be rearranged in this way.

$$\frac{\sin \theta_1}{\sin \theta_2} = \frac{n_2}{n_1}$$

The ratio n_2/n_1 is called the relative index of refraction for the two media.

SAMPLE PROBLEM

The diagram represents a ray of monochromatic light, having a frequency of 5.09×10^{14} hertz, as it is about to emerge from glycerol into air.

(a) On the diagram, use a protractor and a straight edge to draw a normal to the glycerol-air interface. Label the angle of incidence θ_1. Determine its measure to the nearest degree.

(b) Calculate the angle of refraction.

(c) On the diagram, draw the refracted light ray, label the angle of refraction θ_2, and indicate its measure to the nearest degree.

(d) At a boundary between two media, some of the incident light is always reflected. On the diagram, use a protractor and a straight edge to draw the reflected ray, label the angle of reflection θ_r, and indicate its measure to the nearest degree.

(e) Calculate the speed of the light in glycerol.

(f) Calculate the wavelength of the light in air in nanometers.

(g) Calculate the wavelength of the light in glycerol in nanometers.

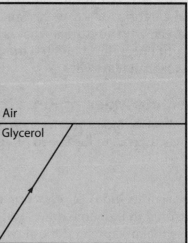

SOLUTION: Identify the known and unknown values.

Known
$f = 5.09 \times 10^{14}$ Hz
$n_1 = 1.47$ (glycerol)
$n_2 = 1.00$ (air)
$v_2 = c = 3.00 \times 10^8$ m/s

Unknown
$\theta_1 = ?°$
$\theta_2 = ?°$
$\theta_r = ?°$
$v_1 = ?$ m/s (glycerol)
$\lambda_2 = ?$ nm (air)
$\lambda_1 = ?$ nm (glycerol)

(a) On the diagram, draw a normal to the surface at the point of incidence. The angle of incidence is measured from the normal. See the diagram that follows. The angle of incidence is 30°.

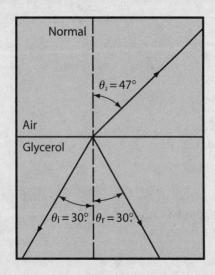

(b) Use the formula $n_1 \sin \theta_1 = n_2 \sin \theta_2$. Note that the subscript 1 refers to the incident medium and the subscript 2 refers to the refractive medium. Solve the equation for $\sin \theta_2$.

$$\sin \theta_2 = \frac{n_1 \sin \theta_1}{n_2}$$

Substitute the known values and solve for θ_2.

$$\sin \theta_2 = \frac{(1.47)(\sin 30.°)}{1.00}$$
$$\theta_2 = 47°$$

(c) The angle of refraction is in air and is measured from the normal using a protractor.

(d) The angle of incidence is equal to the angle of reflection. Thus, the angle of reflection is 30.°, and is measured from the normal.

(e) Solve the formula $n = c/v$ for v.

$$v = \frac{c}{n}$$

Substitute the known values and solve.

$$v = \frac{3.00 \times 10^8 \text{ m/s}}{1.47} = 2.04 \times 10^8 \text{ m/s}$$

(f) Solve the formula $v = f\lambda$ for the wavelength, λ.

$$\lambda = \frac{v}{f}$$

Substitute the known values and solve.

$$\lambda_2 = \frac{3.00 \times 10^8 \text{ m/s}}{5.09 \times 10^{14} \text{ Hz}}$$
$$\lambda_2 = 5.89 \times 10^{-7} \text{ m}$$
$$\lambda_2 = 589 \text{ nm}$$

(g) Write the formula relating absolute indices of refraction and wavelengths.

$$\frac{n_2}{n_1} = \frac{\lambda_1}{\lambda_2}$$

Solve the equation for λ_1.

$$\lambda_1 = \frac{n_2\lambda_2}{n_1}$$

Substitute the known values and solve.

$$\lambda_1 = \frac{(1.00)(589 \text{ nm})}{1.47} = 401 \text{ nm}$$

The Electromagnetic Spectrum

Light waves are **electromagnetic waves** which consist of periodically changing electric and magnetic fields and move through a vacuum at speed $c = 3.00 \times 10^8$ meters per second. All electromagnetic waves, regardless of their frequency and wavelength, are produced by accelerating charged particles. The **electromagnetic spectrum,** which is the complete range of frequencies and wavelengths of electromagnetic waves, is shown in Figure 5-19. Notice that visible light is only a small portion of the spectrum.

There are no sharp divisions between the various kinds of electromagnetic waves. They are classified according to the methods by which they are generated or received. For example, radio waves, used for communication systems, are produced by charges accelerating in a wire. Do not confuse electromagnetic radio waves with longitudinal sound waves.

Microwaves are used in radar systems in air-traffic control, for transmitting long-distance telephone communications in outer space, and to cook food. The frequency of microwaves used in a microwave oven is the same as the natural rotational frequency of water molecules. Resonance is produced in water molecules contained in food and the resulting internal energy due to vibration heats the food.

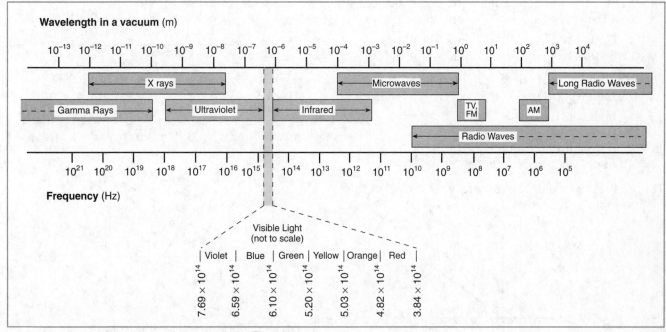

Figure 5-19. The electromagnetic spectrum Ⓡ

Infrared waves appear as heat when absorbed by objects. Practical applications of the infrared portion of the electromagnetic spectrum include heat lamps used in physical therapy and infrared photography.

Visible light is approximately one percent of the electromagnetic spectrum. It is produced by the rearrangement of electrons in atoms and molecules. The wavelengths that the human eye can detect are in the range of approximately 400 to 700 nanometers.

Ultraviolet light is the part of sunlight that causes sunburns. The ozone layer of the atmosphere filters practically all of the high frequency components of ultraviolet radiation from the Sun, but the inner atmosphere readily transmits the remaining lower frequency ultraviolet radiation. Some commercial skin lotions are designed to absorb ultraviolet rays to prevent them from affecting the skin.

X rays are used as diagnostic tools by physicians. Living tissues and organisms can be destroyed by x rays, so precautions should be taken to avoid overexposure.

Gamma rays are emitted by radioactive nuclei. This electromagnetic radiation is harmful to living tissues.

Review Questions

72. How long does it take light to travel a distance of 100. meters?

    (1) 3.00×10^{10} s   (3) 3.33×10^{-7} s
    (2) 3.00×10^{8} s   (4) 3.33×10^{7} s

73. Calculate the wavelength in a vacuum of a light wave having a frequency of 5.3×10^{14} hertz. Express the wavelength in nanometers.

74. What is the frequency of a light wave having a wavelength of 5.00×10^{-7} meter in a vacuum?

    (1) 6.00×10^{-14} Hz   (3) 6.00×10^{15} Hz
    (2) 6.00×10^{14} Hz   (4) 6.00×10^{16} Hz

75. Which form(s) of energy can be transmitted through a vacuum?

    (1) light, only
    (2) sound, only
    (3) both light and sound
    (4) neither light nor sound

76. A ray is reflected from a surface, as shown in the diagram that follows.

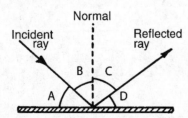

Which letter represents the angle of incidence?

77. The diagram below represents a light ray being reflected from a plane mirror. The angle between the incident and reflected ray is 70°.

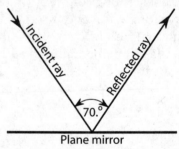

What is the angle of incidence for this ray?

    (1) 20.°   (2) 35°   (3) 55°   (4) 70.°

78. In the diagram below, ray R of monochromatic yellow light is incident upon a glass surface at an angle θ.

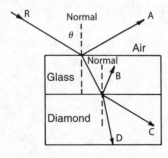

Which resulting ray is *not* possible?

79. Which diagram best represents wave reflection?

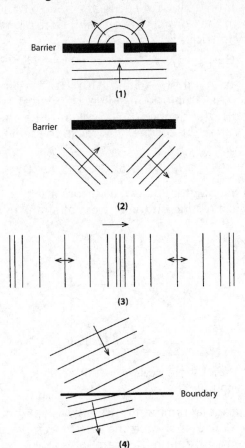

Barrier

(1)

Barrier

(2)

(3)

Boundary

(4)

80. When a ray of light strikes a mirror perpendicular to its surface, what is the angle of reflection?

81. A ray of light passes from air into glass at an angle of incidence of 0°. Which statement best describes the speed and direction of the light ray as it passes into the glass?

(1) Only speed changes.
(2) Only direction changes.
(3) Both speed and direction change.
(4) Neither speed nor direction changes.

82. As a wave enters a new medium, there may be a change in the wave's

(1) frequency   (3) period
(2) speed   (4) phase

83. The speed of a ray of light traveling through a substance having an absolute index of refraction of 1.1 is

(1) 1.1×10^8 s   (3) 3.0×10^8 s
(2) 2.7×10^8 s   (4) 3.3×10^8 s

84. Which arrow best represents the path that a monochromatic ray of light ($f = 5.09 \times 10^{14}$ Hz) travels as it passes through air, corn oil, glycerol, and back into air?

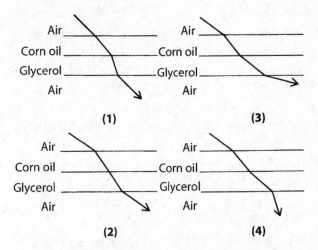

Air
Corn oil
Glycerol
Air

(1)

Air
Corn oil
Glycerol
Air

(3)

Air
Corn oil
Glycerol
Air

(2)

Air
Corn oil
Glycerol
Air

(4)

85. What happens to the speed, wavelength, and frequency of light when it passes from water into flint glass?

(1) Its speed decreases, its wavelength becomes shorter, and its frequency remains the same.
(2) Its speed decreases, its wavelength becomes shorter, and its frequency increases.
(3) Its speed increases, its wavelength becomes longer, and its frequency remains the same.
(4) Its speed increases, its wavelength becomes longer, and its frequency decreases.

86. Which ray diagram best represents the phenomenon of refraction?

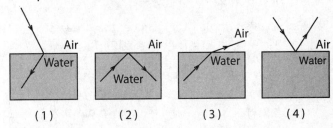

Air
Water

(1)

Air
Water

(2)

Air
Water

(3)

Air
Water

(4)

87. In the diagram below, ray AB is incident on surface XY at point B.

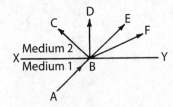

If medium 2 has a lower index of refraction than medium 1, through which point will the ray most likely pass?

88. A beam of monochromatic red light passes obliquely from air into water. Which characteristic of the light does *not* change?

(1) direction   (3) frequency
(2) velocity   (4) wavelength

89. The speed of light ($f = 5.09 \times 10^{14}$ Hz) in corn oil is the same as the speed of light in

(1) diamond   (3) air
(2) flint glass   (4) glycerol

90. The speed of light in a medium is 2.00×10^8 meters per second. Calculate the absolute index of refraction for the medium.

91. In which medium is the wavelength of yellow light the shortest?

(1) flint glass   (3) diamond
(2) crown glass (4) zircon

92. The frequency of a ray of light is 5.09×10^{14} hertz. What is the ratio of the speed of this ray in diamond to its speed in zircon?

93. In the diagram below, monochromatic light ($f = 5.09 \times 10^{14}$ Hz) in air is about to travel through crown glass, water, and diamond.

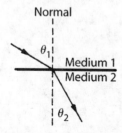

(not drawn to scale)

In which substance does the light travel at the slowest speed?

94. For a given angle of incidence, the greatest change in the direction of a light ray ($f = 5.09 \times 10^{14}$ Hz) is produced when the light ray passes obliquely from air into

(1) Lucite   (3) fused quartz
(2) glycerol   (4) crown glass

95. The diagram below represents a wave traveling from medium 1 to medium 2.

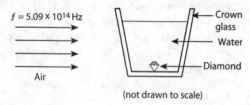

The relative index of refraction may be determined by calculating the ratio of

(1) $\dfrac{\theta_1}{\theta_2}$ (2) $\dfrac{\sin \theta_2}{\sin \theta_1}$ (3) $\dfrac{\sin \theta_1}{\sin \theta_2}$ (4) $\dfrac{n_1}{n_2}$

96. A ray of light ($f = 5.09 \times 10^{14}$ Hz) in air is incident on a block of Lucite at an angle of 60.° from the normal. The angle of refraction of this ray in Lucite is closest to

(1) 35°   (2) 45°   (3) 60.°   (4) 75°

97. A ray of light ($f = 5.09 \times 10^{14}$ Hz) traveling in air strikes a block of sodium chloride at an angle of incidence of 30.°. What is the angle of refraction for the light ray in the sodium chloride?

(1) 19°   (2) 25°   (3) 40.°   (4) 49°

98. In the diagram below, a person observes an object resting on the bottom of a tank of water.

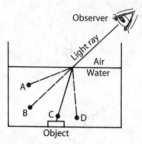

To the observer, the object appears to be at which point?

99. Which diagram best represents the path taken by a ray of monochromatic light as it passes from air through the materials shown?

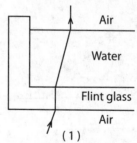

(1)

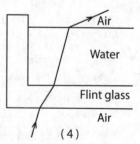

(3)

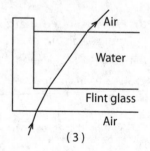

(2)

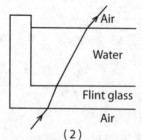

(4)

100. Which electromagnetic radiation has the shortest wavelength?

(1) infrared   (3) gamma
(2) radio   (4) ultraviolet

101. The electromagnetic spectrum does *not* include

(1) light waves   (3) sound waves
(2) radio waves   (4) x rays

102. Electrons oscillating with a frequency of 2.0×10^{10} hertz produce electromagnetic waves. These waves would be classified as

(1) infrared　　(3) microwave
(2) visible　　(4) x ray

103. A microwave and an x ray are traveling in a vacuum. Compared to the wavelength and period of the microwave, the x ray has a wavelength that is

(1) longer and a period that is shorter
(2) longer and a period that is longer
(3) shorter and a period that is longer
(4) shorter and a period that is shorter

104. Which wavelength is in the infrared range of the electromagnetic spectrum?

(1) 100 nm　(2) 100 mm　(3) 100 m　(4) 100 μm

105. Radio waves are propagated through the interaction of

(1) nuclear and electric fields
(2) electric and magnetic fields
(3) gravitational and magnetic fields
(4) gravitational and electric fields

106. In a vacuum, all electromagnetic waves have the same

(1) frequency　　(3) speed
(2) wavelength　　(4) energy

107. A monochromatic beam of light with a frequency of 5.45×10^{14} hertz travels in a vacuum. What is the color of the light?

108. The wavelength of a typical AM radio wave is 3×10^3 meters. Determine the order of magnitude of its frequency.

Base your answers to questions 109 through 112 on the information and diagram below.

When a ray of monochromatic light passes from medium A to medium B, its speed decreases.

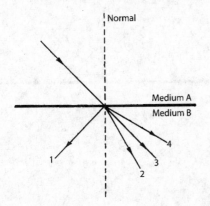

109. Which arrow best represents the path of the ray in medium B?

110. Compared to the frequency of the light in medium A, the frequency of the light in medium B is

(1) lower　　(2) higher　　(3) the same

111. Compared to the wavelength of the light in medium A, the wavelength of the light in medium B is

(1) shorter　　(2) longer　　(3) the same

112. According to information listed in the *Reference Tables for Physical Setting/Physics*, what could be the identity of substance B if medium A is corn oil?

Base your answers to questions 113 through 116 on the information and diagram below.

A ray of light ($f = 5.09 \times 10^{14}$ Hz) moves from air through substance B, through substance C, and back into air. The surfaces of substances B and C are parallel.

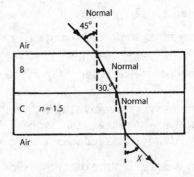

113. Calculate the index of refraction of substance B.

114. Calculate the speed of light in substance C.

115. If the angle of incidence of the light ray in air is increased, what happens to the angle of refraction in substance B?

116. What is the measure of angle X?

Base your answers to questions 117 through 120 on the information and diagram below.

A ray of monochromatic light ($f = 5.09 \times 10^{14}$ Hz) traveling in air is incident upon the surface of plate X. The values of n in the diagram represent absolute indices of refraction.

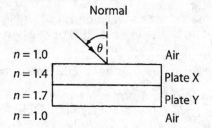

117. What is the relative index of refraction of the light going from plate X to plate Y?

(1) $\dfrac{1.0}{1.7}$ (2) $\dfrac{1.0}{1.4}$ (3) $\dfrac{1.7}{1.4}$ (4) $\dfrac{1.4}{1.7}$

118. Calculate the speed of the light ray in plate X.

119. Compared to angle θ, the angle of refraction of the light ray in plate X is

(1) smaller   (2) greater   (3) the same

120. Compared to angle θ, the angle of refraction of the ray emerging from plate Y into air is

(1) smaller   (2) greater   (3) the same

---

121. A periodic wave travels at speed v through medium A. The wave passes with all its energy into medium B. The speed of the wave through medium B is $\dfrac{v}{2}$. On the diagram below draw the wave as it travels through medium B. [Show at least one full wave.]

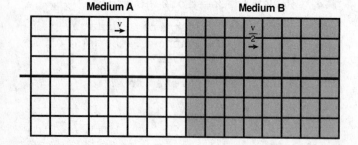

Base your answers to questions 122 through 124 on the information below.

A stationary research ship uses sonar to send a 1.18×10^3-hertz sound wave down through the ocean water. The reflected sound wave from the flat ocean bottom 324 meters below the ship is detected 0.425 second after it was sent from the ship.

122. Calculate the speed of the sound wave in the ocean water.

123. Calculate the wavelength of the sound wave in the ocean water.

124. Determine the period of the sound wave in the ocean water.

Base your answers to questions 125 through 127 on the information below.

A beam of monochromatic light having a wavelength of 5.89×10^{-7} meters in air is incident on the surface of a diamond at an angle of 0°.

125. Calculate the wavelength of this light in the diamond.

126. Determine the angle of refraction of this light as it enters the diamond.

127. Compare the frequency and speed of this light in the diamond to the frequency and speed of this light in air.

Directions

Review the Test-Taking Strategies section of this book. Then answer the following questions. Read each question carefully and answer with a correct choice or response.

Part A

1 A periodic wave travels through a rope, as shown in the diagram below.

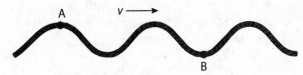

As the wave travels, what is transferred between points A and B?
(1) mass only
(2) energy only
(3) both mass and energy
(4) neither mass nor energy

2 In which wave type is the disturbance parallel to the direction of wave travel?
(1) torsional   (3) transverse
(2) longitudinal   (4) circular

3 A tuning fork oscillates with a frequency of 256 hertz after being struck by a rubber hammer. Which phrase best describes the sound waves produced by this oscillating tuning fork?
(1) electromagetic waves that require no medium for transmission
(2) electromagnetic waves that require a medium for transmission
(3) mechanical waves that require no medium for transmission
(4) mechanical waves that require a medium for transmission

4 The diagram below shows a transverse water wave moving in the direction shown by velocity vector *v*.

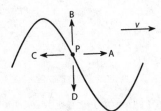

At the instant shown, a cork at point P on the water's surface is moving toward
(1) A   (2) B   (3) C   (4) D

5 The energy of a sound wave is most closely related to its
(1) period   (3) frequency
(2) amplitude   (4) wavelength

6 The product of a wave's frequency and its period is
(1) one   (3) its wavelength
(2) its velocity   (4) Planck's constant

7 What is the period of a wave with a frequency of 250 hertz?
(1) 1.2×10^{-3} s
(2) 2.5×10^{-3} s
(3) 9.0×10^{-3} s
(4) 4.0×10^{-3} s

8 The reciprocal of the frequency of a periodic wave is the wave's
(1) period   (3) intensity
(2) amplitude   (4) speed

9 Two points on a transverse wave that have the same magnitude of displacement from equilibrium are in phase if the points also have
(1) the same direction of displacement and the same direction of motion
(2) the same direction of displacement and the opposite direction of motion
(3) the opposite direction of displacement and the same direction of motion
(4) the opposite direction of displacement and the opposite direction of motion

10 Which wave diagram has *both* wavelength (λ) and amplitude (*A*) labeled correctly?

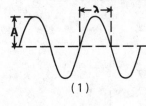
(1)

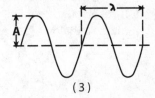
(3)

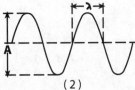
(2)

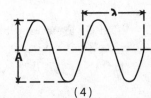
(4)

11 A source of sound waves approaches a stationary observer through a uniform medium. Compared to the frequency and wavelength of the emitted sound, the observer would detect waves with a
(1) higher frequency and shorter wavelength
(2) higher frequency and longer wavelength
(3) lower frequency and shorter wavelength
(4) lower frequency and longer wavelength

12 Which phenomenon is produced by two or more waves passing simultaneously through the same region?
(1) refraction   (3) interference
(2) diffraction   (4) reflection

13 Maximum constructive interference between two waves of the same frequency could occur when their phase difference is
(1) 1λ (2) $\frac{\lambda}{2}$ (3) $\frac{3\lambda}{2}$ (4) $\frac{\lambda}{4}$

14 Which wave phenomenon could *not* be demonstrated with a single wave pulse?
(1) a standing wave   (3) reflection
(2) diffraction   (4) refraction

15 If two identical sound waves arriving at the same point are in phase, the resulting wave has
(1) an increase in speed
(2) an increase in frequency
(3) a larger amplitude
(4) a longer period

16 Standing waves are produced by the interference of two waves of the same
(1) frequency and amplitude, but opposite directions of travel
(2) frequency and direction of travel, but different amplitudes
(3) amplitude and direction of travel, but different frequencies
(4) frequency, amplitude, and direction of travel

17 Two waves of the same wavelength λ interfere to form a standing wave pattern as shown in the diagram below.

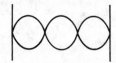

What is the straight-line distance between consecutive nodes?
(1) 1λ (2) 2λ (3) $\frac{1}{2}\lambda$ (4) $\frac{1}{3}\lambda$

18 Two identical guitar strings are tuned to the same pitch. If one string is plucked, the other nearby string vibrates with the same frequency. This phenomenon is called
(1) resonance
(2) reflection
(3) refraction
(4) destructive interference

Base your answers to questions 19 and 20 on the diagram below which represents shallow water waves of constant wavelength passing through two small openings, A and B, in a barrier.

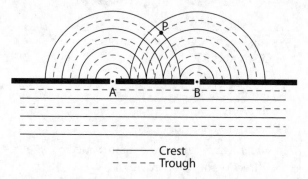

——— Crest
- - - - Trough

19 Compared to the length of path BP, the length of path AP is
(1) 1λ longer   (3) $\frac{1}{2}\lambda$ longer
(2) 2λ longer   (4) the same

20 Which statement best describes the interference at point *P*?
(1) It is constructive, and causes a longer wavelength.
(2) It is constructive, and causes an increase in amplitude.
(3) It is destructive, and causes a shorter wavelength.
(4) It is destructive, and causes a decrease in amplitude.

21 The diagram below shows a light ray interacting with a barrier.

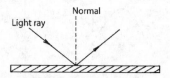

Which light phenomenon is illustrated?
(1) diffraction   (3) refraction
(2) interference   (4) reflection

22 Which diagram best represents the phenomenon of diffraction?

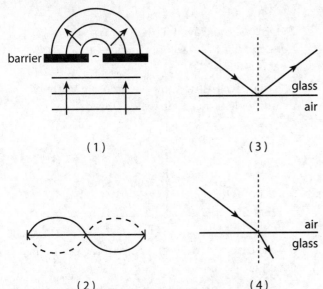

(1)   (3)

(2)   (4)

23 A ray of monochromatic light is incident on a plane mirror at an angle of 30.° The angle of reflection for the light ray is
(1) 15°   (2) 30.°   (3) 60.°   (4) 90.°

24 The diagram below represents wave fronts traveling from medium X into medium Y.

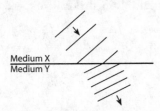

All points on any one wave front shown must be
(1) traveling with the same speed
(2) traveling in the same medium
(3) in phase
(4) superposed

25 What is the approximate speed of light in alcohol?
(1) 1.4×10^8 m/s   (3) 3.0×10^8 m/s
(2) 2.2×10^8 m/s   (4) 4.4×10^8 m/s

26 What is the color of light with a frequency of 5.65×10^{14} hertz?
(1) green   (2) red   (3) violet   (4) yellow

27 Which color of light has the lowest frequency?
(1) violet   (2) green   (3) yellow   (4) red

28 Which waves are *not* electromagnetic?
(1) radio   (3) light
(2) ultraviolet   (4) sound

29 What is the speed of a radio wave in a vacuum?
(1) 0 m/s   (3) 1.13×10^3 m/s
(2) 3.31×10^2 m/s   (4) 3.00×10^8 m/s

30 Electromagnetic radiation is produced by
(1) an accelerating electron
(2) an accelerating neutron
(3) an electron at constant velocity
(4) a neutron at constant velocity

31 Which form of electromagnetic radiation has the shortest wavelength in air?
(1) ultraviolet   (3) infrared
(2) visible   (4) radio

32 How much time does it take light from a flash camera to reach a subject 6.0 meters across a room?
(1) 5.0×10^{-9} s   (3) 5.0×10^{-8} s
(2) 2.0×10^{-8} s   (4) 2.0×10^{-7} s

33 Electromagnetic radiation having a wavelength of 1.3×10^{-7} meter would be classified as
(1) infrared   (3) blue
(2) orange   (4) ultraviolet

Part B

34 Which graph best represents the relationship between the frequency and period of a wave?

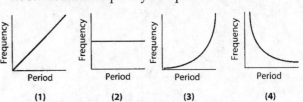

(1)   (2)   (3)   (4)

35 Which graph best represents the relationship between frequency and wavelength for microwaves in a vacuum?

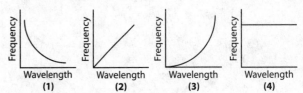

(1)   (2)   (3)   (4)

36 If the period of a wave is doubled, its wavelength is
(1) halved   (3) unchanged
(2) doubled   (4) quartered

37 Periodic waves with a wavelength of 0.50 meter move with a speed of 0.30 meter per second in medium A. When the waves enter medium B, they travel at 0.15 meter per second. Calculate the wavelength of the waves in medium B. [2]

38 In the diagram below, a ray of light enters a transparent medium from air.

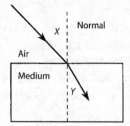

If angle X is 45° and angle Y is 30.°, what is the absolute index of refraction of the medium?

39 Which pair of moving pulses in a rope will produce destructive interference?

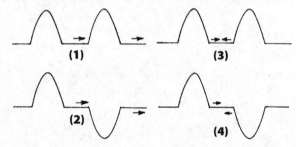

40 A ray of monochromatic light AB in air strikes a piece of glass at an incident angle θ, as shown in the diagram below.

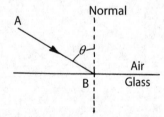

Which diagram best illustrates the ray's interaction with the glass?

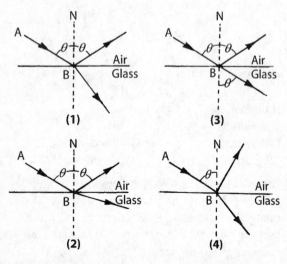

41 Which expression represents a constant for light waves of different frequencies in a vacuum?
(1) $f\lambda$ (2) f/λ (3) λ/f (4) $f+\lambda$

42 Determine the wavelength of x rays with a frequency of 1.5×10^{18} hertz traveling in a vacuum. [1]

43 The diagram below shows a ray of light traveling in air incident on an air-water boundary.

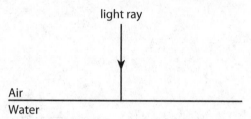

On the diagram, draw the path of the ray in the water. [1]

44 Calculate the time required for light to travel a distance of 1.50×10^{11} meters. [2]

Base your answers to questions 45 and 46 on the information and diagram below. Two plane mirrors are positioned perpendicular to each other as shown. A ray of monochromatic red light is incident on mirror 1 at an angle of 55°. This ray is reflected from mirror 1 and then strikes mirror 2.

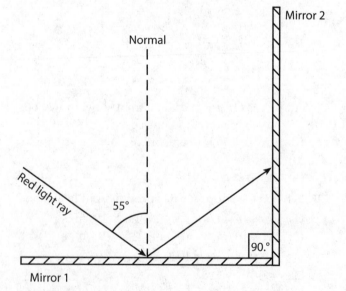

45 Determine the angle at which the ray is incident on mirror 2. [1]

46 On the diagram, use a protractor and a straightedge to draw the ray of light as it is reflected from mirror 2. [1]

47 Determine the speed of a ray of light (f = 5.09×10^{14} Hz) traveling through a block of sodium chloride. [1]

Base your answers to questions 48 through 51 on the diagram below, which represents the wave pattern produced by a vibrating source of constant frequency moving linearly in a shallow tank of water. The pattern is viewed from above and the lines represent crests.

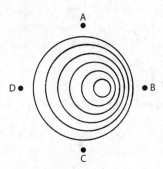

48 Towards which point is the source moving? [1]

49 What wave phenomenon is illustrated by the wave pattern? [1]

50 Compare the frequency of the waves observed at point B to the frequency of the waves observed at point D. [1]

51 Describe the wavelength of the waves observed at point D if the magnitude of the velocity of the source is increased. [1]

Base your answers to questions 52 through 58 on the diagram below, which represents a segment of a periodic wave traveling to the right in a steel spring. A crest passes line XY every 0.40 second.

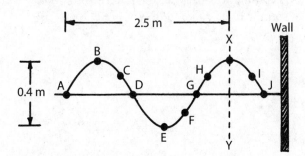

52 What is the amplitude of the wave? [1]

53 What is the wavelength of the wave? [1]

54 How many cycles of the wave are shown? [1]

55 What is the frequency of the wave? [1]

56 Calculate the speed of the wave. [2]

57 Identify two points on the wave that are in phase. [1]

58 In which direction will point H move in the next instant of time? [1]

Base your answers to questions 59 through 64 on the diagram below, which represents two media with parallel surfaces in air and a ray of light (f = 5.09×10^{14} Hz) passing through them.

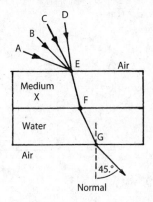

59 Calculate the approximate speed of the light in water. [2]

60 Calculate the angle of incidence in water, if the angle of refraction in air is 45°. [2]

61 Which line best represents the incident ray in air? [1]

62 Compare the speed of light in water to the speed of light in medium X. [1]

63 Identify an absolute index of refraction for medium X that would make ray EFG a straight line. [1]

64 Calculate the wavelength of the light in water. [2]

Base your answers to questions 65 through 69 on the information and diagram below.

A ray of monochromatic light having a wavelength of 4.00×10^{-7} meter in air passes from air through Lucite and then into air again.

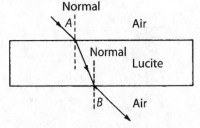

65 Calculate the frequency of the light in air. [2]

66 Identify the color of the light. [1]

67 Calculate the wavelength of the light in Lucite. [2]

68 Compare the measure of angle *A* to the measure of angle *B*. [1]

69 If angle *A* was increased, what would happen to the angle of refraction in the Lucite? [1]

Base your answers to questions 70 through 73 on the diagram below, which represents a ray of monochromatic light ($f = 5.09 \times 10^{14}$ Hz) in air incident on flint glass.

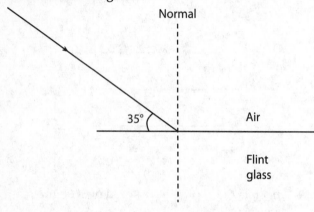

70 Determine the angle of incidence of the light ray in air. [1]

71 Calculate the angle of refraction of the light ray in the flint glass. [2]

72 Using a protractor and straightedge, draw the refracted ray on the diagram. [1]

73 What happens to the light from the incident ray that is *not* refracted or absorbed? [1]

Base your answers to questions 74 through 76 on the information and diagram below.

The sonar of a stationary ship sends a signal with a frequency of 5.0×10^3 hertz down through water. The speed of the signal is 1.5×10^3 meters per second. The echo from the bottom is detected 4.0 seconds later.

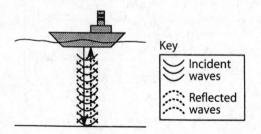

74 Calculate the wavelength of the sonar wave. [2]

75 Calculate the depth of the water under the ship. [2]

76 The echo is an example of which wave phenomenon? [1]

Base your answers to questions 77 through 80 on the information and diagram below.

A vibrating 1,000-hertz tuning fork produces sound waves that travel at 340 meters per second in air. Points A and B are some distance from the tuning fork. Point P is 20. meters from the tuning fork.

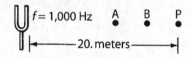

77 Calculate the time required for a sound wave to travel from the tuning fork to point P. [2]

78 Calculate the wavelength of the sound waves produced by the tuning fork. [2]

79 If the waves are in phase at point A and B, what is the minimum distance separating points A and B in terms of λ? [1]

80 If the vibrating tuning fork is accelerated toward point P, what happens to the frequency of the sound observed at P? [1]

81 A sound wave has a wavelength of 5.5 meters as it travels through air at STP. Determine the wavelength of this sound in a medium where its speed is 1,324 meters per second. [1]

82 Explain why, when a rapidly moving fire engine is coming toward you, the pitch of its siren sounds higher than it does when the fire engine is at rest. [1]

Base your answers to questions 83 and 84 on the information and diagram below.

A ray of light passes from air into a block of transparent material X as shown.

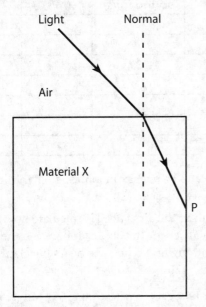

83 Measure the angles of incidence and refraction to the nearest degree for this light ray at the air into material X boundary and write your answers in the appropriate places on the diagram. [2]

84 The refracted light ray is reflected from the material X–air boundary at point P. Using a protractor and straightedge, on the diagram draw the reflected ray from point P. [1]

Part C

Base your answers to questions 85 through 92 on the following information, diagram, and data table.

Seven pairs of students performed an experiment to determine the speed of sound in air in the classroom. The apparatus consisted of a tall cylinder nearly filled with water, a hollow glass tube, a 30-centimeter ruler, a Celsius thermometer, a tuning fork marked 512 hertz, and a rubber mallet. The glass tube was held vertically in the cylinder of water. After striking the tuning fork with the mallet, it was held over the open end of the tube as shown.

Keeping the vibrating fork just above the edge of the tube, the glass tube was slowly moved up and down in the water until the position was located where the sound was loudest. The length of the air column in the glass tube at this point was measured and recorded. The inside diameter of the tube and the temperature of the air inside the tube were also measured and recorded in the incomplete data table that follows. Each pair of students used the same tuning fork and all the data was collected within a 15-minute time interval.

Students were instructed to use the formula $\lambda = 4\ell + 1.6d$ to calculate the wavelength λ of the sound wave that was produced in the air column by the tuning fork. They were also told to use the formula

$$v = 331\sqrt{1 + \frac{T_C}{273}}$$

to determine the accepted value for v, the speed of sound in air in meters per second at a particular Celsius temperature T_C.

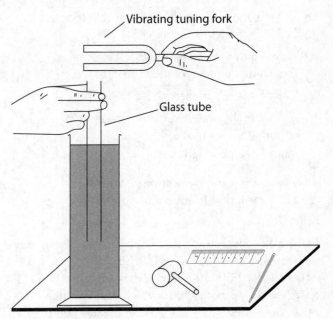

Data Table								
Trial	Length ℓ of air column (m)	Inside diameter d of tube (m)	Wavelength (m)	Frequency (Hz)	Temperature (°C)	Experimental speed of sound (m/s)	Accepted speed of sound, v (m/s)	Relative error (%)
1	0.163	0.032		512	21.5			
2	0.149	0.039		512	21.5			
3	0.150	0.037	0.659	512	20.5	337	343	
4	0.149	0.037		512	21.5			
5	0.152	0.040		512	21.8			
6	0.159	0.038	0.697	512	21.5			
7	0.152	0.040		512	21.8			

85 What type of wave was produced by the vibrating tuning fork? [1]

86 The loudest sound was produced when the natural frequency of the air in the column was the same as that of the vibrating tuning fork. What is the name of this wave phenomenon? [1]

87 What is the range of data collected for the length of the air column? [1]

88 What is the mean of the data collected for the inside diameter of the tube? [1]

89 How many significant digits were reported for the inside diameter of the tube in trial 5? [1]

90 Calculate the wavelength for trial 1. [2]

91 Calculate the accepted value for the speed of sound in air for trial 6. [2]

92 Determine the relative error for trial 3. [1]

Base your answers to questions 93 through 95 on the paragraph that follows and your knowledge of physics.

During a thunderstorm, a single bolt of lightning may develop 3.75 terawatts of power, but the lightning only lasts for 1.5×10^{-3} second. About 75% of the energy is dissipated as heat, which dramatically raises the temperature of the air in the lightning channel, causing the air to expand quickly. The movement creates sound waves that can be heard as thunder for distances up to 30. kilometers. An observer located 30. kilometers from the lightning strike sees the flash of lightning before hearing the clap of thunder.

93 Express in scientific notation the power developed by the lightning bolt in watts. [1]

94 Calculate the energy in joules, the lightning bolt dissipates as heat. [2]

95 Assuming the air is at STP, calculate how much time elapses for the observer between the flash of lightning and when she hears the clap of thunder. [2]

Base your answers to questions 96 through 99 on the information and diagram below.

A ray of monochromatic light ($f = 5.09 \times 10^{14}$ Hz) is traveling in air. The ray is incident on the surface of a block of flint glass at an angle of 40.°, as shown. Part of the light is reflected at the air-glass interface and part is refracted in the glass.

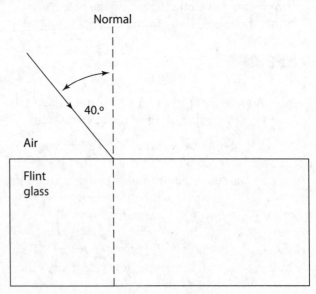

96 On the diagram, draw the reflected ray and label the angle of reflection with its measure in degrees. [2]

97 Calculate the angle of refraction in the flint glass to the nearest degree. [2]

98 On the diagram, draw the refracted ray. Label it "refracted ray." [1]

99 Calculate the wavelength of the light ray in flint glass. [2]

Base your answers to questions 100 and 101 on the diagram below, which shows a light ray ($f = 5.09 \times 10^{14}$ Hz) in air, incident on a boundary with fused quartz. At the boundary, part of the light is refracted and part of the light is reflected.

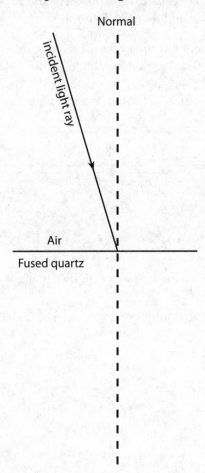

100 Calculate the angle of refraction of the incident light ray. [2]

101 Using a protractor and straightedge, construct the refracted light ray in the fused quartz on the diagram. [1]

102 A ray of monochromatic light ($f = 5.09 \times 10^{14}$ Hz) is incident upon an interface of water and an unknown medium, X. The ray is refracted in medium X as shown in the diagram below.

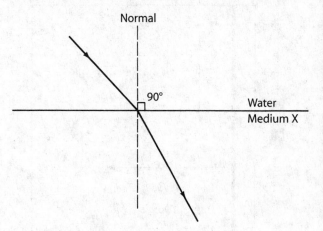

Calculate the speed of light in medium X. [4]

Base your answers to questions 103 through 105 on the following information and diagram.

The diagram represents a wave generator having a constant frequency of 12 hertz and producing parallel wave fronts in a shallow tank of water. The velocity of the wave is v.

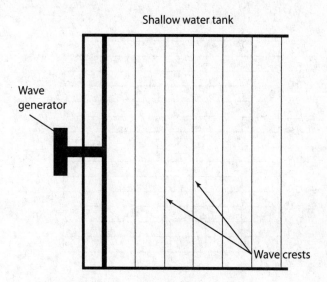

103 Determine the period of the waves. [1]

104 Using a ruler, measure the wavelength of the waves to the nearest tenth of a centimeter. [1]

105 Calculate the speed of the waves in the tank. [2]

106 A barrier is placed in the tank as shown in the following diagram.

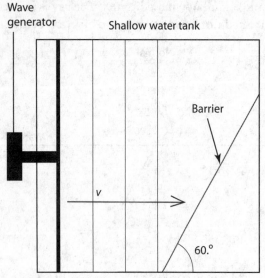

Wave generator
Shallow water tank
Barrier
v
60.°

Use a protractor and a straight edge to construct an arrow to represent the direction of the velocity of the reflected waves. [1]

Base your answers to questions 107 through 109 on the information and diagram below.

Two waves, A and B, travel in the same direction in the same medium at the same time.

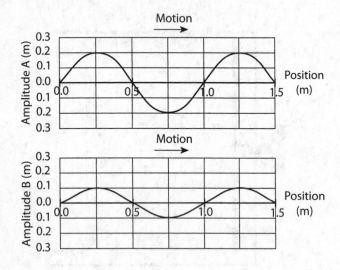

Motion

Amplitude A (m)

Position (m)

Motion

Amplitude B (m)

Position (m)

107 On the grid below draw the resultant wave produced by the superposition of waves A and B. [1]

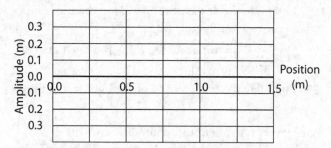

Amplitude (m)

Position (m)

108 What is the amplitude of the resultant wave? [1]

109 What is the wavelength of the resultant wave? [1]

Base your answers to questions 110 and 111 on the information and diagram below.

A student standing on a dock observes a piece of wood floating on the water as shown below. As a water wave passes, the wood moves up and down, rising to the top of a wave crest every 5.0 seconds.

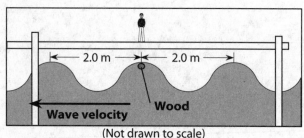

2.0 m   2.0 m

Wave velocity   Wood

(Not drawn to scale)

110 Calculate the frequency of the passing water waves. [2]

111 Calculate the speed of the water waves. [2]

Modern Physics

How **Scientists Study** Modern Physics

? *Are the glass tubes used to make "neon" signs always filled with neon?* **?**

Although these bright lights are commonly called neon lights, the tubes can actually contain other gases such as mercury vapor, the noble gases helium, argon, or krypton, or a combination of gases. The gas inside the tube is at low pressure. When a high potential difference is applied to the metal electrodes at each end of the tube, electrons flow through the tube. This excites the gas atoms. When electrons in the excited atoms fall to lower energy levels, the photons that are emitted possess energies that are characteristic of the gas or gases. Viewed through a spectroscope the light would appear as the bright-line spectrum of the gas or gases present in the tube. To the naked eye, the light appears as a characteristic glow.

When viewed, neon appears as reddish orange, mercury vapor as light blue, argon as lavender, and krypton as grayish green. A variety of different colors is produced by coating the inside of the tubing with a phosphor or by using colored tubing.

Modern Physics

Vocabulary

absorption spectrum	excited state	quantized
antimatter	ground state	quantum
antiparticle	hadron	quantum theory
antiquark	ionization potential	quark
atom	lepton	spectral line
atomic spectrum	meson	Standard Model of Particle Physics
baryon	neutrino	
bright-line spectrum	nucleus	stationary state
emission spectrum	photon	strong nuclear force
energy level	Planck's constant	universal mass unit
energy-level diagram	positron	

Wave-Particle Duality of Energy and Matter

Light, a form of electromagnetic radiation, can be represented as a wave propagated by an interchange of energy between periodically varying electric and magnetic fields. Waves of electromagnetic energy are identified by their frequency, wavelength, amplitude, and velocity. In addition, electromagnetic radiation exhibits the phenomena of diffraction, interference, and the Doppler effect, which are readily explained by a wave model of light.

Waves Have a Particle Nature

The wave model of light, however, cannot explain other phenomena such as interactions of light with matter. In these interactions, light—or other electromagnetic radiation—acts as if it is composed of particles possessing kinetic energy and momentum. For example, when light strikes matter, some of the light's momentum is transferred to the matter. In the latter part of the nineteenth century it was discovered that light having a frequency above some minimum value and incident on certain metals caused electrons to be emitted from the metal. This phenomenon, called the photoelectric effect, could not be explained by a wave model of light. Albert Einstein explained the phenomenon using quantum theory developed by Max Planck.

Quantum Theory

Quantum theory assumes that electromagnetic energy is emitted from and absorbed by matter in discrete amounts or packets. Each packet of electromagnetic energy emitted or absorbed is called a **quantum** (plural, quanta) of energy. The amount of energy E of each quantum is directly proportional to the frequency f of the electromagnetic radiation. The proportionality constant between the energy of a quantum and its frequency is called **Planck's constant**, h. Thus, the energy of a quantum is given by this formula.

$$E = hf$$

The energy E is in joules, the frequency f is in hertz, and Planck's constant h is a universal constant equal to 6.63×10^{-34} joule · second (J · s). The small energy values of quanta are often expressed in electronvolts, eV (1 eV = 1.60×10^{-19} J).

The quantum, or basic unit, of electromagnetic energy is called a **photon**. Although a photon is a massless particle of light, it carries both energy and momentum. The energy of a photon can be found using the previous equation. For light in a vacuum, $f = c/\lambda$ the energy of a photon can also be described in this way.

$$E_{photon} = hf = \frac{hc}{\lambda}$$ ®

The equation states that the energy of a photon is directly proportional to its frequency and inversely proportional to its wavelength.

SAMPLE PROBLEM

The energy of a photon is 2.11 electronvolts.

(a) Determine the energy of the photon in joules.
(b) Calculate the frequency of the photon.
(c) Identify the color of light associated with the photon.

SOLUTION: Identify the known and unknown values.

Known
$E = 2.11$ eV
$h = 6.63 \times 10^{-34}$ J · s
1 eV = 1.60×10^{-19} J

Unknown
$E = ?$ J
$f = ?$ Hz
color = ?

1. Convert electronvolts to joules using the relationship 1 eV = 1.60×10^{-19} J.

$$2.11 \text{ eV}\left(\frac{1.60 \times 10^{-19} \text{ J}}{1 \text{ eV}}\right) = 3.38 \times 10^{-19} \text{ J}$$

2. Solve the formula
$E_{photon} = hf$ for frequency f.

$$f = \frac{E_{photon}}{h}$$

3. Substitute the known values and solve.

$$f = \frac{3.38 \times 10^{-19} \text{ J}}{6.63 \times 10^{-34} \text{ J·s}} = 5.10 \times 10^{14} \text{ Hz}$$

4. According to the electromagnetic spectrum chart found in the *Reference Tables for Physical Setting/Physics*, a frequency of 5.10×10^{14} Hz corresponds to yellow light.

Photon-Particle Collisions

The photoelectric effect demonstrates that when a photon in the visible light range is incident on a metal surface, the photon's energy is completely absorbed and transferred to the emitted electron. However, when X-ray photons, which have much higher frequencies and energies than photons of visible light, strike a metal surface, not only are electrons ejected but electromagnetic radiation of lower frequency is also given off.

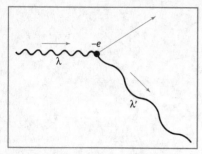

Figure 6-1. A collision of an X-ray photon and an electron in an atom: Besides the electron ejected from the atom, a photon of lower energy (longer wavelength) is also emitted (scattered) by the atom. The energy transferred to the electron equals the difference in energy between the incident photon and the scattered photon. The vector sum of the momentum of the electron and the scattered photon also equals the momentum of the incident photon.

When an X-ray photon and an electron collide, some of the energy of the photon is transferred to the electron and the photon recoils with less energy. Less energy means that the photon has lower frequency. Figure 6-1 illustrates this phenomenon.

Both energy, a scalar quantity, and momentum, a vector quantity, are conserved in this interaction, just as they are in collisions between particles. The incident photon loses energy and momentum, while the electron gains energy and momentum. Photons in a vacuum always travel at the speed of light. Thus, the momentum of a photon depends only on its wavelength or frequency.

Particles Have a Wave Nature

Just as radiation has both wave and particle characteristics, matter in motion has wave as well as particle characteristics. The wavelengths of the waves associated with the motion of ordinary objects, such as a thrown baseball, are too small to be detected. But the waves associated with the motion of particles of atomic or subatomic size, such as electrons, can produce diffraction and interference patterns that can be observed. Diffraction and interference phenomena provide evidence for the wave nature of particles.

Review Questions

1. In which part of the electromagnetic spectrum does a photon have the least energy?

   (1) gamma rays   (3) visible light
   (2) microwaves   (4) ultraviolet

2. The energy of a photon varies inversely with its

   (1) frequency   (3) speed
   (2) momentum   (4) wavelength

3. Compared to the frequency and wavelength of a photon of red light, a photon of blue light has a

   (1) lower frequency and shorter wavelength
   (2) lower frequency and longer wavelength
   (3) higher frequency and shorter wavelength
   (4) higher frequency and longer wavelength

4. A photon has an energy of 8.0×10^{-19} joule. What is this energy expressed in electronvolts?

   (1) 5.0×10^{-38} eV   (3) 8.0×10^{-19} eV
   (2) 1.6×10^{-19} eV   (4) 5.0 eV

5. The slope of a graph of photon energy versus photon frequency represents

   (1) Planck's constant
   (2) the mass of a photon
   (3) the speed of light
   (4) the speed of light squared

6. Which graph best represents the relationship between photon energy and photon frequency?

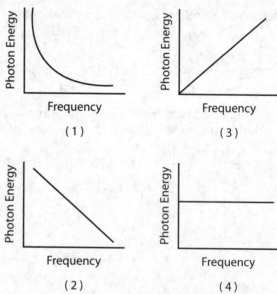

7. A photon of green light has a frequency of 6.0×10^{14} hertz. The energy associated with this photon is

   (1) 1.1×10^{-48} J   (3) 5.0×10^{-7} J
   (2) 6.0×10^{-34} J   (4) 4.0×10^{-19} J

8. Calculate the energy of a photon having a wavelength of 4.00×10^{-7} meter in air.

9. An X-ray photon collides with an electron in an atom, ejecting the electron and emitting another photon. During the collision there is a conservation of
   (1) momentum only
   (2) energy only
   (3) both momentum and energy
   (4) neither momentum nor energy

10. Experiments performed with light indicate that light exhibits
    (1) particle properties only
    (2) wave properties only
    (3) both particle and wave properties
    (4) neither wave nor particle properties

11. A photon of light carries
    (1) energy, but not momentum
    (2) momentum, but not energy
    (3) both energy and momentum
    (4) neither energy nor momentum

Early Models of the Atom

An **atom** is the smallest particle of an element that retains the characteristics of the element. Models for the structure of the atom have evolved over centuries as scientists have developed more sophisticated methods and equipment for studying particles that are too small to be detected by the unaided eye.

Thomson's Model

Over 100 years ago, J. J. Thomson discovered that electrons are relatively low-mass, negatively charged particles present in atoms. Because he knew that atoms are electrically neutral, Thomson concluded that part of the atom must possess a positive charge equal to the total charge of the atom's electrons. Thomson proposed a model in which the atom consists of a uniform distribution of positive charge in which electrons are embedded, like raisins in plum pudding.

Rutherford's Model

Less than two decades later, Ernest Rutherford proposed a different model of the atom. He performed experiments in which he directed a beam of massive, positively charged particles, traveling at approximately 5% of the speed of light, at extremely thin gold foil. Rutherford postulated that if an atom was like those described in Thomson's model, there would be only small net Coulomb forces on a positively charged particle as it passed through or near a gold atom in the foil, and the particle would pass through the foil relatively unaffected. However, he found that, although nearly all the positively charged particles were not deflected from a straight-line path through the gold foil, a small number of particles were scattered at large angles.

To explain the large angles of deflection of those few particles, Rutherford theorized that the massive, energetic, positively charged particles must have collided with other even more massive positively charged particles. Assuming that atoms are symmetrical, he concluded that this concentration of mass and positive charge in the atom, which he called the nucleus, is located at the atom's center. From the relative number of deflected particles, he calculated that the nucleus is only about $\frac{1}{10,000}$ the diameter of the average atom.

Based on the results of these scattering experiments, Rutherford described an atom as being similar to a miniature solar system. The tiny nucleus at the center of the atom contains all the positive charge of the atom and virtually all of its mass. The nucleus is surrounded by enough electrons to balance the positive charge of the nucleus and make the atom electrically neutral. The electrons move in orbits around the nucleus and are held in orbit by Coulomb forces of attraction between their negative charges and the positive charge of the nucleus.

In Rutherford's model, the electrons orbiting the nucleus accelerate due to a change in direction of motion. Rutherford knew that these accelerated charges should radiate electromagnetic energy, lose kinetic energy and momentum in the process, and spiral rapidly to the nucleus. The radiated electromagnetic energy would increase in frequency and produce a continuous spectrum. This expected behavior is contradicted by the observed bright-line spectrum that is characteristic of each element. (Bright-line spectra will be discussed later in this topic.)

The Bohr Model of the Hydrogen Atom

About two years later, Niels Bohr attempted to explain why electrons in atoms can maintain their positions outside the nucleus rather than spiral into the nucleus and cause the atom to collapse. Bohr developed a model of the hydrogen atom based on these assumptions:

- All forms of energy are **quantized,** that is, an electron can gain or lose kinetic energy only in fixed amounts, or quanta.
- The electron in the hydrogen atom can occupy only certain specific orbits of fixed radius and no others.
- The electron can jump from one orbit to a higher one by absorbing a quantum of energy in the form of a photon.
- Each allowed orbit in the atom corresponds to a specific amount of energy. The orbit nearest the nucleus represents the smallest amount of energy that the electron can have. The electron can remain in this orbit without losing energy even though it is being constantly accelerated toward the nucleus by the Coulomb force of attraction.

When the electron is in any particular orbit, it is said to be in a **stationary state.** Each stationary state represents a specific amount of energy and is called an **energy level.** The successive energy levels of the hydrogen atom are assigned integral numbers, denoted by $n = 1$, $n = 2$, etc. When the electron is in the lowest energy level ($n = 1$), the atom is said to be in the **ground state.** When the electron is in any level above $n = 1$, the atom is said to be in an **excited state.**

Energy Levels Any process that raises the energy level of electrons in an atom is called <u>excitation</u>. Excitation can be the result of absorbing the energy of colliding particles of matter, such as electrons, or of photons of electromagnetic radiation. A photon's energy is absorbed by an electron in an atom only if the photon's energy corresponds exactly to an energy-level difference possible for the electron. Excitation energies are different for different elements.

Atoms rapidly lose the energy of their various excited states as their electrons return to the ground state. This lost energy is in the form of photons (radiation) of specific frequencies, which appear as spectral lines in the characteristic spectrum of each element. A **spectral line** is a particular frequency of absorbed or emitted energy characteristic of an atom.

Ionization Potential An atom can absorb sufficient energy to raise an electron to an energy level such that the electron is essentially removed from the atom and an ion is formed. The energy required to remove an electron from an atom to form an ion is called the atom's **ionization potential.** An atom in an excited state requires a smaller amount of energy to become an ion than does an atom in the ground state.

Figure 6-2 shows the energy-level diagram for the hydrogen atom. An **energy-level diagram** is one in which the energy levels of a quantized system are indicated by distances of horizontal lines from a zero energy level. The energy level of an electron that has been completely removed from the atom ($n = \infty$) is defined to be 0.00 eV. Thus, all other energy levels have negative values. As an electron moves closer to the nucleus, the energy associated with the electron becomes smaller. Because an electron in the ground state has the lowest energy, its energy has the largest negative value. The *Physics Reference Tables for Physical Setting/Physics* contain energy level diagrams for hydrogen and mercury.

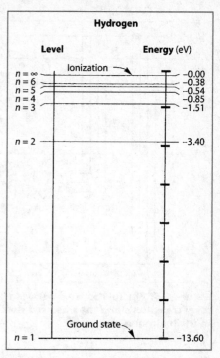

Figure 6-2. Energy levels for the hydrogen atom

Limitations of Bohr's Model Although Bohr's model explained the spectral lines of hydrogen, it could not predict the spectra or explain the electron orbits of elements having many electrons. Nevertheless, Bohr's model with its quantized energy levels set the stage for future atomic models.

The Cloud Model

Bohr's model of the atom has been replaced by the cloud model. In this model, electrons are not confined to specific orbits. Instead, they are spread out in space in a form called an electron cloud. The electron cloud is densest in regions where the probability of finding the electron is highest. Complicated equations describe the shape, location, and density of each electron cloud in an atom. Each cloud corresponds to a particular location for an electron. By incorporating the cloud model into the Rutherford-Bohr model, scientists have been able to construct accurate models of the electron arrangements for all the elements.

Atomic Spectra

When the electrons in excited atoms of an element in the gaseous state return to lower energy levels, they produce a specific series of frequencies of electromagnetic radiation called the **atomic spectrum** of the element. Each element has a characteristic spectrum that differs from that of every other element. Thus, the spectrum can be used to identify the element, even when the element is mixed with other elements.

The element helium was found on the Sun before it was isolated on Earth. Spectral lines of the Sun's corona were studied during a solar eclipse. The lines were not previously reported for any known element, so the new element was named helium from the Greek word for sun, *helios*.

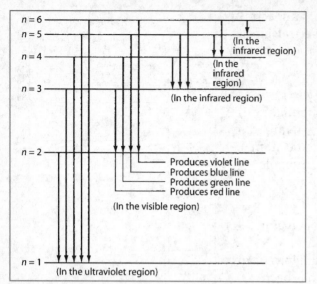

$n = 6$
$n = 5$
$n = 4$ — (In the infrared region)
(In the infrared region)
$n = 3$
(In the infrared region)

$n = 2$
— Produces violet line
— Produces blue line
— Produces green line
— Produces red line
(In the visible region)

$n = 1$
(In the ultraviolet region)

Figure 6-3. The relationship between possible energy level transitions and the observed series of frequencies in the hydrogen spectrum

Emission (Bright-Line) Spectra

Energy levels in an atom, introduced by Bohr, provided an explanation for atomic spectra. When an electron in an atom in an excited state falls to a lower energy level, the energy of the emitted photon is equal to the difference between the energies of the initial and final states. That is

$$E_{photon} = E_i - E_f$$ (R)

where E_i is the initial energy of an electron in the higher energy level and E_f is the final energy of the electron in the lower energy level. Each energy difference between two energy levels corresponds to a photon having a specific frequency. A specific series of frequencies, characteristic of the element, is produced when the electrons of its atoms in excited states fall to lower energy levels and the atoms return to lower states or to the ground state. When these emitted frequencies are viewed in a spectroscope, the frequencies appear as a series of bright lines against a dark background and, therefore, are called a **bright-line spectrum** or an **emission spectrum**. In Figure 6-3 the energy emissions producing various series of lines in the ultraviolet, visible light, and infrared regions are indicated in the energy-level diagram for hydrogen.

Absorption Spectra

As explained earlier, an atom can absorb only photons having energies equal to specific differences in its energy levels. The frequencies and wavelengths of these absorbed photons are exactly the same as those of the photons emitted when electrons lose energy and fall between the same energy levels. If the atoms of an element are subjected to white light, which consists of all the visible frequencies, the atoms will selectively absorb the same frequencies that they emit when excited. The absorbed frequencies appear as dark lines in the otherwise continuous white-light spectrum. This series of dark lines, resulting from the selective absorption of particular frequencies in the white-light spectrum of an atom, is called an **absorption spectrum**. An atom will absorb a photon only if the photon possesses the exact amount of energy required to raise the atom to one of its possible excited states.

Review Questions

12. The lowest energy state of an atom is called its
(1) ground state
(2) ionized state
(3) initial energy state
(4) final energy state

13. Which electron transition in the hydrogen atom results in the emission of a photon with the greatest energy?
(1) $n = 2$ to $n = 1$
(2) $n = 3$ to $n = 2$
(3) $n = 4$ to $n = 2$
(4) $n = 5$ to $n = 3$

14. What is the minimum energy required to ionize a hydrogen atom in the $n = 3$ state?
(1) 13.60 eV
(2) 12.09 eV
(3) 5.52 eV
(4) 1.51 eV

15. Which photon energy could be absorbed by a hydrogen atom that is in the $n = 2$ state?
(1) 0.66 eV
(2) 1.51 eV
(3) 1.89 eV
(4) 2.40 eV

16. Hydrogen atoms undergo a transition from the $n = 3$ excited state to the ground state. What is the total number of different photon energies that may be emitted by these atoms?

17. An electron in a mercury atom jumps from level a to level g by absorbing a single photon. Determine the energy of the photon in joules.

18. Which phenomenon provides evidence that the hydrogen atom has discrete energy levels?

19. A photon having an energy of 9.40 electronvolts strikes a hydrogen atom in the ground state. Why is the photon *not* absorbed by the hydrogen atom?
    (1) The atom's orbital electron is moving too fast.
    (2) The photon striking the atom is moving too fast.
    (3) The photon's energy is too small.
    (4) The photon is being repelled by electrostatic force.

20. Which transition between the energy levels of a mercury atom causes the emission of a photon of highest frequency?
    (1) e to d (2) e to c (3) c to b (4) b to a

21. White light is passed through a cloud of cool hydrogen gas and then examined with a spectroscope. The dark lines observed on a bright background are caused by
    (1) the hydrogen emitting all frequencies in the white light
    (2) the hydrogen absorbing certain frequencies of the white light
    (3) diffraction of the white light
    (4) constructive interference

22. It is possible for an excited hydrogen atom to return to the ground state by the emission of a single photon. Regardless of the initial excited state, this electron transition produces a spectral line in which region of the electromagnetic spectrum?
    (1) ultraviolet   (3) visible light
    (2) infrared   (4) radio waves

23. An electron in a mercury atom changes from energy level b to level e. This energy-level change occurs as the atom
    (1) absorbs a 2.03-eV photon
    (2) absorbs a 5.74-eV photon
    (3) emits a 2.03-eV photon
    (4) emits a 5.74-eV photon

Base your answers to questions 24 through 26 on the information that follows.

A hydrogen atom emits a 2.55-electronvolt photon as its electron changes from one energy level to another.

24. Determine the energy level change for the electron.

25. Express the energy of the emitted photon in joules.

26. Calculate the frequency of the emitted photon.

Base your answers to questions 27 through 29 on the information below.

The light of the "alpha line" in the Balmer series of the hydrogen spectrum has a wavelength of 6.58×10^{-7} meter in air.

27. Calculate the energy of an "alpha line" photon in joules.

28. What is the energy of an "alpha line" photon in electronvolts?

29. Using your answer to question 28, explain whether or not this result verifies that the "alpha line" corresponds to a transition from energy level $n = 3$ to energy level $n = 2$ in a hydrogen atom.

Base your answers to questions 30 through 33 on the following information.

A photon with 14.60 electronvolts of energy collides with a mercury atom in its ground state.

30. Express the energy of the incident photon in joules.

31. Calculate the frequency of the incident photon.

32. In what region of the electromagnetic spectrum is the frequency of the incident photon?
    (1) gamma rays   (3) visible
    (2) infrared   (4) ultraviolet

33. If the photon collision ionizes the atom, what is the maximum energy that the electron removed from the atom can have?
    (1) 0.00 eV   (3) 10.38 eV
    (2) 4.22 eV   (4) 14.60 eV

34. Calculate the frequency of the photon emitted when the electron in an excited hydrogen atom changes from energy level $n = 3$ to $n = 2$.

The Nucleus

Rutherford's experiments showed that all of the atom's positive charge and nearly all of its mass is contained in the nucleus. The **nucleus** is the core of an atom made up of one or more protons and (except for one of the isotopes of hydrogen) one or more neutrons. The protons and neutrons that make up the nucleus of an atom are called <u>nucleons</u>.

Strong Nuclear Force

The positively charged protons in any nucleus containing more than one proton are separated by a distance of 10^{-15} meter. Consequently, a large repulsive Coulomb force exists between them. The gravitational force of attraction between protons is far too weak to counterbalance this electrostatic force of repulsion. Thus, there must exist a very strong attractive nuclear force to keep the protons concentrated in the nucleus of an atom. It is this **strong nuclear force,** which is an attractive force between protons and neutrons in an atomic nucleus, that is responsible for the stability of the nucleus.

The strong nuclear force of attraction between two protons in a nucleus is about 100 times stronger than the electrostatic force of repulsion. At distances greater than a few nucleon diameters, however, the strong nuclear force diminishes rapidly and becomes much less than the gravitational or electrostatic forces. Although the strong nuclear force is the strongest force known to exist, it is effective only over a short distance.

Universal Mass Unit

The mass of an individual atom is a very small fraction of a kilogram. Consequently, for convenience, scientists use another unit called the universal mass unit, u, to express such masses. The **universal mass unit,** or atomic mass unit, is defined as $\frac{1}{12}$ the mass of an atom of carbon-12, which is a carbon atom having 6 protons, 6 neutrons, and 6 electrons. In universal mass units, the mass of the proton is 1.0073 u, the mass of the neutron is 1.0087 u, and the mass of an electron is 0.0005 u. In SI units, a mass of one universal mass unit, or 1 u, equals 1.66×10^{-27} kilogram.

Mass-Energy Relationship

Einstein showed that mass and energy are different forms of the same thing and are equivalent. The energy equivalent of mass is directly proportional to both the mass and the speed of light in a vacuum squared. The following formula expresses this relationship.

$$E = mc^2$$

®

Energy E is in joules, mass m is in kilograms, and c is the speed of light in a vacuum, 3.00×10^8 meters per second. For example, if one kilogram of mass is converted to energy, the amount of energy produced is 9.00×10^{16} joules. Thus, the masses of subatomic particles can be expressed in joules, but more often they are expressed in an equivalent number of electronvolts.

SAMPLE PROBLEM

One universal mass unit equals 1.66×10^{-27} kilogram. Calculate the energy equivalent of one universal mass unit in megaelectronvolts.

SOLUTION: Identify the known and unknown values.

Known
$m = 1.66 \times 10^{-27}$ kg
$c = 3.00 \times 10^8$ m/s
1 eV $= 1.60 \times 10^{-19}$ J
10^6 eV $= 1$ MeV

Unknown
$E = ?$ MeV

1. Write the formula that relates energy and mass.

$$E = mc^2$$

2. Substitute the known values and solve.

$$E = (1.66 \times 10^{-27} \text{ kg})(3.00 \times 10^8 \text{ m/s})^2$$
$$E = 1.49 \times 10^{-10} \text{ J}$$

3. Use the relationship between electronvolts and joules to convert the energy in joules to electronvolts.

$$E = (1.49 \times 10^{-10} \text{ J})\left(\frac{1 \text{ eV}}{1.60 \times 10^{-19} \text{ J}}\right)$$

$$E = 9.31 \times 10^8 \text{ eV}$$

4. Use the relationship between eV and Mev to convert eV to MeV.

$$E = (9.31 \times 10^8 \text{ eV})\left(\frac{1 \text{ MeV}}{10^6 \text{ eV}}\right)$$

$$E = 931 \text{ MeV}$$

Nuclear Mass and Energy

According to Einstein's mass-energy equation, any change in energy results in an equivalent change in mass. Mass-energy is conserved at all levels from cosmic to subatomic. For example, in a chemical reaction in which one kilogram of carbon combines with oxygen to form carbon dioxide, the amount of energy released is 3.3×10^7 joules. Even though this is a significant amount of energy, it is equivalent to only 4×10^{-10} kilogram of mass. The mass of the carbon dioxide formed in the reaction is slightly less than the mass of the carbon and oxygen before they reacted. This change in mass is too small to detect or measure. The same is true for all chemical reactions and other ordinary energy changes. However, in reactions involving the nuclei of atoms, the changes in energy relative to the masses involved are much larger, and the corresponding changes in mass can be measured.

The mass of a proton is 1.0073 u and the mass of a neutron is 1.0087 u. Thus, the total mass of two protons and two neutrons is 2(1.0073 u + 1.0087 u), or 4.0320 u. However, the mass of a helium-4 nucleus, which consists of two protons and two neutrons, is only 4.0016 u. Thus, the mass of the atomic nucleus is less than the sum of the masses of its individual nucleons when measured separately. This is true of every nucleus, with the exception of hydrogen-1, which has only one nucleon.

When nucleons come together to form a nucleus, energy is released and an equivalent amount of matter is lost. To break up the nucleus and separate the nucleons, work must to be done against the strong nuclear force of attraction. The energy needed to separate the nucleons appears as an equivalent increase in their total mass.

SAMPLE PROBLEM

A helium nucleus consisting of two protons and two neutrons has a mass of 4.0016 universal mass units. The mass of a proton is 1.0073 universal mass units and the mass of a neutron is 1.0087 universal mass units.

(a) Find the difference between the mass of the helium nucleus and the total mass of its constituents.
(b) Find the energy equivalent of this mass difference in electronvolts.

SOLUTION: Identify the known and unknown values.

Known
mass of helium
   nucleus = 4.0016 u
mass of proton = 1.0073 u
mass of neutron = 1.0087 u
1 u = 931 MeV

Unknown
mass difference = ? u
E = ? eV

1. Determine the mass of the two protons and two neutrons.

   mass of 2 protons = 2(1.0073 u) = 2.0146 u
   mass of 2 neutrons = 2(1.0087 u) = 2.0174 u

Find the total mass of the four individual nucleons.
total mass = 2.0146 u + 2.0174 u = 4.0320 u

Find the difference between the masses of the individual nucleons and a helium nucleus.
mass difference = 4.0320 u − 4.0016 u = 0.0304 u

2. Use the relationship between the universal mass unit and MeV, 1 u = 931 MeV.

   E = (0.0304 u)(931 MeV/u) = 28.3 MeV

Studying Atomic Nuclei

The structure of the atomic nucleus and the nature of matter have been investigated using particle accelerators. These devices use electric and magnetic fields to increase the kinetic energies of charged particles, such as electrons and protons, and project them at speeds near the speed of light in a vacuum into samples of matter. Collisions between the high speed particles and atomic nuclei may disrupt the nuclei and release new particles. The study of these ejected particles can give useful information about the structure and forces within the nucleus. Scientists continue to study the atomic nucleus because the nucleus, and thus the atomic structure of an atom of an element determines the particular physical and chemical properties of the element. Each type of atom is different and distinct. A growing understanding of nuclear forces and structure will increase understanding of matter and its interactions.

Review Questions

35. Which particles are most likely to be found in an atomic nucleus?

   (1) neutrons, only
   (2) protons, only
   (3) both protons and neutrons
   (4) both neutrons and electrons

36. Which description of the interaction which binds a nucleus together is most accurate?

   (1) long-range and weak
   (2) long-range and strong
   (3) short-range and weak
   (4) short-range and strong

37. What force holds protons and neutrons together in an atom?

   (1) strong force   (3) gravitational force
   (2) magnetic force   (4) electrostatic force

38. Which fundamental force is primarily responsible for the attraction between protons and electrons?

   (1) strong   (3) gravitational
   (2) weak   (4) electromagnetic

39. The energy produced by the complete conversion of 2.0×10^{-5} kilogram of mass into energy is

   (1) 1.8 TJ   (2) 6.0 GJ   (3) 1.8 MJ   (4) 6.0 kJ

40. In the equation $E = mc^2$, E may be expressed in

   (1) newtons/coulomb   (3) electronvolts
   (2) joules/second   (4) coulombs

41. If a deuterium nucleus has a mass of 1.53×10^{-3} universal mass unit less than its components, this mass represents an energy of

   (1) 1.38 MeV   (3) 1.53 MeV
   (2) 1.42 MeV   (4) 3.16 MeV

42. Calculate the amount of energy in joules that would be produced if 2.50×10^{-3} kilogram of matter was entirely converted to energy.

43. If the mass of one proton was totally converted into energy, the yield would be

   (1) 2.79×10^{-38} J   (3) 1.50×10^{-10} J
   (2) 5.01×10^{-19} J   (4) 9.00×10^{16} J

44. In a nuclear reaction, 9.90×10^{-13} joule of energy was released. Calculate the mass equivalent of this energy.

45. Which graph best represents the relationship between energy and mass when matter is converted into energy?

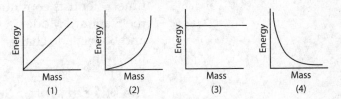

  (1)   (2)   (3)   (4)

46. The chart below shows the masses of selected particles.

Particle	Mass
$^{235}_{92}\text{U}$	235.0 u
$^{138}_{56}\text{Ba}$	137.9 u
$^{95}_{36}\text{Kr}$	94.9 u
$^{1}_{0}\text{n}$	1.0 u

Consider the following equation.

$$^{235}_{92}\text{U} + {}^{1}_{0}\text{n} \rightarrow {}^{138}_{56}\text{Ba} + {}^{95}_{36}\text{Kr} + 3{}^{1}_{0}\text{n} + E$$

The energy E is equivalent to a mass of

   (1) 0.2 u   (2) 2.0 u   (3) 2.2 u   (4) 0.0 u

The Standard Model of Particle Physics

Today, particle physicists are in the process of building a model of the structure of the nucleus. The current model, called the **Standard Model of Particle Physics,** is a theory, not a law, that is used to explain the existence of all the particles that have been observed and the forces that hold atoms together or lead to their decay.

The Fundamental Forces in Nature

Force can be defined as a push or pull on a mass, or explained as a vector quantity causing an object to accelerate. In modern physics, scientists refer to particles as force carriers, because forces are brought about as a result of an exchange of particles.

There are four fundamental forces in nature: strong (nuclear), electromagnetic, weak, and gravitational. Table 6-1 gives an overview of the important characteristics of these four forces. The weak force, which has not yet been discussed, is another short-range nuclear force that is responsible for the decay of some nuclear particles.

Table 6-1. The Fundamental Forces of Nature

Force	Relative Strength	Range of Force
strong (nuclear)	1	$\approx 10^{-15}$ m
electromagnetic	10^{-2}	proportional to $\frac{1}{r^2}$
weak	10^{-13}	$<10^{-18}$ m
gravitational	10^{-38}	proportional to $\frac{1}{r^2}$

Electric and magnetic forces are often treated independently, but they are actually combined as electromagnetic force. The weak force has successfully been combined with the electromagnetic force to produce a single electroweak force. Grand unification theories (GUTs) attempt to add the strong force to this combination. Theories of everything (TOEs), which would combine gravity with all the other forces, are not developed at this time. Scientists continue to try to resolve questions and inconsistencies in the Standard Model in much the same manner as Thomson, Rutherford, and Bohr made changes and amendments to the model for the structure of the atom.

Classification of Subatomic Particles

Particles can be classified according to the types of interactions they have with other particles. If the force carrier particles are excluded, all particles can be classified into two groups according to the types of interactions they have with other particles. A particle that interacts through the strong nuclear force, as well as the electromagnetic, weak, and gravitational forces, is called a **hadron.** Protons and neutrons are hadrons. A particle that interacts through the electromagnetic, weak, and gravitational forces, but *not* the strong nuclear force, is called a **lepton.** A lepton has a mass less than that of a proton. Electrons, positrons, and neutrinos are classified as leptons. A **positron** is a particle whose mass is equal to the mass of the electron, and whose positive electric charge is equal in magnitude to the negative charge of the electron. A **neutrino** is a neutral particle that has little, if any, mass but does possess both energy and momentum. The *Reference Tables for Physical Setting/Physics* give the names, symbols, and charges of the six members of the lepton family.

Ⓡ

The hadron group can be subdivided into baryons and mesons. A **baryon** is an elementary particle that can be transformed into a proton or neutron and some number of mesons and lighter particles. Baryons are also known as heavy particles because their masses are equal to or greater than the mass of a proton. A **meson** is a particle of intermediate mass. Mesons decay into electrons, positrons, neutrinos, and photons.

An antiparticle is associated with each particle. An **antiparticle** is a particle having mass, lifetime, and spin identical to the associated particle, but with charge of opposite sign (if charged) and magnetic moment reversed in sign. An antiparticle is denoted by a bar over the symbol for the particle. For example, an antiproton, the antiparticle of a proton p, is denoted by the symbol $\overline{\pi}$. Thus, the antiproton would be described as a stable baryon carrying a unit negative charge, but having the same mass as a proton. The positron, noted earlier, is thus the antiparticle of the electron. The antineutron, the antiparticle of the neutron, has the same mass as the neutron and is also electrically neutral. However the magnetic moment and spin of the antineutron are in the same direction, whereas, the magnetic moment and spin of the neutron are in opposite directions. An antiparticle exists for the neutrino; the two are identical except for their direction of spin. **Antimatter** is material consisting of atoms that are composed of antiprotons, antineutrons, and positrons.

The Quark Baryons and mesons are composed of more fundamental particles called quarks. A **quark** is one of the basic particles, having charges of $\pm\frac{1}{3}e$ or $\pm\frac{2}{3}e$, from which many of the elementary particles may be built up. This implies that the charge on the electron is no longer considered to be the smallest nonzero charge that a particle may possess. The quarks are named *up, down, charm, strange, top,* and *bottom*. Every baryon is a combination of three quarks and every meson is a combination of a quark and an antiquark. An **antiquark** is the antiparticle of a quark, having electric charge, baryon number, and strangeness opposite in sign to that of the corresponding quark. An antibaryon consists of three antiquarks. The *Reference Tables for Physical Setting/Physics* give the names, symbols, and Ⓡ charges of the six members of the quark family. The quark content of a proton is *uud* (up, up, down) and the quark content of a neutron is *udd* (up, down, down). When quarks combine to form baryons, their charges add algebraically to a total of 0e, +1e, or −1e. When quarks and antiquarks combine to form mesons, their charges add algebraically to a total of 0e, +1e, or −1e.

Review Questions

Base your answers to questions 47 through 49 on information given in Table 6-1.

47. Express the range of the strong force in picometers.

48. Express the range of the weak force in nanometers.

49. How many times stronger than the gravitational force is the electromagnetic force?

50. What is the total number of quarks in a helium nucleus consisting of 2 protons and 2 neutrons?

(1) 16   (2) 12   (3) 8   (4) 4

Base your answers to questions 51 and 52 on the information and equation below.

During the process of beta (β^-) emission, a neutron in the nucleus of an atom is converted into a proton, an electron, an electron antineutrino, and energy.

neutron → proton + electron + electron antineutrino + energy

51. Based on conservation laws, how does the mass of the neutron compare to the mass of the proton?

52. Since charge must be conserved in the reaction shown, what charge must an electron antineutrino carry?

53. A baryon may have a charge of

(1) $-\frac{1}{3}e$ (2) 0 e   (3) $+\frac{2}{3}e$ (4) $+\frac{4}{3}e$

54. An antibaryon is composed of

(1) three quarks
(2) one quark and two antiquarks
(3) three antiquarks
(4) two quarks and one antiquark

55. What is the electric charge on a pion having quark composition $u\bar{d}$?

56. What is the electric charge on a particle having quark composition $d\bar{b}$?

57. A particle has a quark composition of *dds*. What is the charge on and classification of the particle?

(1) −1e, baryon   (3) −1e, meson
(2) +1e, baryon   (4) +1e, meson

58. A particle has a quark composition of $s\bar{u}$. What is the charge on and classification of the particle?

(1) −1e, baryon
(2) +1e, baryon
(3) −1e, meson
(4) +1e, meson

59. What is the mass of an antineutron in kilograms?

Directions

Review the Test-Taking Strategies section of this book. Then answer the following questions. Read each question carefully and answer with a correct choice or response.

Part A

1 A photon of light traveling through space with a wavelength of 6.0×10^{-7} meter has an energy of
(1) 4.0×10^{-40} J
(3) 5.4×10^{10} J
(2) 3.3×10^{-19} J
(4) 5.0×10^{14} J

2 The energy of a photon varies directly with its
(1) frequency
(2) wavelength
(3) speed
(4) rest mass

3 A variable-frequency light source emits a series of photons. As the frequency of the photon increases, what happens to the energy and wavelength of the photon?
(1) The energy decreases and the wavelength decreases.
(2) The energy decreases and the wavelength increases.
(3) The energy increases and the wavelength decreases.
(4) The energy increases and the wavelength increases.

4 When a photon and a free electron collide there is conservation of
(1) velocity, only
(2) both velocity and energy
(3) momentum, only
(4) both momentum and energy

5 The concept that electrons exhibit wave properties can best be demonstrated by the
(1) collisions between photons and electrons
(2) existence of an electron antiparticle
(3) production of electron interference patterns
(4) classification of the electron as a lepton

6 The bright-line emission spectrum of an element can best be explained by
(1) electrons transitioning between discrete energy levels in the atoms of that element
(2) protons acting as both particles and waves
(3) electrons being located in the nucleus
(4) protons being dispersed uniformly throughout the atoms of that element

7 A hydrogen atom is excited to the $n = 3$ state. In returning to the ground state, the atom could *not* emit a photon with an energy of
(1) 1.89 eV
(3) 12.09 eV
(2) 10.20 eV
(4) 12.75 eV

8 During which energy level change for the electron in a hydrogen atom does the emitted photon have the shortest wavelength?
(1) $n = 5$ directly to $n = 2$
(2) $n = 4$ directly to $n = 2$
(3) $n = 2$ directly to $n = 4$
(4) $n = 2$ directly to $n = 5$

9 How much energy would be generated if a 1.00×10^{-3}-kilogram mass was completely converted to energy?
(1) 9.31×10^{-1} MeV
(3) 9.00×10^{13} J
(2) 9.31×10^{2} MeV
(4) 9.00×10^{16} J

10 The energy equivalent of the rest mass of an electron is approximately
(1) 5.1×10^{5} J
(3) 2.7×10^{-22} J
(2) 8.2×10^{-14} J
(4) 8.5×10^{-28} J

11 In the nuclear reaction

$$^{3}_{1}\text{H} + ^{1}_{1}\text{H} \rightarrow ^{4}_{2}\text{He} + \text{energy}$$

the masses of the nuclei are:
$^{1}_{1}\text{H} = 1.008\ 13$ u
$^{3}_{1}\text{H} = 3.016\ 95$ u
$^{4}_{2}\text{He} = 4.003\ 88$ u

How much energy is released during the reaction?
(1) 3.39×10^{-21} MeV
(3) 1.97×10^{1} MeV
(2) 2.12×10^{-2} MeV
(4) 1.91×10^{15} MeV

12 Which statement is true of the strong nuclear force?
(1) It acts over very great distances.
(2) It holds protons and neutrons together.
(3) It is much weaker than gravitational forces.
(4) It repels neutral charges.

13 A meson may *not* have a charge of
(1) $+1e$
(3) $0e$
(2) $+2e$
(4) $-1e$

14 The charge of an antistrange quark is approximately
(1) $+ 5.33 \times 10^{-20}$ C   (3) $+ 5.33 \times 10^{20}$ C
(2) $- 5.33 \times 10^{-20}$ C   (4) $- 5.33 \times 10^{20}$ C

Part B

15 A proton has a quark content of *uud* and a neutron has a quark content of *udd*. What is the quark content of an antiproton? [1]

16 Calculate the energy of a photon with a frequency of 5.00×10^{15} hertz. [2]

17 On the axes below sketch a line to represent the relationship between photon energy and wavelength for a series of photons. [1]

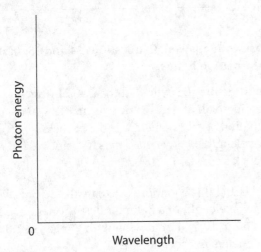

Base your answers to questions 18 and 19 on the following information and diagram.

The diagram represents the collision of an X-ray photon having wavelength λ with an electron -*e* in an atom. The electron is ejected from the atom, and a photon having a longer wavelength λ' than the incident photon is also emitted.

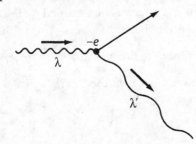

18 Calculate the wavelength λ of an incident photon which has a frequency of 1.00×10^{18} hertz. [2]

19 Energy is conserved in the collision. Write an expression in terms of photon wavelength to represent the electron's increase in energy as a result of the collision. [1]

Base your answers to questions 20 through 23 on the information that follows.

An electron in a mercury atom makes a direct transition from energy level *e* to energy level *b*.

20 Determine the energy in electronvolts that is given off in this transition. [1]

21 Determine the energy in joules of the photon emitted in the transition. [1]

22 Calculate the frequency of the radiation corresponding to the emitted photon. [2]

23 Explain what would happen if a 4.50-electronvolt photon was incident on a mercury atom in the ground state. [1]

24 An electron in a mercury atom drops from energy level *i* to the ground state by emitting a single photon. This photon has an energy of
(1) 2.50×10^{-19} J   (3) 1.66×10^{-18} J
(2) 1.41×10^{-18} J   (4) 1.91×10^{-18} J

25 The following graph represents the relationship between mass and its energy equivalent.

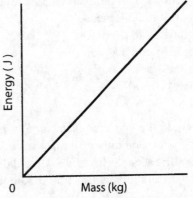

What is the physical signficance of the slope of the line? [1]

26 If c is the speed of light in a vacuum, which is an acceptable unit for the mass of a subatomic particle?
(1) GeV
(2) GeV $\cdot$ c
(3) GeV/c
(4) GeV/c^2

27 Express Planck's constant in fundamental units. [1]

Base your answers to questions 28 and 29 on the information in the following chart.

Particle	Rest Mass
proton	1.0073 u
neutron	1.0087 u

28 Calculate the energy equivalent of the rest mass of a neutron in megaelectronvolts. [2]

29 A tritium nucleus consists of one proton and two neutrons and has a total mass of 3.0170 universal mass units. Determine the difference in mass between the total mass of the nucleons and the mass of the tritium nucleus. [2]

30 A tau lepton decays into an electron, an electron antineutrino, and a tau neutrino, as represented in the reaction below.

$$\tau \rightarrow e + \bar{\nu}_e + \nu_\tau$$

Complete the equation below to show how this reaction obeys the Law of Conservation of Charge by indicating the amount of charge on each particle. [1]

_____ e $\rightarrow$ _____ e + _____ e + _____ e

31 A lithium atom consists of 3 protons, 4 neutrons, and 3 electrons. This atom contains a total of
(1) 9 quarks and 7 leptons
(2) 12 quarks and 6 leptons
(3) 14 quarks and 3 leptons
(4) 21 quarks and 3 leptons

Part C

32 According to the *Reference Tables for Physical Setting/Physics*, one universal mass unit is equal to 9.31×10^2 megaelectronvolts. Calculate the value for the universal mass unit in kilograms. [2]

33 The diagram that follows is the energy-level diagram for a fictitious element. Draw arrows on the diagram to represent all possible electron transitions that would cause photons to be emitted from atoms of this element in the $n = 5$ excited state. [2]

```
_____  n = 6
_____  n = 5

_____  n = 4

_____  n = 3


_____  n = 2




Ground  _____  n = 1
state
```

Base your answers to questions 34 and 35 on the information below.

Louis de Broglie extended the idea of wave-particle duality to all of nature with his matter-wave equation, $\lambda = \frac{h}{mv}$, where λ is the particle's wavelength, m is its mass, v is its velocity, and h is Planck's constant.

34 Using this equation, calculate the de Broglie wavelength of a helium nucleus (mass = 6.7×10^{-27} kg) moving with a speed of 2.0×10^6 meters per second. [2]

35 The wavelength of this particle is of the same order of magnitude as which type of electromagnetic radiation? [1]

Base your answers to questions 36 through 38 on the following information.

According to Bohr's model of the hydrogen atom, the electron can exist only in certain allowed orbits each having radius r_n, which is determined by the energy level n. The equation for calculating this radius is $r_n = \dfrac{n^2 h^2}{4\pi^2 m_e k e^2}$ where the quantities are represented by the same symbols as in the *Reference Tables for Physical Setting/Physics*.

36 Calculate the radius in meters of the hydrogen atom in the ground state. [3]

37 Express the radius of the hydrogen atom in the ground state in nanometers to the proper number of significant digits. [1]

38 Express, in lowest terms, the ratio of the radius of a hydrogen atom in excited state $n = 4$ to the radius of a hydrogen atom in excited state $n = 2$. [1]

Base your answers to questions 39 through 42 on the following statement.

Under certain conditions an electron and a positron can annihilate each other and produce two photons. Annihilation is a process in which a particle and its antiparticle are converted into energy.

39 Calculate the combined energy in joules of the photons created when an electron and a positron annihilate each other. [2]

40 Assuming the photons are identical, express the energy of one photon in electronvolts. [1]

41 Assuming the photons are identical, calculate the frequency of one photon. [2]

42 According to information in the electromagnetic spectrum chart in the *Reference Tables for Physical Setting/Physics*, how would one of these photons be classified? [1]

Base your answers to questions 43 through 50 on the following information and diagram.

A student performed an experiment using a diffraction grating to measure the wavelengths of the bright lines in mercury's spectrum. A diffraction grating is a device consisting of numerous parallel lines ruled on a glass plate. The device causes light that passes through it from a source to act as individual sources. Where the light interferes constructively, bright lines are produced.

The apparatus used in the experiment included a mercury vapor lamp, exposed by only a thin vertical slit, placed at one corner of a lab table, and a diffraction grating positioned at an adjacent corner. A meter stick was placed at right angles to the line joining the slit and the center of the grating. The rod of a ring stand was used as a guide to mark the distance x of the bright line observed by the student when looking through the grating from the source, as shown. A two-meter stick was used to measure the distance z from the grating to the location of the bright line.

The student was told that the equation $\lambda = d\sin\theta$ could be used to determine the wavelength of the bright line. In the equation, d is the distance between the lines on the glass diffraction grating and θ is the angle between the line joining the source and grating and the line joining the bright line and the grating.

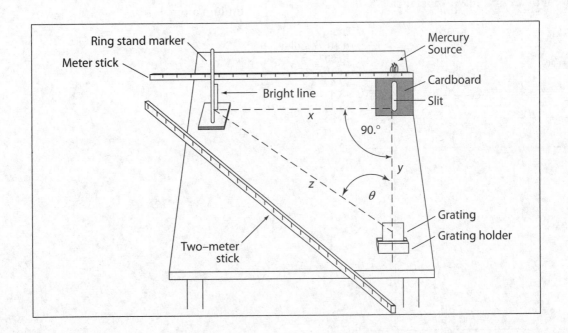

The student was given the value of d. She measured x and z three times and recorded the average x and z, as shown below.

$$d = 1.67 \times 10^{-4} \text{ cm}$$
$$x = 50.4 \text{ cm}$$
$$z = 193.9 \text{ cm}$$

43 Express d in meters. [1]

44 Write an expression that represents the sine of angle θ. [1]

45 Calculate the wavelength of the bright line. [2]

46 According to *the Handbook of Chemistry and Physics*, the accepted value for the wavelength of this line is 4358.33 Å (angstrom units). If 1 Å = 10^{-10} m, what is the accepted value for the wavelength in meters? [1]

47 Calculate the student's percent error for this bright line measurement. [2]

48 Calculate the energy in joules associated with the student's measured wavelength. [2]

49 Express the energy of the measured line in electronvolts. [1]

50 Refer to the energy level diagram for mercury in the *Reference Tables for Physical Setting/Physics*. Which electron transition is most likely to be the one that the student measured? [1]

Base your answers to questions 51 and 52 on the diagram below, which shows some energy levels for an atom of an unknown substance.

51 Determine the minimum energy necessary for an electron to change from the B energy level to the F energy level. [1]

52 Calculate the frequency of the photon emitted when an electron in this atom changes from the F energy level to the B energy level. [2]

Base your answers to questions 53 and 54 on the information and data table below.

In the first nuclear reaction using a particle accelerator, accelerated protons bombarded lithium atoms, producing alpha particles and energy. The energy resulted from the conversion of mass into energy. The reaction can be written as shown below.

$$^{1}_{1}\text{H} + ^{7}_{3}\text{Li} \rightarrow ^{4}_{2}\text{He} + ^{4}_{2}\text{He} + \text{energy}$$

Data Table		
Particle	**Symbol**	**Mass (u)**
proton	$^{1}_{1}\text{H}$	1.007 83
lithium atom	$^{7}_{3}\text{Li}$	7.016 00
alpha particle	$^{4}_{2}\text{He}$	4.002 60

53 Determine the difference between the total mass of a proton plus a lithium atom, $^{1}_{1}\text{H} + ^{7}_{3}\text{Li}$, and the total mass of two alpha particles, $^{4}_{2}\text{He} + ^{4}_{2}\text{He}$, in universal mass units. [1]

54 Determine the energy in megaelectronvolts produced in the reaction of a proton with a lithium atom. [1]

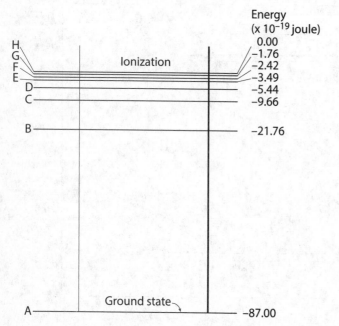

Energy
(x 10^{-19} joule)
0.00
H
G   −1.76
F   Ionization
E   −2.42
     −3.49
D   −5.44
C   −9.66

B   −21.76

Ground state

A   −87.00

Appendix
Reference Tables for Physical Setting/Physics

Strategies to Help Answer Questions

You should become thoroughly familiar with all details of these tables. Look for the (R) in the text to see where the content is enhanced by the reference tables.

Some of the ways these reference tables are used in Regents Examination questions include:

- finding a specific fact, such as the value of an electronvolt expressed in joules

- using an equation on the reference tables to solve a problem, such as determining the kinetic energy of a moving object

- graphing or recognizing the correct graph of data on the reference tables, such as the absolute index of refraction of a substance

- decoding a graphic symbol in a question, such as a quark or lepton

- performing a procedure using part of the reference tables, such as approximating the wavelength of red light from the frequency data given in the electromagnetic spectrum

- interpreting data in the reference tables, such as the ionization energies for mercury

Reference Tables for Physical Setting/PHYSICS
2006 Edition

List of Physical Constants

Name	Symbol	Value
Universal gravitational constant	G	6.67×10^{-11} N•m²/kg²
Acceleration due to gravity	g	9.81 m/s²
Speed of light in a vacuum	c	3.00×10^{8} m/s
Speed of sound in air at STP		3.31×10^{2} m/s
Mass of Earth		5.98×10^{24} kg
Mass of the Moon		7.35×10^{22} kg
Mean radius of Earth		6.37×10^{6} m
Mean radius of the Moon		1.74×10^{6} m
Mean distance—Earth to the Moon		3.84×10^{8} m
Mean distance—Earth to the Sun		1.50×10^{11} m
Electrostatic constant	k	8.99×10^{9} N•m²/C²
1 elementary charge	e	1.60×10^{-19} C
1 coulomb (C)		6.25×10^{18} elementary charges
1 electronvolt (eV)		1.60×10^{-19} J
Planck's constant	h	6.63×10^{-34} J•s
1 universal mass unit (u)		9.31×10^{2} MeV
Rest mass of the electron	m_e	9.11×10^{-31} kg
Rest mass of the proton	m_p	1.67×10^{-27} kg
Rest mass of the neutron	m_n	1.67×10^{-27} kg

Prefixes for Powers of 10

Prefix	Symbol	Notation
tera	T	10^{12}
giga	G	10^{9}
mega	M	10^{6}
kilo	k	10^{3}
deci	d	10^{-1}
centi	c	10^{-2}
milli	m	10^{-3}
micro	μ	10^{-6}
nano	n	10^{-9}
pico	p	10^{-12}

Approximate Coefficients of Friction

	Kinetic	Static
Rubber on concrete (dry)	0.68	0.90
Rubber on concrete (wet)	0.58	
Rubber on asphalt (dry)	0.67	0.85
Rubber on asphalt (wet)	0.53	
Rubber on ice	0.15	
Waxed ski on snow	0.05	0.14
Wood on wood	0.30	0.42
Steel on steel	0.57	0.74
Copper on steel	0.36	0.53
Teflon on Teflon	0.04	

The Electromagnetic Spectrum

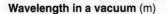

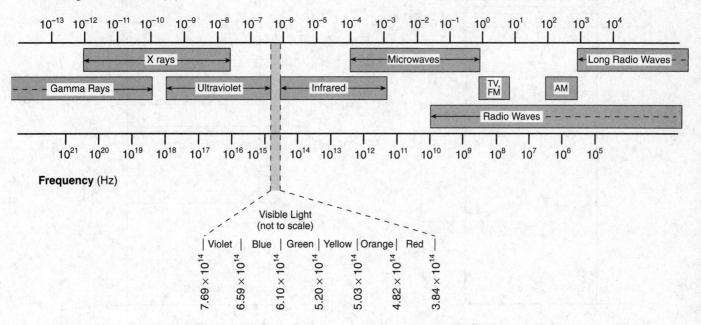

Absolute Indices of Refraction	
($f = 5.09 \times 10^{14}$ Hz)	
Air	1.00
Corn oil	1.47
Diamond	2.42
Ethyl alcohol	1.36
Glass, crown	1.52
Glass, flint	1.66
Glycerol	1.47
Lucite	1.50
Quartz, fused	1.46
Sodium chloride	1.54
Water	1.33
Zircon	1.92

Energy Level Diagrams

Hydrogen

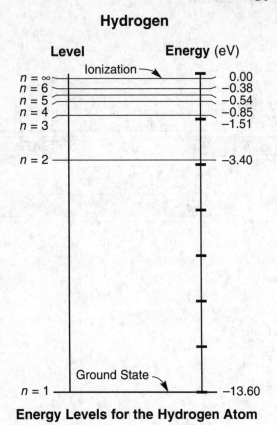

Energy Levels for the Hydrogen Atom

Mercury

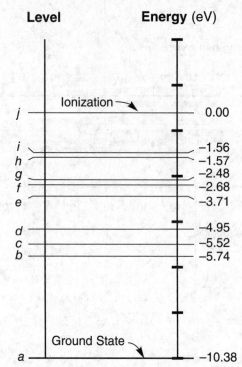

A Few Energy Levels for the Mercury Atom

Classification of Matter

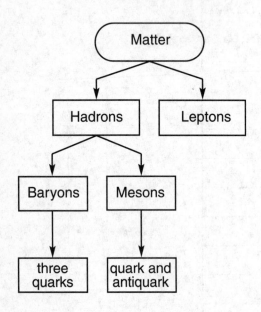

Particles of the Standard Model

Quarks

Name	up	charm	top
Symbol	u	c	t
Charge	$+\frac{2}{3}\,e$	$+\frac{2}{3}\,e$	$+\frac{2}{3}\,e$

down	strange	bottom
d	s	b
$-\frac{1}{3}\,e$	$-\frac{1}{3}\,e$	$-\frac{1}{3}\,e$

Leptons

electron	muon	tau
e	μ	τ
$-1e$	$-1e$	$-1e$

electron neutrino	muon neutrino	tau neutrino
ν_e	ν_μ	ν_τ
0	0	0

Note: For each particle, there is a corresponding antiparticle with a charge opposite that of its associated particle.

Electricity

$$F_e = \frac{kq_1q_2}{r^2}$$

$$E = \frac{F_e}{q}$$

$$V = \frac{W}{q}$$

$$I = \frac{\Delta q}{t}$$

$$R = \frac{V}{I}$$

$$R = \frac{\rho L}{A}$$

$$P = VI = I^2R = \frac{V^2}{R}$$

$$W = Pt = VIt = I^2Rt = \frac{V^2t}{R}$$

A = cross-sectional area
E = electric field strength
F_e = electrostatic force
I = current
k = electrostatic constant
L = length of conductor
P = electrical power
q = charge
R = resistance
R_{eq} = equivalent resistance
r = distance between centers
t = time
V = potential difference
W = work (electrical energy)
Δ = change
ρ = resistivity

Series Circuits

$$I = I_1 = I_2 = I_3 = \ldots$$

$$V = V_1 + V_2 + V_3 + \ldots$$

$$R_{eq} = R_1 + R_2 + R_3 + \ldots$$

Parallel Circuits

$$I = I_1 + I_2 + I_3 + \ldots$$

$$V = V_1 = V_2 = V_3 = \ldots$$

$$\frac{1}{R_{eq}} = \frac{1}{R_1} + \frac{1}{R_2} + \frac{1}{R_3} + \ldots$$

Circuit Symbols

cell

battery

switch

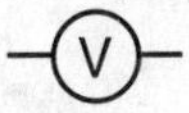

voltmeter

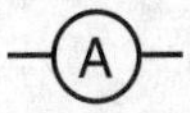

ammeter

resistor

variable resistor

lamp

Resistivities at 20°C	
Material	**Resistivity ($\Omega \bullet$m)**
Aluminum	2.82×10^{-8}
Copper	1.72×10^{-8}
Gold	2.44×10^{-8}
Nichrome	$150. \times 10^{-8}$
Silver	1.59×10^{-8}
Tungsten	5.60×10^{-8}

Waves

$v = f\lambda$

$T = \dfrac{1}{f}$

$\theta_i = \theta_r$

$n = \dfrac{c}{v}$

$n_1 \sin \theta_1 = n_2 \sin \theta_2$

$\dfrac{n_2}{n_1} = \dfrac{v_1}{v_2} = \dfrac{\lambda_1}{\lambda_2}$

c = speed of light in a vacuum
f = frequency
n = absolute index of refraction
T = period
v = velocity or speed
λ = wavelength
θ = angle
θ_i = angle of incidence
θ_r = angle of reflection

Modern Physics

$E_{photon} = hf = \dfrac{hc}{\lambda}$

$E_{photon} = E_i - E_f$

$E = mc^2$

c = speed of light in a vacuum
E = energy
f = frequency
h = Planck's constant
m = mass
λ = wavelength

Geometry and Trigonometry

Rectangle

$A = bh$

Triangle

$A = \frac{1}{2}bh$

Circle

$A = \pi r^2$

$C = 2\pi r$

Right Triangle

$c^2 = a^2 + b^2$

$\sin \theta = \dfrac{a}{c}$

$\cos \theta = \dfrac{b}{c}$

$\tan \theta = \dfrac{a}{b}$

A = area
b = base
C = circumference
h = height
r = radius

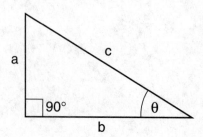

Mechanics

$$\bar{v} = \frac{d}{t}$$

$$a = \frac{\Delta v}{t}$$

$$v_f = v_i + at$$

$$d = v_i t + \frac{1}{2}at^2$$

$$v_f^2 = v_i^2 + 2ad$$

$$A_y = A \sin \theta$$

$$A_x = A \cos \theta$$

$$a = \frac{F_{net}}{m}$$

$$F_f = \mu F_N$$

$$F_g = \frac{Gm_1 m_2}{r^2}$$

$$g = \frac{F_g}{m}$$

$$p = mv$$

$$p_{before} = p_{after}$$

$$J = F_{net}\,t = \Delta p$$

$$F_s = kx$$

$$PE_s = \frac{1}{2}kx^2$$

$$F_c = ma_c$$

$$a_c = \frac{v^2}{r}$$

$$\Delta PE = mg\Delta h$$

$$KE = \frac{1}{2}mv^2$$

$$W = Fd = \Delta E_T$$

$$E_T = PE + KE + Q$$

$$P = \frac{W}{t} = \frac{Fd}{t} = F\bar{v}$$

a = acceleration

a_c = centripetal acceleration

A = any vector quantity

d = displacement or distance

E_T = total energy

F = force

F_c = centripetal force

F_f = force of friction

F_g = weight or force due to gravity

F_N = normal force

F_{net} = net force

F_s = force on a spring

g = acceleration due to gravity or gravitational field strength

G = universal gravitational constant

h = height

J = impulse

k = spring constant

KE = kinetic energy

m = mass

p = momentum

P = power

PE = potential energy

PE_s = potential energy stored in a spring

Q = internal energy

r = radius or distance between centers

t = time interval

v = velocity or speed

$\bar{v}$ = average velocity or average speed

W = work

x = change in spring length from the equilibrium position

Δ = change

θ = angle

μ = coefficient of friction

Glossary

absolute error the difference between an experimental value and the accepted value of a measured quantity

absolute index of refraction a property of a material medium equal to the ratio of the speed of light in a vacuum to the speed of light in the material medium

absorption spectrum a series of dark lines resulting from the selective absorption of particular frequencies of the continuous spectrum produced by white light

acceleration the time rate of change of velocity; a vector quantity

accepted value the most probable value for a measured quantity, which is usually published in reference books

accurate describes a measurement that is the same or very close to the accepted value

ammeter a device for measuring electric current when connected in series in an electrical circuit

ampere (A) the fundamental SI unit of electric current; equal to one coulomb per second

amplitude the magnitude of the maximum displacement of a particle of a medium from its rest or equilibrium position

angle of incidence the angle between an incident ray and the normal to the surface at the point where the ray strikes the surface

angle of reflection the angle between a reflected ray and the normal to the surface at the point where the ray is reflected

angle of refraction the angle between a ray emerging from the interface of two media and the normal to that interface at the point where the ray emerges

antimatter material consisting of atoms which are composed of antiprotons, antineutrons, and positrons

antinode the point of maximum displacement of a medium when two waves are interacting

antiparticle a particle having mass, lifetime, and spin identical to the associated particle, but with charge of opposite sign (if charged) and magnetic moment reversed in sign

antiquark the antiparticle of a quark, having electric charge, baryon number, and strangeness opposite in sign to those of the corresponding quark

atom the smallest particle of an element

atomic spectrum a specific series of frequencies of electromagnetic radiation produced when electrons in excited atoms of an element in the gaseous state return to lower energy levels

baryon a heavy particle composed of three quarks; an elementary particle which can be transformed into a proton or neutron and some number of mesons and lighter particles

battery a combination of two or more electrochemical cells; also, a direct-current voltage source which converts chemical, thermal, nuclear, or solar energy into electrical energy

bright-line spectrum an emission spectrum or a series of bright lines against a dark background that results from the emission of radiation of specific frequencies by a heated gas

cell a device that converts chemical energy to electrical energy

centripetal acceleration the acceleration that results in the uniform motion of an object in a circular path; a vector quantity directed toward the center of curvature

centripetal force the force needed to keep an object moving in a circular path; a vector quantity directed toward the center of curvature

closed system a group of objects, not acted upon by any external force

coefficient of friction the ratio of the frictional force to the normal force

compression a decrease in spring length from its equilibrium position or length

condensation a region of maximum compression in a longitudinal wave

conductivity a property of a material that describes the availability of charges that are free to move under the influence of an electric field

conductor a material, usually a metal, in which electric charge moves easily

conservative force name given to a force when work done against it is independent of the path taken

constant proportion the relationship that exists between two quantities when an increase in one causes no change in the other

constructive interference the effect produced when two in-phase waves pass simultaneously through a medium causing an increase in amplitude

coulomb (C) the derived SI unit of electric charge equal to a current of one ampere passing through a given area in one second; 6.25×10^{18} elementary charges

Coulomb's law states that the magnitude of the electrostatic force that one point charge exerts on another point charge is directly proportional to the product of the charges and inversely proportional to the square of the distance between them

crest in a transverse wave, the position of maximum displacement of a particle of the medium in the positive direction (for example, upward)

current in an electric circuit, the rate at which charge passes a given point; a scalar quantity

dependent variable the quantity that changes in an experiment as a result of changes made by the experimenter

derived unit a combination of two or more fundamental units used to simplify notation

destructive interference the effect produced when two waves of equal frequency and amplitude, whose phase difference is $180°$ or $\frac{1}{2}\lambda$, pass simultaneously through a medium

diffraction the spreading of wave fronts into the region behind a barrier in a wave's path

direct squared proportion the relationship that exists between two quantities in which an increase in one causes a squared increase in the other

directly proportional applies to the relationship between two quantities in which an increase in one quantity causes an increase in the other; the quotient of the quantities in a non-zero constant

displacement the change in position of an object described by the vector that begins at the initial position of the object and ends at its final position

distance the total length of the path that an object travels; a scalar quantity

Doppler effect a change in observed frequency and wavelength due to the relative motion of a wave source and an observer

dynamics the branch of mechanics dealing with how forces affect an object's motion

elastic potential energy the energy stored in a spring when work is done in compressing or stretching it; a scalar quantity

electric circuit a closed path along which charged particles move

electric field the region around a charged particle through which a force is exerted on another charged particle

electric field line the imaginary line along which a positive test charge would move in an electric field

electric field strength the force per unit charge on a stationary positive test charge in an electric field; a vector quantity

electrical energy the total amount of energy in an electric circuit; equal to the product of power consumed and the time of the charge flow; a scalar quantity

electrical power the rate at which electrical energy is converted into other forms; a scalar quantity

electromagnetic energy the energy associated with electric or magnetic fields

electromagnetic induction the process of generating a potential difference in a conductor due to the relative motion between the conductor and a magnetic field

electromagnetic spectrum the complete range of frequencies and wavelengths of electromagnetic waves

electromagnetic wave periodically changing electric and magnetic fields that move through a vacuum at speed $c = 3.00 \times 10^8$ m/s

electron the fundamental negatively charged $(-)$ subatomic particle of matter; particle charge is equal in magnitude to that of a proton; mass is negligible compared to the mass of a proton

electronvolt (eV) a unit of energy equal to the work done in moving an elementary charge through a potential difference of one volt

electrostatic force the force that one point charge exerts on another point charge; magnitude of force is directly proportional to the product of the charges and inversely proportional to the square of the distance between them; a vector quantity

elementary charge denoted by e, the charge equal in magnitude to the charge of an electron $(-e)$ or the charge of a proton $(+e)$

elongation an increase in spring length from its equilibrium length or position

emission spectrum a series of bright lines against a dark background, resulting from the emission of radiation of specific frequencies

energy level a stationary state of the electrons in an atom which represents a specific amount of energy

energy the ability to do work; a scalar quantity

energy-level diagram diagram in which the energy levels of a quantized system are indicated by distances of horizontal lines from a zero energy level

equilibrium state of an object when the net force acting on it is zero

equivalent resistance the single resistance that could replace several resistors in a circuit

excitation any process that raises the energy level of electrons in an atom

excited state the condition of an atom when its electron is in any level above the lowest energy level because of the absorption of a quantum of energy

experimental value measurement made during laboratory work which may stand alone or be incorporated into one or more formulas to yield a value for a physical quantity

extrapolation the extension of a graphed line beyond the region in which data was taken

force a push or pull on a mass; a vector quantity

free fall the ideal falling motion of an object acted upon only by the force of gravity

free-body diagram a sketch, or scale drawing, that shows all the forces acting concurrently on an object

frequency the number of cycles per unit time of an oscillating particle; a scalar quantity

friction the force that opposes the relative motion of two objects in contact; a vector quantity

fundamental unit one of a set of units in which all quantities measured by physicists can be expressed

generator device that converts mechanical energy into electrical energy by rotating a large coil of wire in a magnetic field

gravitational field a region in space where a test particle would experience a gravitational force

gravitational field strength the force per unit mass at a given point in a gravitational field; a vector quantity

gravitational force the attractive force that one object exerts on another object due to their masses; the magnitude of force is directly proportional to the product of the masses and inversely proportional to the square of the distance between their centers; a vector quantity

gravitational potential energy the work done on or the energy change of an object resulting from lifting the object to a height above Earth's surface; a scalar quantity

gravity the force between the mass of Earth and the mass of any object in the vicinity of Earth; a vector quantity

ground state the condition of an atom when its electron is in the lowest energy level and the atom is not absorbing or radiating energy

hadron a particle that interacts through the strong nuclear force, as well as electromagnetic, weak, and gravitational forces

hertz (Hz) derived SI unit of frequency equivalent to one cycle per second; in fundamental units, 1 Hz equals 1/s

horizontal component (of velocity) a component velocity vector whose direction is parallel to the horizon

ideal mechanical system a closed system in which no friction or other nonconservative force is acting

impulse the product of the net force acting on an object and the time during which the force acts; a vector quantity

incident ray a ray that originates in a medium and strikes a boundary or an interface with another medium

independent variable the quantity that the experimenter changes in an experiment

indirect squared proportion the relationship that exists between two quantities in which an increase in one causes a squared decrease in the other

induced potential difference the difference in potential created in a conductor due to its relative motion in a magnetic field

inertia the resistance of an object to a change in its motion; directly proportional to the object's mass

instantaneous velocity the velocity of an object at any particular instant in time; a vector quantity

insulator a substance, usually a compound or a nonmetallic element, in which electric charge flows poorly

interference the superposition of one wave on another

internal energy the total potential and kinetic energy possessed by the particles that make up an object, but excluding the potential and kinetic energy of the system as a whole

inversely proportional applies to the relationship between two quantities in which an increase in one quantity causes a decrease in the other; the product of the quantities is a non-zero constant

ionization potential the energy required to remove an electron from an atom to form an ion

joule (J) a derived SI unit equal to the work done when a force of one newton produces a displacement of one meter; the unit for electrical energy

kilogram (kg) the fundamental SI unit of mass

kinetic energy the energy of an object due to its motion; a scalar quantity

kinetic friction the friction of motion between objects in contact; a vector quantity

law of conservation of charge states that in a closed, isolated system, the total charge of the system remains constant

law of conservation of energy states that energy can be neither created nor destroyed

law of conservation of momentum states that the total momentum of the objects in a closed system is constant

law of reflection states that the angle of incidence is equal to the angle of reflection

lepton a particle that interacts through the electromagnetic, weak, and gravitational forces, but not the strong nuclear force

line of best fit a straight or curved line on a graph which approximates the relationship among a set of data points

linear motion an object's change of position along a straight line

longitudinal wave a wave in which the motion of the vibratory disturbance is parallel to the direction of propagation or travel of the wave through the medium

magnet a material in which the spinning electrons of its atoms are aligned with one another

magnetic field the region where magnetic force exists around a magnet or any moving charged object

magnetic field (flux) lines the imaginary lines that map out the magnetic field around a magnet

magnetic field strength the number of magnetic flux lines per unit area passing through a plane perpendicular to the direction of the lines; a vector quantity

magnetic force the force produced by the motion of charges relative to each other; a vector quantity

magnetism the force of attraction or repulsion between magnetic poles

mass the amount of matter contained in an object; a scalar quantity

mean the average, $\bar{x}$, of a set of n measurements, where x_i is the individual measurement and f_i is the frequency of measurement,

$$\bar{x} = \frac{\sum\limits_{i=1}^{n} x_i f_i}{\sum f_i}$$

mechanical energy the sum of the kinetic and potential energies in a system; a scalar quantity

mechanics the branch of physics that deals with forces and their effects in producing and changing motion

medium a body of matter through which waves propagate

meson a particle of intermediate mass composed of a quark and an antiquark

meter (m) the fundamental SI unit of length

momentum the product of an object's mass and velocity; a vector quantity

motor device that converts electrical energy into mechanical energy as a result of forces on a current-carrying conductor in a magnetic field

natural frequency a particular frequency at which every elastic body will vibrate if disturbed

net force the vector sum of the concurrent forces acting on an object; a vector quantity

neutrino a neutral particle that possesses both energy and momentum but has little, if any, mass

neutron subatomic particle with no charge and a mass approximately equal to that of a proton

newton (N) the force that imparts an acceleration of one meter per second^2 to a one-kilogram mass

node region of zero displacement of the medium produced by maximum destructive interference of waves

nonconservative force name given to a force when work done against it is dependent on the path taken

non-ideal mechanical system a system in which a nonconservative force such as friction is acting

normal a line drawn perpendicular to a surface

normal force the force pressing two contacting surfaces together; on a horizontal surface, the normal force is equal in magnitude but opposite in direction to the weight of an object resting on the surface; a vector quantity

north magnetic pole the magnetic pole from which the magnetic flux of a magnet is considered to emerge

nuclear energy the energy released by nuclear fission, the division of a heavy atomic nucleus into parts of comparable mass, or by nuclear fusion, the combining of two light nuclei to form a heavier nucleus; a scalar quantity

nucleon name given to protons and neutrons that make up the nucleus of an atom

nucleus the core of an atom which is made up of one or more protons and (except for one of the isotopes of hydrogen) one or more neutrons

ohm (Ω) the derived SI unit of electrical resistance equivalent to one volt per ampere

ohm·meter ($\Omega \cdot m$) the SI unit for resistivity

Ohm's law states that at constant temperature the resistance of a conductor is equal to the ratio of the potential difference applied across it to the current that flows through it

parallel circuit an electric circuit in which the circuit elements are connected between two points, with one end of each component connected to each point

pendulum a mass (bob) attached to one end of a string or wire that is attached at the other end to a pivot point

percent error a measure of the reliability of an experimental result calculated by dividing the absolute error by the accepted value and multiplying the quotient by 100

period (of a pendulum) the time required for a displaced pendulum to complete one cycle of motion; a scalar quantity

period (of a wave) the time required for one complete vibration to pass a given point in the medium; a scalar quantity

periodic wave a series of regularly repeated disturbances of a field or medium

phase the position of a point on a wave relative to another point on the same wave; two points on a wave are in phase when they are displaced from their rest position by the same amount in the same direction and are moving in the same direction

photocell a device that converts light, a form of electromagnetic radiation, into electrical energy

photon the quantum, or basic unit, of electromagnetic energy

Planck's constant (h) the proportionality constant in the mathematical relationship between the energy of a quantum and its frequency

positron a particle having mass equal to the mass of the electron, and positive electric charge equal in magnitude to the negative charge of the electron

potential difference the difference in potential energy per unit charge between two points in an electric field; a scalar quantity

potential energy the energy possessed by an object due to its position or condition; a scalar quantity

power the rate at which work is done or energy is consumed; a scalar quantity

precise describes several measurements taken of the same event that are nearly identical

principle of superposition states that the resultant displacement at any point on two or more superimposed waves is the algebraic sum of the displacements of the individual waves

proton the fundamental positively charged (+) subatomic particle of matter; particle charge is equal in magnitude to that of an electron; particle has a mass of approximately one universal mass unit

pulse a single short disturbance that moves from one position to another in a field or medium

quantized condition that restricts a system to the absorption or radiation of energy only in fixed amounts, or quanta

quantum a discrete packet of electromagnetic energy emitted or absorbed

quantum theory the theory that assumes that electromagnetic energy is emitted from and absorbed by matter in discrete amounts or packets of energy

quark one of the basic particles, having charges of $\pm\frac{1}{3}e$ or $\pm\frac{2}{3}e$, from which many of the elementary particles may be built up

range (in data analysis) the difference between the highest and lowest values in a data set

range the horizontal distance traveled by a projectile

rarefaction a region of maximum expansion in a longitudinal wave

ray a straight line that is drawn at right angles to a wave front and points in the direction of wave travel

reflected ray a ray that rebounded from a boundary or interface

reflection the rebounding of a pulse or wave as it strikes a barrier

refracted ray a ray that results from an incident ray entering a second medium of different optical density obliquely

refraction the change in direction of a wave due to a change in speed at the boundary between two media with different densities (different absolute indices of refraction)

resistance a measure of the opposition that a device or conductor offers to the flow of electric current

resistivity characteristic of a material that depends on its electronic structure and temperature

resistor a device designed to have a definite amount of resistance

resolution of forces the process of determining the magnitude and direction of the components of a force; usually two components at right angles to each other

resonance the vibration of a body at its natural frequency due to the action of a vibrating source of the same frequency

resultant the single vector that is equivalent to the combined effect of two or more vectors

scalar a quantity that has magnitude only, with no direction specified

scientific notation a way of expressing quantities which consists of a number equal to or greater than one and less than ten followed by a multiplication sign and the base ten raised to some integral power

second (s) the fundamental SI unit of time

series circuit an electric circuit in which all parts are connected end to end to provide a single path for current

SI prefix a prefix combined with an SI base unit to form a new unit that is larger or smaller than the base unit by a multiple or submultiple of 10

SI system (Système International) provides standardized units for scientific measurements

significant figures the digits in a measured quantity that are known with certainty plus the one digit whose value has been estimated

slope the inclination of a graphed line, determined as the ratio $\frac{\Delta y}{\Delta x}$ for any two points on the line

Snell's law the mathematical relationship that governs the refraction of light as it passes obliquely from one medium to another of different optical density; $n_1 \sin\theta_1 = n_2 \sin\theta_2$

spectral line a particular frequency of absorbed or emitted energy characteristic of an atom

speed the distance that an object moves in a unit of time; a scalar quantity

speed (of a wave) equal to the product of its wavelength and frequency; a scalar quantity

spring constant the constant of proportionality between the applied force and the compression or elongation of a spring

standard deviation the square root of the variance of a set of data

Standard Model of Particle Physics a theory used to explain the existence of all the particles that have been observed and the forces that hold atoms together or lead to their decay

standing wave a pattern of wave crests and troughs that remains stationary in a medium when two waves of equal frequency and amplitude pass through the medium in opposite directions

static friction the force that opposes the start of motion; a vector quantity

statics the branch of mechanics that treats forces that act on objects at rest

static equilibrium state of an object at rest

stationary state any particular orbit that can be occupied by an electron in an atom

strong nuclear force an attractive force between protons and neutrons in an atomic nucleus which is responsible for the stability of the nucleus; a vector quantity

superposition occurs when two or more waves travel through the same medium simultaneously

switch a device for making, breaking, or changing the connections in an electric circuit

tangent a line on a graph which passes through a point and has a slope equal to the slope of the curve at that point

thermal energy also called heat; is the total kinetic energy possessed by the individual particles that comprise an object

transverse wave a wave in which the motion of the vibratory disturbance is perpendicular to the direction of travel of the wave

trough in a transverse wave, the position of maximum displacement in the negative direction (downward)

unbalanced force a nonzero net force acting on an object; a vector quantity

uniform circular motion the motion of an object traveling in a circular path at constant speed

uniform motion the motion of an object moving at constant speed

unit a standard quantity with which other similar quantities can be compared

universal mass unit or atomic mass unit; one-twelfth the mass of a carbon-12 atom

vacuum a region of empty space

variable resistor a coil of resistance wire whose effective resistance can be varied by sliding a contact point

variance the sum of the squares of the differences of the measurements in a set of data from the mean of the set, divided by the number of measurements

vector a quantity that has both magnitude and direction, often shown graphically as an arrow with definite length and direction

vector components (of a force) the two or more concurrent forces whose vector sum is the acting force

velocity the time rate of change of an object's displacement; a vector quantity

vertical component (of velocity) a component velocity vector whose direction is at right angles to the horizon

volt (V) the derived SI unit of electric potential difference; equal to one joule per coulomb

voltmeter a device for measuring potential difference across an element when connected in parallel with it in an electric circuit

watt (W) the derived SI unit of power equal to one joule per second

wave a vibratory disturbance that propagates through a medium or field

wave front all adjacent points on a wave that are in phase with each other

wavelength the distance between any two successive points in phase with one another in a periodic wave

weight the gravitational force with which a planet attracts a mass; a vector quantity

work the transfer of energy to an object when the object moves due to the application of a force that is entirely in the direction of motion or has a component in the direction of the object's motion; a scalar quantity

Index

and electromagnetic induction 135–136
units of measurement 3, 120
electric fields 118–119
around a point charge 118
between charged plates 119
and electric current 121
electric field line 118
electric field strength 118
electricity 114–129
electrochemical cells 121
electromagnetic energy 85, 184–185
quantum theory 184–185
electromagnetic force 195
electromagnetic induction 135–136
electromagnetic radiation 136, 168
and the photoelectric effect 185–186
electromagnetic waves 136, 147, 167
light 162–168
spectrum 167–168
electron clouds 189
electrons 114–115, 183
and charged objects 114–115
charge on 114–116
and current flow 121
and electromagnetic induction 135
and magnetism 133, 135
and models of the atom 187, 190
electronvolts 119
electrostatic force 116, 118
electrostatics 114–116
electroweak force 196
elementary charge 114
elevators
weight in 52
emission spectra
of atoms 189–190
energy 80–96
conservation of 95
conversions 85
elastic potential energy 88–90
electrical 127–128
forms of 85–86
gravitational potential energy 85–86, 94–96
kinetic 92–93, 95–96
mass-energy relationship 192–193

potential 85–86, 88–90, 95–96
transfers 84–85, 148
units of measurement 3, 80, 129
wave-particle duality 184–186
and waves 148, 151
and work 80, 94–98
energy levels
of atoms 188
diagrams of 189, 193
equations
solving 21–22
equilibrium
static 36–37
dynamic 38
estimation 13
excitation energies 188–190
excited states 188, 190
experimental values 16
extrapolation 17

fields
electric 118–119
gravitational 50–51
magnetic 134
forces 33–37
adding 34–35
centripetal 47–48
component 35–36
concurrent 33–35
conservative 94
dynamics 38–41
electromagnetic 195
electrostatic 116, 118
and equilibrium 36–37
friction 53–55, 94, 96
fundamental 195
gravitational 50, 195–196
kinematics 24–30
magnetic 133–134
measuring 5
net 34, 36
and Newton's laws of motion 38–41, 47
nonconservative 94, 96
normal 53
on a pendulum 60
and power 81
resolution of 35–36
and springs 88–90
statics 33–37
strong nuclear 192
unbalanced 38–39
units of measurement 3, 39
universal law of gravitation 50–52

weak force 195
and work 80
free-body diagram 37
free fall 30, 42, 95
frequency
and the Doppler effect 156–157
in measurement 14
natural 158–159
of pendulums 60
and periodic waves 150, 152
and photon energy 185
and quantum energy 184–185
and refraction 163, 164
and spectral lines 189, 190
units of measurement 3, 150
friction 53–55, 94, 96
coefficient of 53–54
on an inclined surface 54–55, 94–95
fluid 55
kinetic 54–55
static 54–55
fuses 127

gamma rays 168
generators 85
grand unification theories (GUTs) 196
graphing data 17–19
about springs 88–89
and acceleration 27–29
and distances traveled 28–29
and impulse 57
linear motion 26–27
and Newton's second law 39
resolving forces into components 35–36
solving displacement problems 25–27
gravitational field 50–51
gravitational field strength 51
gravitational force 195
gravitational potential energy 85–86, 94
gravity 30, 85, 94–96
and other fundamental forces 195–196
and projectile motion 43–45
universal law of gravitation 50–52
ground states 188–190

hadrons 196
heat 85, 167–168

Acknowledgments

Author Acknowledgments:
For my daughter, Heather, and granddaughters, Julia and Adrianne

Independent Reviewer: Tom Good

Photographs:
Every effort has been made to secure permission and provide appropriate credit for photographic material. The publisher deeply regrets any omission and pledges to correct errors called to its attention in subsequent editions.

Unless otherwise acknowledged, all photographs are the property of Pearson Education, Inc.

Photo locators denoted as follows: Top (T), Center (C), Bottom (B), Left (L), Right (R), Background (Bkgd)

Cover suravid/Shutterstock; **i** suravid/Shutterstock; **154** Steve Gorton/ DK Images; **1086 B** Lawrence Berkeley National Laboratory.

New York Regents Examinations

The following New York Regents Examinations are provided so that you can practice a Regents Examination for The Physical Setting/Physics.

Using the Regents Examinations

The best way to use these examinations is to take an entire test after you have reviewed the course content. Use the tests to determine if you have reviewed enough to do well on the Regents Examination and to determine where further review will be helpful.

Before beginning a test, make sure you have a copy of the *Reference Tables for Physical Setting/Physics,* a protractor, a centimeter ruler, and a pencil for making graphs and diagrams.

Do not look up any information or answers while you take the examination. Answer each question just as you would during a real test. As you take the examination, use the margin of the paper to note any question where you are just guessing. Leave the more difficult questions for last, but be sure to answer each question. Every credit counts so do not skip over a long question that is worth only a credit or two. A long question could be easier than it initially appears and a correct answer to it may make the difference between earning an A or a B or between passing and failing.

Many multiple-choice questions and constructed-response questions will have a numerical answer. Although a detailed solution is not required for a multiple-choice question, it is still in your best interest to use the problem-solving skills you have acquired throughout the course to determine the answer. You should represent all known quantities given in the statement with proper symbols and units, and determine the proper symbol for the quantity being sought. Determine the appropriate formula for solving the problem by referring to the *Reference Tables for Physical Setting/Physics.* Solve the equation for the unknown variable and substitute the known quantities with their units. Perform the calculations and simplify the units. You should not merely take values given in a problem and punch numbers into a calculator to determine answers to multiple choice questions. An incorrect answer you may obtain by this careless method will usually be one of the possible answer choices.

When you finish, have your teacher score your examination and help you determine the areas where you need the most work. Also review the "guesses" you noted in the margin to find out what you need to study to ensure that you will be able to answer similar questions on the next test. Once you have determined your weaknesses, you can focus your review on those topics in this book.

Reviewing the areas where you know the least will give you the best chance of improving your final score. Spending time on areas where you are doing quite well will not produce much improvement in your total score, but is still important if time permits.

Answer Key All answers to these Regents Examinations are included in the Answer Key, which also includes Diagnostic Tests to help you assess what you know before starting to study a topic.

Part A

Answer all questions in this part.

Directions (1–35): For *each* statement or question, choose the word or expression that, of those given, best completes the statement or answers the question. Some questions may require the use of the *2006 Edition Reference Tables for Physical Setting/Physics*. Record your answers on your separate answer sheet.

1 A unit used for a vector quantity is
(1) watt
(2) newton
(3) kilogram
(4) second

2 A displacement vector with a magnitude of 20. meters could have perpendicular components with magnitudes of
(1) 10. m and 10. m
(2) 12 m and 8.0 m
(3) 12 m and 16 m
(4) 16 m and 8.0 m

3 A hiker travels 1.0 kilometer south, turns and travels 3.0 kilometers west, and then turns and travels 3.0 kilometers north. What is the total distance traveled by the hiker?
(1) 3.2 km
(2) 3.6 km
(3) 5.0 km
(4) 7.0 km

4 A car with an initial velocity of 16.0 meters per second east slows uniformly to 6.0 meters per second east in 4.0 seconds. What is the acceleration of the car during this 4.0-second interval?
(1) 2.5 m/s^2 west
(2) 2.5 m/s^2 east
(3) 4.0 m/s^2 west
(4) 4.0 m/s^2 east

5 On the surface of planet X, a body with a mass of 10. kilograms weighs 40. newtons. The magnitude of the acceleration due to gravity on the surface of planet X is
(1) 4.0×10^3 m/s^2
(2) 4.0×10^2 m/s^2
(3) 9.8 m/s^2
(4) 4.0 m/s^2

6 A car traveling in a straight line at an initial speed of 8.0 meters per second accelerates uniformly to a speed of 14 meters per second over a distance of 44 meters. What is the magnitude of the acceleration of the car?
(1) 0.41 m/s^2
(2) 1.5 m/s^2
(3) 3.0 m/s^2
(4) 2.2 m/s^2

7 An object starts from rest and falls freely for 40. meters near the surface of planet P. If the time of fall is 4.0 seconds, what is the magnitude of the acceleration due to gravity on planet P?
(1) 0 m/s^2
(2) 1.3 m/s^2
(3) 5.0 m/s^2
(4) 10. m/s^2

8 If a block is in equilibrium, the magnitude of the block's acceleration is
(1) zero
(2) decreasing
(3) increasing
(4) constant, but not zero

9 The diagram below shows a light ray striking a plane mirror.

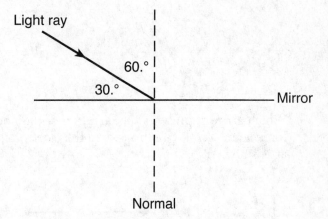

What is the angle of reflection?
(1) 30.°
(2) 60.°
(3) 90.°
(4) 120.°

10 An electric field exerts an electrostatic force of magnitude 1.5×10^{-14} newton on an electron within the field. What is the magnitude of the electric field strength at the location of the electron?
(1) 2.4×10^{-33} N/C
(2) 1.1×10^{-5} N/C
(3) 9.4×10^4 N/C
(4) 1.6×10^{16} N/C

11 A 7.0-kilogram cart, A, and a 3.0-kilogram cart, B, are initially held together at rest on a horizontal, frictionless surface. When a compressed spring attached to one of the carts is released, the carts are pushed apart. After the spring is released, the speed of cart B is 6.0 meters per second, as represented in the diagram below.

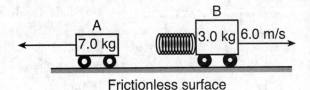

Frictionless surface

What is the speed of cart A after the spring is released?

(1) 14 m/s   (3) 3.0 m/s
(2) 6.0 m/s   (4) 2.6 m/s

12 An electron in a magnetic field travels at constant speed in the circular path represented in the diagram below.

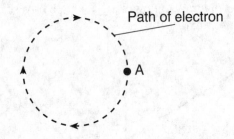

Path of electron

Which arrow represents the direction of the net force acting on the electron when the electron is at position A?

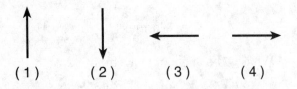

(1)   (2)   (3)   (4)

13 The potential difference between two points, A and B, in an electric field is 2.00 volts. The energy required to move a charge of 8.00×10^{-19} coulomb from point A to point B is

(1) 4.00×10^{-19} J   (3) 6.25×10^{17} J
(2) 1.60×10^{-18} J   (4) 2.50×10^{18} J

14 Which statement describes the gravitational force and the electrostatic force between two charged particles?

(1) The gravitational force may be either attractive or repulsive, whereas the electrostatic force must be attractive.
(2) The gravitational force must be attractive, whereas the electrostatic force may be either attractive or repulsive.
(3) Both forces may be either attractive or repulsive.
(4) Both forces must be attractive.

15 An electrostatic force exists between two $+3.20 \times 10^{-19}$-coulomb point charges separated by a distance of 0.030 meter. As the distance between the two point charges is *decreased*, the electrostatic force of

(1) attraction between the two charges decreases
(2) attraction between the two charges increases
(3) repulsion between the two charges decreases
(4) repulsion between the two charges increases

16 What is the energy of the photon emitted when an electron in a mercury atom drops from energy level f to energy level b?

(1) 8.42 eV   (3) 3.06 eV
(2) 5.74 eV   (4) 2.68 eV

17 An observer counts 4 complete water waves passing by the end of a dock every 10. seconds. What is the frequency of the waves?

(1) 0.40 Hz   (3) 40. Hz
(2) 2.5 Hz   (4) 4.0 Hz

18 Copper is a metal commonly used for electrical wiring in houses. Which metal conducts electricity better than copper at 20°C?

(1) aluminum   (3) nichrome
(2) gold   (4) silver

19 A motor does 20. joules of work on a block, accelerating the block vertically upward. Neglecting friction, if the gravitational potential energy of the block increases by 15 joules, its kinetic energy

(1) decreases by 5 J   (3) decreases by 35 J
(2) increases by 5 J   (4) increases by 35 J

20 When only one lightbulb blows out, an entire string of decorative lights goes out. The lights in this string must be connected in

(1) parallel with one current pathway
(2) parallel with multiple current pathways
(3) series with one current pathway
(4) series with multiple current pathways

21 An electric toaster is rated 1200 watts at 120 volts. What is the total electrical energy used to operate the toaster for 30. seconds?

(1) 1.8×10^3 J   (3) 1.8×10^4 J
(2) 3.6×10^3 J   (4) 3.6×10^4 J

22 What is the rate at which work is done in lifting a 35-kilogram object vertically at a constant speed of 5.0 meters per second?

(1) 1700 W   (3) 180 W
(2) 340 W   (4) 7.0 W

23 When a wave travels through a medium, the wave transfers

(1) mass, only
(2) energy, only
(3) both mass and energy
(4) neither mass nor energy

24 Glass may shatter when exposed to sound of a particular frequency. This phenomenon is an example of

(1) refraction   (3) resonance
(2) diffraction   (4) the Doppler effect

25 Which waves require a material medium for transmission?

(1) light waves   (3) sound waves
(2) radio waves   (4) microwaves

26 Which type of oscillation would most likely produce an electromagnetic wave?

(1) a vibrating tuning fork
(2) a washing machine agitator at work
(3) a swinging pendulum
(4) an electron traveling back and forth in a wire

27 If monochromatic light passes from water into air with an angle of incidence of 35°, which characteristic of the light will remain the same?

(1) frequency   (3) speed
(2) wavelength   (4) direction

28 The absolute index of refraction of medium Y is twice as great as the absolute index of refraction of medium X. As a light ray travels from medium X into medium Y, the speed of the light ray is

(1) halved   (3) quartered
(2) doubled   (4) quadrupled

29 The diagram below shows a transverse wave moving toward the right along a rope.

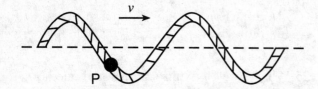

At the instant shown, point *P* on the rope is moving toward the

(1) bottom of the page   (3) left
(2) top of the page   (4) right

30 When an isolated conductor is placed in the vicinity of a positive charge, the conductor is attracted to the charge. The charge of the conductor

(1) must be positive
(2) must be negative
(3) could be neutral or positive
(4) could be neutral or negative

31 The quarks that compose a baryon may have charges of

(1) $+\frac{2}{3}e, +\frac{2}{3}e,$ and $-\frac{1}{3}e$

(2) $+\frac{1}{3}e, -\frac{1}{3}e,$ and $+\frac{2}{3}e$

(3) $-1e, -1e,$ and 0

(4) $+\frac{2}{3}e, +\frac{2}{3}e,$ and 0

32 A rubber block weighing 60. newtons is resting on a horizontal surface of dry asphalt. What is the magnitude of the minimum force needed to start the rubber block moving across the dry asphalt?

(1) 32 N   (3) 51 N
(2) 40. N   (4) 60. N

33 The data table below lists the mass and speed of four different objects.

Object	Mass (kg)	Speed (m/s)
A	2.0	6.0
B	4.0	5.0
C	6.0	4.0
D	8.0	2.0

Which object has the greatest inertia?

(1) A   (3) C
(2) B   (4) D

34 The electroscope shown in the diagram below is made completely of metal and consists of a knob, a stem, and leaves. A positively charged rod is brought near the knob of the electroscope and then removed.

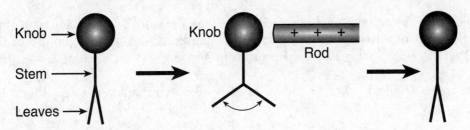

The motion of the leaves results from electrons moving from the

(1) leaves to the knob, only
(2) knob to the leaves, only
(3) leaves to the knob and then back to the leaves
(4) knob to the leaves and then back to the knob

35 Which circuit diagram represents the correct way to measure the current in a resistor?

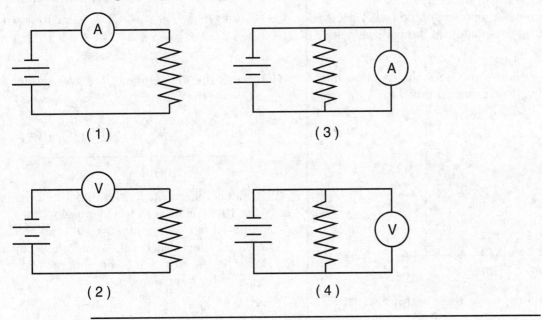

(1)

(3)

(2)

(4)

[6]

Part B–1

Answer all questions in this part.

Directions (36–50): For *each* statement or question, choose the word or expression that, of those given, best completes the statement or answers the question. Some questions may require the use of the *2006 Edition Reference Tables for Physical Setting/Physics*. Record your answers on your separate answer sheet.

36 The height of a typical kitchen table is approximately

(1) 10^{-2} m   (3) 10^1 m
(2) 10^0 m   (4) 10^2 m

37 A ball is thrown with a velocity of 35 meters per second at an angle of 30.° above the horizontal. Which quantity has a magnitude of zero when the ball is at the highest point in its trajectory?

(1) the acceleration of the ball
(2) the momentum of the ball
(3) the horizontal component of the ball's velocity
(4) the vertical component of the ball's velocity

38 The graph below represents the relationship between velocity and time of travel for a toy car moving in a straight line.

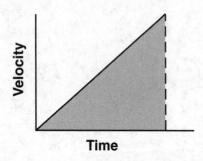

The shaded area under the line represents the toy car's

(1) displacement   (3) acceleration
(2) momentum   (4) speed

39 A spring stores 10. joules of elastic potential energy when it is compressed 0.20 meter. What is the spring constant of the spring?

(1) 5.0×10^1 N/m   (3) 2.5×10^2 N/m
(2) 1.0×10^2 N/m   (4) 5.0×10^2 N/m

Base your answers to questions 40 and 41 on the information below and on your knowledge of physics.

A cannonball with a mass of 1.0 kilogram is fired horizontally from a 500.-kilogram cannon, initially at rest, on a horizontal, frictionless surface. The cannonball is acted on by an average force of 8.0×10^3 newtons for 1.0×10^{-1} second.

40 What is the magnitude of the change in momentum of the cannonball during firing?

(1) 0 kg•m/s   (3) 8.0×10^3 kg•m/s
(2) 8.0×10^2 kg•m/s   (4) 8.0×10^4 kg•m/s

41 What is the magnitude of the average net force acting on the cannon?

(1) 1.6 N   (3) 8.0×10^3 N
(2) 16 N   (4) 4.0×10^6 N

42 A metal sphere, X, has an initial net charge of -6×10^{-6} coulomb and an identical sphere, Y, has an initial net charge of $+2 \times 10^{-6}$ coulomb. The spheres touch each other and then separate. What is the net charge on sphere X after the spheres have separated?

(1) 0 C   (3) -4×10^{-6} C
(2) -2×10^{-6} C   (4) -6×10^{-6} C

43 A constant eastward horizontal force of 70. newtons is applied to a 20.-kilogram crate moving toward the east on a level floor. If the frictional force on the crate has a magnitude of 10. newtons, what is the magnitude of the crate's acceleration?

(1) 0.50 m/s^2 (3) 3.0 m/s^2
(2) 3.5 m/s^2 (4) 4.0 m/s^2

44 Which graph represents the relationship between the energy of photons and the wavelengths of photons in a vacuum?

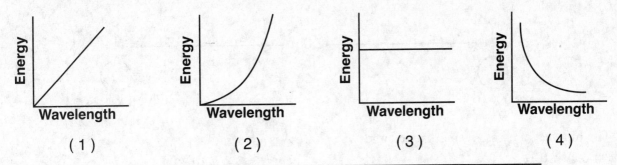

(1)   (2)   (3)   (4)

Base your answers to questions 45 and 46 on the information and diagram below and on your knowledge of physics.

One end of a long spring is attached to a wall. A student vibrates the other end of the spring vertically, creating a wave that moves to the wall and reflects back toward the student, resulting in a standing wave in the spring, as represented below.

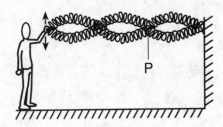

45 What is the phase difference between the incident wave and the reflected wave at point P?

(1) 0°   (3) 180°
(2) 90°   (4) 270°

46 What is the total number of antinodes on the standing wave in the diagram?

(1) 6   (3) 3
(2) 2   (4) 4

47 The diagrams below represent four pieces of copper wire at 20.°C. For each piece of wire, ℓ represents a unit of length and A represents a unit of cross-sectional area.

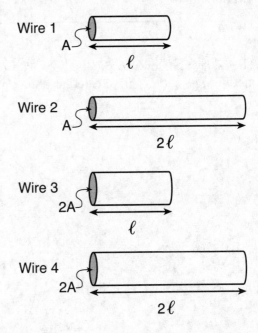

The piece of wire that has the greatest resistance is

(1) wire 1   (3) wire 3
(2) wire 2   (4) wire 4

Base your answers to questions 48 and 49 on the diagram below, which represents two charged, identical metal spheres, and on your knowledge of physics.

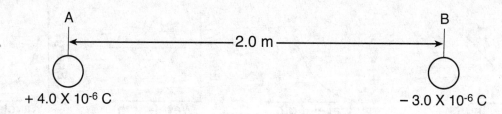

48 The number of excess elementary charges on sphere A is

(1) 6.4×10^{-25}

(2) 6.4×10^{-19}

(3) 2.5×10^{13}

(4) 5.0×10^{13}

49 What is the magnitude of the electric force between the two spheres?

(1) 3.0×10^{-12} N

(2) 1.0×10^{-6} N

(3) 2.7×10^{-2} N

(4) 5.4×10^{-2} N

50 The diagram below represents the wave fronts produced by a point source moving to the right in a uniform medium. Observers are located at points A and B.

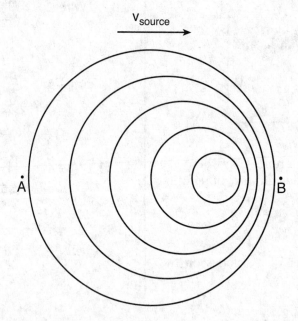

Compared to the wave frequency and wavelength observed at point A, the wave observed at point B has a

(1) higher frequency and a shorter wavelength
(2) higher frequency and a longer wavelength
(3) lower frequency and a shorter wavelength
(4) lower frequency and a longer wavelength

June '17   Regents Examination

Part B–2

Answer all questions in this part.

Directions (51–65): Record your answers in the spaces provided in your answer booklet. Some questions may require the use of the *2006 Edition Reference Tables for Physical Setting/Physics*.

51 On the diagram *in your answer booklet*, sketch *at least four* magnetic field lines of force around a bar magnet. [Include arrows to show the direction of each field line.]   [1]

Base your answers to questions 52 through 54 on the information below and on your knowledge of physics.

Tritium is a radioactive form of the element hydrogen. A tritium nucleus is composed of one proton and two neutrons. When a tritium nucleus decays, it emits a beta particle (an electron) and an antineutrino to create a stable form of helium. During beta decay, a neutron is spontaneously transformed into a proton, an electron, and an antineutrino.

52 What is the total number of quarks in a tritium nucleus?   [1]

53 What is the total charge, in elementary charges, of a proton, an electron, and an antineutrino?   [1]

54 What fundamental interaction is responsible for binding together the protons and neutrons in a helium nucleus?   [1]

---

55 The diagram below represents a ball projected horizontally from a cliff at a speed of 10. meters per second. The ball travels the path shown and lands at time *t* and distance *d* from the base of the cliff. [Neglect friction.]

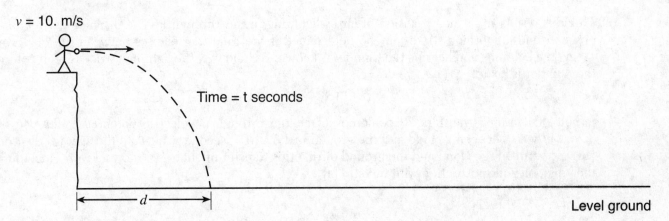

A second, identical ball is projected horizontally from the cliff at 20. meters per second. Determine the distance the second ball lands from the base of the cliff in terms of *d*.   [1]

56–57 An operating television set draws 0.71 ampere of current when connected to a 120-volt outlet. Calculate the time it takes the television to consume 3.0×10^5 joules of electric energy. [Show all work, including the equation and substitution with units.] [2]

58–59 On the centimeter grid *in your booklet*, draw *at least one* cycle of a periodic transverse wave with an amplitude of 2.0 centimeters and a wavelength of 6.0 centimeters. [2]

60 The diagram below represents a 35-newton block hanging from a vertical spring, causing the spring to elongate from its original length.

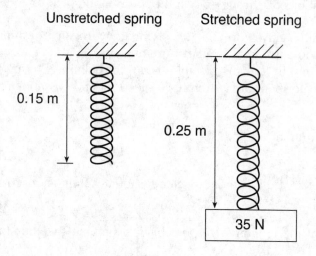

Determine the spring constant of the spring. [1]

61 Determine the amount of matter, in kilograms, that must be converted to energy to yield 1.0 gigajoule. [1]

62 Thunder results from the expansion of air as lightning passes through it. The distance between an observer and a lightning strike may be determined if the time that elapses between the observer seeing the lightning and hearing the thunder is known. Explain why the lightning strike is seen before the thunder is heard. [1]

63–64 A bolt of lightning transfers 28 coulombs of charge through an electric potential difference of 3.2×10^7 volts between a cloud and the ground in 1.5×10^{-3} second. Calculate the average electric current between the cloud and the ground during this transfer of charge. [Show all work, including the equation and substitution with units.] [2]

65 The diagram below represents two pulses traveling toward each other in a uniform medium.

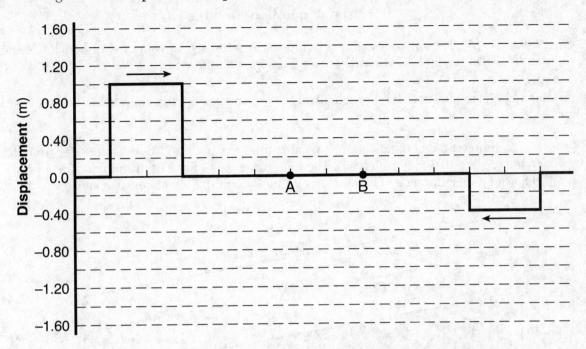

On the grid *in your answer booklet*, draw the resultant displacement of the medium when both pulses are located between points *A* and *B*. [1]

Part C

Answer all questions in this part.

Directions (66–85): Record your answers in the spaces provided in your answer booklet. Some questions may require the use of the *2006 Edition Reference Tables for Physical Setting/Physics*.

Base your answers to questions 66 through 70 on the information and diagram below and on your knowledge of physics.

As represented in the diagram, a ski area rope-tow pulls a 72.0-kilogram skier from the bottom to the top of a 40.0-meter-high hill. The rope-tow exerts a force of magnitude 158 newtons to move the skier a total distance of 230. meters up the side of the hill at constant speed.

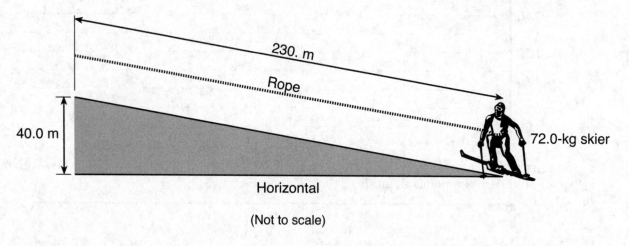

(Not to scale)

66 Determine the total amount of work done by the rope on the skier. [1]

67–68 Calculate the total amount of gravitational potential energy gained by the skier while moving up the hill. [Show all work, including the equation and substitution with units] [2]

69 Describe what happens to the internal energy of the skier-hill system as the skier is pulled up the hill. [1]

70 Describe what happens to the total mechanical energy of the skier-hill system as the skier is pulled up the hill. [1]

_____

Base your answers to questions 71 through 76 on the diagram and information below and on your knowledge of physics.

A 15-ohm resistor, 30.-ohm resistor, and an ammeter are connected as shown with a 60.-volt battery.

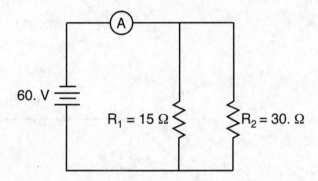

71–72 Calculate the equivalent resistance of R_1 and R_2. [Show all work, including the equation and substitution with units.] [2]

73 Determine the current measured by the ammeter. [1]

74–75 Calculate the rate at which the battery supplies energy to the circuit. [Show all work, including the equation and substitution with units.] [2]

76 If another resistor were added in parallel to the original circuit, what effect would this have on the current through resistor R_1? [1]

_____

Base your answers to questions 77 through 80 on the information below and on your knowledge of physics.

A gas-powered model airplane has a mass of 2.50 kilograms. A student exerts a force on a cord to keep the airplane flying around her at a constant speed of 18.0 meters per second in a horizontal, circular path with a radius of 25.0 meters.

77–78 Calculate the kinetic energy of the moving airplane. [Show all work, including the equation and substitution with units.] [2]

79–80 Calculate the magnitude of the centripetal force exerted on the airplane to keep it moving in this circular path. [Show all work, including the equation and substitution with units.] [2]

_____

Base your answers to questions 81 through 85 on the information and diagram below and on your knowledge of physics.

A ray of light with a frequency of 5.09×10^{14} hertz traveling in medium X is refracted at point P. The angle of refraction is 90.°, as represented in the diagram.

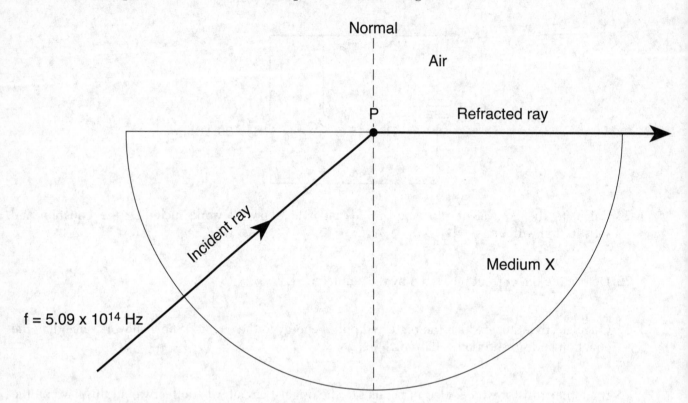

81–82 Calculate the wavelength of the light ray in air. [Show all work, including the equation and substitution with units.] [2]

83 Measure the angle of incidence for the light ray incident at point P and record the value *in your answer booklet*. [1]

84–85 Calculate the absolute index of refraction for medium X. [Show all work, including the equation and substitution with units.] [2]

PHYSICAL SETTING PHYSICS

Thursday, June 15, 2017 — 1:15 to 4:15 p.m., only

ANSWER BOOKLET

☐ Male

Student . . . . Sex: ☐ Female

Teacher . . . .

School . . . . Grade . . . .

Record your answers for Part B–2 and Part C in this booklet.

Part B–2

51

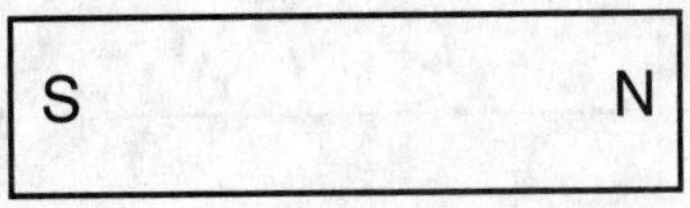

52 _____ quarks

53 _____ e

54 _____

55 _____

56–57

58-59

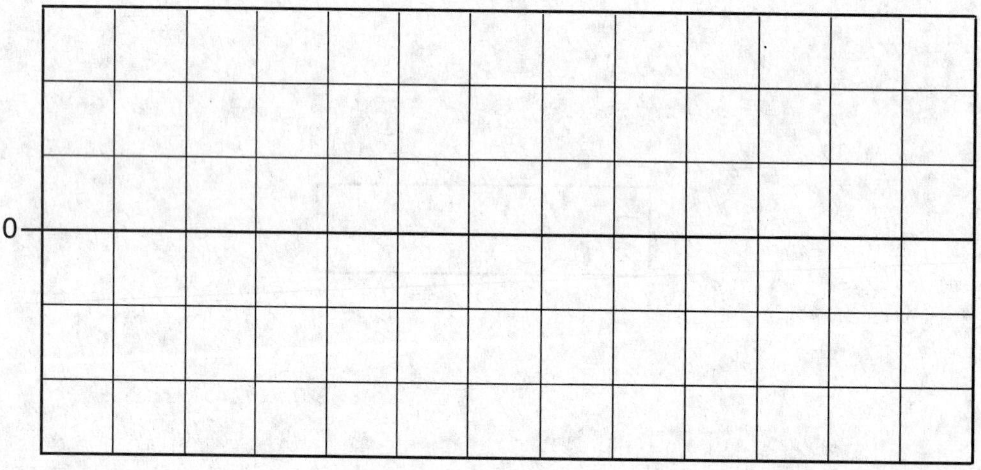

60 _____ **N/m**

61 _____ **kg**

62 _____

_____

June '17 Regents Examination

65

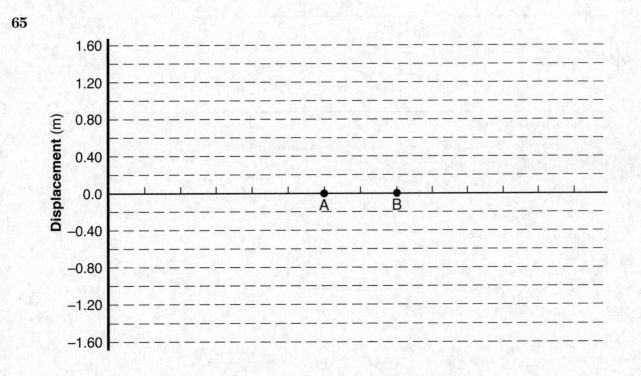

June '17   Regents Examination

Part C

66 _____ **J**

67–68

69 _____

70 _____

June '17   Regents Examination

71–72

73 _____ **A**

74–75

76 _____

June '17   Regents Examination

77–78

79–80

June '17   Regents Examination

81–82

83 _____ °

84–85

Part A

Answer all questions in this part.

Directions (1–35): For *each* statement or question, choose the word or expression that, of those given, best completes the statement or answers the question. Some questions may require the use of the *2006 Edition Reference Tables for Physical Setting/Physics*. Record your answers on your separate answer sheet.

1 Which quantity is a vector?

(1) power   (3) speed
(2) kinetic energy   (4) weight

2 A 65.0-kilogram astronaut weighs 638 newtons at the surface of Earth. What is the mass of the astronaut at the surface of the Moon, where the acceleration due to gravity is 1.62 meters per second squared?

(1) 10.7 kg   (3) 105 N
(2) 65.0 kg   (4) 638 N

3 When the sum of all the forces acting on a block on an inclined plane is zero, the block

(1) must be at rest
(2) must be accelerating
(3) may be slowing down
(4) may be moving at constant speed

4 The greatest increase in the inertia of an object would be produced by increasing the

(1) mass of the object from 1.0 kg to 2.0 kg
(2) net force applied to the object from 1.0 N to 2.0 N
(3) time that a net force is applied to the object from 1.0 s to 2.0 s
(4) speed of the object from 1.0 m/s to 2.0 m/s

5 A 100.-kilogram cart accelerates at 0.50 meter per second squared west as a horse exerts a force of 60. newtons west on the cart. What is the magnitude of the force that the cart exerts on the horse?

(1) 10. N   (3) 60. N
(2) 50. N   (4) 110 N

6 Sound waves are described as

(1) mechanical and transverse
(2) mechanical and longitudinal
(3) electromagnetic and transverse
(4) electromagnetic and longitudinal

7 An electrical force of 8.0×10^{-5} newton exists between two point charges, q_1 and q_2. If the distance between the charges is doubled, the new electrical force between the charges will be

(1) 1.6×10^{-4} N   (3) 3.2×10^{-4} N
(2) 2.0×10^{-5} N   (4) 4.0×10^{-5} N

8 A blue lab cart is traveling west on a track when it collides with and sticks to a red lab cart traveling east. The magnitude of the momentum of the blue cart before the collision is 2.0 kilogram • meters per second, and the magnitude of the momentum of the red cart before the collision is 3.0 kilogram • meters per second. The magnitude of the total momentum of the two carts after the collision is

(1) 1.0 kg • m/s   (3) 3.0 kg • m/s
(2) 2.0 kg • m/s   (4) 5.0 kg • m/s

9 The diagram below represents the path of a thrown ball through the air.

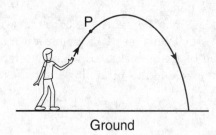

Which arrow best represents the direction in which friction acts on the ball at point *P*?

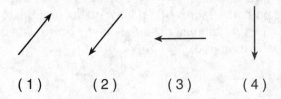

10 A magnetic field would be produced by a beam of

(1) x rays   (3) protons
(2) gamma rays   (4) neutrons

11 The diagram below represents the electric field in the region of two small charged spheres, A and B.

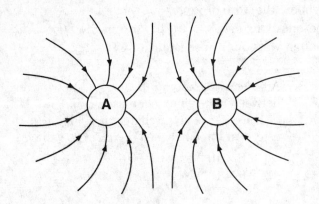

What is the sign of the net charge on A and B?

(1) A is positive and B is positive.
(2) A is positive and B is negative.
(3) A is negative and B is negative.
(4) A is negative and B is positive.

12 A horizontal force of 20 newtons eastward causes a 10-kilogram box to have a displacement of 5 meters eastward. The total work done on the box by the 20-newton force is

(1) 40 J   (3) 200 J
(2) 100 J   (4) 1000 J

13 A block initially at rest on a horizontal, frictionless surface is accelerated by a constant horizontal force of 5.0 newtons. If 15 joules of work is done on the block by this force while accelerating it, the kinetic energy of the block increases by

(1) 3.0 J   (3) 20. J
(2) 15 J   (4) 75 J

14 Two objects, A and B, are held one meter above the horizontal ground. The mass of B is twice as great as the mass of A. If PE is the gravitational potential energy of A relative to the ground, then the gravitational potential energy of B relative to the ground is

(1) PE   (3) $\frac{PE}{2}$

(2) 2PE   (4) 4PE

15 What is the kinetic energy of a 55-kilogram skier traveling at 9.0 meters per second?

(1) 2.5×10^2 J   (3) 2.2×10^3 J
(2) 5.0×10^2 J   (4) 4.9×10^3 J

16 A 5.09×10^{14}-hertz electromagnetic wave is traveling through a transparent medium. The main factor that determines the speed of this wave is the

(1) nature of the medium
(2) amplitude of the wave
(3) phase of the wave
(4) distance traveled through the medium

17 A motor does a total of 480 joules of work in 5.0 seconds to lift a 12-kilogram block to the top of a ramp. The average power developed by the motor is

(1) 8.0 W   (3) 96 W
(2) 40. W   (4) 2400 W

18 A 5.8×10^4-watt elevator motor can lift a total weight of 2.1×10^4 newtons with a maximum constant speed of

(1) 0.28 m/s   (3) 2.8 m/s
(2) 0.36 m/s   (4) 3.6 m/s

19 A stationary police officer directs radio waves emitted by a radar gun at a vehicle moving toward the officer. Compared to the emitted radio waves, the radio waves reflected from the vehicle and received by the radar gun have a

(1) longer wavelength   (3) longer period
(2) higher speed   (4) higher frequency

20 A light wave strikes the Moon and reflects toward Earth. As the light wave travels from the Moon toward Earth, the wave carries

(1) energy, only
(2) matter, only
(3) both energy and matter
(4) neither energy nor matter

21 The time required to produce one cycle of a wave is known as the wave's

(1) amplitude   (3) period
(2) frequency   (4) wavelength

22 A magnetic compass is placed near an insulated copper wire. When the wire is connected to a battery and a current is created, the compass needle moves and changes its position. Which is the best explanation for the production of a force that causes the needle to move?

(1) The copper wire magnetizes the compass needle and exerts the force on the compass needle.
(2) The compass needle magnetizes the copper wire and exerts the force on the compass needle.
(3) The insulation on the wire becomes charged, which exerts the force on the compass needle.
(4) The current in the wire produces a magnetic field that exerts the force on the compass needle.

23 A beam of monochromatic light ($f = 5.09 \times 10^{14}$ Hz) has a wavelength of 589 nanometers in air. What is the wavelength of this light in Lucite?

(1) 150 nm   (3) 589 nm
(2) 393 nm   (4) 884 nm

24 If the amplitude of a sound wave is increased, there is an increase in the sound's

(1) loudness   (3) velocity
(2) pitch   (4) wavelength

25 In the diagram below, point P is located in the electric field between two oppositely charged parallel plates.

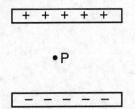

Compared to the magnitude and direction of the electrostatic force on an electron placed at point P, the electrostatic force on a proton placed at point P has

(1) the same magnitude and the same direction
(2) the same magnitude, but the opposite direction
(3) a greater magnitude, but the same direction
(4) a greater magnitude and the opposite direction

26 The effect produced when two or more sound waves pass through the same point simultaneously is called

(1) interference   (3) refraction
(2) diffraction   (4) resonance

27 A gamma ray photon and a microwave photon are traveling in a vacuum. Compared to the wavelength and energy of the gamma ray photon, the microwave photon has a

(1) shorter wavelength and less energy
(2) shorter wavelength and more energy
(3) longer wavelength and less energy
(4) longer wavelength and more energy

28 According to the Standard Model of Particle Physics, a neutrino is a type of

(1) lepton   (3) meson
(2) photon   (4) baryon

29 Which combination of quarks produces a neutral baryon?

(1) cts   (3) uds
(2) dsb   (4) uct

30 When 2.0×10^{-16} kilogram of matter is converted into energy, how much energy is released?

(1) 1.8×10^{-1} J   (3) 6.0×10^{-32} J
(2) 1.8×10^{1} J   (4) 6.0×10^{-8} J

31 A ball is hit straight up with an initial speed of 28 meters per second. What is the speed of the ball 2.2 seconds after it is hit? [Neglect friction.]

(1) 4.3 m/s   (3) 22 m/s
(2) 6.4 m/s   (4) 28 m/s

32 A particle with a charge of 3.00 elementary charges moves through a potential difference of 4.50 volts. What is the change in electrical potential energy of the particle?

(1) 1.07×10^{-19} eV   (3) 1.50 eV
(2) 2.16×10^{-18} eV   (4) 13.5 eV

33 Which circuit has the largest equivalent resistance?

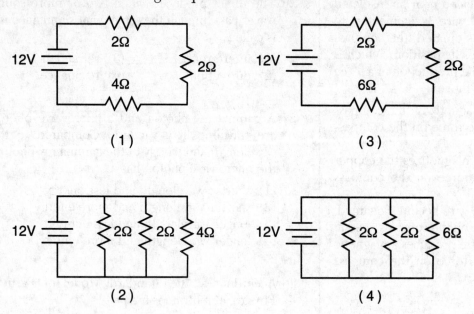

(1)

(3)

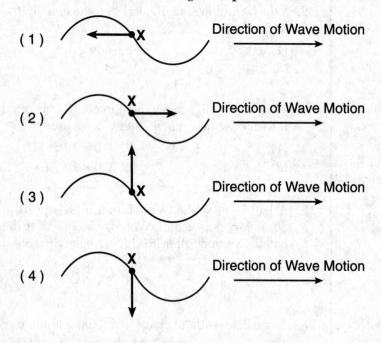

(2)

(4)

34 A transverse wave is moving toward the right in a uniform medium. Point X represents a particle of the uniform medium. Which diagram represents the direction of the motion of particle X at the instant shown?

(1) Direction of Wave Motion

(2) Direction of Wave Motion

(3) Direction of Wave Motion

(4) Direction of Wave Motion

June '16 Regents Examination

35 Which diagram represents magnetic field lines between two north magnetic poles?

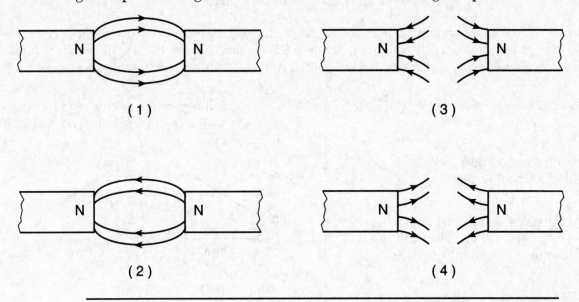

Part B–1

Answer all questions in this part.

Directions (36–50): For *each* statement or question, choose the word or expression that, of those given, best completes the statement or answers the question. Some questions may require the use of the *2006 Edition Reference Tables for Physical Setting/Physics.* Record your answers on your separate answer sheet.

36 Which measurement is closest to 1×10^{-2} meter?

(1) diameter of an atom
(2) width of a student's finger
(3) length of a football field
(4) height of a schoolteacher

37 Which graph represents the relationship between the speed of a freely falling object and the time of fall of the object near Earth's surface?

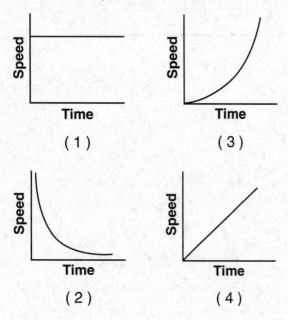

38 A hair dryer with a resistance of 9.6 ohms operates at 120 volts for 2.5 minutes. The total electrical energy used by the dryer during this time interval is

(1) 2.9×10^3 J   (3) 1.7×10^5 J
(2) 3.8×10^3 J   (4) 2.3×10^5 J

39 A box weighing 46 newtons rests on an incline that makes an angle of 25° with the horizontal. What is the magnitude of the component of the box's weight perpendicular to the incline?

(1) 19 N   (3) 42 N
(2) 21 N   (4) 46 N

40 Which graph represents the motion of an object traveling with a positive velocity and a negative acceleration?

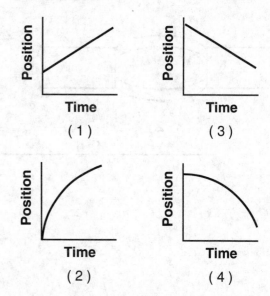

41 Car *A*, moving in a straight line at a constant speed of 20. meters per second, is initially 200 meters behind car *B*, moving in the same straight line at a constant speed of 15 meters per second. How far must car *A* travel from this initial position before it catches up with car *B*?

(1) 200 m   (3) 800 m
(2) 400 m   (4) 1000 m

42 A 2700-ohm resistor in an electric circuit draws a current of 2.4 milliamperes. The total charge that passes through the resistor in 15 seconds is

(1) 1.6×10^{-4} C   (3) 1.6×10^{-1} C
(2) 3.6×10^{-2} C   (4) 3.6×10^{1} C

43 A 1000.–kilogram car traveling 20.0 meters per second east experiences an impulse of 2000. newton • seconds west. What is the final velocity of the car after the impulse has been applied?

(1) 18.0 m/s east   (3) 20.5 m/s west
(2) 19.5 m/s east   (4) 22.0 m/s west

44 Which graph represents the relationship between the potential difference applied to a copper wire and the resulting current in the wire at constant temperature?

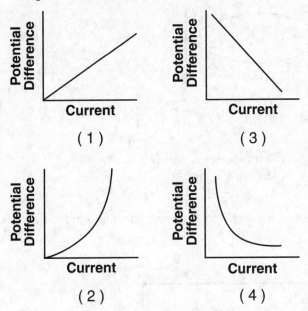

(1)

(3)

(2)

(4)

45 A tungsten wire has resistance R at 20°C. A second tungsten wire at 20°C has twice the length and half the cross-sectional area of the first wire. In terms of R, the resistance of the second wire is

(1) $\frac{R}{2}$

(3) $2R$

(2) R

(4) $4R$

46 After an incandescent lamp is turned on, the temperature of its filament rapidly increases from room temperature to its operating temperature. As the temperature of the filament increases, what happens to the resistance of the filament and the current through the filament?

(1) The resistance increases and the current decreases.

(2) The resistance increases and the current increases.

(3) The resistance decreases and the current decreases.

(4) The resistance decreases and the current increases.

47 Parallel wave fronts are incident on an opening in a barrier. Which diagram shows the configuration of wave fronts and barrier opening that will result in the greatest diffraction of the waves passing through the opening? [Assume all diagrams are drawn to the same scale.]

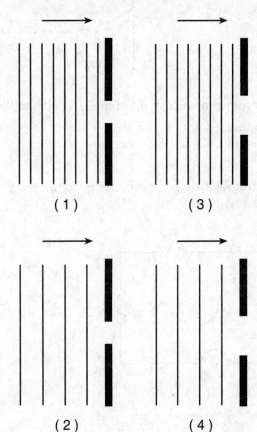

(1)

(3)

(2)

(4)

48 A singer demonstrated that she could shatter a crystal glass by singing a note with a wavelength of 0.320 meter in air at STP. What was the natural frequency of the glass?

(1) 9.67×10^{-4} Hz

(3) 1.03×10^{3} Hz

(2) 1.05×10^{2} Hz

(4) 9.38×10^{8} Hz

[8]

49 The diagram below represents a standing wave in a string.

Standing Wave

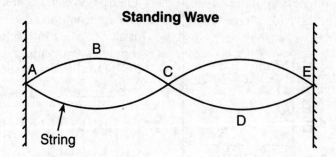

Maximum constructive interference occurs at the

(1) antinodes *A*, *C*, and *E*

(2) nodes *A*, *C*, and *E*

(3) antinodes *B* and *D*

(4) nodes *B* and *D*

50 Which circuit diagram represents voltmeter *V* connected correctly to measure the potential difference across resistor R_2?

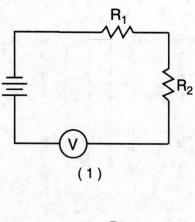

(1)

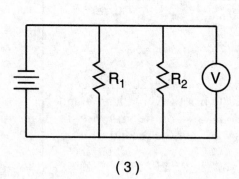

(3)

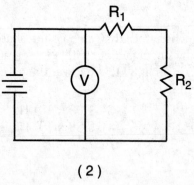

(2)

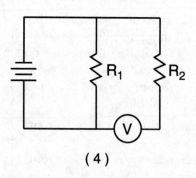

(4)

Part B–2

Answer all questions in this part.

Directions (51–65): Record your answers in the spaces provided in your answer booklet. Some questions may require the use of the *2006 Edition Reference Tables for Physical Setting/Physics*.

Base your answers to questions 51 through 53 on the information and diagram below and on your knowledge of physics.

As represented in the diagram below, a constant 15-newton force, *F*, is applied to a 2.5-kilogram box, accelerating the box to the right at 2.0 meters per second squared across a rough horizontal surface.

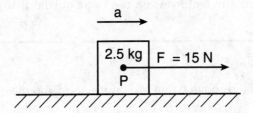

51–52 Calculate the magnitude of the net force acting on the box. [Show all work, including the equation and substitution with units.] [2]

53 Determine the magnitude of the force of friction on the box. [1]

Base your answers to questions 54 and 55 on the information and diagram below and on your knowledge of physics.

A ray of light ($f = 5.09 \times 10^{14}$ Hz) is traveling through a mineral sample that is submerged in water. The ray refracts as it enters the water, as shown in the diagram below.

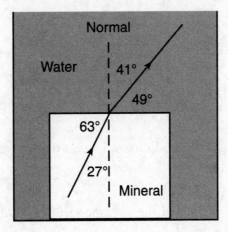

54–55 Calculate the absolute index of refraction of the mineral. [Show all work, including the equation and substitution with units.] [2]

Base your answers to questions 56 through 58 on the information below and on your knowledge of physics.

A ball is rolled twice across the same level laboratory table and allowed to roll off the table and strike the floor. In each trial, the time it takes the ball to travel from the edge of the table to the floor is accurately measured. [Neglect friction.]

56–57 In trial A, the ball is traveling at 2.50 meters per second when it reaches the edge of the table. The ball strikes the floor 0.391 second after rolling off the edge of the table. Calculate the height of the table. [Show all work, including the equation and substitution with units.] [2]

58 In trial B, the ball is traveling at 5.00 meters per second when it reaches the edge of the table. Compare the time it took the ball to reach the floor in trial B to the time it took the ball to reach the floor in trial A. [1]

Base your answers to questions 59 through 61 on the information and diagram below and on your knowledge of physics.

A toy airplane flies clockwise at a constant speed in a horizontal circle of radius 8.0 meters. The magnitude of the acceleration of the airplane is 25 meters per second squared. The diagram shows the path of the airplane as it travels around the circle.

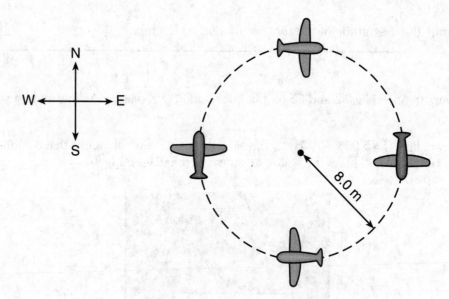

59–60 Calculate the speed of the airplane. [Show all work, including the equation and substitution with units.] [2]

61 State the direction of the velocity of the airplane at the instant the acceleration of the airplane is southward. [1]

Base your answers to questions 62 through 64 on the information and graph below and on your knowledge of physics.

The graph below represents the speed of a marble rolling down a straight incline as a function of time.

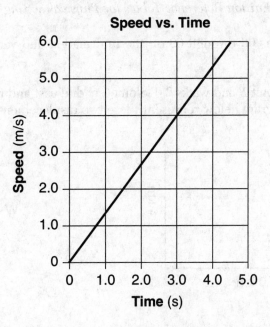

62 What quantity is represented by the slope of the graph? [1]

63–64 Calculate the distance the marble travels during the first 3.0 seconds. [Show all work, including the equation and substitution with units.] [2]

65 The graph below represents the relationship between weight and mass for objects on the surface of planet X.

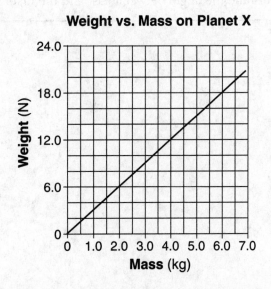

Determine the acceleration due to gravity on the surface of planet X. [1]

Part C

Answer all questions in this part.

Directions (66–85): Record your answers in the spaces provided in your answer booklet. Some questions may require the use of the *2006 Edition Reference Tables for Physical Setting/Physics*.

Base your answers to questions 66 through 69 on the information and vector diagram below and on your knowledge of physics.

A hiker starts at point *P* and walks 2.0 kilometers due east and then 1.4 kilometers due north. The vectors in the diagram below represent these two displacements.

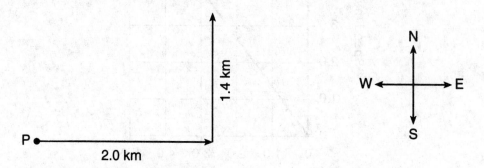

66 Using a metric ruler, determine the scale used in the vector diagram. [1]

67 On the diagram *in your answer booklet,* use a ruler to construct the vector representing the hiker's resultant displacement. [1]

68 Determine the magnitude of the hiker's resultant displacement. [1]

69 Using a protractor, determine the angle between east and the hiker's resultant displacement. [1]

Base your answers to questions 70 through 74 on the information and diagram below and on your knowledge of physics.

A jack-in-the-box is a toy in which a figure in an open box is pushed down, compressing a spring. The lid of the box is then closed. When the box is opened, the figure is pushed up by the spring. The spring in the toy is compressed 0.070 meter by using a downward force of 12.0 newtons.

70–71 Calculate the spring constant of the spring. [Show all work, including the equation and substitution with units.] [2]

72–73 Calculate the total amount of elastic potential energy stored in the spring when it is compressed. [Show all work, including the equation and substitution with units.] [2]

74 Identify *one* form of energy to which the elastic potential energy of the spring is converted when the figure is pushed up by the spring. [1]

Base your answers to questions 75 through 80 on the information below and on your knowledge of physics.

A 12-volt battery causes 0.60 ampere to flow through a circuit that contains a lamp and a resistor connected in parallel. The lamp is operating at 6.0 watts.

75 Using the circuit symbols shown on the *Reference Tables for Physical Setting/Physics,* draw a diagram of the circuit in the space provided *in your answer booklet.* [1]

76–77 Calculate the current through the lamp. [Show all work, including the equation and substitution with units.] [2]

78 Determine the current in the resistor. [1]

79–80 Calculate the resistance of the resistor. [Show all work, including the equation and substitution with units.] [2]

_____

Base your answers to questions 81 through 85 on the information below and on your knowledge of physics.

The Great Nebula in the constellation Orion consists primarily of excited hydrogen gas. The electrons in the atoms of excited hydrogen have been raised to higher energy levels. When these atoms release energy, a frequent electron transition is from the excited $n = 3$ energy level to the $n = 2$ energy level, which gives the nebula one of its characteristic colors.

81 Determine the energy, in electronvolts, of an emitted photon when an electron transition from $n = 3$ to $n = 2$ occurs. [1]

82 Determine the energy of this emitted photon in joules. [1]

83–84 Calculate the frequency of the emitted photon. [Show all work, including the equation and substitution with units.] [2]

85 Identify the color of light associated with this photon. [1]

_____

The University of the State of New York

REGENTS HIGH SCHOOL EXAMINATION

PHYSICAL SETTING PHYSICS

Tuesday, June 21, 2016 — 1:15 to 4:15 p.m., only

ANSWER BOOKLET

☐ Male

Student .... Sex: ☐ Female

Teacher ....

School .... Grade ....

Record your answers for Part B–2 and Part C in this booklet.

Part B–2

51–52

53 ______________________ **N**

54–55

56–57

58 _____

_____

June '16   Regents Examination

59–60

61 _____

62 _____

63–64

65 _____ m/s^2

June '16 Regents Examination

Part C

66 1.0 cm = _____ **km**

67

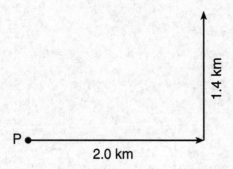

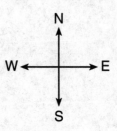

68 _____ **km**

69 _____ °

70–71

72–73

74 _____

June '16   Regents Examination

75

76–77

78 _____ **A**

79–80

June '16   Regents Examination

81 _____ eV

82 _____ J

83–84

85 _____

Part A

Answer all questions in this part.

Directions (1–35): For *each* statement or question, choose the word or expression that, of those given, best completes the statement or answers the question. Some questions may require the use of the *2006 Edition Reference Tables for Physical Setting/Physics*. Record your answers on your separate answer sheet.

1 Which quantities are scalar?
(1) speed and work
(2) velocity and force
(3) distance and acceleration
(4) momentum and power

2 A 3.00-kilogram mass is thrown vertically upward with an initial speed of 9.80 meters per second. What is the maximum height this object will reach? [Neglect friction.]
(1) 1.00 m   (3) 9.80 m
(2) 4.90 m   (4) 19.6 m

3 An airplane traveling north at 220. meters per second encounters a 50.0-meters-per-second crosswind from west to east, as represented in the diagram below.

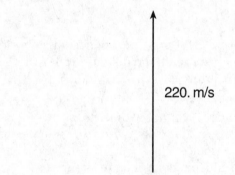

220. m/s

50.0 m/s

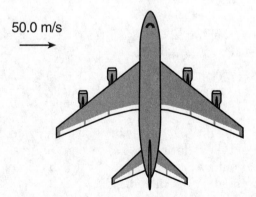

What is the resultant speed of the plane?
(1) 170. m/s   (3) 226 m/s
(2) 214 m/s   (4) 270. m/s

4 A 160.-kilogram space vehicle is traveling along a straight line at a constant speed of 800. meters per second. The magnitude of the net force on the space vehicle is
(1) 0 N   (3) 8.00×10^2 N
(2) 1.60×10^2 N   (4) 1.28×10^5 N

5 A student throws a 5.0-newton ball straight up. What is the net force on the ball at its maximum height?
(1) 0.0 N   (3) 5.0 N, down
(2) 5.0 N, up   (4) 9.8 N, down

6 A vertical spring has a spring constant of 100. newtons per meter. When an object is attached to the bottom of the spring, the spring changes from its unstretched length of 0.50 meter to a length of 0.65 meter. The magnitude of the weight of the attached object is
(1) 1.1 N   (3) 50. N
(2) 15 N   (4) 65 N

7 A 1.5-kilogram cart initially moves at 2.0 meters per second. It is brought to rest by a constant net force in 0.30 second. What is the magnitude of the net force?
(1) 0.40 N   (3) 10. N
(2) 0.90 N   (4) 15 N

8 Which characteristic of a light wave must increase as the light wave passes from glass into air?
(1) amplitude   (3) period
(2) frequency   (4) wavelength

9 As a 5.0×10^2-newton basketball player jumps from the floor up toward the basket, the magnitude of the force of her feet on the floor is 1.0×10^3 newtons. As she jumps, the magnitude of the force of the floor on her feet is

(1) 5.0×10^2 N   (3) 1.5×10^3 N
(2) 1.0×10^3 N   (4) 5.0×10^5 N

10 A 0.0600-kilogram ball traveling at 60.0 meters per second hits a concrete wall. What speed must a 0.0100-kilogram bullet have in order to hit the wall with the same magnitude of momentum as the ball?

(1) 3.60 m/s   (3) 360. m/s
(2) 6.00 m/s   (4) 600. m/s

11 The Hubble telescope's orbit is 5.6×10^5 meters above Earth's surface. The telescope has a mass of 1.1×10^4 kilograms. Earth exerts a gravitational force of 9.1×10^4 newtons on the telescope. The magnitude of Earth's gravitational field strength at this location is

(1) 1.5×10^{-20} N/kg   (3) 8.3 N/kg
(2) 0.12 N/kg   (4) 9.8 N/kg

12 When two point charges are a distance d apart, the magnitude of the electrostatic force between them is F. If the distance between the point charges is increased to $3d$, the magnitude of the electrostatic force between the two charges will be

(1) $\dfrac{1}{9}F$ (3) $2F$

(2) $\dfrac{1}{3}F$ (4) $4F$

13 A radio operating at 3.0 volts and a constant temperature draws a current of 1.8×10^{-4} ampere. What is the resistance of the radio circuit?

(1) 1.7×10^4 Ω   (3) 5.4×10^{-4} Ω
(2) 3.0×10^1 Ω   (4) 6.0×10^{-5} Ω

14 Which energy transformation occurs in an operating electric motor?

(1) electrical → mechanical
(2) mechanical → electrical
(3) chemical → electrical
(4) electrical → chemical

15 A block slides across a rough, horizontal tabletop. As the block comes to rest, there is an increase in the block-tabletop system's

(1) gravitational potential energy
(2) elastic potential energy
(3) kinetic energy
(4) internal (thermal) energy

16 How much work is required to move an electron through a potential difference of 3.00 volts?

(1) 5.33×10^{-20} J   (3) 3.00 J
(2) 4.80×10^{-19} J   (4) 1.88×10^{19} J

17 During a laboratory experiment, a student finds that at 20° Celsius, a 6.0-meter length of copper wire has a resistance of 1.3 ohms. The cross-sectional area of this wire is

(1) 7.9×10^{-8} m²   (3) 4.6×10^0 m²
(2) 1.1×10^{-7} m²   (4) 1.3×10^7 m²

18 A net charge of 5.0 coulombs passes a point on a conductor in 0.050 second. The average current is

(1) 8.0×10^{-8} A   (3) 2.5×10^{-1} A
(2) 1.0×10^{-2} A   (4) 1.0×10^2 A

19 If several resistors are connected in series in an electric circuit, the potential difference across each resistor

(1) varies directly with its resistance
(2) varies inversely with its resistance
(3) varies inversely with the square of its resistance
(4) is independent of its resistance

20 The amplitude of a sound wave is most closely related to the sound's

(1) speed   (3) loudness
(2) wavelength   (4) pitch

21 A duck floating on a lake oscillates up and down 5.0 times during a 10.-second interval as a periodic wave passes by. What is the frequency of the duck's oscillations?

(1) 0.10 Hz   (3) 2.0 Hz
(2) 0.50 Hz   (4) 50. Hz

June '15 Regents Examination

22 Which diagram best represents the position of a ball, at equal time intervals, as it falls freely from rest near Earth's surface?

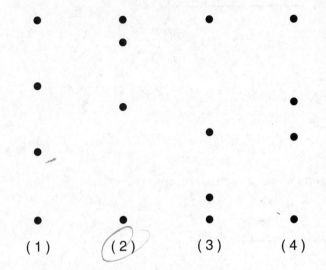

(1)   (2)   (3)   (4)

23 A gamma ray and a microwave traveling in a vacuum have the same
(1) frequency   (3) speed
(2) period   (4) wavelength

24 A student produces a wave in a long spring by vibrating its end. As the frequency of the vibration is doubled, the wavelength in the spring is
(1) quartered   (3) unchanged
(2) halved   (4) doubled

25 Which two points on the wave shown in the diagram below are in phase with each other?

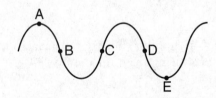

(1) A and B   (3) B and C
(2) A and E   (4) B and D

26 As a longitudinal wave moves through a medium, the particles of the medium
(1) vibrate parallel to the direction of the wave's propagation
(2) vibrate perpendicular to the direction of the wave's propagation
(3) are transferred in the direction of the wave's motion, only
(4) are stationary

27 Wind blowing across suspended power lines may cause the power lines to vibrate at their natural frequency. This often produces audible sound waves. This phenomenon, often called an Aeolian harp, is an example of
(1) diffraction   (3) refraction
(2) the Doppler effect   (4) resonance

28 A student listens to music from a speaker in an adjoining room, as represented in the diagram below.

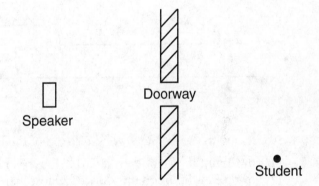

She notices that she does not have to be directly in front of the doorway to hear the music. This spreading of sound waves beyond the doorway is an example of
(1) the Doppler effect   (3) refraction
(2) resonance   (4) diffraction

29 What is the minimum energy required to ionize a hydrogen atom in the $n = 3$ state?
(1) 0.00 eV   (3) 1.51 eV
(2) 0.66 eV   (4) 12.09 eV

Base your answers to questions 30 and 31 on the diagram below and on your knowledge of physics. The diagram represents two small, charged, identical metal spheres, A and B that are separated by a distance of 2.0 meters.

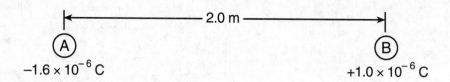

30 What is the magnitude of the electrostatic force exerted by sphere A on sphere B?
   (1) 7.2×10^{-3} N
   (2) 3.6×10^{-3} N
   (3) 8.0×10^{-13} N
   (4) 4.0×10^{-13} N

31 If the two spheres were touched together and then separated, the charge on sphere A would be
   (1) -3.0×10^{-7} C
   (2) -6.0×10^{-7} C
   (3) -1.3×10^{-6} C
   (4) -2.6×10^{-6} C

---

32 The horn of a moving vehicle produces a sound of constant frequency. Two stationary observers, A and C, and the vehicle's driver, B, positioned as represented in the diagram below, hear the sound of the horn.

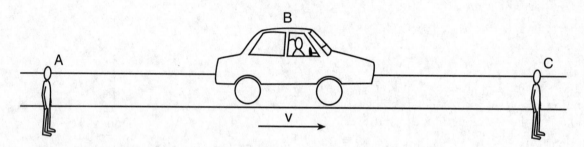

   Compared to the frequency of the sound of the horn heard by driver B, the frequency heard by observer A is

   (1) lower and the frequency heard by observer C is lower
   (2) lower and the frequency heard by observer C is higher
   (3) higher and the frequency heard by observer C is lower
   (4) higher and the frequency heard by observer C is higher

33 A different force is applied to each of four different blocks on a frictionless, horizontal surface. In which diagram does the block have the greatest inertia 2.0 seconds after starting from rest?

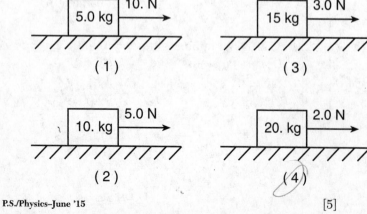

34 The diagram below shows a ray of monochromatic light incident on a boundary between air and glass.

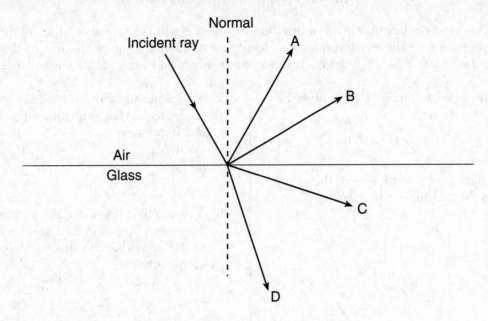

Which ray best represents the path of the reflected light ray?

(1) A

(2) B

(3) C

(4) D

35 Two pulses approach each other in the same medium. The diagram below represents the displacements caused by each pulse.

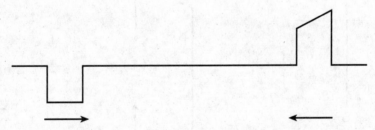

Which diagram best represents the resultant displacement of the medium as the pulses pass through each other?

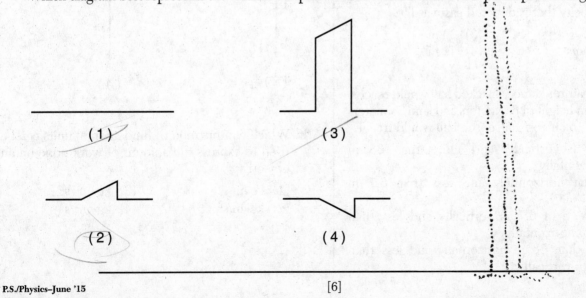

(1)

(2)

(3)

(4)

Part B–1

Answer all questions in this part.

Directions (36–50): For *each* statement or question, choose the word or expression that, of those given, best completes the statement or answers the question. Some questions may require the use of the *2006 Edition Reference Tables for Physical Setting/Physics*. Record your answers on your separate answer sheet.

36 The diameter of an automobile tire is closest to

- (1) 10^{-2} m
- (2) 10^0 m
- (3) 10^1 m
- (4) 10^2 m

37 The vector diagram below represents the velocity of a car traveling 24 meters per second 35° east of north.

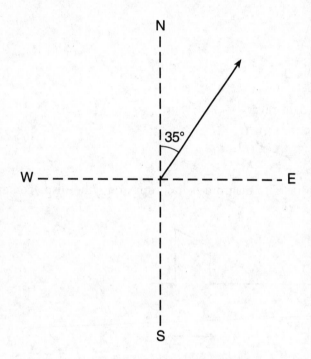

What is the magnitude of the component of the car's velocity that is directed eastward?
- (1) 14 m/s
- (2) 20. m/s
- (3) 29 m/s
- (4) 42 m/s

38 Without air resistance, a kicked ball would reach a maximum height of 6.7 meters and land 38 meters away. With air resistance, the ball would travel
- (1) 6.7 m vertically and more than 38 m horizontally
- (2) 38 m horizontally and less than 6.7 m vertically
- (3) more than 6.7 m vertically and less than 38 m horizontally
- (4) less than 38 m horizontally and less than 6.7 m vertically

39 A car is moving with a constant speed of 20. meters per second. What total distance does the car travel in 2.0 minutes?
- (1) 10. m
- (2) 40. m
- (3) 1200 m
- (4) 2400 m

40 A car, initially traveling at 15 meters per second north, accelerates to 25 meters per second north in 4.0 seconds. The magnitude of the average acceleration is
- (1) 2.5 m/s²
- (2) 6.3 m/s²
- (3) 10. m/s²
- (4) 20. m/s²

41 An object is in equilibrium. Which force vector diagram could represent the force(s) acting on the object?

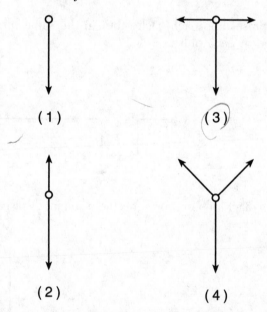

42 Which combination of fundamental units can be used to express the amount of work done on an object?
- (1) kg•m/s
- (2) kg•m/s²
- (3) kg•m²/s²
- (4) kg•m²/s³

June '15 Regents Examination

43 Which graph best represents the relationship between the potential energy stored in a spring and the change in the spring's length from its equilibrium position?

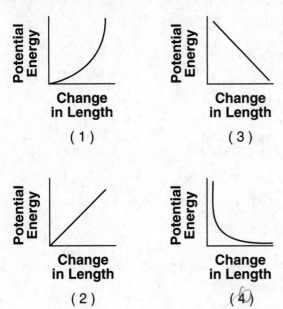

44 An electric motor has a rating of 4.0×10^2 watts. How much time will it take for this motor to lift a 50.-kilogram mass a vertical distance of 8.0 meters? [Assume 100% efficiency.]

(1) 0.98 s   (3) 98 s
(2) 9.8 s   (4) 980 s

45 A compressed spring in a toy is used to launch a 5.00-gram ball. If the ball leaves the toy with an initial horizontal speed of 5.00 meters per second, the minimum amount of potential energy stored in the compressed spring was

(1) 0.0125 J   (3) 0.0625 J
(2) 0.0250 J   (4) 0.125 J

46 A ray of yellow light ($f = 5.09 \times 10^{14}$ Hz) travels at a speed of 2.04×10^8 meters per second in

(1) ethyl alcohol   (3) Lucite
(2) water   (4) glycerol

47 A blue-light photon has a wavelength of 4.80×10^{-7} meter. What is the energy of the photon?

(1) 1.86×10^{22} J   (3) 4.14×10^{-19} J
(2) 1.44×10^2 J   (4) 3.18×10^{-26} J

48 The graph below represents the relationship between the force exerted on an elevator and the distance the elevator is lifted.

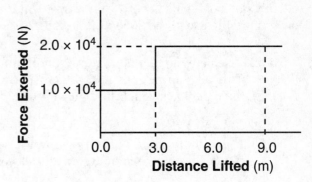

How much total work is done by the force in lifting the elevator from 0.0 m to 9.0 m?

(1) 9.0×10^4 J   (3) 1.5×10^5 J
(2) 1.2×10^5 J   (4) 1.8×10^5 J

49 The diagram below shows waves A and B in the same medium.

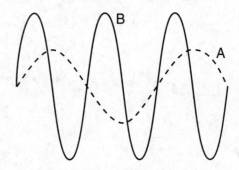

Compared to wave A, wave B has

(1) twice the amplitude and twice the wavelength
(2) twice the amplitude and half the wavelength
(3) the same amplitude and half the wavelength
(4) half the amplitude and the same wavelength

50 What is the quark composition of a proton?

(1) uud   (3) csb
(2) udd   (4) uds

Part B–2

Answer all questions in this part.

Directions (51–65): Record your answers in the spaces provided in your answer booklet. Some questions may require the use of the *2006 Edition Reference Tables for Physical Setting/Physics*.

51–52 Calculate the minimum power output of an electric motor that lifts a 1.30×10^4-newton elevator car vertically upward at a constant speed of 1.50 meters per second. [Show all work, including the equation and substitution with units.] [2]

53–54 A microwave oven emits a microwave with a wavelength of 2.00×10^{-2} meter in air. Calculate the frequency of the microwave. [Show all work, including the equation and substitution with units.] [2]

55–56 Calculate the energy equivalent in joules of the mass of a proton. [Show all work, including the equation and substitution with units.] [2]

Base your answers to questions 57 through 59 on the information and diagram below and on your knowledge of physics.

A 1.5×10^3-kilogram car is driven at a constant speed of 12 meters per second counterclockwise around a horizontal circular track having a radius of 50. meters, as represented below.

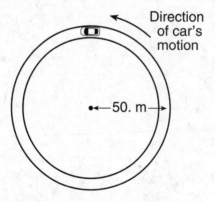

Track, as Viewed from Above

57 On the diagram *in your answer booklet*, draw an arrow to indicate the direction of the velocity of the car when it is at the position shown. Start the arrow on the car. [1]

58–59 Calculate the magnitude of the centripetal acceleration of the car. [Show all work, including the equation and substitution with units.] [2]

Base your answers to questions 60 through 62 on the information below and on your knowledge of physics.

A football is thrown at an angle of 30.° above the horizontal. The magnitude of the horizontal component of the ball's initial velocity is 13.0 meters per second. The magnitude of the vertical component of the ball's initial velocity is 7.5 meters per second. [Neglect friction.]

60 On the axes *in your answer booklet*, draw a graph representing the relationship between the horizontal displacement of the football and the time the football is in the air. [1]

61–62 The football is caught at the same height from which it is thrown. Calculate the total time the football was in the air. [Show all work, including the equation and substitution with units.] [2]

Base your answers to questions 63 through 65 on the information and diagram below and on your knowledge of physics.

A ray of light ($f = 5.09 \times 10^{14}$ Hz) traveling through a block of an unknown material, passes at an angle of incidence of 30.° into air, as shown in the diagram below.

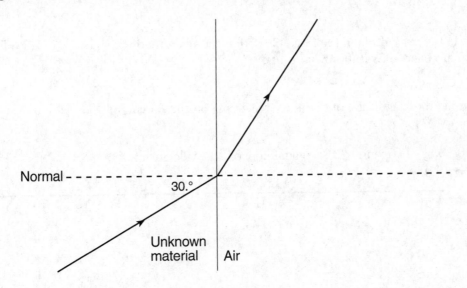

63 Use a protractor to determine the angle of refraction of the light ray as it passes from the unknown material into air. [1]

64–65 Calculate the index of refraction of the unknown material. [Show all work, including the equation and substitution with units.] [2]

Part C

Answer all questions in this part.

Directions (66–85): Record your answers in the spaces provided in your answer booklet. Some questions may require the use of the *2006 Edition Reference Tables for Physical Setting/Physics.*

Base your answers to questions 66 through 70 on the information below and on your knowledge of physics.

The diagram below represents a 4.0-newton force applied to a 0.200-kilogram copper block sliding to the right on a horizontal steel table.

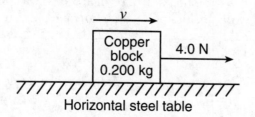

66 Determine the weight of the block.   [1]

67–68 Calculate the magnitude of the force of friction acting on the moving block. [Show all work, including the equation and substitution with units.]   [2]

69 Determine the magnitude of the net force acting on the moving block.   [1]

70 Describe what happens to the magnitude of the velocity of the block as the block slides across the table.   [1]

_____

Base your answers to questions 71 through 75 on the information and diagram below and on your knowledge of physics.

Two conducting parallel plates 5.0×10^{-3} meter apart are charged with a 12-volt potential difference. An electron is located midway between the plates. The magnitude of the electrostatic force on the electron is 3.8×10^{-16} newton.

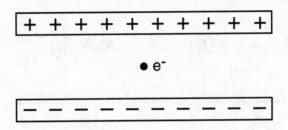

71 On the diagram *in your answer booklet*, draw *at least three* field lines to represent the direction of the electric field in the space between the charged plates. [1]

72 Identify the direction of the electrostatic force that the electric field exerts on the electron. [1]

73–74 Calculate the magnitude of the electric field strength between the plates, in newtons per coulomb. [Show all work, including the equation and substitution with units.] [2]

75 Describe what happens to the magnitude of the net electrostatic force on the electron as the electron is moved toward the positive plate. [1]

___

Base your answers to questions 76 through 80 on the information below and on your knowledge of physics.

An electron in a mercury atom changes from energy level *b* to a higher energy level when the atom absorbs a single photon with an energy of 3.06 electronvolts.

76 Determine the letter that identifies the energy level to which the electron jumped when the mercury atom absorbed the photon. [1]

77 Determine the energy of the photon, in joules. [1]

78–79 Calculate the frequency of the photon. [Show all work, including the equation and substitution with units.] [2]

80 Classify the photon as one of the types of electromagnetic radiation listed in the electromagnetic spectrum. [1]

___

Base your answers to questions 81 through 85 on the information and circuit diagram below and on your knowledge of physics.

Three lamps are connected in parallel to a 120.-volt source of potential difference, as represented below.

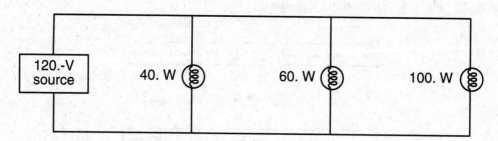

81–82 Calculate the resistance of the 40.-watt lamp. [Show all work, including the equation and substitution with units.] [2]

83 Describe what change, if any, would occur in the power dissipated by the 100.-watt lamp if the 60.-watt lamp were to burn out. [1]

84 Describe what change, if any, would occur in the equivalent resistance of the circuit if the 60.-watt lamp were to burn out. [1]

85 The circuit is disassembled. The same three lamps are then connected in series with each other and the source. Compare the equivalent resistance of this series circuit to the equivalent resistance of the parallel circuit. [1]

The University of the State of New York

REGENTS HIGH SCHOOL EXAMINATION

PHYSICAL SETTING
PHYSICS

Wednesday, June 17, 2015 — 1:15 to 4:15 p.m., only

ANSWER BOOKLET

Student .... Sex: ☐ Male ☐ Female

Teacher ....

School .... Grade ....

Record your answers for Part B–2 and Part C in this booklet.

Part B–2

51–52

53–54

55–56

June '15   Regents Examination

57

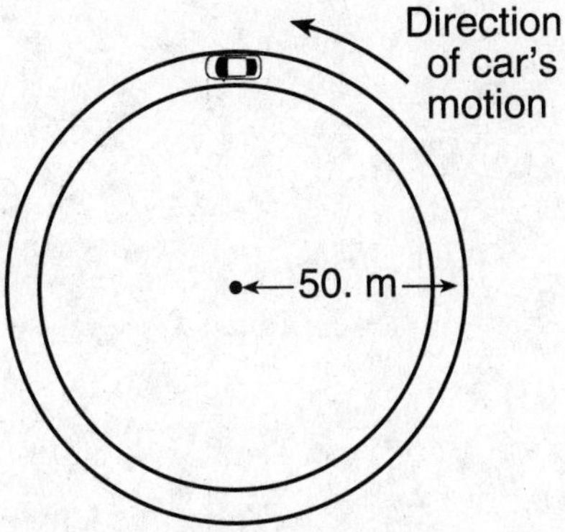

Direction
of car's
motion

•←—50. m—→

Track, as Viewed from Above

58–59

60

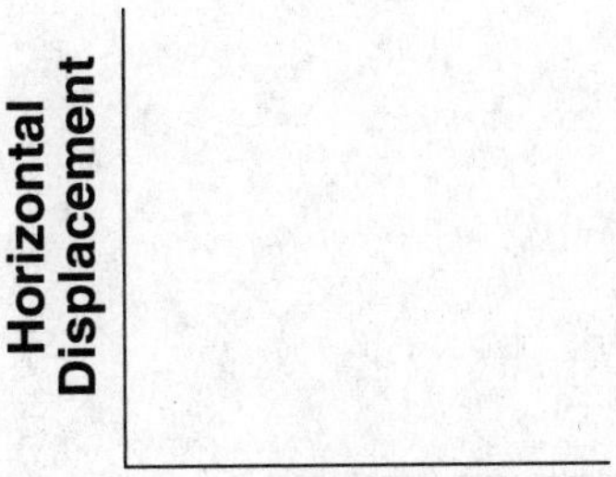

Horizontal
Displacement

Time

June '15 Regents Examination

61–62

63 _____ °

64–65

June '15   Regents Examination

66 _____ **N**

67–68

69 _____ **N**

70 _____

_____

71

+ + + + + + + + + +

● e⁻

– – – – – – – – – –

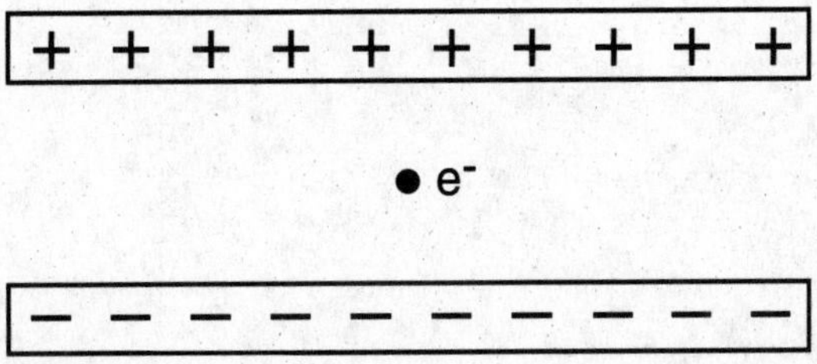

72 _____

73–74

75 _____

_____

76 _____

77 _____ **J**

78–79

80 _____

June '15   Regents Examination

81–82

83 _____

_____

84 _____

_____

85 _____

_____

Part A

Answer all questions in this part.

Directions (1–35): For *each* statement or question, choose the word or expression that, of those given, best completes the statement or answers the question. Some questions may require the use of the *2006 Edition Reference Tables for Physical Setting/Physics*. Record your answers on your separate answer sheet.

1 Which quantity is scalar?

(1) mass   (3) momentum

(2) force   (4) acceleration

2 What is the final speed of an object that starts from rest and accelerates uniformly at 4.0 meters per second^2 over a distance of 8.0 meters?

(1) 8.0 m/s   (3) 32 m/s

(2) 16 m/s   (4) 64 m/s

3 The components of a 15-meters-per-second velocity at an angle of 60.° above the horizontal are

(1) 7.5 m/s vertical and 13 m/s horizontal

(2) 13 m/s vertical and 7.5 m/s horizontal

(3) 6.0 m/s vertical and 9.0 m/s horizontal

(4) 9.0 m/s vertical and 6.0 m/s horizontal

4 What is the time required for an object starting from rest to fall freely 500. meters near Earth's surface?

(1) 51.0 s   (3) 10.1 s

(2) 25.5 s   (4) 7.14 s

5 A baseball bat exerts a force of magnitude F on a ball. If the mass of the bat is three times the mass of the ball, the magnitude of the force of the ball on the bat is

(1) F (3) $3F$

(2) $2F$ (4) $F/3$

6 A 2.0-kilogram mass is located 3.0 meters above the surface of Earth. What is the magnitude of Earth's gravitational field strength at this location?

(1) 4.9 N/kg   (3) 9.8 N/kg

(2) 2.0 N/kg   (4) 20. N/kg

7 A truck, initially traveling at a speed of 22 meters per second, increases speed at a constant rate of 2.4 meters per second^2 for 3.2 seconds. What is the total distance traveled by the truck during this 3.2-second time interval?

(1) 12 m   (3) 70. m

(2) 58 m   (4) 83 m

8 A 750-newton person stands in an elevator that is accelerating downward. The upward force of the elevator floor on the person must be

(1) equal to 0 N   (3) equal to 750 N

(2) less than 750 N   (4) greater than 750 N

9 A 3.0-kilogram object is acted upon by an impulse having a magnitude of 15 newton•seconds. What is the magnitude of the object's change in momentum due to this impulse?

(1) 5.0 kg•m/s   (3) 3.0 kg•m/s

(2) 15 kg•m/s   (4) 45 kg•m/s

10 An air bag is used to safely decrease the momentum of a driver in a car accident. The air bag reduces the magnitude of the force acting on the driver by

(1) increasing the length of time the force acts on the driver

(2) decreasing the distance over which the force acts on the driver

(3) increasing the rate of acceleration of the driver

(4) decreasing the mass of the driver

11 An electron moving at constant speed produces

(1) a magnetic field, only

(2) an electric field, only

(3) both a magnetic and an electric field

(4) neither a magnetic nor an electric field

12 A beam of electrons passes through an electric field where the magnitude of the electric field strength is 3.00×10^3 newtons per coulomb. What is the magnitude of the electrostatic force exerted by the electric field on each electron in the beam?

(1) 5.33×10^{-23} N   (3) 3.00×10^3 N

(2) 4.80×10^{-16} N   (4) 1.88×10^{22} N

13 How much work is required to move 3.0 coulombs of electric charge a distance of 0.010 meter through a potential difference of 9.0 volts?

(1) 2.7×10^3 J   (3) 3.0 J

(2) 27 J   (4) 3.0×10^{-2} J

14 What is the resistance of a 20.0-meter-long tungsten rod with a cross-sectional area of 1.00×10^{-4} meter^2 at 20°C?

(1) 2.80×10^{-5} Ω   (3) 89.3 Ω

(2) 1.12×10^{-2} Ω   (4) 112 Ω

15 Two pieces of flint rock produce a visible spark when they are struck together. During this process, mechanical energy is converted into

(1) nuclear energy and electromagnetic energy

(2) internal energy and nuclear energy

(3) electromagnetic energy and internal energy

(4) elastic potential energy and nuclear energy

16 A 15-kilogram cart is at rest on a horizontal surface. A 5-kilogram box is placed in the cart. Compared to the mass and inertia of the cart, the cart-box system has

(1) more mass and more inertia

(2) more mass and the same inertia

(3) the same mass and more inertia

(4) less mass and more inertia

17 Transverse waves are to radio waves as longitudinal waves are to

(1) light waves   (3) ultraviolet waves

(2) microwaves   (4) sound waves

18 As a monochromatic light ray passes from air into water, two characteristics of the ray that will *not* change are

(1) wavelength and period

(2) frequency and period

(3) wavelength and speed

(4) frequency and speed

19 When a mass is placed on a spring with a spring constant of 60.0 newtons per meter, the spring is compressed 0.500 meter. How much energy is stored in the spring?

(1) 60.0 J   (3) 15.0 J

(2) 30.0 J   (4) 7.50 J

20 A boy pushes his sister on a swing. What is the frequency of oscillation of his sister on the swing if the boy counts 90. complete swings in 300. seconds?

(1) 0.30 Hz   (3) 1.5 Hz

(2) 2.0 Hz   (4) 18 Hz

21 What is the period of a sound wave having a frequency of 340. hertz?

(1) 3.40×10^2 s   (3) 9.73×10^{-1} s

(2) 1.02×10^0 s   (4) 2.94×10^{-3} s

22 An MP3 player draws a current of 0.120 ampere from a 3.00-volt battery. What is the total charge that passes through the player in 900. seconds?

(1) 324 C   (3) 5.40 C

(2) 108 C   (4) 1.80 C

23 A beam of light has a wavelength of 4.5×10^{-7} meter in a vacuum. The frequency of this light is

(1) 1.5×10^{-15} Hz   (3) 1.4×10^2 Hz

(2) 4.5×10^{-7} Hz   (4) 6.7×10^{14} Hz

24 When x-ray radiation and infrared radiation are traveling in a vacuum, they have the same

(1) speed   (3) wavelength

(2) frequency   (4) energy per photon

25 The diagram below represents two identical pulses approaching each other in a uniform medium.

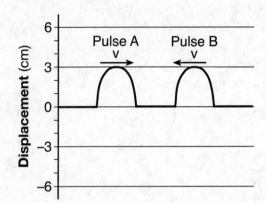

As the pulses meet and are superposed, the maximum displacement of the medium is

(1) −6 cm   (3) 3 cm
(2) 0 cm   (4) 6 cm

26 As a car approaches a pedestrian crossing the road, the driver blows the horn. Compared to the sound wave emitted by the horn, the sound wave detected by the pedestrian has a

(1) higher frequency and a lower pitch
(2) higher frequency and a higher pitch
(3) lower frequency and a higher pitch
(4) lower frequency and a lower pitch

27 When air is blown across the top of an open water bottle, air molecules in the bottle vibrate at a particular frequency and sound is produced. This phenomenon is called

(1) diffraction   (3) resonance
(2) refraction   (4) the Doppler effect

28 An antibaryon composed of two antiup quarks and one antidown quark would have a charge of

(1) +1e   (3) 0e
(2) −1e   (4) −3e

29 Which force is responsible for producing a stable nucleus by opposing the electrostatic force of repulsion between protons?

(1) strong   (3) frictional
(2) weak   (4) gravitational

30 What is the total energy released when 9.11×10^{-31} kilogram of mass is converted into energy?

(1) 2.73×10^{-22} J   (3) 9.11×10^{-31} J
(2) 8.20×10^{-14} J   (4) 1.01×10^{-47} J

31 A shopping cart slows as it moves along a level floor. Which statement describes the energies of the cart?

(1) The kinetic energy increases and the gravitational potential energy remains the same.
(2) The kinetic energy increases and the gravitational potential energy decreases.
(3) The kinetic energy decreases and the gravitational potential energy remains the same.
(4) The kinetic energy decreases and the gravitational potential energy increases.

32 Two identically-sized metal spheres, A and B, are on insulating stands, as shown in the diagram below. Sphere A possesses an excess of 6.3×10^{10} electrons and sphere B is neutral.

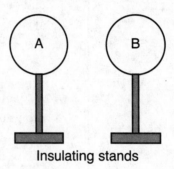

Insulating stands

Which diagram best represents the charge distribution on sphere B?

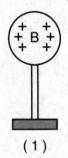   

(1)   (2)   (3)   (4)

33 Two points, A and B, are located within the electric field produced by a −3.0 nanocoulomb charge. Point A is 0.10 meter to the left of the charge and point B is 0.20 meter to the right of the charge, as shown in the diagram below.

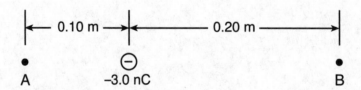

Compared to the magnitude of the electric field strength at point A, the magnitude of the electric field strength at point B is

(1) half as great
(2) twice as great

(3) one-fourth as great
(4) four times as great

June '14   Regents Examination

34 The diagram below represents two waves, *A* and *B*, traveling through the same uniform medium.

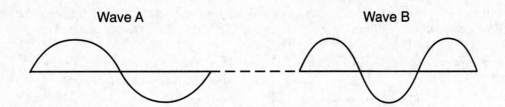

Which characteristic is the same for both waves?

(1) amplitude

(2) frequency

(3) period

(4) wavelength

35 The diagram below shows a periodic wave.

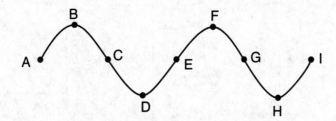

Which two points on the wave are 180.° out of phase?

(1) *A* and *C*

(2) *B* and *E*

(3) *F* and *G*

(4) *D* and *H*

Part B–1

Answer all questions in this part.

Directions (36–50): For *each* statement or question, choose the word or expression that, of those given, best completes the statement or answers the question. Some questions may require the use of the *2006 Edition Reference Tables for Physical Setting/Physics*. Record your answers on your separate answer sheet.

36 The height of a 30-story building is approximately
  (1) 10^0 m   (3) 10^2 m
  (2) 10^1 m   (4) 10^3 m

37 Two identically-sized metal spheres on insulating stands are positioned as shown below. The charge on sphere A is -4.0×10^{-6} coulomb and the charge on sphere B is -8.0×10^{-6} coulomb.

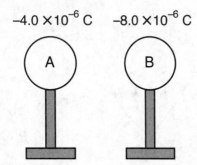

-4.0×10^{-6} C -8.0×10^{-6} C

The two spheres are touched together and then separated. The total number of excess electrons on sphere A after the separation is
  (1) 2.5×10^{13} (3) 5.0×10^{13}
  (2) 3.8×10^{13} (4) 7.5×10^{13}

38 A 1.0×10^3-kilogram car travels at a constant speed of 20. meters per second around a horizontal circular track. The diameter of the track is 1.0×10^2 meters. The magnitude of the car's centripetal acceleration is
  (1) 0.20 m/s^2 (3) 8.0 m/s^2
  (2) 2.0 m/s^2 (4) 4.0 m/s^2

39 Which combination of units can be used to express electrical energy?
  (1) $\dfrac{\text{volt}}{\text{coulomb}}$

  (2) $\dfrac{\text{coulomb}}{\text{volt}}$

  (3) volt•coulomb

  (4) volt•coulomb•second

40 The total amount of electrical energy used by a 315-watt television during 30.0 minutes of operation is
  (1) 5.67×10^5 J   (3) 1.05×10^1 J
  (2) 9.45×10^3 J   (4) 1.75×10^{-1} J

41 Which graph best represents the relationship between the absolute index of refraction and the speed of light ($f = 5.09 \times 10^{14}$ Hz) in various media?

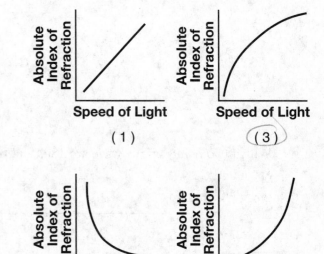

42 A 25-gram paper cup falls from rest off the edge of a tabletop 0.90 meter above the floor. If the cup has 0.20 joule of kinetic energy when it hits the floor, what is the total amount of energy converted into internal (thermal) energy during the cup's fall?
  (1) 0.02 J   (3) 2.2 J
  (2) 0.22 J   (4) 220 J

43 Which electron transition between the energy levels of hydrogen causes the emission of a photon of visible light?
  (1) $n = 6$ to $n = 5$ (3) $n = 5$ to $n = 2$
  (2) $n = 5$ to $n = 6$ (4) $n = 2$ to $n = 5$

44 Which graph best represents an object in equilibrium moving in a straight line?

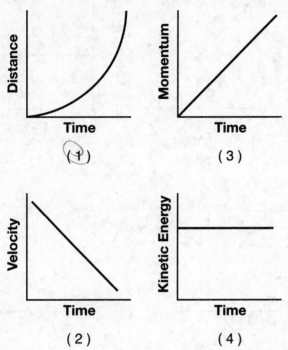

(1)

(3)

(2)

(4)

45 A body, B, is moving at constant speed in a horizontal circular path around point P. Which diagram shows the direction of the velocity (v) and the direction of the centripetal force (F_c) acting on the body?

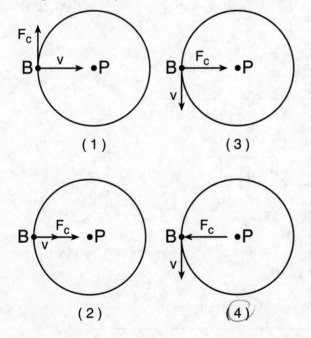

(1)

(3)

(2)

(4)

46 Which graph best represents the relationship between photon energy and photon wavelength?

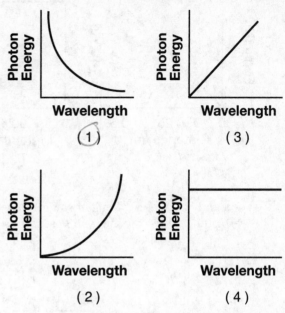

(1)

(3)

(2)

(4)

47 Which combination of initial horizontal velocity, (v_H) and initial vertical velocity, (v_v) results in the greatest horizontal range for a projectile over level ground? [Neglect friction.]

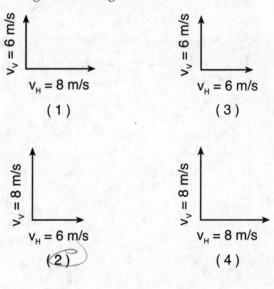

(1)

(3)

(2)

(4)

48 Which graph best represents the greatest amount of work?

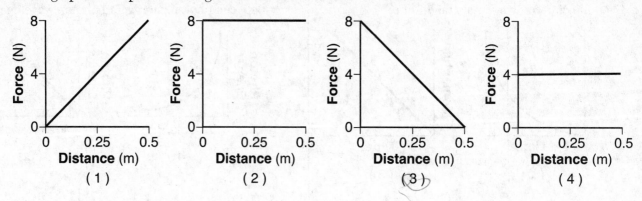

(1)　　　　(2)　　　　(3)　　　　(4)

49 When a ray of light traveling in water reaches a boundary with air, part of the light ray is reflected and part is refracted. Which ray diagram best represents the paths of the reflected and refracted light rays?

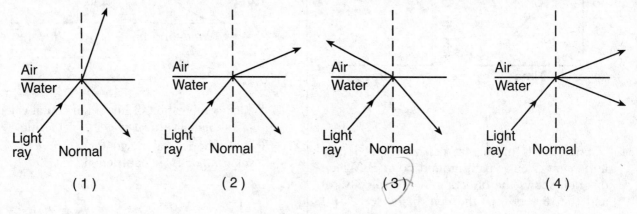

(1)　　　　(2)　　　　(3)　　　　(4)

50 The graph below represents the work done against gravity by a student as she walks up a flight of stairs at constant speed.

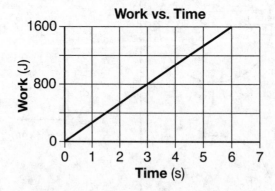

Compared to the power generated by the student after 2.0 seconds, the power generated by the student after 4.0 seconds is

(1) the same　　　　(3) half as great
(2) twice as great　　　(4) four times as great

Part B–2

Answer all questions in this part.

Directions (51–65): Record your answers in the spaces provided in your answer booklet. Some questions may require the use of the *2006 Edition Reference Tables for Physical Setting/Physics*.

Base your answers to questions 51 through 54 on the information below and the scaled vector diagram in your answer booklet and on your knowledge of physics.

      Two forces, a 60.-newton force east and an 80.-newton force north, act concurrently on an object located at point *P*, as shown.

51 Using a ruler, determine the scale used in the vector diagram. [1]

52 Draw the resultant force vector to scale on the diagram *in your answer booklet*. Label the vector "*R*." [1]

53 Determine the magnitude of the resultant force, *R*. [1]

54 Determine the measure of the angle, in degrees, between north and the resultant force, *R*. [1]

55–56 A 3.00-newton force causes a spring to stretch 60.0 centimeters. Calculate the spring constant of this spring. [Show all work, including the equation and substitution with units.] [2]

57 A 7.28-kilogram bowling ball traveling 8.50 meters per second east collides head-on with a 5.45 kilogram bowling ball traveling 10.0 meters per second west. Determine the magnitude of the total momentum of the two-ball system after the collision. [1]

58–59 Calculate the average power required to lift a 490-newton object a vertical distance of 2.0 meters in 10. seconds. [Show all work, including the equation and substitution with units.] [2]

60 The diagram *in your answer booklet* shows wave fronts approaching an opening in a barrier. The size of the opening is approximately equal to one-half the wavelength of the waves. On the diagram *in your answer booklet*, draw the shape of *at least three* of the wave fronts after they have passed through this opening. [1]

61 The diagram *in your answer booklet* shows a mechanical transverse wave traveling to the right in a medium. Point *A* represents a particle in the medium. Draw an arrow originating at point *A* to indicate the initial direction that the particle will move as the wave continues to travel to the right in the medium. [1]

June '14 Regents Examination

62 Regardless of the method used to generate electrical energy, the amount of energy provided by the source is always greater than the amount of electrical energy produced. Explain why there is a difference between the amount of energy provided by the source and the amount of electrical energy produced. [1]

Base your answers to questions 63 through 65 on the graph below, which represents the relationship between velocity and time for a car moving along a straight line, and your knowledge of physics.

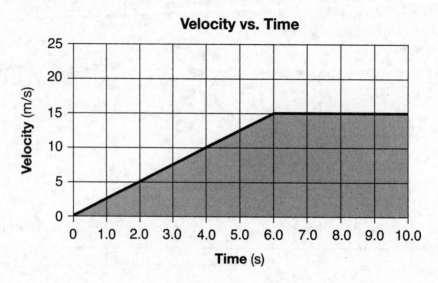

63 Determine the magnitude of the average velocity of the car from $t = 6.0$ seconds to $t = 10.$ seconds. [1]

64 Determine the magnitude of the car's acceleration during the first 6.0 seconds. [1]

65 Identify the physical quantity represented by the shaded area on the graph. [1]

Part C

Answer all questions in this part.

Directions (66–85): Record your answers in the spaces provided in your answer booklet. Some questions may require the use of the *2006 Edition Reference Tables for Physical Setting/Physics*.

Base your answers to questions 66 through 70 on the information below and on your knowledge of physics.

A student constructed a series circuit consisting of a 12.0-volt battery, a 10.0-ohm lamp, and a resistor. The circuit does *not* contain a voltmeter or an ammeter. When the circuit is operating, the total current through the circuit is 0.50 ampere.

66 In the space *in your answer booklet*, draw a diagram of the series circuit constructed to operate the lamp, using symbols from the *Reference Tables for Physical Setting/Physics*. [1]

67 Determine the equivalent resistance of the circuit. [1]

68 Determine the resistance of the resistor. [1]

69–70 Calculate the power consumed by the lamp. [Show all work, including the equation and substitution with the units.] [2]

Base your answers to questions 71 through 75 on the information below and on your knowledge of physics.

Pluto orbits the Sun at an average distance of 5.91×10^{12} meters. Pluto's diameter is 2.30×10^{6} meters and its mass is 1.31×10^{22} kilograms.

Charon orbits Pluto with their centers separated by a distance of 1.96×10^{7} meters. Charon has a diameter of 1.21×10^{6} meters and a mass of 1.55×10^{21} kilograms.

71–72 Calculate the magnitude of the gravitational force of attraction that Pluto exerts on Charon. [Show all work, including the equation and substitution with units.] [2]

73–74 Calculate the magnitude of the acceleration of Charon toward Pluto. [Show all work, including the equation and substitution with units.] [2]

75 State the reason why the magnitude of the Sun's gravitational force on Pluto is greater than the magnitude of the Sun's gravitational force on Charon. [1]

Base your answers to questions 76 through 80 on the information below and on your knowledge of physics.

A horizontal 20.-newton force is applied to a 5.0-kilogram box to push it across a rough, horizontal floor at a constant velocity of 3.0 meters per second to the right.

76 Determine the magnitude of the force of friction acting on the box.   [1]

77–78 Calculate the weight of the box. [Show all work, including the equation and substitution with units.]   [2]

79–80 Calculate the coefficient of kinetic friction between the box and the floor. [Show all work, including the equation and substitution with units]   [2]

_____

Base your answers to questions 81 through 85 on the information below and on your knowledge of physics.

An electron traveling with a speed of 2.50×10^6 meters per second collides with a photon having a frequency of 1.00×10^{16} hertz. After the collision, the photon has 3.18×10^{-18} joule of energy.

81–82 Calculate the original kinetic energy of the electron. [Show all work, including the equation and substitution with units.]   [2]

83 Determine the energy in joules of the photon before the collision.   [1]

84 Determine the energy lost by the photon during the collision.   [1]

85 Name *two* physical quantities conserved in the collision.   [1]

_____

The University of the State of New York

REGENTS HIGH SCHOOL EXAMINATION

PHYSICAL SETTING
PHYSICS

Friday, June 20, 2014 — 1:15 to 4:15 p.m., only

ANSWER BOOKLET

Sex: ☐ Male
☐ Female

Student . . . .

Teacher . . . .

School . . . .   Grade . . . .

Record your answers for Part B–2 and Part C in this booklet.

Part B–2

51 1.0 cm = _____ N

52

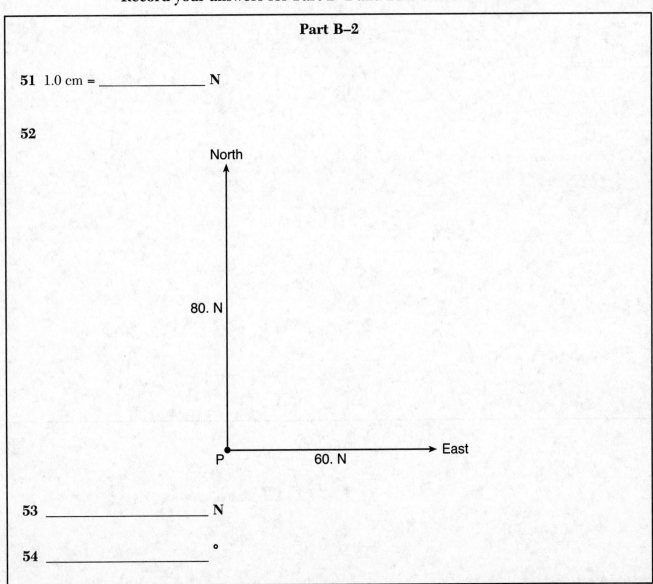

53 _____ N

54 _____ °

55–56

57 _____ kg•m/s

58–59

60

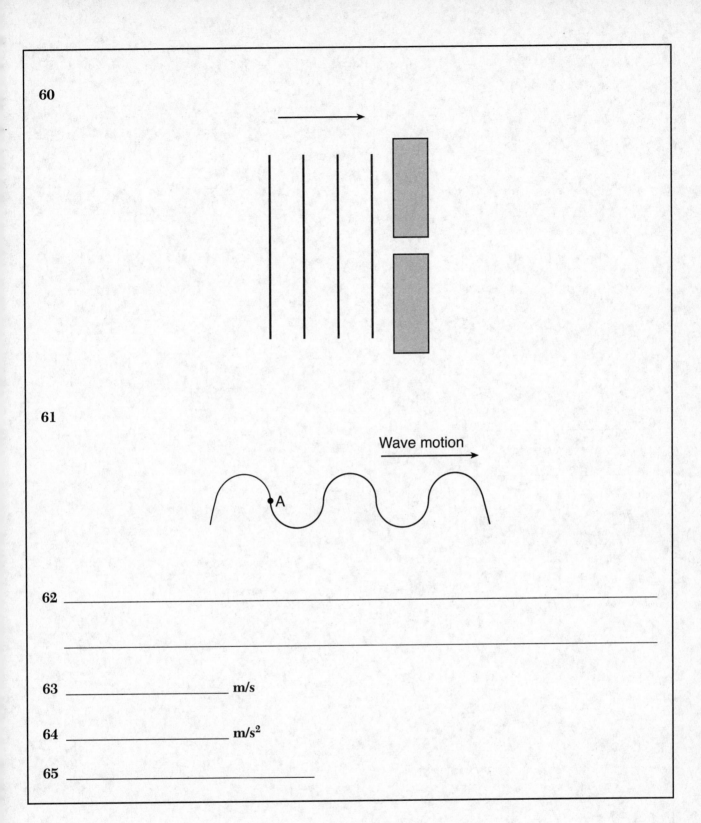

61

Wave motion

• A

62 _____

_____

63 _____ m/s

64 _____ m/s²

65 _____

66

67 _____ Ω

68 _____ Ω

69–70

71–72

73–74

75 _____

_____

June '14   Regents Examination

76 _____ N

77–78

79–80

June '14   Regents Examination

81–82

83 _____ J

84 _____ J

85 _____ and _____

Part A

Answer all questions in this part.

Directions (1–35): For *each* statement or question, choose the word or expression that, of those given, best completes the statement or answers the question. Some questions may require the use of the *2006 Edition Reference Tables for Physical Setting/Physics*. Record your answers on your separate answer sheet.

1 Which term identifies a scalar quantity?

(1) displacement (3) velocity
(2) momentum (4) time

2 Two 20.-newton forces act concurrently on an object. What angle between these forces will produce a resultant force with the greatest magnitude?

(1) 0° (3) 90.°
(2) 45° (4) 180.°

3 A car traveling west in a straight line on a highway decreases its speed from 30.0 meters per second to 23.0 meters per second in 2.00 seconds. The car's average acceleration during this time interval is

(1) 3.5 m/s² east (3) 13 m/s² east
(2) 3.5 m/s² west (4) 13 m/s² west

4 In a race, a runner traveled 12 meters in 4.0 seconds as she accelerated uniformly from rest. The magnitude of the acceleration of the runner was

(1) 0.25 m/s² (3) 3.0 m/s²
(2) 1.5 m/s² (4) 48 m/s²

5 A projectile is launched at an angle above the ground. The horizontal component of the projectile's velocity, v_x, is initially 40. meters per second. The vertical component of the projectile's velocity, v_y, is initially 30. meters per second. What are the components of the projectile's velocity after 2.0 seconds of flight? [Neglect friction.]

(1) v_x = 40. m/s and v_y = 10. m/s
(2) v_x = 40. m/s and v_y = 30. m/s
(3) v_x = 20. m/s and v_y = 10. m/s
(4) v_x = 20. m/s and v_y = 30. m/s

6 A ball is thrown with an initial speed of 10. meters per second. At what angle above the horizontal should the ball be thrown to reach the greatest height?

(1) 0° (3) 45°
(2) 30.° (4) 90.°

7 Which object has the greatest inertia?

(1) a 0.010-kg bullet traveling at 90. m/s
(2) a 30.-kg child traveling at 10. m/s on her bike
(3) a 490-kg elephant walking with a speed of 1.0 m/s
(4) a 1500-kg car at rest in a parking lot

8 An 8.0-newton wooden block slides across a horizontal wooden floor at constant velocity. What is the magnitude of the force of kinetic friction between the block and the floor?

(1) 2.4 N (3) 8.0 N
(2) 3.4 N (4) 27 N

9 Which situation represents a person in equilibrium?

(1) a child gaining speed while sliding down a slide
(2) a woman accelerating upward in an elevator
(3) a man standing still on a bathroom scale
(4) a teenager driving around a corner in his car

10 A rock is thrown straight up into the air. At the highest point of the rock's path, the magnitude of the net force acting on the rock is

(1) less than the magnitude of the rock's weight, but greater than zero
(2) greater than the magnitude of the rock's weight
(3) the same as the magnitude of the rock's weight
(4) zero

11 The diagram below shows a compressed spring between two carts initially at rest on a horizontal, frictionless surface. Cart A has a mass of 2 kilograms and cart B has a mass of 1 kilogram. A string holds the carts together.

The string is cut and the carts move apart. Compared to the magnitude of the force the spring exerts on cart A, the magnitude of the force the spring exerts on cart B is

(1) the same   (3) twice as great
(2) half as great   (4) four times as great

12 An 8.0-newton block is accelerating down a frictionless ramp inclined at 15° to the horizontal, as shown in the diagram below.

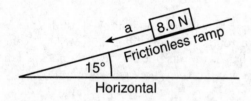

What is the magnitude of the net force causing the block's acceleration?

(1) 0 N   (3) 7.7 N
(2) 2.1 N   (4) 8.0 N

13 At a certain location, a gravitational force with a magnitude of 350 newtons acts on a 70.-kilogram astronaut. What is the magnitude of the gravitational field strength at this location?

(1) 0.20 kg/N   (3) 9.8 m/s^2
(2) 5.0 N/kg   (4) 25 000 N•kg

14 A spring gains 2.34 joules of elastic potential energy as it is compressed 0.250 meter from its equilibrium position. What is the spring constant of this spring?

(1) 9.36 N/m   (3) 37.4 N/m
(2) 18.7 N/m   (4) 74.9 N/m

15 When a teacher shines light on a photocell attached to a fan, the blades of the fan turn. The brighter the light shone on the photocell, the faster the blades turn. Which energy conversion is illustrated by this demonstration?

(1) light → thermal → mechanical
(2) light → nuclear → thermal
(3) light → electrical → mechanical
(4) light → mechanical → chemical

16 Which statement describes a characteristic common to all electromagnetic waves and mechanical waves?

(1) Both types of waves travel at the same speed.
(2) Both types of waves require a material medium for propagation.
(3) Both types of waves propagate in a vacuum.
(4) Both types of waves transfer energy.

17 An electromagnetic wave is produced by charged particles vibrating at a rate of 3.9×10^8 vibrations per second. The electromagnetic wave is classified as

(1) a radio wave   (3) an x ray
(2) an infrared wave   (4) visible light

18 The energy of a sound wave is most closely related to the wave's

(1) frequency   (3) wavelength
(2) amplitude   (4) speed

19 A sound wave traveling eastward through air causes the air molecules to

(1) vibrate east and west
(2) vibrate north and south
(3) move eastward, only
(4) move northward, only

20 What is the speed of light ($f = 5.09 \times 10^{14}$ Hz) in ethyl alcohol?

(1) 4.53×10^{-9} m/s   (3) 1.24×10^8 m/s
(2) 2.43×10^2 m/s   (4) 2.21×10^8 m/s

21 In the diagram below, an ideal pendulum released from position *A* swings freely to position *B*.

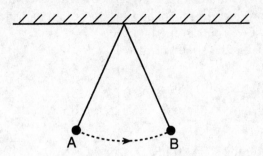

As the pendulum swings from *A* to *B*, its total mechanical energy
(1) decreases, then increases
(2) increases, only
(3) increases, then decreases
(4) remains the same

22 The diagram below represents a periodic wave.

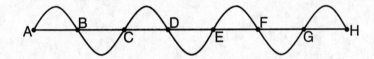

Which two points on the wave are out of phase?
(1) *A* and *C*
(2) *B* and *F*
(3) *C* and *E*
(4) *D* and *G*

23 A dry plastic rod is rubbed with wool cloth and then held near a thin stream of water from a faucet. The path of the stream of water is changed, as represented in the diagram below.

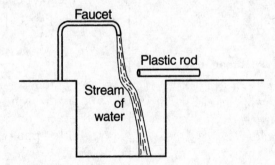

Which force causes the path of the stream of water to change due to the plastic rod?
(1) nuclear
(2) magnetic
(3) electrostatic
(4) gravitational

24 A distance of 1.0×10^{-2} meter separates successive crests of a periodic wave produced in a shallow tank of water. If a crest passes a point in the tank every 4.0×10^{-1} second, what is the speed of this wave?

(1) 2.5×10^{-4} m/s   (3) 2.5×10^{-2} m/s
(2) 4.0×10^{-3} m/s   (4) 4.0×10^{-1} m/s

25 One vibrating 256-hertz tuning fork transfers energy to another 256-hertz tuning fork, causing the second tuning fork to vibrate. This phenomenon is an example of

(1) diffraction   (3) refraction
(2) reflection   (4) resonance

26 Sound waves are produced by the horn of a truck that is approaching a stationary observer. Compared to the sound waves detected by the driver of the truck, the sound waves detected by the observer have a greater

(1) wavelength   (3) period
(2) frequency   (4) speed

27 The electronvolt is a unit of

(1) energy
(2) charge
(3) electric field strength
(4) electric potential difference

28 Which particle would produce a magnetic field?

(1) a neutral particle moving in a straight line
(2) a neutral particle moving in a circle
(3) a stationary charged particle
(4) a moving charged particle

29 A physics student takes her pulse and determines that her heart beats periodically 60 times in 60 seconds. The period of her heartbeat is

(1) 1 Hz   (3) 1 s
(2) 60 Hz   (4) 60 s

30 Moving 4.0 coulombs of charge through a circuit requires 48 joules of electric energy. What is the potential difference across this circuit?

(1) 190 V   (3) 12 V
(2) 48 V   (4) 4.0 V

31 The diagram below shows currents in a segment of an electric circuit.

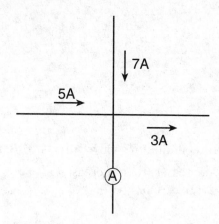

What is the reading of ammeter A?

(1) 1 A   (3) 9 A
(2) 5 A   (4) 15 A

32 An electric dryer consumes 6.0×10^6 joules of electrical energy when operating at 220 volts for 1.8×10^3 seconds. During operation, the dryer draws a current of

(1) 10. A   (3) 9.0×10^2 A
(2) 15 A   (4) 3.3×10^3 A

33 Which net charge could be found on an object?

(1) $+4.80 \times 10^{-19}$ C   (3) -2.40×10^{-19} C
(2) $+2.40 \times 10^{-19}$ C   (4) -5.60×10^{-19} C

34 A photon is emitted as the electron in a hydrogen atom drops from the $n = 5$ energy level directly to the $n = 3$ energy level. What is the energy of the emitted photon?

(1) 0.85 eV   (3) 1.51 eV
(2) 0.97 eV   (4) 2.05 eV

35 In a process called pair production, an energetic gamma ray is converted into an electron and a positron. It is *not* possible for a gamma ray to be converted into two electrons because

(1) charge must be conserved
(2) momentum must be conserved
(3) mass-energy must be conserved
(4) baryon number must be conserved

Part B–1

Answer all questions in this part.

Directions (36–50): For *each* statement or question, choose the word or expression that, of those given, best completes the statement or answers the question. Some questions may require the use of the *2006 Edition Reference Tables for Physical Setting/Physics.* Record your answers on your separate answer sheet.

36 The approximate length of an unsharpened No. 2 pencil is

(1) 2.0×10^{-2} m   (3) 2.0×10^0 m

(2) 2.0×10^{-1} m   (4) 2.0×10^1 m

37 The diagram below shows an 8.0-kilogram cart moving to the right at 4.0 meters per second about to make a head-on collision with a 4.0-kilogram cart moving to the left at 6.0 meters per second.

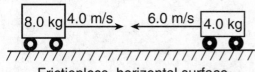

Frictionless, horizontal surface

After the collision, the 4.0-kilogram cart moves to the right at 3.0 meters per second. What is the velocity of the 8.0-kilogram cart after the collision?

(1) 0.50 m/s left   (3) 5.5 m/s left

(2) 0.50 m/s right   (4) 5.5 m/s right

38 Four forces act concurrently on a block on a horizontal surface as shown in the diagram below.

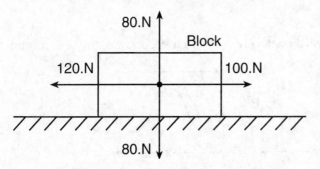

As a result of these forces, the block

(1) moves at constant speed to the right

(2) moves at constant speed to the left

(3) accelerates to the right

(4) accelerates to the left

39 If a motor lifts a 400.-kilogram mass a vertical distance of 10. meters in 8.0 seconds, the *minimum* power generated by the motor is

(1) 3.2×10^2 W   (3) 4.9×10^3 W

(2) 5.0×10^2 W   (4) 3.2×10^4 W

40 A 4.0-kilogram object is accelerated at 3.0 meters per second² north by an unbalanced force. The same unbalanced force acting on a 2.0-kilogram object will accelerate this object toward the north at

(1) 12 m/s²   (3) 3.0 m/s²

(2) 6.0 m/s²   (4) 1.5 m/s²

41 An electron is located in an electric field of magnitude 600. newtons per coulomb. What is the magnitude of the electrostatic force acting on the electron?

(1) 3.75×10^{21} N   (3) 9.60×10^{-17} N

(2) 6.00×10^2 N   (4) 2.67×10^{-22} N

42 The current in a wire is 4.0 amperes. The time required for 2.5×10^{19} electrons to pass a certain point in the wire is

(1) 1.0 s   (3) 0.50 s

(2) 0.25 s   (4) 4.0 s

43 When two point charges of magnitude q_1 and q_2 are separated by a distance, r, the magnitude of the electrostatic force between them is F. What would be the magnitude of the electrostatic force between point charges $2q_1$ and $4q_2$ when separated by a distance of $2r$?

(1) F (3) $16F$

(2) $2F$ (4) $4F$

44 The composition of a meson with a charge of −1 elementary charge could be

(1) $s\bar{c}$ (3) $u\bar{b}$

(2) $d\,s\,s$ (4) $\bar{u}\,\bar{c}\,\bar{d}$

45 Which graph represents the relationship between the kinetic energy and the speed of a freely falling object?

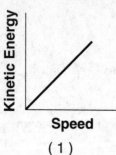
(1)

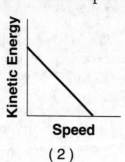
(2)

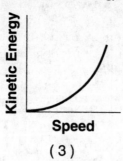
(3)

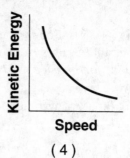
(4)

46 Which diagram represents the electric field between two oppositely charged conducting spheres?

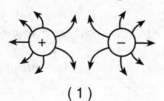
(1)

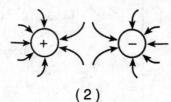
(2)

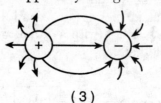
(3)

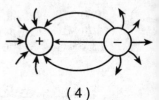
(4)

47 Which graph represents the relationship between the magnitude of the gravitational force, F_g, between two masses and the distance, r, between the centers of the masses?

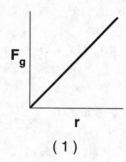
(1)

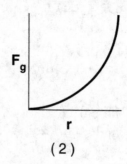
(2)

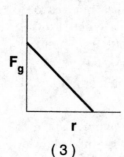
(3)

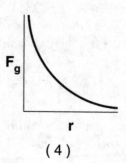
(4)

48 The diagram below shows two waves traveling toward each other at equal speed in a uniform medium.

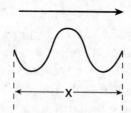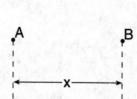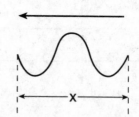

When both waves are in the region between points A and B, they will undergo

(1) diffraction

(2) the Doppler effect

(3) destructive interference

(4) constructive interference

49 The diagram below shows a series of straight wave fronts produced in a shallow tank of water approaching a small opening in a barrier.

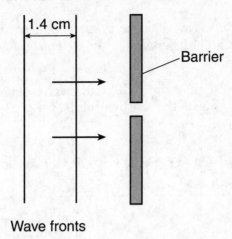

Wave fronts

Which diagram represents the appearance of the wave fronts after passing through the opening in the barrier?

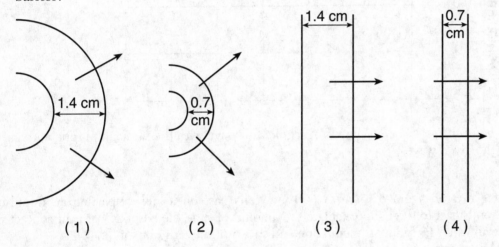

(1)   (2)   (3)   (4)

50 The graph below represents the relationship between energy and the equivalent mass from which it can be converted.

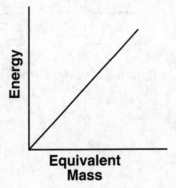

The slope of this graph represents

(1) c (3) g
(2) c^2 (4) g^2

June '13   Regents Examination

Part B–2

Answer all questions in this part.

Directions (51–65): Record your answers in the spaces provided in your answer booklet. Some questions may require the use of the *2006 Edition Reference Tables for Physical Setting/Physics*.

51–52 A 25.0-meter length of platinum wire with a cross-sectional area of 3.50×10^{-6} meter^2 has a resistance of 0.757 ohm at 20°C. Calculate the resistivity of the wire. [Show all work, including the equation and substitution with units.] [2]

53 The diagram below represents a periodic wave moving along a rope.

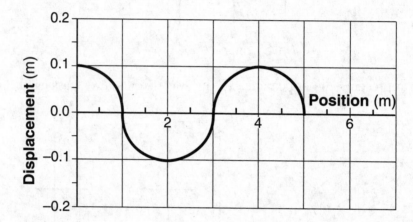

On the grid *in your answer booklet*, draw *at least one* full wave with the same amplitude and half the wavelength of the given wave. [1]

54–55 A baseball bat exerts an average force of 600. newtons east on a ball, imparting an impulse of 3.6 newton•seconds east to the ball. Calculate the amount of time the baseball bat is in contact with the ball. [Show all work, including the equation and substitution with units.] [2]

56 The diagram below shows the north pole of one bar magnet located near the south pole of another bar magnet.

$$\boxed{\text{N}} \qquad \boxed{\text{S}}$$

On the diagram *in your answer booklet*, draw *three* magnetic field lines in the region between the magnets. [1]

Base your answers to questions 57 through 59 on the information and graph below.

The graph below shows the relationship between speed and elapsed time for a car moving in a straight line.

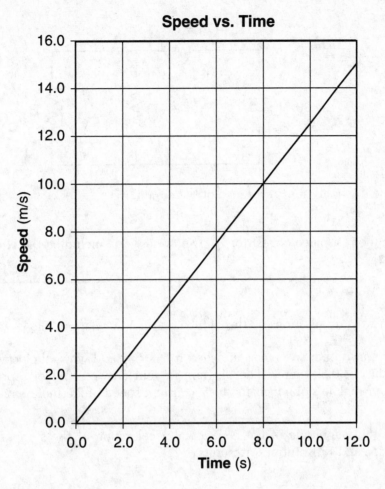

Speed vs. Time

57 Determine the magnitude of the acceleration of the car. [1]

58–59 Calculate the total distance the car traveled during the time interval 4.0 seconds to 8.0 seconds. [Show all work, including the equation and substitution with units.] [2]

Base your answers to questions 60 through 62 on the information below.

A 20.-ohm resistor, R_1, and a resistor of unknown resistance, R_2, are connected in parallel to a 30.-volt source, as shown in the circuit diagram below. An ammeter in the circuit reads 2.0 amperes.

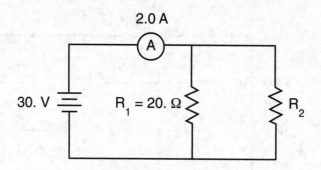

60 Determine the equivalent resistance of the circuit. [1]

61–62 Calculate the resistance of resistor R_2. [Show all work, including the equation and substitution with units.] [2]

_____

Base your answers to questions 63 through 65 on the information below.

A 28-gram rubber stopper is attached to a string and whirled clockwise in a horizontal circle with a radius of 0.80 meter. The diagram in your answer booklet represents the motion of the rubber stopper. The stopper maintains a constant speed of 2.5 meters per second.

63–64 Calculate the magnitude of the centripetal acceleration of the stopper. [Show all work, including the equation and substitution with units.] [2]

65 On the diagram *in your answer booklet*, draw an arrow showing the direction of the centripetal force acting on the stopper when it is at the position shown. [1]

_____

Part C

Answer all questions in this part.

Directions (66–85): Record your answers in the spaces provided in your answer booklet. Some questions may require the use of the *2006 Edition Reference Tables for Physical Setting/Physics*.

Base your answers to questions 66 through 69 on the information below.

Auroras over the polar regions of Earth are caused by collisions between charged particles from the Sun and atoms in Earth's atmosphere. The charged particles give energy to the atoms, exciting them from their lowest available energy level, the ground state, to higher energy levels, excited states. Most atoms return to their ground state within 10. nanoseconds.

In the higher regions of Earth's atmosphere, where there are fewer interatom collisions, a few of the atoms remain in excited states for longer times. For example, oxygen atoms remain in an excited state for up to 1.0 second. These atoms account for the greenish and red glows of the auroras. As these oxygen atoms return to their ground state, they emit green photons ($f = 5.38 \times 10^{14}$ Hz) and red photons ($f = 4.76 \times 10^{14}$ Hz). These emissions last long enough to produce the changing aurora phenomenon.

66 What is the order of magnitude of the time, in seconds, that most atoms spend in an excited state? [1]

67–68 Calculate the energy of a photon, in joules, that accounts for the red glow of the aurora. [Show all work, including the equation and substitution with units.] [2]

69 Explain what is meant by an atom being in its ground state. [1]

Base your answers to questions 70 through 75 on the information below.

A girl rides her bicycle 1.40 kilometers west, 0.70 kilometer south, and 0.30 kilometer east in 12 minutes. The vector diagram in your answer booklet represents the girl's first two displacements in sequence from point P. The scale used in the diagram is 1.0 centimeter = 0.20 kilometer.

70–71 On the vector diagram *in your answer booklet*, using a ruler and a protractor, construct the following vectors:

• Starting at the arrowhead of the second displacement vector, draw a vector to represent the 0.30 kilometer east displacement. Label the vector with its magnitude. [1]

• Draw the vector representing the resultant displacement of the girl for the entire bicycle trip *and* label the vector R. [1]

72–73 Calculate the girl's average speed for the entire bicycle trip. [Show all work, including the equation and substitution with units.] [2]

74 Determine the magnitude of the girl's resultant displacement for the entire bicycle trip, in kilometers. [1]

75 Determine the measure of the angle, in degrees, between the resultant and the 1.40-kilometer displacement vector. [1]

_____

Base your answers to questions 76 through 80 on the information below.

A light ray with a frequency of 5.09×10^{14} hertz traveling in water has an angle of incidence of 35° on a water-air interface. At the interface, part of the ray is reflected from the interface and part of the ray is refracted as it enters the air.

76 What is the angle of reflection of the light ray at the interface? [1]

77 On the diagram *in your answer booklet*, using a protractor and a straightedge, draw the reflected ray. [1]

78–79 Calculate the angle of refraction of the light ray as it enters the air. [Show all work, including the equation and substitution with units.] [2]

80 Identify *one* characteristic of this light ray that is the same in *both* the water and the air. [1]

_____

Base your answers to questions 81 through 85 on the information and diagram below.

A 30.4-newton force is used to slide a 40.0-newton crate a distance of 6.00 meters at constant speed along an incline to a vertical height of 3.00 meters.

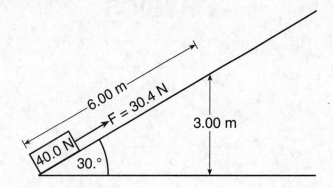

81 Determine the total work done by the 30.4-newton force in sliding the crate along the incline. [1]

82–83 Calculate the total increase in the gravitational potential energy of the crate after it has slid 6.00 meters along the incline. [Show all work, including the equation and substitution with units.] [2]

84 State what happens to the kinetic energy of the crate as it slides along the incline. [1]

85 State what happens to the internal energy of the crate as it slides along the incline. [1]

The University of the State of New York

REGENTS HIGH SCHOOL EXAMINATION

PHYSICAL SETTING PHYSICS

Thursday, June 13, 2013 — 1:15 to 4:15 p.m., only

ANSWER BOOKLET

☐ Male

Student .... Sex: ☐ Female

Teacher ....

School .... Grade ....

Record your answers for Part B–2 and Part C in this booklet.

Part B–2

51–52

53

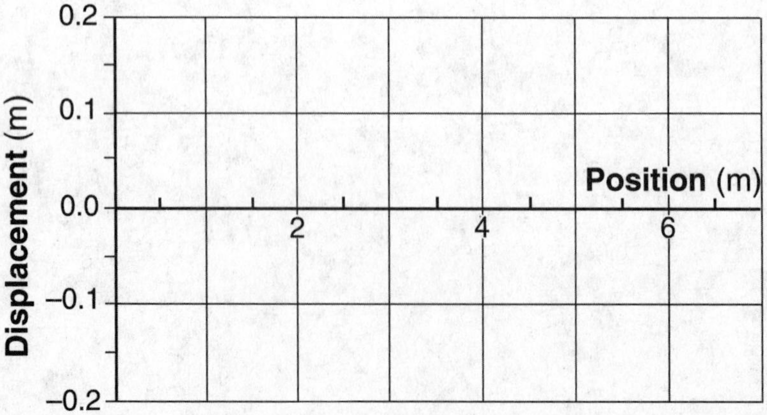

56

```
┌─────┐     ┌─────┐
│  N  │     │  S  │
└─────┘     └─────┘
```

[2]

57 _____ m/s^2

58–59

60 _____ Ω

61–62

June '13   Regents Examination

65

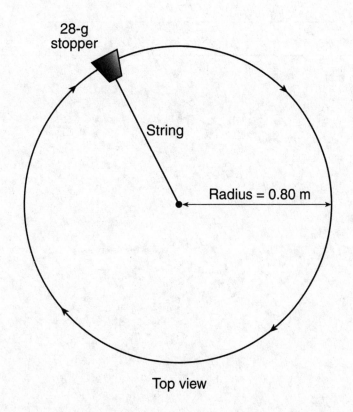

28-g
stopper

String

Radius = 0.80 m

Top view

Part C

66 _____

67–68

69 _____

_____

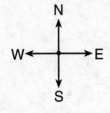

Scale
1.0 cm = 0.20 km

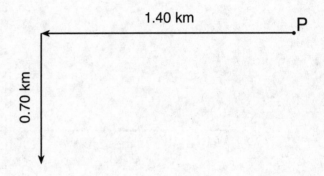

72–73

74 _____ **km**

75 _____ °

76 _____ °

77

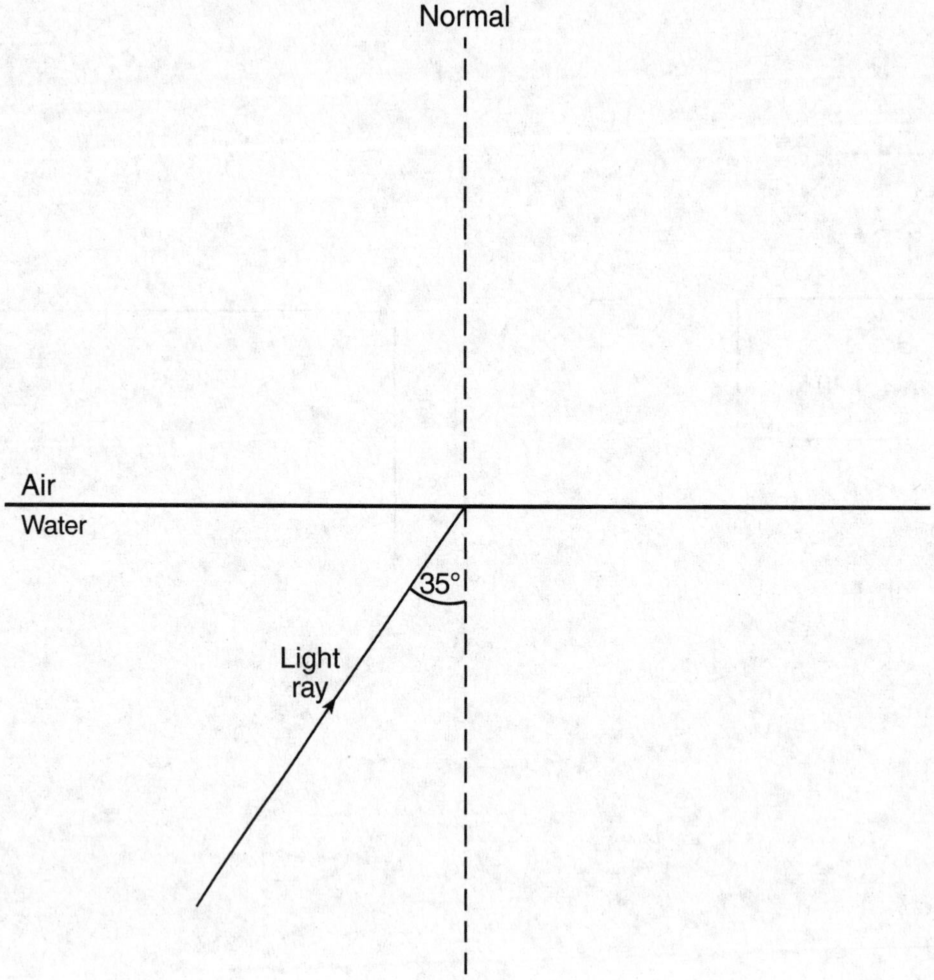

Normal

Air
Water

35°

Light
ray

78–79

80 _____

June '13   Regents Examination

P.S./PHYSICS

81 _____ **J**

82–83

84 _____

85 _____

Part A

Answer all questions in this part.

Directions (1–35): For *each* statement or question, choose the word or expression that, of those given, best completes the statement or answers the question. Some questions may require the use of the *2006 Edition Reference Tables for Physical Setting/Physics*. Record your answers on your separate answer sheet.

Base your answers to questions 1 and 2 on the information below.

In a drill during basketball practice, a player runs the length of the 30.-meter court and back. The player does this three times in 60. seconds.

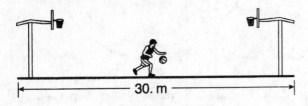

(Not drawn to scale)

1 The magnitude of the player's total displacement after running the drill is
(1) 0.0 m
(2) 30. m
(3) 60. m
(4) 180 m

2 The average speed of the player during the drill is
(1) 0.0 m/s
(2) 0.50 m/s
(3) 3.0 m/s
(4) 30. m/s

3 A baseball is thrown at an angle of 40.0° above the horizontal. The horizontal component of the baseball's initial velocity is 12.0 meters per second. What is the magnitude of the ball's initial velocity?
(1) 7.71 m/s
(2) 9.20 m/s
(3) 15.7 m/s
(4) 18.7 m/s

4 A particle could have a charge of
(1) 0.8×10^{-19} C
(2) 1.2×10^{-19} C
(3) 3.2×10^{-19} C
(4) 4.1×10^{-19} C

5 Which object has the greatest inertia?
(1) a 15-kg mass traveling at 5.0 m/s
(2) a 10.-kg mass traveling at 10. m/s
(3) a 10.-kg mass traveling at 5.0 m/s
(4) a 5.0-kg mass traveling at 15 m/s

6 A car, initially traveling east with a speed of 5.0 meters per second, is accelerated uniformly at 2.0 meters per second² east for 10. seconds along a straight line. During this 10.-second interval the car travels a total distance of
(1) 50. m
(2) 60. m
(3) 1.0×10^2 m
(4) 1.5×10^2 m

7 Which situation describes an object that has *no* unbalanced force acting on it?
(1) an apple in free fall
(2) a satellite orbiting Earth
(3) a hockey puck moving at constant velocity across ice
(4) a laboratory cart moving down a frictionless 30.° incline

8 A child riding a bicycle at 15 meters per second accelerates at −3.0 meters per second² for 4.0 seconds. What is the child's speed at the end of this 4.0-second interval?
(1) 12 m/s
(2) 27 m/s
(3) 3.0 m/s
(4) 7.0 m/s

9 An unbalanced force of 40. newtons keeps a 5.0-kilogram object traveling in a circle of radius 2.0 meters. What is the speed of the object?
(1) 8.0 m/s
(2) 2.0 m/s
(3) 16 m/s
(4) 4.0 m/s

10 A 5.00-kilogram block slides along a horizontal, frictionless surface at 10.0 meters per second for 4.00 seconds. The magnitude of the block's momentum is
(1) 200. kg•m/s
(2) 50.0 kg•m/s
(3) 20.0 kg•m/s
(4) 12.5 kg•m/s

11 A 0.50-kilogram puck sliding on a horizontal shuffleboard court is slowed to rest by a frictional force of 1.2 newtons. What is the coefficient of kinetic friction between the puck and the surface of the shuffleboard court?
(1) 0.24
(2) 0.42
(3) 0.60
(4) 4.1

12 A number of 1.0-newton horizontal forces are exerted on a block on a frictionless, horizontal surface. Which top-view diagram shows the forces producing the greatest magnitude of acceleration of the block?

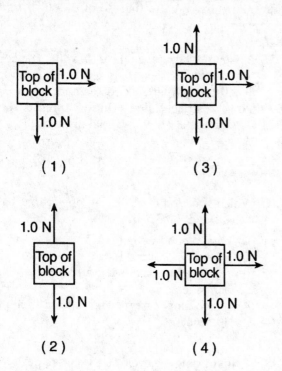

(1)

(2)

(3)

(4)

13 On a small planet, an astronaut uses a vertical force of 175 newtons to lift an 87.5-kilogram boulder at constant velocity to a height of 0.350 meter above the planet's surface. What is the magnitude of the gravitational field strength on the surface of the planet?

(1) 0.500 N/kg   (3) 9.81 N/kg
(2) 2.00 N/kg   (4) 61.3 N/kg

14 A car uses its brakes to stop on a level road. During this process, there must be a conversion of kinetic energy into

(1) light energy
(2) nuclear energy
(3) gravitational potential energy
(4) internal energy

15 Which change decreases the resistance of a piece of copper wire?

(1) increasing the wire's length
(2) increasing the wire's resistivity
(3) decreasing the wire's temperature
(4) decreasing the wire's diameter

16 A stone on the end of a string is whirled clockwise at constant speed in a horizontal circle as shown in the diagram below.

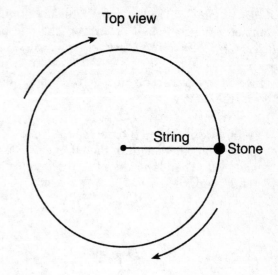

Top view

Which pair of arrows best represents the directions of the stone's velocity, v, and acceleration, a, at the position shown?

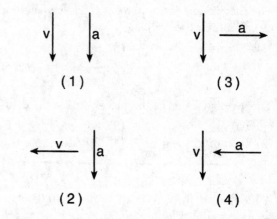

(1)   (3)

(2)   (4)

17 How much work is done by the force lifting a 0.1-kilogram hamburger vertically upward at constant velocity 0.3 meter from a table?

(1) 0.03 J   (3) 0.3 J
(2) 0.1 J   (4) 0.4 J

18 Two electrons are separated by a distance of 3.00×10^{-6} meter. What are the magnitude and direction of the electrostatic forces each exerts on the other?

(1) 2.56×10^{-17} N away from each other
(2) 2.56×10^{-17} N toward each other
(3) 7.67×10^{-23} N away from each other
(4) 7.67×10^{-23} N toward each other

June '12   Regents Examination

19 Which object will have the greatest change in electrical energy?

(1) an electron moved through a potential difference of 2.0 V
(2) a metal sphere with a charge of 1.0×10^{-9} C moved through a potential difference of 2.0 V
(3) an electron moved through a potential difference of 4.0 V
(4) a metal sphere with a charge of 1.0×10^{-9} C moved through a potential difference of 4.0 V

20 The resistance of a circuit remains constant. Which graph best represents the relationship between the current in the circuit and the potential difference provided by the battery?

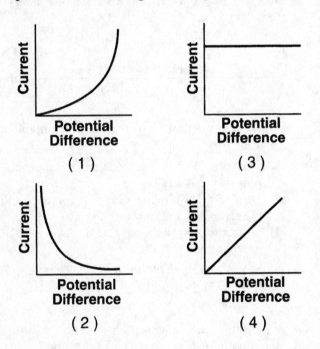

21 The wavelength of a wave doubles as it travels from medium *A* into medium *B*. Compared to the wave in medium *A*, the wave in medium *B* has

(1) half the speed
(2) twice the speed
(3) half the frequency
(4) twice the frequency

22 The watt•second is a unit of

(1) power
(2) energy
(3) potential difference
(4) electric field strength

23 Which quantity has both a magnitude and a direction?

(1) energy   (3) power
(2) impulse   (4) work

24 A tuning fork vibrates at a frequency of 512 hertz when struck with a rubber hammer. The sound produced by the tuning fork will travel through the air as a

(1) longitudinal wave with air molecules vibrating parallel to the direction of travel
(2) transverse wave with air molecules vibrating parallel to the direction of travel
(3) longitudinal wave with air molecules vibrating perpendicular to the direction of travel
(4) transverse wave with air molecules vibrating perpendicular to the direction of travel

25 A 3-ohm resistor and a 6-ohm resistor are connected in parallel across a 9-volt battery. Which statement best compares the potential difference across each resistor?

(1) The potential difference across the 6-ohm resistor is the same as the potential difference across the 3-ohm resistor.
(2) The potential difference across the 6-ohm resistor is twice as great as the potential difference across the 3-ohm resistor.
(3) The potential difference across the 6-ohm resistor is half as great as the potential difference across the 3-ohm resistor.
(4) The potential difference across the 6-ohm resistor is four times as great as the potential difference across the 3-ohm resistor.

26 A 3.6-volt battery is used to operate a cell phone for 5.0 minutes. If the cell phone dissipates 0.064 watt of power during its operation, the current that passes through the phone is

(1) 0.018 A   (3) 19 A
(2) 5.3 A   (4) 56 A

27 A monochromatic beam of light has a frequency of 7.69×10^{14} hertz. What is the energy of a photon of this light?

(1) 2.59×10^{-40} J   (3) 5.10×10^{-19} J
(2) 6.92×10^{-31} J   (4) 3.90×10^{-7} J

28 A 3.00×10^{-9}-coulomb test charge is placed near a negatively charged metal sphere. The sphere exerts an electrostatic force of magnitude 6.00×10^{-5} newton on the test charge. What is the magnitude and direction of the electric field strength at this location?

(1) 2.00×10^4 N/C directed away from the sphere
(2) 2.00×10^4 N/C directed toward the sphere
(3) 5.00×10^{-5} N/C directed away from the sphere
(4) 5.00×10^{-5} N/C directed toward the sphere

29 What is characteristic of both sound waves and electromagnetic waves?

(1) They require a medium.
(2) They transfer energy.
(3) They are mechanical waves.
(4) They are longitudinal waves.

30 A small object is dropped through a loop of wire connected to a sensitive ammeter on the edge of a table, as shown in the diagram below.

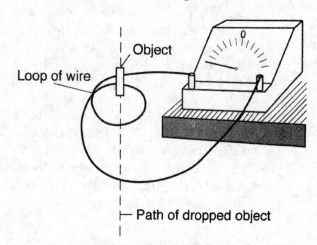

A reading on the ammeter is most likely produced when the object falling through the loop of wire is a

(1) flashlight battery   (3) brass mass
(2) bar magnet   (4) plastic ruler

31 What is the wavelength of a 2.50-kilohertz sound wave traveling at 326 meters per second through air?

(1) 0.130 m   (3) 7.67 m
(2) 1.30 m   (4) 130. m

32 Ultrasound is a medical technique that transmits sound waves through soft tissue in the human body. Ultrasound waves can break kidney stones into tiny fragments, making it easier for them to be excreted without pain. The shattering of kidney stones with specific frequencies of sound waves is an application of which wave phenomenon?

(1) the Doppler effect   (3) refraction
(2) reflection   (4) resonance

33 In the diagram below, a stationary source located at point S produces sound having a constant frequency of 512 hertz. Observer A, 50. meters to the left of S, hears a frequency of 512 hertz. Observer B, 100. meters to the right of S, hears a frequency lower than 512 hertz.

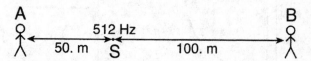

Which statement best describes the motion of the observers?

(1) Observer A is moving toward point S, and observer B is stationary.
(2) Observer A is moving away from point S, and observer B is stationary.
(3) Observer A is stationary, and observer B is moving toward point S.
(4) Observer A is stationary, and observer B is moving away from point S.

34 While sitting in a boat, a fisherman observes that two complete waves pass by his position every 4 seconds. What is the period of these waves?

(1) 0.5 s   (3) 8 s
(2) 2 s   (4) 4 s

35 A wave passes through an opening in a barrier. The amount of diffraction experienced by the wave depends on the size of the opening and the wave's

(1) amplitude   (3) velocity
(2) wavelength   (4) phase

Part B–1

Answer all questions in this part.

Directions (36–50): For *each* statement or question, choose the word or expression that, of those given, best completes the statement or answers the question. Some questions may require the use of the *2006 Edition Reference Tables for Physical Setting/Physics*. Record your answers on your separate answer sheet.

36 The length of a football field is closest to
- (1) 1000 cm
- (2) 1000 dm
- (3) 1000 km
- (4) 1000 mm

37 A student on an amusement park ride moves in a circular path with a radius of 3.5 meters once every 8.9 seconds. The student moves at an average speed of
- (1) 0.39 m/s
- (2) 1.2 m/s
- (3) 2.5 m/s
- (4) 4.3 m/s

38 When a 1.0-kilogram cart moving with a speed of 0.50 meter per second on a horizontal surface collides with a second 1.0-kilogram cart initially at rest, the carts lock together. What is the speed of the combined carts after the collision? [Neglect friction.]
- (1) 1.0 m/s
- (2) 0.50 m/s
- (3) 0.25 m/s
- (4) 0 m/s

39 Two elevators, *A* and *B*, move at constant speed. Elevator *B* moves with twice the speed of elevator *A*. Elevator *B* weighs twice as much as elevator *A*. Compared to the power needed to lift elevator *A*, the power needed to lift elevator *B* is
- (1) the same
- (2) twice as great
- (3) half as great
- (4) four times as great

40 What is the maximum height to which a motor having a power rating of 20.4 watts can lift a 5.00-kilogram stone vertically in 10.0 seconds?
- (1) 0.0416 m
- (2) 0.408 m
- (3) 4.16 m
- (4) 40.8 m

41 What is the current in a wire if 3.4×10^{19} electrons pass by a point in this wire every 60. seconds?
- (1) 1.8×10^{-18} A
- (2) 3.1×10^{-11} A
- (3) 9.1×10^{-2} A
- (4) 11 A

42 Which graph represents the relationship between the magnitude of the gravitational force exerted by Earth on a spacecraft and the distance between the center of the spacecraft and center of Earth? [Assume constant mass for the spacecraft.]

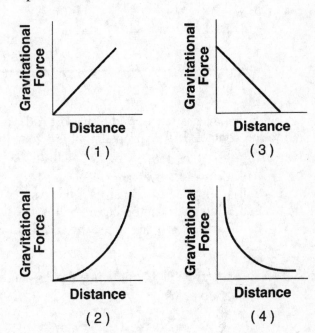

43 To increase the brightness of a desk lamp, a student replaces a 50-watt incandescent lightbulb with a 100-watt incandescent lightbulb. Compared to the 50-watt lightbulb, the 100-watt lightbulb has
- (1) less resistance and draws more current
- (2) less resistance and draws less current
- (3) more resistance and draws more current
- (4) more resistance and draws less current

44 Electrons in excited hydrogen atoms are in the $n = 3$ energy level. How many different photon frequencies could be emitted as the atoms return to the ground state?
- (1) 1
- (2) 2
- (3) 3
- (4) 4

45 The diagram below represents a setup for demonstrating motion.

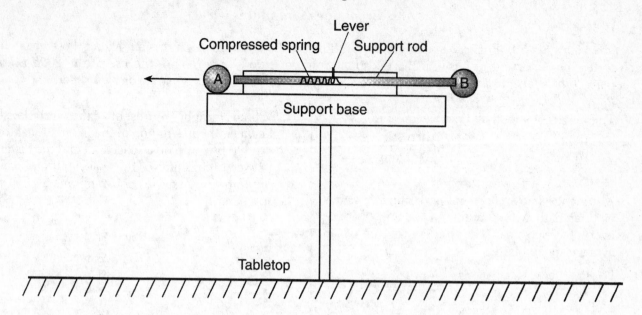

When the lever is released, the support rod withdraws from ball B, allowing it to fall. At the same instant, the rod contacts ball A, propelling it horizontally to the left. Which statement describes the motion that is observed after the lever is released and the balls fall? [Neglect friction.]

(1) Ball A travels at constant velocity.
(2) Ball A hits the tabletop at the same time as ball B.
(3) Ball B hits the tabletop before ball A.
(4) Ball B travels with an increasing acceleration.

46 Two speakers, S_1 and S_2, operating in phase in the same medium produce the circular wave patterns shown in the diagram below.

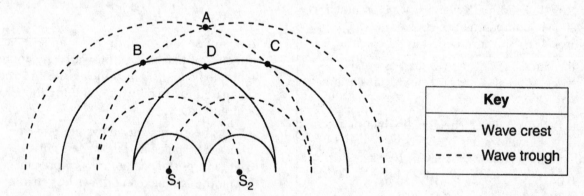

Key	
——	Wave crest
- - - -	Wave trough

At which two points is constructive interference occurring?

(1) A and B
(2) A and D

(3) B and C
(4) B and D

47 A 100.0-kilogram boy and a 50.0-kilogram girl, each holding a spring scale, pull against each other as shown in the diagram below.

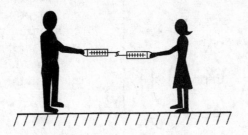

The graph below shows the relationship between the magnitude of the force that the boy applies on his spring scale and time.

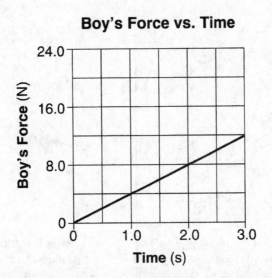

Which graph best represents the relationship between the magnitude of the force that the girl applies on her spring scale and time?

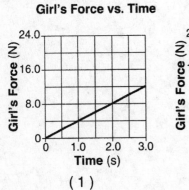

(1)

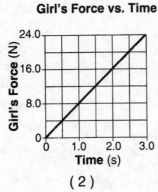

(2)

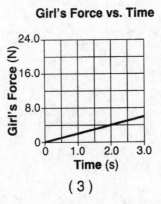

(3)

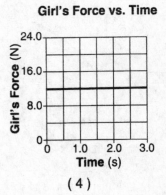

(4)

48 In which diagram do the field lines best represent the gravitational field around Earth?

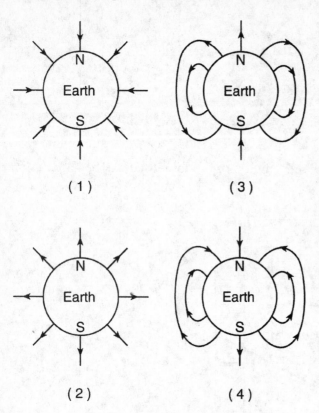

(1)   (3)

(2)   (4)

49 A ray of light ($f = 5.09 \times 10^{14}$ Hz) travels through various substances. Which graph best represents the relationship between the absolute index of refraction of these substances and the corresponding speed of light in these substances?

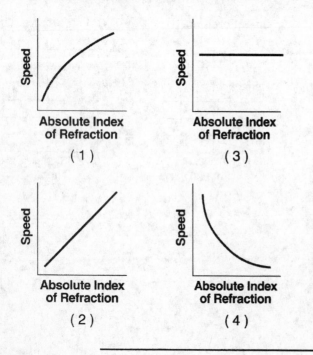

(1)   (3)

(2)   (4)

50 A pendulum is made from a 7.50-kilogram mass attached to a rope connected to the ceiling of a gymnasium. The mass is pushed to the side until it is at position A, 1.5 meters higher than its equilibrium position. After it is released from rest at position A, the pendulum moves freely back and forth between positions A and B, as shown in the diagram below.

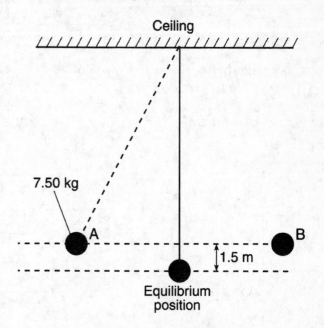

What is the total amount of kinetic energy that the mass has as it swings freely through its equilibrium position? [Neglect friction.]

(1) 11 J
(2) 94 J
(3) 110 J
(4) 920 J

June '12   Regents Examination

Part B–2

Answer all questions in this part.

Directions (51–65): Record your answers in the spaces provided in your answer booklet. Some questions may require the use of the *2006 Edition Reference Tables for Physical Setting/Physics*.

Base your answers to questions 51 through 53 on the information below.

A student produced various elongations of a spring by applying a series of forces to the spring. The graph below represents the relationship between the applied force and the elongation of the spring.

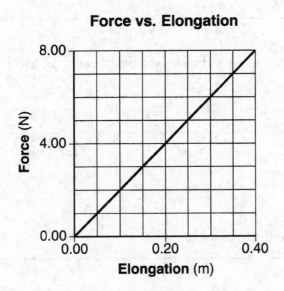

Force vs. Elongation

51 Determine the spring constant of the spring. [1]

52–53 Calculate the energy stored in the spring when the elongation is 0.30 meter. [Show all work, including the equation and substitution with units.] [2]

_____

54–55 Calculate the time required for a 6000.-newton net force to stop a 1200.-kilogram car initially traveling at 10. meters per second. [Show all work, including the equation and substitution with units.] [2]

56–57 A toy rocket is launched twice into the air from level ground and returns to level ground. The rocket is first launched with initial speed v at an angle of 45° above the horizontal. It is launched the second time with the same initial speed, but with the launch angle increased to 60.° above the horizontal. Describe how *both* the total horizontal distance the rocket travels and the time in the air are affected by the increase in launch angle. [Neglect friction.] [2]

58–59 Calculate the magnitude of the average gravitational force between Earth and the Moon. [Show all work, including the equation and substitution with units.] [2]

June '12 Regents Examination

Base your answers to questions 60 through 63 on the information below.

A 15-ohm resistor and a 20.-ohm resistor are connected in parallel with a 9.0-volt battery. A single ammeter is connected to measure the total current of the circuit.

60–61 In the space *in your answer booklet*, draw a diagram of this circuit using symbols from the *Reference Tables for Physical Setting/Physics*. [Assume the availability of any number of wires of negligible resistance.] [2]

62–63 Calculate the equivalent resistance of the circuit. [Show all work, including the equation and substitution with units.] [2]

Base your answers to questions 64 and 65 on the diagram below, which shows a wave in a rope.

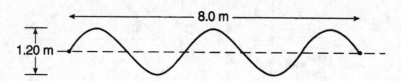

64 Determine the wavelength of the wave. [1]

65 Determine the amplitude of the wave. [1]

Part C

Answer all questions in this part.

Directions (66–85): Record your answers in the spaces provided in your answer booklet. Some questions may require the use of the *2006 Edition Reference Tables for Physical Setting/Physics*.

Base your answers to questions 66 through 70 on the information below.

A runner accelerates uniformly from rest to a speed of 8.00 meters per second. The kinetic energy of the runner was determined at 2.00-meter-per-second intervals and recorded in the data table below.

Data Table

Speed (m/s)	Kinetic Energy (J)
0.00	0.00
2.00	140.
4.00	560.
6.00	1260
8.00	2240

Directions (66–67): Using the information in the data table, construct a graph on the grid *in your answer booklet* following the directions below.

66 Plot the data points for kinetic energy of the runner versus his speed. [1]

67 Draw the line or curve of best fit. [1]

68–69 Calculate the mass of the runner. [Show all work, including the equation and substitution with units.] [2]

70 A soccer player having less mass than the runner also accelerates uniformly from rest to a speed of 8.00 meters per second. Compare the kinetic energy of the less massive soccer player to the kinetic energy of the more massive runner when both are traveling at the same speed. [1]

Base your answers to questions 71 through 75 on the information below.

A river has a current flowing with a velocity of 2.0 meters per second due east. A boat is 75 meters from the north riverbank. It travels at 3.0 meters per second relative to the river and is headed due north. In the diagram below, the vector starting at point P represents the velocity of the boat relative to the river water.

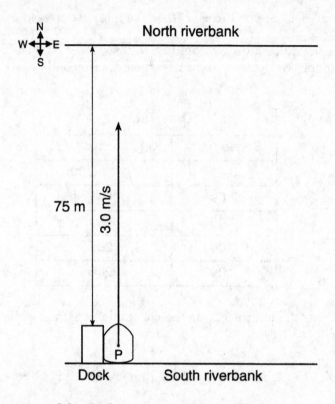

71–72 Calculate the time required for the boat to cross the river. [Show all work, including the equation and substitution with units.] [2]

73 On the diagram *in your answer booklet*, use a ruler and protractor to construct a vector representing the velocity of the river current. Begin the vector at point P and use a scale of 1.0 centimeter = 0.50 meter per second. [1]

74–75 Calculate *or* find graphically the magnitude of the resultant velocity of the boat. [Show all work, including the equation and substitution with units *or* construct the resultant velocity vector *in your answer booklet* for question 73, using a scale of 1.0 centimeter = 0.50 meter per second. The value of the magnitude must be written *in your answer booklet* in the space for questions 74–75.] [2]

Base your answers to questions 76 through 80 on the information below.

A light ray ($f = 5.09 \times 10^{14}$ Hz) is refracted as it travels from water into flint glass. The path of the light ray in the flint glass is shown in the diagram below.

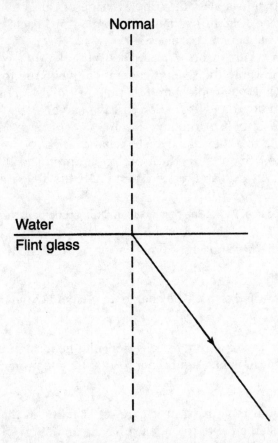

76 Using a protractor, measure the angle of refraction of the light ray in the flint glass. [1]

77–78 Calculate the angle of incidence for the light ray in water. [Show all work, including the equation and substitution with units.] [2]

79 Using a protractor and straightedge, on the diagram *in your answer booklet*, draw the path of the incident light ray in the water. [1]

80 Identify *one* physical event, other than transmission or refraction, that occurs as the light interacts with the water-flint glass boundary. [1]

Base your answers to questions 81 through 85 on the information below.

Two experiments running simultaneously at the Fermi National Accelerator Laboratory in Batavia, Ill., have observed a new particle called the cascade baryon. It is one of the most massive examples yet of a baryon—a class of particles made of three quarks held together by the strong nuclear force—and the first to contain one quark from each of the three known families, or generations, of these elementary particles.

Protons and neutrons are made of up and down quarks, the two first-generation quarks. Strange and charm quarks constitute the second generation, while the top and bottom varieties make up the third. Physicists had long conjectured that a down quark could combine with a strange and a bottom quark to form the three-generation cascade baryon.

On June 13, the scientists running Dzero, one of two detectors at Fermilab's Tevatron accelerator, announced that they had detected characteristic showers of particles from the decay of cascade baryons. The baryons formed in proton-antiproton collisions and lived no more than a trillionth of a second. A week later, physicists at CDF, the Tevatron's other detector, reported their own sighting of the baryon...

Source: D.C., "Pas de deux for a three-scoop particle," *Science News*, Vol. 172, July 7, 2007

81 Which combination of *three* quarks will produce a neutron? [1]

82 What is the magnitude and sign of the charge, in elementary charges, of a cascade baryon? [1]

83 The Tevatron derives its name from teraelectronvolt, the maximum energy it can impart to a particle. Determine the energy, in joules, equivalent to 1.00 teraelectronvolt. [1]

84–85 Calculate the maximum total mass, in kilograms, of particles that could be created in the head-on collision of a proton and an antiproton, each having an energy of 1.60×10^{-7} joule. [Show all work, including the equation and substitution with units.] [2]

The University of the State of New York

REGENTS HIGH SCHOOL EXAMINATION

PHYSICAL SETTING PHYSICS

Wednesday, June 13, 2012 — 1:15 to 4:15 p.m., only

ANSWER BOOKLET

☐ Male

Student .... Sex: ☐ Female

Teacher ....

School .... Grade ....

Record your answers for Part B–2 and Part C in this booklet.

Part B–2

51 ________________________ **N/m**

52–53

54–55

56–57 _____

_____

58–59

June '12   Regents Examination

60–61

62–63

64 _____ m

65 _____ m

66–67

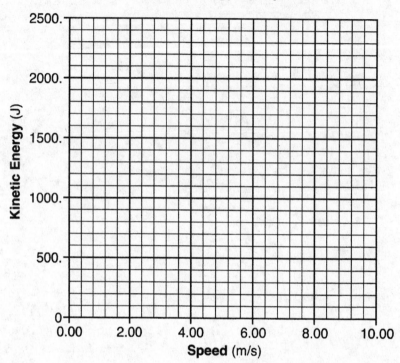

Kinetic Energy vs. Speed

68–69

70 _____

_____

June '12   Regents Examination

73

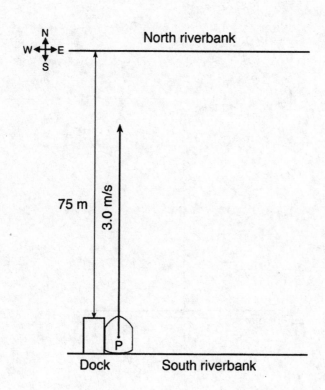

74–75

June '12   Regents Examination

76 _____ °

77–78

79

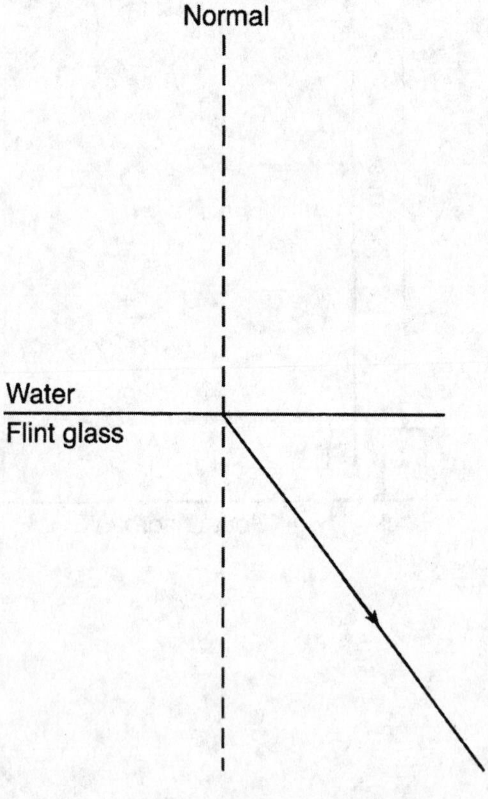

Normal

Water
Flint glass

80 _____

_____

June '12   Regents Examination

81 _____

82 _____ e

83 _____ J

84–85